# OUR SECRET DISCIPLINE

# HELEN VENDLER

# OUR SECRET DISCIPLINE

*ᐓ Yeats and Lyric Form*

THE BELKNAP PRESS OF HARVARD UNIVERSITY PRESS

Cambridge, Massachusetts · 2007

Title page photograph of Yeats (1923) by Spicer-Simson / Hulton Archive / Getty Images.

*Library of Congress Cataloging-in-Publication Data*

Vendler, Helen Hennessy.
   Our secret discipline : Yeats and lyric form / Helen Vendler.
      p. cm.
   Includes bibliographical references and index.
   ISBN-13: 978-0-674-02695-7 (alk. paper)
   ISBN-10: 0-674-02695-0 (alk. paper)
   1. Yeats, W. B. (William Butler), 1865–1939—Criticism and interpretation.
      2. English literature—Irish authors—History and criticism.   3. Lyric
      poetry—History and criticism.   I. Title.

PR5907.V37   2007
821.8—dc22        2007023744

For Seamus Heaney and Marie Heaney,
friends that have been friends indeed.

"They had changed their throats and had the throats of birds."

# Contents

## ᧒— Acknowledgments

Teachers, fellow scholars, and poets have helped me to understand Yeats. Professor Morton Berman of Boston University, who closed his Victorian Literature course with the early poems of Yeats, encouraged me to write my first essay on the poet. The late Professor John Kelleher of Harvard University taught me the poetry and plays of Yeats and directed the dissertation that became my first book on Yeats; he became a lifelong friend and an example of how distinctly the mind of a poet-historian could illuminate Yeats's works.

I have learned a great deal from my participation in the Yeats International Summer School at Sligo, Ireland, and I want to thank the members of the Sligo Yeats Committee, who have kept the School alive and well since 1960, and who have made Sligo a second home for many of the lecturers. Among the lecturers at the Yeats School who enlarged my understanding of the poet were several former directors of the School, now dead—Professor Augustine Martin of the National University of Ireland, who knew almost all of Yeats's poems by heart; the admirable poet and critic Donald Davie; and the devoted Professor A. Norman Jeffares, editor of the indispensable *Commentary* on Yeats's poems. Among many others at the Yeats School who have educated me about the poet's life, I especially thank Yeats's biographer, Professor Roy Foster of Hertford College, Oxford, whose lectures at Harvard University and the Yeats School whetted my appetite for his magisterial *W. B. Yeats: A Life,* and George Yeats's biographer, Professor Ann Saddlemyer of the University of Toronto, who has brought to light many unknown facets of Yeats's experience. I thank, too, for their collegial spirit and their learning, the following Yeatsians: Jonathan Allison of the University of Kentucky, a recent Director of the Yeats School; Massimo Bacigalupo of the University of Genoa; Vereen Bell of Vanderbilt University; George Bornstein of the University of Michigan; Terence Brown of Trinity College, Dublin; Elizabeth Butler Cullingford of the University of Texas; Meg Harper of Georgia State University, Atlanta; Alasdair Macrae of Stirling

University; Jahan Ramazani of the University of Virginia; William Murphy of Union College; Tom Paulin of Hertford College, Oxford; Ronald Schuchard of Emory University; and George Watson of the University of Aberdeen.

Four of the chapters in this book (Chapters III, VII, XI, and XII) were originally presented as the Clarendon Lectures at Oxford University. Professor John Kelly of St. John's College, Oxford, who was Director of the Yeats School when I first lectured there in 1972 (and who has since taken on, with impeccable erudition, the general editorship of Yeats's *Collected Letters*), was my host when I gave the Clarendon Lectures; he and his wife Christine made those weeks at St. John's memorably enjoyable ones, as did the writer Andrew McNeillie, editor at Oxford University Press. The poet Seamus Heaney (whom I first met when he read his poems at the Yeats School in 1975) has enlightened me over many years by his telling observations on Yeats's poetry, voiced in books and essays and in his Nobel Prize Lecture. Professor Warwick Gould of London University, a colleague at the Yeats School and also editor of the *Yeats Annual* (who has permitted me to reprint here two chapters which appeared there in earlier form, Chapters IV and X), offered to read this book before I submitted it for publication, and gave generous and invaluable help to me (as he has to so many Yeatsians) by his critique. I owe to his learning more than I can say, as my many notes mentioning his suggestions will attest. Professor Stephen Burt of Macalester College also read the manuscript and gave helpful comments.

Professor Eamon Duffy of Magdalene College, Cambridge, who was my attentive host while I lived in College for a term as the Parnell Lecturer, presided over my lecture on Yeats's relation to the sonnet, later published in the occasional papers of the College. Some of the material in this book was given as the 2005 Oberlin College Lectures in English and American Literature; I also drew on the book when I gave the Yeats Lecture at the National University of Ireland at Cork, and when I lectured elsewhere. I am grateful to all those who extended hospitality to me during these visits.

All writers on Yeats feel a heartfelt debt to Professor Stephen Parrish of Cornell University, who has seen the magnificent edition of the Yeats manuscript materials through publication (and who, when I was his young colleague, rescued my professional life at a crucial moment of discouragement). I also want to thank Karen Hwa, Senior Manuscript Editor at Cornell University Press, who kindly sent me the page proofs of the Manuscript Materials for *The Tower* in advance of publication. Finally, I recall with admiration and gratitude the late Professor Richard Ellmann, the eminent

Yeatsian of my youth, who was the external reader for my first book on Yeats, and who revealed his identity through the kindness of a jacket comment; his confidence in me as a writer on Yeats was a great gift at that early time.

This book is dependent on the biographical, editorial, scholarly, and critical labors of those Yeatsians who have preceded me; they have substantially added to my comprehension of the poet's work. The relative paucity of citations of other critical studies in this book reflects the impossibility of debating in these pages the innumerable readings that Yeats's poems have received; but it also reflects the simple lack of materials substantially treating Yeatsian form, even in the now numerous books and articles on the poet.

I thank the National Endowment for the Humanities for a fellowship supporting my work on Yeats. I have been aided as well by research funding from Harvard University and from the Department of English. The former Dean of the Faculty of Arts and Sciences at Harvard, William Kirby, together with the former President of the University, Lawrence Summers, generously supplemented my NEH grant for my sabbatical year, 2005–2006, during which I finished this study. While working on Yeats over the past years, I have been awarded month-long residencies by the Bogliasco Foundation, the Foundation of Yaddo, the National Humanities Center, and the American Academy of Berlin. I thank those who made the residencies possible: the poet Henri Cole, who, as a Board member, first invited me to Yaddo, and who told me about Bogliasco and Berlin; Kent Mullikin, Executive Director of the National Humanities Center, who has warmly welcomed me there over the years; Geoffrey Galt Harpham, Director of the Center, who approved my residency at the NHC; Dr. Assad Meymandi, whose gift to the NHC supported that residency; and Gary Smith, Director of the American Academy in Berlin, who invited me to apply for a fellowship there. I am acutely aware of my good fortune in having been granted these residencies. I am also grateful to Dr. Heinrich Meier of the Siemens Stiftung, Munich, for sponsoring my lecture there on Yeats's "Supernatural Songs." The Honorable Mark Wolf of the Massachusetts District Court actively supported my work with generosity of heart.

As always, I am indebted to the libraries of Harvard University. Margaretta Fulton, former Senior Humanities Editor at Harvard University Press, was the inerrant, inspiring (and astonishingly young) copy editor for my first book on Yeats, and was the acquisition editor for this one; her belief in all of my ventures has been a constant helpful influence. Dr.

Sharmila Sen, Senior Humanities Editor at Harvard University Press, and my former student and colleague, has encouragingly seen the book through to publication and helped me substantially in my obtaining of permissions, as has William Sisler, the Director of the Press. My copy editor, Mary Ellen Geer, and the designers for this book, Tim Jones and Marianne Perlak, have turned a collection of chapters into an actual and satisfying object. My former assistant, Alicia Peralta, helped me with library work and manuscript preparation with deft capability and intelligent helpfulness. My present assistant, Amanda Gareis, has taken up, with care and good will, the last bits of work in assembling the manuscript. Jeff Berg has been an exemplary solver of computer problems.

Quotations from the poetry of W. B. Yeats are used with the kind permission of A. P. Watt Ltd., Simon & Schuster, and the estate of Michael B. Yeats.

Finally, I thank David, Xianchun, Killian, and Céline Vendler, as well as the other members of my family and my close friends, for giving me while this book was under way not only much happiness but also help and understanding at times when life became difficult. Among those friends are Seamus Heaney and Marie Heaney, to whom this book is affectionately dedicated in gratitude for decades of kindness, hospitality, companionship, and conversation in Ireland, England, and the United States.

I grew up with my mother's books of poetry; they stopped with the Victorians. The first book I bought for myself was Oscar Williams's *Little Treasury of Modern Poetry,* in which I found Eliot, Thomas, and Auden. Somehow, I missed Yeats, and it was not until I was twenty-two that I read his work and was astonished by it. In my first year of graduate school, I eagerly took a seminar on Yeats's poetry and found that a seminar paper was not nearly long enough to contain what I wanted to say. I decided to write my dissertation on Yeats, but on reflection I realized that I was too young to write about the poems, even though, in the conventional sense, I "understood" (and loved) them, could paraphrase their assertions and register their forms. But I knew that someone who was twenty-two could not write convincingly on the emotions and motives of someone who wrote until he was seventy-three. Perhaps, I thought, once I had lived through the stages of life that had, in Yeats, produced the great late poems, I might aim to write about them. So I reluctantly put the poems aside, and embarked on a dissertation that studied Yeats's *Vision* and the later plays. It was still possible then to read not only all the published work of Yeats but also everything of value that had been written about him.

In 1972 I agreed to lecture at the Yeats International Summer School in Sligo, Ireland, and the lectures I went on to give in subsequent years at that exceptional gathering kept my hand in as a Yeatsian. I thought of collecting those lectures into a book, but I abandoned the idea because in writing for a general audience I could not go as far into the poems as I wished. Some years ago the editor of the *Yeats Annual,* Warwick Gould, invited me to contribute to a volume in memory of Richard Ellmann, and on that occasion I wrote an essay on technique in Yeats's early poetry (now Chapter IV in this book); that essay became a provocation to further study. Aside from a few books on Yeats's style (mostly written by poets such as Tom Parkinson and Jon Stallworthy), there had been little thought given to the formal properties of the poems; but to my eyes, Yeats's style was the most important of his qualities, since it was what would make the poems last. Yeats himself said, after all, "Books live almost entirely because of their style."[1] To undertake a book that was taxonomically focused on Yeats's lyric styles was not entirely what I wanted to do (since it meant that commentary on other features of the poems would have to be abbreviated), but it was what I thought needed to be done. I have had to include a good deal of factual material about inner and outer verse forms (explaining them for scholars and students unfamiliar with prosody and stylistics), and I have had to subordinate more general comments on the Yeatsian imagination to comments on its chosen formal vessels (ultimately to point out, I hope, the intent of that imagination in making its choices). I ask the reader's pardon for the occasional duplication of such factual material; I wanted to make my chapters free-standing ones.

I have put myself here in the position of the writer of the poems, attempting to track his hand and mind as he writes. I do not, therefore, argue with Yeats's ideological or aesthetic positions (which in any case changed over time, and were never anything but complex; as my teacher John Kelleher once said, "Yeats is a poet who moved, like General Sherman, on a wide and constantly shifting front"). I take as my defense for this position Yeats's remarks in a 1927 letter to T. Sturge Moore: "Schopenhauer can do no wrong in my eyes—I no more quarrel with his errors than I do with a mountain cattaract [*sic*]. Error is but the abyss into which he precipitates his truth" (#5060).[2] Here, as I comment on a poem, I aim to follow the poet's creative thinking as it motivates the evolution of the poem. Nor do I want to argue with the poems; poems are hypothetical sites of speculation, not position papers. They do not exist on the same plane as actual life; they are not votes, they are not uttered from a podium or a pulpit, they are not essays. They are products of reverie. They are expert experiments in imagining symbols for a state of affairs, and of arranging language to suit; they are not propositions to be agreed or disagreed with. Each poem is a new personal venture made functional by technical expertise; the poet's moral urgency in writing is as real, needless to say, as his technical skill, but moral urgency alone never made a poem. On the other hand, technical expertise alone does not suffice, either. Form is the necessary and skilled embodiment of the poet's moral urgency, the poet's method of self-revelation.

This book is in every sense a preliminary clearing of the ground of Yeatsian stylistics. Many of Yeats's poems, even great ones, are not discussed here, for reasons of space. Readers can, I trust, apply to other poems the methods that I have put into play here, and will I hope ratify the conclusions I have reached on the importance of form to the poet and the ideological import of various forms. Yeats asserted (in his elegy for the painter Robert Gregory) that the gazing heart "doubled its might" by having recourse to the artist's "secret discipline" of form. He singled out, with respect to painting, "that stern colour and that delicate line"—an emotional palette and structural draftsmanship—as the ingredients of that "secret discipline." In poetry, as in all the arts, "the gazing heart" remains the center, but it doubles its might by its own proper means: diction, prosody, structural evolution, a sense of perfected shape.

Poetic form has become to the ordinary modern reader a discipline indeed secret, one that has remained unmentioned even in the standard *Commentary* on the poetry of Yeats. There has been no volume in which students can find descriptions of the inner and outer formal choices Yeats made, the cultural significance his forms bore for him, or the way his forms—in all their astounding variety—became the material body of his thoughts and emotions. This book goes some small way toward filling that present gap on library shelves, but there is much more to be perceived, and more ground to be canvassed, by future commentators. The shortcomings of these pages are likely to be those that belong to any beginning; but at least I am now old enough to feel that it is not absurd—as it would have been when I was twenty-two—to say something about the great complicated artifacts of Yeats's verbal imagination.

Quotations of Yeats's poems are taken from W. B. Yeats, *The Variorum Edition of the Poems,* ed. Peter Allt and Russell K. Alspach (New York: Macmillan, 1940; 4th printing, 1968), identified by page numbers in the text. The volumes from which manuscript materials are cited are identified separately in the notes. For convenience, I have regularized the capitalization of the titles of Yeats's poems.

I have cited three versions of Yeats's letters. The first *(L)* is the old single-volume edition edited by Allan Wade; this is the one printed selection of letters from Yeats's entire career still available to readers. The second *(CL)* is the ongoing print edition of Yeats's letters under the general editorship of John Kelly: several volumes have been published, but many more are still to come. The third version that I have cited is the InteLex database of the complete letters, issued by Oxford University Press in 2002; although the later letters have not been corrected or annotated, they are cited for their interest. Letters from the database are cited by accession number, preceded by the number sign.

We dreamed that a great painter had been born
To cold Clare rock and Galway rock and thorn,
To that stern colour and that delicate line
That are our secret discipline
Wherein the gazing heart doubles her might.

"In Memory of Major Robert Gregory"

Metrical composition is always very difficult to me, nothing is done upon the first day, not a rhyme is in its place; and when at last the rhymes begin to come, the first rough draft of a six-line stanza takes the whole day.

*Autobiographies* (1955), 202

I said: 'A line will take us hours maybe;
Yet if it does not seem a moment's thought,
Our stitching and unstitching has been naught.'

"Adam's Curse"

Books live almost entirely because of their style.

*Memoirs,* 211

Art only begins after all when something has finally gone down the rat hole after banging about the room.

WBY to R. B. Cunninghame Graham, January 1914

You do not work at your technique. You take the easiest course—
leave out the rhymes or choose the most hackneyed rhymes,
because—damn you—you are lazy . . . When your technique is
sloppy your matter grows second-hand; there is no difficulty to force
you down under the surface. Difficulty is our plough.

WBY to Margot Collis, early April 1936

Go on writing, that is the only thing that matters. Beardsley said to
me "I make a blot & shove it about till something comes."

WBY to Dorothy Wellesley, August 13, 1936

I confess I have often felt both surprise and delight at the means
which he employed to make, little by little, the faulty good, the good
better, and the better perfect. Nothing can be more instructive than
such comparisons.

Johann Nikolaus Forkel, On Johann Sebastian Bach's Life,<br>
Genius, and Works (1802)

At the entrance of the third subject [of the unfinished Art of Fugue]
he mentions himself by name [in the notes B-A-C-H, i.e.,
B-flat–A–C–B-natural].

"Notice" on the back of the title page of the first edition of<br>
The Art of Fugue, 1751

# ৩— Lyric Form in Yeats's Poetry:
## Prophecy, Love, and Revolution

"Whatever I do," Yeats cried out in a 1926 letter, "poetry will remain a torture" (#4952). Over and over, in the intervals he had set aside for writing poems, he complained of the "strain" of writing lyrics, of the "exhaustion" they caused. "Creative work always ruins one's nerves for a time," he said as early as 1908 (#936). Yeats's best-known comment of this sort appears in "Adam's Curse," as he asserts that getting a single line right can take hours. In "The Circus Animals' Desertion," he claims (and his letters bear it out) that for six weeks he has sought in vain for a theme; he speaks elsewhere of having to wait until his mind "fills up" again, as if he had drained it dry. Even when he could not actually compose verse because of the pressure of other work, he often felt themes running through his head; at such times he entered "paragraphs" or "sketches" into a notebook summarizing the theme (and sometimes the internal evolution) of poems to be written up later in verse form. What tormented him was the putting of his themes (and even the words used in the prose sketches) into verse.

In his belief that a profound and passionate inner life was the prerequisite to composition, Yeats made his famous distinction between rhetoric and poetry: rhetoric comes from the quarrel with others (and looks outward to that audience as it shapes its sentences), but poetry issues from the self's quarrel with itself, which the poem exists to express (and sometimes to resolve). Expression, however, depends entirely on the adequacy of the poet's technique: about that Yeats was very clear. In addressing technique he emphasized, in his maturity, three necessary qualities: that the poet's sentences should sound like speech, that words must be put into their "natural order," and that an emotional unity should connect the parts of a work of art. "I always try for the most natural order possible, largely to make thought which being poetical always is difficult to modern people as plain as I can" (#1263). The lack of one or more of these qualities was what he generally criticized in the work of others. "I cannot say" (he wrote to one would-be poet who had sent Yeats some of his verses) "that any of these poems have the perfection of form, the emotional unity, that is lasting poetry" (#1190). Mastering technique, he thought, was the obligation of a young poet; after that, as life deepened, the poetry would have a set of technical resources to depend on, and could perhaps attain that perfection of aesthetic form denoting emotional unity. And he was certain that style must derive from the traditional literary resources that had preceded it. In "The Tragic Theatre" (1910), Yeats declared that "the real world" occupied but a minor part of a work of art; it was technique that created the major part, enabling it to leave the merely personal and become timeless:

> If [in poetry] the real world is not altogether rejected, it is but touched here and there, and into the places we have left empty we summon rhythm, balance, pattern, images that remind us of vast passions, the vagueness of past times. . . . We shall express personal emotion through . . . a style that remembers many masters that it may escape contemporary suggestion.[1]

Biographers, scholars, and critics have on the whole neglected Yeats's labor as a master of formidable techniques of "rhythm, balance, pattern, images," a composer of stylized works of art. A few scholarly books—by Curtis Bradford and Marjorie Perloff—and a few critical studies—those of Jon Stallworthy and Thomas Parkinson—remain the honorable exceptions to this rule, but these authors had limited aims: to study certain drafts, to examine the nature of Yeats's rhymes. There exists no general book examining the sorts of lyrics Yeats wrote, the imaginative impulses that dictated the choice of stanza for his subjects, the poet's development within particular formal genres (the sonnet, the ballad, the *ottava rima* poem), or the ideological meaning for him of certain rhythms or stanza forms. Exterior container-forms (such as individual stanza shapes, line lengths, or entire forms such as the sonnet) were of deep interest to him as vehicles of feeling; but even more meaning could be carried by structural form, by which I mean the architecture of a poem—how it begins, how it ends, how it conducts itself as it invents a path from beginning to end, and how it determines the proportions allotted to its several parts. Genre, too, brings historical meaning along with it, and offers a template for imitation or divagation. Because Yeats used so many different stanzas, meters, and genres, almost every poem poses anew such questions of import; and each poem of course offers an example of inner structural form. The evolution of form, in short, is the content of one of the many stories we can tell about Yeats's long life of writing.

When I first began to read Yeats, I wanted, like any young reader, to understand the "message" of each poem—what it would say in paraphrase. And I felt I needed to comprehend Yeats's idiosyncratic "system" of beliefs—its lunar structures, its historical gyres, its geometric abstractions. Such efforts to master Yeats's thought have to be the preliminary steps taken by all Yeatsians. The number of different verse forms in the *Collected Poems*, when that feature inevitably came to my attention, seemed so great as to defy categorization. Even after teaching Yeats's poetry for some years, and publishing essays on some Yeatsian topics, I knew that there were principles of architectonics in Yeats that I did not yet comprehend. I could not, for instance, account for the bizarre variety of verse forms thrown (as it seemed) together in the Yeatsian sequences. When I went to the library seeking explanations of such phenomena, they were not to be found. And since there is no better motive for writing on a subject than a gap on library shelves, I began in earnest, some years ago, to study Yeats's lyric style.

Yeats's belief in form was so intense that he was willing to endure anxiety, headaches, indigestion, and insomnia to achieve it. It was not writing down the *content* of a germinating poem that troubled him; his prose sketches are sometimes eerily close in content to the finished poem. But in the prose, spirit has not yet found its appropriate body. The stanza form remains to be chosen; the rhythms must be established; the rhymes await discovery; throughout, the envisaged "emotional unity" demands the addition of this, the excision of that. It was the second phase of composition—in which an already-imagined theme found its poetics—that so exhausted Yeats. Now that Cornell University Press has published the drafts of Yeats's finished poems, we can confirm the truthfulness of the poet's account of the pains he took. A look at the multiple drafts for merely the first stanza of "The Wild Swans at Coole" engenders respect for Yeats's unwillingness to settle for anything less than the form of words that would conform to, and convey, the emotional "color" or "aura" that the subject possessed in his mind. There was never a more tireless seeker of the exact word.

But poetry does not consist merely of words. It also consists of a repertoire of stanza forms and line lengths and rhythmic variants. At the same time that he was seeking the right adjective for the kind of beauty he saw in the Coole trees, Yeats was seeking the right stanza form for his plangent subject, and developing a rhyme scheme flexible enough to serve both his grieving self and the alternately drifting and powerful swans. He was also seeking the "right" architectonic form: his well-known rearrangement of the completed stanzas of "The Wild Swans at Coole" to create an entirely different ending is merely one instance of his keen critical awareness of the import of different structural shapes. And these complicated decisions had to be repeated for every poem he wrote. Yeats loved the traditional forms (the ballad, the sonnet), but he also was pleased to find (and adapt to his own purposes) an eccentric stanza discovered in an old poem—in Cowley's elegy for Sir John Hervey, for example, or Donne's "A Nocturnall on St. Lucie's Day."

Not much has been written about how poets decide on the forms, inner and outer, technical and generic, of their poems. In the case of Yeats, the historical and personal drama attending the work has outranked in interest, for scholars, the forms in which the work was cast. Investigation is not helped by the author himself: Yeats rarely says anything in his letters, for instance, about his formal choices. At most, he remarks to a correspondent "I have written a poem" or "I have several poems in my head," and leaves it at that; occasionally he may say that the poem is in "eight-line stanzas." With respect to his rhythms, he writes, "I find it extraordinarily difficult to explain to any, my own system of scansion for I have very little but an instinct" (#2048). The intellectual concentration necessary to "hammer thoughts into a unity" is simply taken as self-evident. Even in his essays, Yeats addresses the larger workings of the poetic imagination far more than questions of technique.

Nor has much been written about when and why a new form enters a poet's volumes. Which forms appear early, which are discovered late, which last throughout the whole career, and why? How does a poet create a fresh handling of an immemorial English form (the ballad, for instance)? And why are some long-standing forms (for example, blank verse) relatively rare in our poet's work? A poem's form, after all, is the chief factor that distinguishes one poem from another. Without a registering of form, poems treating similar subjects begin to seem indistinguishable from each other. I want to raise awareness of the individual "inscapes," both evolutionary and final, of Yeats's poems, not merely because they are there, but because they are indispensable to a full understanding of the work.

My grouping of poems by rhythmic and stanzaic forms (the trimeter, *ottava rima*, the ballad-stanza) will restore, I hope, not only a knowledge of the burden of meaning intrinsic to such forms but also a sense of how Yeats's poems sound in the ear. We are now so accustomed to reading poetry only by eye that it is difficult to recall, in silent reading, that poetry is crucially directed to the ear, and no poetry more so than Yeats's. Yeats heard, rather than saw, words (as we can often tell from his eccentric spell-

ing; he writes "tortoise-shell," for instance, as "tortashel," ignoring its ety-
mology in favor of its sound). The rhythms of Yeats's poetry have largely
been ignored by critics (who can write about a sequence without ever men-
tioning that it changes rhythms and verse forms dramatically as it goes).
Rhythms are the urgency of poetry, and they vary in Yeats from the instruc-
tional emphases of blank verse to the quick-march of the trimeter to the
narrative pacing of the ballad stanza. Yeats's poems are written in tradi-
tional rhythms, from dimeter to hexameter, and they need to be described
accordingly. It is useless, however, to comment on stanza form and meter
without connecting them to content. It tells us nothing to say that "After
Long Silence" (discussed below) is written in embraced quatrains, or that its
lines are iambic pentameters; we have to say why such a poem might take
such a form (or, rather, what Yeats had in mind when he adopted—after
some effort—that form for that content).

So, to begin this account of Yeats's "secret discipline," I want to de-
scribe, and account for, the forms he adopted for three poems which are
plain and clear in speech (and require no esoteric knowledge); in doing this I
hope to persuade readers to understand and ratify my claim of the sig-
nificance of inner and outer forms to the import of the poet's work. A
poem is an experience in time activated by its forms, from the phonetic to
the structural. Approaching poems by verse form, rather than by theme or
by biographical origin or by order of composition, offers a fresh way of in-
quiring into Yeats's work as a poet. To me, the formal shapes of a temporal
art—as they appear, gather force, evolve into coherence and climax, and
round themselves into completion—are beautiful and revealing to contem-
plate, and the poet's decisions as he invents and revises and finishes such
shapes deserve investigation. Of the three poems I take as examples, one is
a prophecy ("An Irish Airman Foresees His Death"), one a love poem ("After
Long Silence"), and one a group elegy ("Easter 1916"). In the case of "After
Long Silence," I will look at Yeats's drafts for evidence of the successive re-
visions that make a poem "come alive," but in the other two cases I will re-
strict my comments, for the sake of brevity, to the finished poem.


Yeats wrote four poems, three of them elegies, about Robert Gregory.
Gregory—the only son, the only child, of Yeats's dear friend Augusta Lady
Gregory—was killed (ironically, by "friendly fire") when his plane was shot
down in World War I. Of the four poems, "An Irish Airman" is the "sim-
plest," but it serves to illustrate the intricacy of Yeats's aesthetic planning,

even in an apparently artless poem (one often anthologized for school children). Because there was no conscription in Ireland, there was no compulsion for Robert Gregory to enlist in the British armed forces; because he was an only son, and the heir to Coole Park, there were family reasons against his joining up. In the poem, Yeats seeks to explain why such a man would have volunteered as a pilot in wartime, and in order to do so, the poet—in a daring gesture—"resurrects" Gregory himself. That is, Yeats decides to assume "Robert Gregory's" voice, all the while keeping the speaker anonymous as "*an* Irish airman" (the title originally read "The Irish Airman," then was despecified to "An").[2] Among the four Gregory poems, it is only in "An Irish Airman Foresees His Death" that Yeats locates the moment of the poem before Gregory's tragic death, so that the airman can prophesy (and, in the event, justify) his dangerous decision to take to the air. Yeats here reverses the traditional after-death stance of elegy, giving us instead the pre-death vision in which the elegiac subject chooses and foresees his fate.

How should Gregory speak? What would be a suitable rhythmic measure for a young man going off to war? Yeats takes up a four-beat march rhythm, one of steady advance, in which the airman predicts his end in the first line:

> I know that I shall meet my fate
> Somewhere among the clouds above[.]

And what rhyme pattern will Gregory use? Yeats chooses the "perfect" *abab* quatrain-rhyme ("perfect" by contrast to the "imperfect" *abcb* form) and accentuates the airman's simplicity of voice by using strong, mostly monosyllabic end-words: *fate, above, hate, love.* Gregory is forthright, independent, a soldier, and this form of four-beat march-step, with its emphatic masculine rhymes, will serve to express his nature. How many quatrains will the airman need to make his declaration? Four, decides Yeats. Four quatrains of four beats each (4 x 4) constitute a "perfect square," which is, like the airman's "perfect" rhyme, one of Yeats's symbols of impregnable and unchangeable "rightness." The poem ends where it "should," on the completion of its perfect square. By such formal means Yeats confirms that the airman's choice is the correct one for his soul:

> I know that I shall meet my fate
> Somewhere among the clouds above;

> Those that I fight I do not hate,
> Those that I guard I do not love;
> My country is Kiltartan Cross,
> My countrymen Kiltartan's poor,
> No likely end could bring them loss
> Or leave them happier than before.[3]
> Nor law, nor duty bade me fight,
> Nor public men, nor cheering crowds,
> A lonely impulse of delight
> Drove to this tumult in the clouds;
> I balanced all, brought all to mind,
> The years to come seemed waste of breath,
> A waste of breath the years behind
> In balance with this life, this death.
>
> (328)[4]

In addition to this poem's tetrameter rhythms, its perfect quatrains, and its four-square "perfect" structure, what else should we notice about Gregory's lines? Although his verse form is the quatrain, his syntax (before the final quatrain) springs forth in two-line units, reinforced by strong verbal repetitions ("Those that," "My country," "Nor") that create the thought-couplets. The use of such a terse two-line "cage" of utterance tells us that the airman has thought through his decision sufficiently to formulate it in succinct and definite statements (which are all the more noticeable because they play *against* the four-line rhyme-pull of the quatrains). The airman's initial reflections on his choice (disregarding Yeats's arrangement of them in two-line "cages") might be summarized as follows: "I neither hate the Germans nor love the British; nor am I defending my own country; nor do I hope for a benefit to my countrymen from victory in this war. Neither conscripted nor obliged to fight by duty, I was not swayed by politicians or by any war-enthusiasm in the society around me." Because these are all "negative" positions, they finally force the airman to a "positive" explanation of his action, one that arises, it seems, from his placing solitary "delight" above social considerations, and spontaneous "impulse" before considered reflection.[5] This declaration of aesthetic choice (more Yeatsian perhaps than Gregorian) "ought" to have ended the poem at the close of quatrain 3, now that the positive words "impulse" and "delight" have replaced the airman's negations of other motives for his enlistment.

There is another reason why the poem "should" end at the close of quatrain 3. We are made conscious, there, of the poem's coming full circle when the phrase "this tumult in the clouds" is made to echo the poem's second line, "Somewhere among the clouds above." When we recognize the echo, and compare the two phrases, we realize—with a start at Yeats's ingenuity—that the early phrase is spoken on the ground: before the airman takes off, the clouds are "above." By the end of the third quatrain, he is up in the sky, feeling "*this* tumult *in* the clouds." To make an airplane lift off within a poem (this is, after all, the first era in which an airplane-poem could be written) is a majestic piece of sleight-of-hand. Another reason why the poem "should" end with quatrain 3 is that the arrival of a proximal modifier in "*this* tumult" (after the repeated distancing pronouns "those" and "them" earlier) brings the poem into the critical "now" and "here" of the lyric moment. The indefinite "somewhere" of the opening has become definite in "this tumult": the change of the airman's position from "among" to "in," the repetition of the word "clouds," and the offered positive motive of delight make the poem thematically complete.

Why, then, does Yeats feel the need to append another quatrain? What can it add to the "full circle" of the airman's ascent from the ground into his place in the air? Does his recognition of his "impulse of delight" need further explanation? The verb "Drove"—with its strong initial stress in a reversed opening foot—suggests an absence of voluntary choice: a form of aesthetic passion "drove" the airman, by his own statement, into the risky exaltation of the sky. But Yeats (in the psychologically essential addendum of quatrain 4) asserts that human passion, to be worthy of human notice, must be integrated into the reflective mind of its subject; that intellect must be joined to passion to dignify passion as an act of the whole person. The chief figure of intellectual forethought offered by English poetry (and much used by Yeats) is the figure of chiasmus, in which words are arranged, not linearly (1, 2, 3, 4), but in "crossed" fashion (1, 2, 2, 1). Such a deliberate, "foreseeing" ordering betokens not a spontaneous, linear, "driven" action, but rather an intellectually meditated decision. To emphasize the conscious choosing by Gregory of the airman's life, Yeats gives him, in his coda—the final, "intellectual," quatrain—a triple chiasmus, in which mind confirms passion:

| 1 | 2 | 3 | | 3 | 2 | 1 |
|---|---|---|---|---|---|---|
| (balanced | years to come | waste of breath | . . . | waste of breath | years behind | balance) |

After the rare triple chiasmus rounds itself off, we are left with the quatrain's "surplus"—the "extra-chiastic" end-words, "this life, this death" (their proximal "this" echoing "this tumult in the clouds"). The superposition of the two "this's" fuses into a single event the airman's life-death apotheosis. The difference between the "linear" movements of the airman's earlier two-line utterances and the final triply chiastic quatrain—1, 2, 3, 3, 2, 1—is the difference between ordinary musing and conscious will.

The airman has taken alert notice not only of his "country" and countrymen but also of the laws and duties of British citizenship (even if they do not bind him); he has registered as well the speeches of politicians and the cheers of patriotic crowds. He is a person fully aware of his social matrix; before he can indulge in his "lonely" impulse, he must weigh all the social factors around him. He is not merely an artist, free to indulge in impulses of delight; he is also a social being, one complicated by the martial temperament externalized in his march-rhythm. The quarrel within himself is one between the social being and the artist, spelled out in his original denials followed by his positive motive. His imaginative world is (as Yeats makes us see in the coda) one of intellect as well as passion, and he must reconcile the two elements if his passionate "impulse" is to be a personally responsible one.

Would we understand all this if we did not take into account the poet's reasons for assuming Gregory's voice, the martial pace, the forthright end-rhymes, the circular return to the word "clouds," the takeoff of the airplane, the "coda" in the triple chiasmus of meditation, the "perfect square" of the whole poem? Does taking into consideration Yeats's labor in making it all turn out "right" help to make the poem seem not merely a statement but also a shape—and a suitable shape—for the airman's statement, evolving through passion to intellectual reflection? The shape, we remind ourselves, is that of a single 16-line block of verse: the quatrains are not made into four "stanzas" by being separated by white space; they are not even made into two 8-line stanzas, with white space between the two sentences of the poem. By running all of its potential "stanzas" together, Yeats declares of this poem that it inscribes a single arc of decision from beginning to end, confirming the "foreseeing" of the airman announced in the title. If, in retrospect, we "delete" all we have discovered about the forms (rhythmic, syntactic, verbal, structural) that Yeats chose, we can still "hear" Gregory's declaration, but we will not understand why it has taken the shapes it has; we will understand it as a speech rather than as a poem, as a statement rather than as an embodiment of an inner quarrel. We give Yeats credit as a poet only by understanding his shaping work. That work begins with a cast of the imagination: "How shall I elegize Robert Gregory?" and proceeds with the basic imaginative decision: "I'll speak in his voice, justifying his decision to become an airman." Everything else follows from this grounding choice—rhythm, syntax, rhyme, diction, length, phrasing, figuration.

Even Yeats's "simpler" poems, then, reward investigation into their patterning—require it, in fact, for adequate registering of their import. In my second example we gain some idea, from the drafts of this poem, of Yeats's repeated efforts during composition to arrange a convincing pattern. Here is "After Long Silence," a touching late love-poem written when the poet was sixty-four:

> Speech after long silence; it is right,
> All other lovers being estranged or dead,
> Unfriendly lamplight hid under its shade,
> The curtains drawn upon unfriendly night,
> That we descant and yet again descant
> Upon the supreme theme of Art and Song:
> Bodily decrepitude is wisdom; young
> We loved each other and were ignorant.
>
> (523)

In the drama of the poem, two people, once a sexual couple—in actual life, Yeats and his first lover, Olivia Shakespear—meet in old age.[6] (Yeats will eventually discover the imaginative form for this meeting: he will cast it as a tryst, a tryst no longer of bodies but of minds, consisting not of a physical embrace but rather of mutual antiphonal speech; however, that conceit is not arrived at right away.) The former lovers have arranged to meet in a restaurant or café, and as the speaker of the poem enters, he is shocked at the change that age has wrought upon his friend—her hair has turned white. And in fact, that is the first thing he says to her: "Your hair is white." He then realizes, wincing, that she must be noting the same appalling change in him: "My hair is white." Before composing his poem, Yeats writes down what he calls his "Subject," an unpromising kernel for what is to come:[7]

> Your hair is white
> My hair is white
> Come let us talk of love
> What other [theme?] do we know
> When we were young

> We were in love with one another
> And therefore ignorant.

The bathos of the white hair, although briefly present in the next draft ("friendly light / hair is white"), is put aside, as Yeats, momentarily at a loss, postpones working on this unbeautiful recognition-scene in favor of progressing to his second theme, the couple's conversation ("Come let us talk of love"). Soon, he has developed his basic form for the latter half of the poem: the original dimeters and trimeters of the "Subject" produce a pentameter embraced-rhyme quatrain, for which he immediately finds the rhymes. These bring in the third theme—the mutual love of the couple in their youth. The rhymes have arrived in *abba* form—*descant, song, young, ignorant*—and keep an interesting balance between the "naïve" internal monosyllables (*song, young*) and the bracketing sophisticated polysyllables (*descant, ignorant*):

> on love descant          descant
> upon the sole theme      supreme theme of art & song
> Wherein there's theme so fitting for the aged; young
> We loved each other and were ignorant.

With his second quatrain more or less in shape, Yeats returns to attempting the first part of his poem. This proves more difficult, as he tries to include the sound of his initial word *white* without using the word itself. He has already abortively rhymed *white* with *light*: now, trying out *right* in place of *white*, he triumphantly finds a key phrase of judgment—"It is right"— from which he can hang his poem. He seeks a new way (other than the white hair) to say that he and Olivia have met—"Once more I have kissed your hand"—but he must (for this tryst where it is minds that meet) drop that memento of physical touch, just as he had dropped the white hair of the physical body. He proceeds to invent the grim and marvelous line, "All other lovers being estranged or dead" (voiced more feebly, at first, with a cliché: "Those other lovers being dead and gone"). The painful reach of the line—"all" other lovers are inaccessible through estrangement or death—accounts for his joy in finding Olivia still at hand, still his friend. (Yeats is estranged from Maud Gonne as a lover, and the keen pain of that estrangement is shown by its being placed first among the causes of loss, before death itself.)

Unfortunately, the rhymes of the first quatrain, as Yeats has now achieved them, turn out not to match the embraced form in which he had already composed the second quatrain. Instead, he has cast the first quatrain in alternate rhyme, *abab;* and this draft reads, as a whole:

> Once more I have kissed your hand & it is right—
> All other lovers being estranged or dead
> The heavy curtains drawn—the candle light
> Waging a doubtful battle with the shade
> We call upon our wisdom and descant
> Upon the supreme theme of art and song—
> Decrepitude increases wisdom—young
> We loved each other and were ignorant.

At least Yeats now has the eight-line length needed to complete the poem he has had in mind to write. However, the battle between the candlelight and the unspecified "shade"—in the room? outside? a lampshade?—is phrased in the Latinate cliché "a doubtful battle"; since this is normally used of actual military engagements, it is hardly suitable in a love-poem, and Yeats drops it.

In the next draft, a palimpsest of what the editor calls "purple crayon" over ink, Yeats originally attempted, while reinserting the candle, to dim it by writing "The candle hidden by its friendly shade." But if the shade is friendly, then the candle is not, and its light should not be allowed to radiate by being, as it now is, an end-word and a rhyme-word. Yeats begins to tinker, and comes up with a rhyme-word for *right* that will be more suitable to a tryst: *night.* The *night* line begins in ink as "The curtains drawn on the unfriendly night," then mutates in purple crayon into "Those curtains drawn upon the deepening night" (with a brief moment in which the noisy phrase "shutters clapped" was the alternative to the softness of "curtains drawn"). Which is truer of the night—that it is "deepening" or that it is "unfriendly"? And where shall the poet put the candle, the shade, and the light?

"The friendly lamplight hidden by its shade," says one revision. Why might the lamplight be thought "friendly"? Because it enables the poet to see his friend. But then why does he want its light to be hidden by a shade? Because if it were not, he could see too clearly in Olivia's face, as she could see in his, the ravages of age (previously embarrassingly over-specified in his shock at her white hair). Finally, he understands that nothing about the lamplight is "friendly": with one of those insights in which poets find that the truth is exactly the opposite of what they have just written, "*unfriendly*" becomes the adjective representing *both* lamplight and night—the light un-friendly because it would expose their age, night unfriendly because it sym-bolizes the death awaiting them. With the double "unfriendly," Yeats hap-pily finds a way to make his first quatrain mutate into the embraced rhyme scheme that he had already settled on for his second quatrain:

> Speech after long silence; it is right—
> All other lovers being estranged or dead,
> Unfriendly lamp-light hid under its shade,
> The curtains drawn upon unfriendly night . . .

Not only does Yeats achieve here a matching embraced-rhyme quatrain, he also, in the graphic masterstroke of the chiasmus-brackets—"Unfriendly lamp-light . . . shade . . . curtains . . . unfriendly night"—poses the reunited couple as isolated in space and time, endangered on the one hand by light and on the other by night, saved from the perilous encroachments only by the fragile veils of shade and curtains.

In an earlier draft, Yeats had written that "Bodily decrepitude increases wisdom," implying that some wisdom preexisted the arrival of decrepitude. Now, suspecting that before decrepitude enlightens us we have no wisdom at all, he revises the line to say, uncompromisingly, that "Bodily decrepitude is wisdom"—and with that, he has completed his poem.[8]

Now that we have seen some of Yeats's struggles to get "After Long Si-lence" right, we can take in the form of the completed whole, and perceive that (because no white space separates its two quatrains) it has taken a form, with its embraced-rhyme quatrains, resembling that of the octave of an Italian sonnet; but whereas the sonnet would rhyme *abbaabba,* Yeats's oc-tave rhymes *abbacddc.* By deciding on this pentameter rhyme-unit, Yeats brings his tribute to Olivia into the precincts of the Petrarchan love-sonnet, where some words of the second quatrain—*descant, supreme theme of art and song*—would not be out of place. The poem that began in gratitude for re-sumed speech has elevated itself to a higher plane, that of a repeated musi-cal descant on the subject of love, that "supreme theme of Art and Song." The long prelude to this ecstatic mutuality, created by the exclusion of dan-gerous light and menacing night, has at last evolved into the actual tryst of spirits who engage in praise of love, Art, and Song.

How can the poem end? The wisdom of knowing the full dimensions of love and recalling its age-old expression in art and song is paid for by "bodily decrepitude"—felt as seven heavy syllables intruding on the enchanted descant. The last two lines, if we summarize them abstractly, set age against youth, and wisdom against ignorance. But it would not do justice to Yeats's feelings about being sixty-four to call that state merely "age": no, it is horrible "bodily decrepitude." And it would not do justice to the couple's past to dismiss it with the generalized term "youth": instead the wonderful "young" hangs over the line break as if to prolong, as much as possible, a reminiscence of that moment. The simple monosyllables "We loved each other" stand linguistically for the innocence and naïveté of youth, just as the complex polysyllables of "bodily decrepitude" stand for the debility and wisdom of age. "Young / We loved each other" reads as narrative fact, and we might wish that the poem could end with that nostalgic backward look. But Yeats resumes his "wise" voice with the dismissive ironic comment: "And were ignorant." The judgment pronounced in these words reminds us that the poet has uttered a judgment earlier: "It is right . . . that we descant [on love as the supreme theme of Art and Song]." "It is right" (with its echo of the liturgical "Justum est" ) offers a strange observation: what is "right" about their descant-speech on love as the supreme theme of aesthetic expression? The judgment is pronounced so solemnly, and in such high language, that Yeats must be implying that a different sort of speech after long silence would *not* be right, might even be "wrong." There are many things that the old friends could have talked about—events since they last met, mutual acquaintances, bodily decrepitude. But if they are to renew their past trysts of love in the present tryst of minds, their speech should dwell not on the past but on the present, not on the accidents of body (white hair, decrepitude), but rather on the subject that unites their minds, their mutual valuing of Art and Song and love.

In writing about his meeting with Olivia Shakespear, Yeats's first word adds the crucial information of "speech" to the title "After Long Silence." Yeats is not primarily rejoicing at seeing Olivia once more; it is not "Sight after long absence" that he announces (in fact, the actual seeing of her with white hair is a cause of pain). Rather, he rejoices that he can exchange speech with a dear friend whom he has not seen for some time. (And it is not the case that he and she have not been in communication: he and Olivia, though the poem does not say so, exchanged letters frequently.) When the poet says in grateful relief "*Speech* after long silence" (as one might say "*Water* after long thirst"), it is the physical descant of voices (absent from letters) in the felt proximity of an actual meeting that he celebrates. The very intonation, with its spondee on "long silence," conveys his gratitude.

Although in sketching the "Subject," Yeats had conceived of the poem as a direct address to Olivia—"Your hair is white"—the final poem, celebrating the precious mutual interchange of talk, uses solely the mutual "We." After the initial judgment, "It is right," Yeats inserts, in a triumph of syntax, a long three-line participial prelude-arc of the conditions clouding their tryst: other lovers estranged or dead, lamplight (in courtesy) hid, curtains drawn against the darkness encircling them. All these sad contexts have to be summoned up in order for us to understand the fragility and emphasis of the poem's rise to the "noble" topics of love, Art, and Song.

Had the poem ended with line 6, we would have known all the crucial information about the couple's meeting: that all their other lovers are unavailable, that the tryst between poet and former lover is one of the mind, that the speech they exchange is not mundane but musical and philosophical, that they have in common their reverence for Art and Song and for the theme that supremely generates aesthetic effort. What is added by the last two lines? It is not something about the actual event of "speech after long silence." That narrative has been completed. The last lines begin with a reflective epigram uttered from "outside" the present tryst: "Bodily decrepitude is wisdom." Although Yeats has seen that age alone has made their present high discourse possible, would that epigrammatic recognition suffice as a judgment on this meeting? Hardly: it leaves out the personal past of the protagonists, the original physical tryst on which this mental one is modeled. Almost as an apology for his bitter epigram, the poet appends the narrative of the long-past love that has generated this late meeting: "young / We loved each other." Old-age decrepitude is poised between two narratives—the present-tense one of mutual speech, the past-tense one of mutual youthful love. Then there arrives, in coordinate form, the harsh last phrase: "and were ignorant." "Ignorant" is a word that does not belong in a Petrarchan octave: it is too graphic, too scornful (as we can see from its appearance in "Easter 1916"). Yeats's bold use of "ignorant" to end his poem puts us on a new plane entirely—not the factual plane of grateful summary, as in the poem's first clause; not the symbolic plane of the "unfriendly" external conditions, light and night; not the "noble" plane of the descant nor the sage one of the epigram; not the rueful retrospective plane of the brief glance at their early love; but rather a plane of acerbic forgiveness for their lack of wisdom in youth: "What could we have known then, ignorant as we were, of the deep dimensions and aesthetic history of love?" "Art" and "Song" are forgotten, here at the end, in the resigned pairing of early sexuality and life-ignorance, the one not possible without the other.

The whole of "After Long Silence" is a single sentence (its syntactic form a partial explanation of the lack of white space between its quatrains).

As Yeats explains in the "General Introduction to My Work," he sought, as an ideal of perfect verse-making, "a complete coincidence between period and stanza":

> It was a long time before I had made a language to my liking; I began to make it when I discovered some twenty years ago that I must seek, not as Wordsworth thought words in common use, but a powerful and passionate syntax, and a complete coincidence between period and stanza. Because I need a passionate syntax for passionate subject-matter I compel myself to accept those traditional metres that have developed with the language.[9]

 We shall see further examples of Yeats's belief in the coincidence of period and stanza (most remarkably in his invented ten-line stanza as it is used in parts II and III of "Nineteen Hundred and Nineteen").

If we read "After Long Silence" without seeing it as a quasi-Petrarchan octave suitable to love; if we ignore the long syntactic arc of suspense before the liturgical "It is right" can complete itself; if we are unconscious of the chiasmus warding off light and night from the couple's protected encounter; if we miss contrasts in diction, syntax, and syllabic arrangement (the sagely Latinate copula, "bodily decrepitude is wisdom," versus the blunt narrative "we loved each other," the one polysyllabic, the other chiefly monosyllabic); if we neglect the collapse from the high discourse of "descant" to the low discourse of its rhyme-word "ignorant," and if we do not see all these separate feelings bound into a single sentence by a powerful syntax, then we have missed Yeats's shaping of his awkward "Subject" into memorable poetry. And when, with the aid of the drafts, we follow Yeats's concentrated internal processes of revision, we see even more closely the variety of intermediate choices he had to make to progress from the blank "Subject" to the accomplished poem—choices in rhyme, in syntax, in figures of speech, and in diction (descending even to the contrasts of décor and sound in "shutters clapped" versus "curtains drawn"). Seen as an old-age reminiscence and judgment, the poem is moving in human terms; seen as a work of art, it is moving as a problem solved: how to make a conclusive shape for a passing moment, how to retain the atmosphere of an endangered love-tryst while removing physical conjunction.

The more complicated Yeats's own feelings about his subject become, the more varied are the thought-forms that arise in response. In "Easter

1916"—my third and final example of how an understanding of the poet's forms increases our comprehension of his poems—Yeats recorded his own tumultuous changes of attitude toward the "rebels" who proclaimed an Irish Republic (Yeats referred to the poem in the English fashion as a "Rebellion" poem, rather than calling it a poem about the Easter "Rising").[10] Unable to approve of the rebels' endorsement of violent means, willing to trust that after the War the English parliament might "keep faith" and permit Home Rule, Yeats had become politically estranged even from his fellow poets Padraic Pearse and Thomas MacDonagh, not to speak of his beloved Maud Gonne. He had despised John MacBride, Maud Gonne's former husband, for his abusive treatment of Maud and her daughter Iseult. But the Easter Rising and the subsequent British executions of its leaders impelled Yeats to write a group elegy for these men (and for the woman he knew among them, Constance Gore-Booth Markiewicz, who does not, however, figure in the poem's close because as a woman she escaped execution). Even if Yeats wanted to praise the rebels' bravery, their love of Ireland, and their faith in proclaiming a Republic that did not yet exist, how could he praise them, since he had refused to condone their turn to armed violence? How could he write a poem reflecting on their actions that would not be propaganda for their attitudes? In the event, of course, he wrote something so ambivalent that Maud Gonne would write to him "I don't like your poem."[11]

Yeats chooses, for his elegy, a quick <u>trimeter march-rhythm</u> suitable both to military enterprise and to the second subject of the poem, the rapidity of natural change. The trimeter *abab* "perfect" quatrain, a form that Yeats revived, became for him, as we shall see in Chapter VII, closely identified with nationalist endeavor. In stanzas 1 and 2 of "Easter 1916," Yeats carefully keeps his rebels anonymous (although his contemporary Irish audience would have recognized them all). After first presenting a collective "them," he next points out individuals—"That woman," "This man," "This other," "This other man"—but persistently refrains from naming them:

> I have met them at close of day
> Coming with vivid faces
> From counter or desk among grey
> Eighteenth-century houses.
> I have passed with a nod of the head
> Or polite meaningless words,
> Or have lingered awhile and said

Polite meaningless words,
And thought before I had done
Of a mocking tale or a gibe
To please a companion
Around the fire at the club,
Being certain that they and I
But lived where motley is worn:
All changed, changed utterly:
A terrible beauty is born.

That woman's days were spent
In ignorant good-will,
Her nights in argument
Until her voice grew shrill.
What voice more sweet than hers
When, young and beautiful,
She rode to harriers?
This man had kept a school
And rode our winged horse;
This other his helper and friend
Was coming into his force;
He might have won fame in the end,
So sensitive his nature seemed,
So daring and sweet his thought.
This other man I had dreamed
A drunken, vainglorious lout.
He had done most bitter wrong
To some who are near my heart,
Yet I number him in the song;
He, too, has resigned his part
In the casual comedy;
He, too, has been changed in his turn,
Transformed utterly:
A terrible beauty is born.

Critics, in an exception to their usual indifference to form in Yeats, have had to take notice of the third stanza of "Easter 1916," since it is so startlingly different, in form and in theme, from the other stanzas. First of all, it suppresses the ballad-refrain ("A terrible beauty is born") that closes (and therefore determines the final quatrain-rhyme of) all the other stanzas. Moreover, unlike stanzas 1, 2, and 4, stanza 3 departs from history into nature,[12] and from realism into symbol, as it transforms the plural "real" people of stanza 2 into the single inorganic form of a stone. Finally, by its unexpected intrusion, stanza 3 sharply alters the course of the poem. Up to this point Yeats has emphasized passive "changed-ness" as if the rebels have been transformed by wizardly power, "enchanted" to a stone, but stanza 3 counters that passive political changed-ness with the *active* changingness of natural life. Here is the stanza of natural change, standing alone against the other three:

> Hearts with one purpose alone
> Through summer and winter seem
> Enchanted to a stone
> To trouble the living stream.
> The horse that comes from the road,
> The rider, the birds that range
> From cloud to tumbling cloud,
> Minute by minute they change;
> A shadow of cloud on the stream
> Changes minute by minute;[13]
> A horse-hoof slides on the brim,
> And a horse plashes within it;
> The long-legged moor-hens dive,
> And hens to moor-cocks call;
> Minute by minute they live:
> The stone's in the midst of all.

In nature, constant change rules everything, including those human beings who live in accordance with the rhythms of nature (such as the rider of the horse in Yeats's quick-drawn scene). The single item in the scene that does *not* change is the "stone" that "troubles" the living stream. The symbolic stone is biblically allusive (Ezekiel 36:26: "I will take away the stony heart out of your flesh, and I will give you an heart of flesh"); the allusion generates Yeats's judgment in the fourth stanza that "Too long a sacrifice / Can make a stone of the heart."[14] Hearts of stone in ideologues are contrasted to hearts of flesh in those who fluctuate with natural life. As Yeats had written in "J. M. Synge and the Ireland of His Time," "Minds, whose patriotism is perhaps great enough to carry them to the scaffold, cry down natural impulse with the morbid persistence of minds unsettled by some fixed idea. . . . [A woman will be deflected from truth by] a solitary thought which has turned a portion of her mind to stone" (*E & I*, 313–314).

As we have seen, the collective vague "they" of stanza 1 ("I have met them at close of day"), who became individual *dramatis personae* in the equally anonymous, but "realistic," vignettes of stanza 2, are aggregated in stanza 3 into a single inorganic symbolic form—"The stone's in the midst of all." They return, as we shall see, to being a collective anonymous plural pronoun in stanza 4: "We know their dream." But at the close of stanza 4, the hitherto unidentified people of the poem are, finally, named—and not named as "Thomas MacDonagh," "John MacBride," "James Connolly," and "Padraic Pearse"—their names as persons—but rather by last names alone, the names they will bear in the history books: "MacDonagh and MacBride / And Connolly and Pearse." Yeats's technique in delaying these historic names—by his generalizing plurals and his anonymous vignettes—grants them, when they appear, particular weight. But perhaps more crucially, Yeats at last gives these hitherto anonymous persons, by naming them, an existential equality with himself, the famous speaker of the poem, identified from the beginning by his authorial signature and his authoritative "I."

Although "Easter 1916" is composed in four parts—"changed, transformed, *changes,* changed"—its inmost structure is that of a fundamental conflict: the antagonism between changing (stanza 3) and being changed (stanzas 1, 2, and 4). The scherzo on change takes place on the plane of nature, while the stanzas about *being* changed occur on the plane of society. Fate is in charge of the "social stanzas": the persons in them have been "changed" or "transformed" into martyrs by having been executed by the British authorities. (Had they merely been imprisoned, the rebels would not have been "utterly" transformed.) I believe that Yeats here borrows his formula for the sublime—"a terrible beauty"—from Blake. In the "fearful symmetry" of the fiery tiger (by contrast to the agreeable symmetry of the lamb), Blake yokes an adjective of emotional response to a noun from the vocabulary of aesthetics; in "terrible beauty" Yeats does the same.[15] By attaching the refrain "A terrible beauty is born" to every stanza *except* the third, Yeats singles out the stanza about nature's active changingness as an example of the beautiful, in contrast to the revolutionary sublime of the other three stanzas. And since the other stanzas are placed within the narrative ballad-tradition by their persisting refrain, the refrain-less stanza of change is thereby put outside narrative and into the genre of meditation. The truly unchanging quality, ever-present in nature, is change.

If stanza 3 is to exemplify the natural and the beautiful under the rubric of active change, what sort of shapes will Yeats find for it? He drops, first of all, the "I" of the other three stanzas: the stanza of nature is external, objective. The immobile stone, opening and closing the passage, brackets the natural, leaving Yeats with only eleven lines for the ephemerally beautiful— the counter-truth to the "terrible" beauty of the other stanzas. His eleven lines of change exhibit linear form in their three assertions, chiasmic form in their center, and recursive form in their diction. The first assertion is a list of organic creatures governing the verb "change": horse, rider, birds—"minute by minute they change." The second assertion departs from the organic to the inorganic, without altering the verb: "A shadow . . . changes minute by minute." But Yeats has created—by repeating, in reverse order, the central verb and adverb—the figure of speech, a chiasmus, that always (as we saw in "An Irish Airman" and "After Long Silence") denotes forethought. The self-reversing patterning—"Minute by minute: change :: changes: minute by minute"—announces that there is a flux and reflux to nature's changes: forward or backward, they are all ephemeral. The third set of assertions, returning to the organic (horse, moor-hens, moor-cocks) drops the earlier generalizing governing verb "change" in favor of its local rapid minute-by-minute instantiations: "slides," "plashes," "dive," "call," and—above all— "live" (the root of this last verb repeated from "the living stream").

Why does Yeats need *three* sets of assertions to make his point about active change? In part, he offers them to guide the reader's eye over his landscape: "horse" takes us to "rider," "rider" takes us to "birds," "birds" lifts us to "cloud," while "a shadow of cloud on the stream" brings the eye back down to earth, thereby allowing the close focus of "horse-hoof," "brim," and "moor-hens," the latter bringing in, by their calls to moor-cocks, the essential role in natural change played by sexual generation. Yeats's third stanza is the most musical in the poem, as it plays, "minute by minute," its delightful recursive changes on apparently "realistic" natural motifs— stream, horse, birds, clouds, and active "change." As it rises from the minatory stone to its musicality, its recursiveness, and its insistence on many active-voice appearances of the verb "change," the stanza mimics the transient livingness of nature. On the other hand, the initial and final "blockage" of natural life by the stone—especially in the last, obstructive, line, "The stone's in the midst of all"—tells us that the stone is an irremovably permanent part of the scene, that the "living stream" can never rid itself of the troubling stone, that natural fluency and ideological fixity are perpetually present and perpetually antagonistic. Yeats's stanza of tender recursive relish of the natural and the beautiful—placed, as it is, between the socio-political stanzas 2 and 4—is "blocked" by the ideological challenge of the martyrs. In one of his most successful poetic techniques, noticed long ago by Paul de Man, Yeats—by means of one clearly allegorical item, here the blocking stone—renders all the "realistic" earthly entities surrounding it symbolic as well, each an illumination, here, of the fluctuating nature of the inhabited natural world. The stream is its fluidity, the rider its transient human denizen, the birds its intermittency, the clouds its indefiniteness of outline, the shadow its fluctuating light-effects, the moor-hens and moor-cocks its seasonal sexuality, the plash and bird-calls its unforeseeable and changing music.

Throughout the poem, Yeats's constantly shifting attitudes toward both himself and the heroes of 1916 serve in their own right to exemplify natural change, demonstrating the mobility of an imaginative mind prepared to consider a form of beauty it had not previously recognized. Yeats allows us to see several states of his mind: his regret (at the moment of writing) for his own earlier alienated posture toward the rebels as he committed the worst fault for a poet, uttering (twice) "polite meaningless words"; his pain at the loss of those who had been friends or fellow poets, conveyed in stanza 2 as he sketches each in turn; his inability to interpret their "stoni-ness"—have they been "enchanted" like characters in a fairy tale, or have they voluntarily chosen, by too long a sacrifice, to turn their hearts to stone? The poet's recollections of earlier emotions evolve toward his tense questioning and hypothesizing at the end. As the first stanza of "Easter 1916" sketched a narrative, the second a set of *dramatis personae,* and the third a condition of natural changingness, so the fourth attempts to render a judgment. Judgment thrusts itself forward in the poet's first two words of estimation, "Too long":

> Too long a sacrifice
> Can make a stone of the heart.
> O when may it suffice?
> That is heaven's part, our part
> To murmur name upon name,
> As a mother names her child
> When sleep at last has come
> On limbs that had run wild.
> What is it but nightfall?
> No, no, not night but death;

Was it needless death after all?
For England may keep faith
For all that is done and said.
We know their dream; enough
To know they dreamed and are dead;
And what if excess of love
Bewildered them till they died?
I write it out in a verse—
MacDonagh and MacBride
And Connolly and Pearse
Now and in time to be,
Wherever green is worn,
Are changed, changed utterly:
A terrible beauty is born.

(391–394)

In this superbly managed stanza of attempted judgment, the poet's ambivalent and constantly changing attitudes crowd pell-mell upon each other. In a strong moral assertion, he claims that one can engage in "too long" a sacrifice, petrifying the heart; then (as he asks how long is too long) he repents of his own query, as he recalls old Hamlet's words forbidding his son to judge Gertrude's guilt or innocence, which can be evaluated only by God: "Leave her to heaven." "That is heaven's part," echoes Yeats (revising his draft from "God" to "heaven" to create the allusion). Although he has ostensibly resigned judgment to heaven, Yeats immediately falls to judging the patriots once again, this time by a patronizing vision in which the poet, as in a pietà, presides over adolescent children whose limbs had "run wild." Yeats then attempts to evade final judgment altogether by pretending that this is only "nightfall," but quickly rebukes himself back to sternness in "No, no, not night but death." In his next judgment, Yeats questions the patriots' actions by defending his own preference for a postwar parliamentary establishment of Home Rule—"England may keep faith"—which would render the rebels' premature deaths "needless." Finally—finally—the poet discovers an alternative to adverse judgments by admitting something in the patriots' actions that he knows from his own life: like himself, the rebels were "dreamers," "bewildered" by an "excess of love," resembling in this his own Oisin, bewildered by an excess of love for his "faery bride."

In a characteristically telling syntactic alteration, Yeats turns away from his search for the agent (fate, the British administration) that has "changed" the patriots; now he simply observes the consequences for them of dreaming and loving. External agency with respect to their death vanishes along with the past participles "changed" and "transformed": instead, Yeats writes, "they dreamed and *are dead*"; love bewildered them "till they *died*." These variants make the deaths "natural" rather than violent, springing from internal motives (dream, love) rather than from external execution. At this point, the poet can at last establish a stance for himself that is not false. The patronizing maternal oral "murmuring" is silently repudiated: the poet will not murmur, but write; and write not in prose but in verse. He will create a durable artifact, not merely an ephemeral murmur of natural lament. (To this extent, Yeats qualifies his praise of the merely "natural": the nature in stanza 3 has no place for the human artifact of verse, a different form of "stone" from ideological fixity, but still something stable and lasting.) In the military roll call of the patriots—"MacDonagh and MacBride / And Connolly and Pearse"—Yeats substitutes their permanent chronicle-names for their ideological "fixity." They will survive under these names as the transformed founders of the Republic for which they were willing to die.

In his final homage, "Wherever green is worn," Yeats humbles himself by gesturing to a piece of popular poetry (which echoes earlier verses mentioning the phrase), "The Wearing of the Green." It says of Ireland:

She's the most distressful country that ever yet was seen,
They are hanging men and women for the wearing of the green.[16]

Conceding that such patriotic street-ballads have a popular power his own verse does not possess, Yeats borrows the patriotic slogan to prophesy that "now and in time to be, / Wherever green is worn," the men of the Easter Rising will be remembered, not as their quotidian selves, but as they were "changed, changed utterly" by their deaths. (To appreciate the force of this gesture, we have to recall Yeats's unremitting hatred of green as a political symbol; he forbade it as a color for the binding of his books.)

"Easter 1916" has survived as Yeats's most famous political poem because of its long-meditated means (Yeats dated the poem "September 25, 1916," a full five months after the Rising, when the significance of the Rising and the subsequent executions had become manifest). Surprisingly— since he is alluding by his refrain to an essentially narrative form, the ballad—he retells neither the events of the armed conflict nor the fact of the executions, nor does he name, until the end, his *dramatis personae.* What he has done in "Easter 1916" is to render his own changing attitudes toward the characters of the Rising, from well before the event to after the executions. Once he had decided on the fundamental contrast between the rebels and himself—ideological fixity versus mobility of thought—he had to decide how he would structure that contrast, and chose to nestle natural mobility in the center of the poem, flanked within its own stanza by the two brief appearances of the stone, and bracketed more generally by the sociopolitical stanzas 1, 2, and 4. In structuring the changes in his own responses, he displayed in the opening pre-Rising stanza his cynical and alienated stance, in the second stanza his disappointment in his friends and acquaintances as their commitment to violence became the crucial hinge between their past lives and their new fixity, and in the final stanza his mixed feelings, expressed in queries and hypotheses, about their armed resistance.

To ingest a large historical event with a substantial cast of characters, to find a way to sketch not only its phases and actors but oneself among them, is not usually the task of lyric. But Yeats creates a means to treat the Rising by using anonymous psychological characterizations added to symbols of nature and stone, abstractions that will fit the multiple aspects of the Rising and make them manageable in lyric. And I must mention here the most invisible, but the most certain abstraction of all, to me a striking instance of Yeats's belief in guiding his poem by a form of unseen control—in this case, the date of the Rising: April 24, 1916.[17] In "Easter 1916," the "16" of the year and the "24" of the date are commemorated in the lengths of the poem's four stanzas, arranged in alternating line-groupings of 16, 24, 16, 24 (nowhere else does Yeats employ two stanza-lengths arranged in regular alternation). Because April's number among the months is 4, the poem rhymes in 4-line groups: *abab,* and so on. As far as we know, Yeats never mentioned the poem's emblematic form: it was his own secret, long unobserved, like his other structural inventions. He must have felt that embedding the date of the Rising in his poem about it guaranteed the fit of the work to its subject.[18]

Beginnings and endings are, in poems, highly significant. Yeats's present-perfect habitual verb—"I have met them"—situates the beginning of the poem in a past continuous quotidian life, pervaded by a sardonic certainty that is violently disrupted by the birth of the "terrible beauty." The end—"I write it out in a verse"—brings the lyric from that prewar past into the immediate present, as the poet assumes a traditional historical task of the Irish bard—to celebrate heroes. If we miss the fundamental antagonism of fixity and change that structures the poem; if we overlook Yeats's surprised discovery that although fixity cannot change, it can *be* changed; if we do not wonder about the intrusion of the natural world in stanza 3, with its suppression of both the "I" and the refrain, together with its figures of reiteration, flux, and recursion; if we do not ask the reason for both the opening anonymity of the *dramatis personae* and the counter-move of a closing roll call of surnames; if we forget that the closing stanza of judgment takes the paradoxical form of a plethora of questions; if we do not perceive the invisible numbers guiding the poem—then we cannot properly describe Yeats's set of attitudes toward the Rising and its patriots, or indeed value how he has enlarged the genre of modern elegy by this difficult venture into elegizing not a single subject, but a specific and varied group of people.

In a letter to Olivia Shakespear, Yeats called "After Long Silence" "this little poem" (*L*, 772). But even Yeats's "little" poems come into being only by an ardent and arduous passage from conception to execution. The three short poems I have taken up here reveal how Yeats works in each case toward inner and outer forms that will bring about that "unity of being" characteristic, as he argued, of all achieved art. The historical drama of Yeats's era has, until now, distracted commentators from his patient and meticulous work as a poet; to read him well, we need to enter, with him, the parallel drama of the creation of art.

## ⌒ Antechamber and Afterlife:
## Byzantium and the Delphic Oracle

Nothing more quickly reveals Yeats's acute sense of form—the inner form of a poem's evolution and the outer form of its metrical and stanzaic shape—than to see the poet writing the "same" poem twice. Twice, Yeats situates himself in Byzantium, death's antechamber; and twice—in the person of Plotinus—he travels to the afterlife-realm of the Immortals. In these four poems, Yeats brackets the event of death itself, in the first pair by imagining himself reflecting, before the fact, on death; and in the second pair by imagining himself, after the fact, as having survived death. In the Byzantium poems, he wonders what sort of after-death state he might aspire to, and conjures up two distinct forms of life to choose between once he is "out of nature"—the one emphasizing wisdom, the other, art. In the poems about Plotinus's fate, he first adopts the description of the land of the Immortals offered by the Delphic Oracle, and then—in "News for the Delphic Oracle"—repudiates that orthodox description. Because Yeats conferred such very different shapes on these four poems—two pairs of two— they can provide, more amply than the individual short poems of Chapter I, answers to the fundamental question of this book: Can a consideration of lyric form, inner and outer, help us to a better understanding of Yeats's poems? Written in Yeats's last decade, these four "afterlife" poems—"Sailing to Byzantium," "Byzantium," "The Delphic Oracle upon Plotinus," and "News for the Delphic Oracle"—have been much commented on, but they are, I think, still imperfectly understood, or even misunderstood, because Yeats scholars have not posed questions about either their external or internal lyric form. I will spend more time on these famous poems than on subsequent ones in later chapters in order to alert readers to the details of Yeats's meticulous originality in the choice and deployment of forms.

The late Professor John Kelleher of Harvard University was the first scholar (to my knowledge) to link the two later poems concerning Plotinus with the two earlier poems about Byzantium, and I follow his insight here. The four poems concern what Yeats called in a letter "the search for the spiritual life." In that letter, written just after the composition of the earliest of these poems, Yeats refers to his own mood as oscillating "between spiritual excitement and the sexual torture and the knowledge that they are somehow inseparable" (L, 720–721). The sexual torture relevant here is that of sexual impotence, of desire without the capacity to act. This state provokes, according to Yeats, an unexpected excitement as he reflects on the imminent supervening of the spiritual life over the physical one. (The mixture of the sexual and the spiritual underlies all four poems, but it takes different expression in each.) The second poem of each pair is an afterword to its predecessor. Each pair of two is a diptych in which left and right stand as proposal and counter-proposal. Finally, each poem has an independent and unique existence in its own right.

## The Byzantium Poems

The 1927 "Sailing to Byzantium" is a four-stanza Roman-numeraled sequence written in *ottava rima* (a stanza of eight pentameter lines rhyming *abababcc*).

### Sailing to Byzantium

#### I

That is no country for old men. The young
In one another's arms, birds in the trees
—Those dying generations—at their song,
The salmon-falls, the mackerel-crowded seas,
Fish, flesh, or fowl, commend all summer long
Whatever is begotten, born, and dies.
Caught in that sensual music all neglect
Monuments of unageing intellect.

#### II

An aged man is but a paltry thing,
A tattered coat upon a stick, unless
Soul clap its hands and sing, and louder sing
For every tatter in its mortal dress,
Nor is there singing school but studying
Monuments of its own magnificence;
And therefore I have sailed the seas and come
To the holy city of Byzantium.

III

O sages standing in God's holy fire
As in the gold mosaic of a wall,
Come from the holy fire, perne in a gyre,
And be the singing-masters of my soul.
Consume my heart away; sick with desire
And fastened to a dying animal
It knows not what it is; and gather me
Into the artifice of eternity.

IV

Once out of nature I shall never take
My bodily form from any natural thing,
But such a form as Grecian goldsmiths make
Of hammered gold and gold enamelling
To keep a drowsy Emperor awake;
Or set upon a golden bough to sing
To lords and ladies of Byzantium
Of what is past, or passing, or to come.

(407–408)

I call "Sailing to Byzantium" a "sequence" because I am convinced that when Yeats prefaced single stanzas or groups of stanzas with a Roman numeral, he meant each numeral to indicate a marked change in "station" (that is, physical or mental location). Each time a Yeats poem is interrupted by a Roman numeral, the reader is asked to move to (or think within) a new location.[1] The four stations of "Sailing to Byzantium," as I understand them, are:

   I. "That *country*" of sensual music from which the speaker has bitterly departed;
  II. "The holy *city* of Byzantium" where the speaker hopes to learn a singing proper to the soul;
 III. A *cathedral* with a wall-mosaic of named male personages presented against a gold background symbolizing the fire of eternity;
  IV. The Emperor's *palace* where a golden bird sings to a courtly audience of men and women.

Each station, as has long been noticed, has some variant of the word "sing" in it, denoting not only the poet's pain at having to leave the song of sensu-

ality behind but also his urgent quest to find a new form of song to substi-
tute for the song of the flesh:

> I. Birds . . . at their *song;* that sensual music;
> II. Soul *sing* . . . louder *sing* for every tatter; *singing* school;
> III. Sages . . . *singing*-masters of the soul;
> IV. Golden bird set on a golden bough to *sing* to lords and ladies.

Since each of the stations of "Sailing to Byzantium" consists of a single
stanza of *ottava rima,* Yeats is affirming that all of his self-placements, as he
faces this end-of-life crisis, are "equal" in psychic weight. Some other se-
quences among his poems present stations of very different individual
lengths (for example, "Vacillation"); or a sequence can group several stanzas
under a single station, as in "The Circus Animals' Desertion," where the
middle station, II, is composed of three stanzas, while the other stations, I
and III, have only one stanza apiece. These structural differences in the
Yeatsian concept of a numbered part make it necessary to remark that all
the stations in "Sailing to Byzantium" have equal length. As we shall see,
there are no such "stations" in its companion poem, "Byzantium," where
the speaker stays in one place.

Is there a reason for the order of the stations in Yeats's Roman-numeraled
poem? Or could the stations of "Sailing to Byzantium" be shuffled into a
different order? Especially when all the stations are equal in weight, this
question becomes inevitable. Since poetry is a *temporal* art, we tend to feel
that there exists a temporal advance in a poem: first this, then this, then this.
Although this is so, poems are also structured *spatially* (as when stanzas be-
have like "rooms," as their name implies, or exist on different "levels"—
heaven, earth, hell). Temporality and spatiality both contribute to the "ar-
gument" or set of successive implicit assertions in any poem. Having the
"last word" is important in a poem, as in life. And the opening "word"—
the first station—is always crucial in setting the conditions of the poem's
thought-world. But could the last stanza have served as the first? Or could
the third and fourth stanzas have changed places? Could "Sailing to Byzan-
tium" have opened with "An aged man is but a paltry thing"? Could it have
ended with "And gather me / Into the artifice of eternity"? In interpreting a
poem, we must assess the poet's choices by imagining that they might have
been different.[2]

A poem—at least in the Yeatsian universe—is a set of symbolic abstrac-
tions which become verbal equivalents of a mental construct. (We can see
the process of symbolic abstraction in action as Yeats changes a prose "Sub-

ject" into a poem, as in "After Long Silence," described in Chapter I.) Often we do not know what has provoked the chosen symbols of a poem until the poem has been unfolding itself for some time. The crisis that has led to the poem reveals itself sooner or later, but we must not assume that it will be evident in the first line (or, even if it is, that it will be fully exposed there; we do not know the terms of the crisis of "Sailing to Byzantium" until its third stanza). Critics have long been aware of many of the more conspicuous symbolic "moves" of "Sailing to Byzantium": An old man (whom I will call, for convenience, here as elsewhere, "Yeats") sums up in the first station his jaundiced view of the country of sensual music that he has left behind; it is "no country for old men." His own sexual impotence has sexualized for the sufferer the entire world of nature. Wherever he looked, in his former home (identified as Catholic Ireland in the manuscript drafts, but purged of specific reference in revision-toward-abstraction), he saw only spawning, fertilizing, and lovemaking, heard only mating calls. In that country, all animate orders—fish, flesh, and fowl—representing all habitable elements—water, earth, and air—unite in a chorus of self-congratulatory songs of begetting and giving birth. Only the impotent man interjects his sour note: "those dying generations," he says, sing of "whatever is begotten, born, and dies." His vindictive insistence on the generations' decay, his unfair summation of existence in which death arrives at the moment after birth, are sublimely ignored by the summer singers, who are living out that flourishing middle of life—the period of adult sexual experience—omitted in the old man's brutal juxtaposition of beginning and end. Frustrated by not being able to join in the secular choir of the pastoral "country" of the young, he has fled to the "holy city" of Byzantium (concealing his desperation by rendering his progress in stately and orotund iambics: "And therefore I have sailed the seas and come / To the holy city of Byzantium"). A "paltry" figure among the vigorous young, he hopes to regain respect by emphasizing the power of the rigid Byzantine "monuments of unageing intellect" to inspire his soul to a new song. He has gone, then, from erotic country to holy city; and from the sensual music of the flesh to music appropriate to the "unageing intellect." The rhyme "come . . . Byzantium" closes the evocation of the first two stations. There is a critical consensus on the thematic evolution of the poem up to this point.

And although everyone has agreed that in the third station Yeats addresses a group of "sages," it has not been seen that these sages are not *in* Byzantium; they are located far above the city, in the invisible realm of eternity, standing in "God's holy fire" (fire is the element missing in the first station, because it is not, on earth, a habitable element). It is in this third station that the deepest crisis of the poem, occluded earlier within the speaker's jealous denigration of the mating young, is nakedly exposed, as the poet admits to the sages that his heart is still "sick with desire"—the same desire that animates "the young in one another's arms, birds in the trees . . . at their song." But his flesh no longer rises (as it once did) in response to the desire of the heart. The speaker interprets his sexual impotence to mean that his animal being has already begun to die (no other infirmities of the body except impotence are instanced to justify the bitter epithet "a dying animal"; we see now that it is the speaker's own sense of dying that has made him project the words "dying" and "dies" onto the young). Because his heart, as full of desire as when he lived in the country of the young, is unhappily and unnaturally "fastened" to his failing body, "it knows not what it is." Yeats's crisis is therefore one of identity: what will be the new identity to replace his former, now dysfunctional, sexual one?

The first new possible identity for himself—that after his death he will be considered (by his readers) as a sage and admired for his wisdom—occurs to Yeats in this third station as he stands (we infer) in the Byzantine cathedral, Hagia Sophia, the church of the Holy Wisdom (the cathedral's name probably suggests the name "sages" given to the persons the speaker now addresses). Yeats is contemplating a mural mosaic that shows sages standing against a background of gold, which, as the iconographic symbol for "God's holy fire," informs the observer that the sages addressed by the poet are located in heaven. (The actual mosaics that Yeats saw were in Ravenna, where there is a frieze of prophets identified by name; the imagined mosaic, we deduce, must also identify its personages by name—"Isaiah," "Hosea," "Jeremiah"—or the speaker would not know that these holy figures were "sages," by contrast, say, to martyrs.) "When my body ends its existence, I could belong among these sages," thinks Yeats, but knowing he cannot rise to heaven unaided, he implores their help. By addressing them as living beings, he looks "through" the mosaic before him to the "reality" that it represents—eternity and its inhabitants. This is the devotional practice recommended to believers—that they use the icon before them as a window to the celestial, praying to the "real" Virgin as they contemplate a sacred image of the Virgin. The other way of responding to an image—the way of the connoisseur, dwelling on manner and medium—does not treat the people in the image as really existing elsewhere, able to be addressed. As George Herbert says in "The Elixir":

A man may look on glass,
And on it stay his eye;
Or, if he pleaseth, through it pass,
And then the heavens espy.

Yeats chooses to "pass through" the mosaic (by demoting it to a simile) and "espy" the heaven beyond, so that he can cry out directly: "O sages standing in God's holy fire / As in the gold mosaic of a wall." His prayer to the sages is composed of a series of verbs begging that they will descend to save him and "gather" him back to their realm so that he can learn to sing under their instruction. The sages are to *come* (from the holy fire), *perne* (in a gyre), *be* the singing-masters of his soul, *consume* his heart away, and *gather* him—where?—into the *artifice* representing them and their eternal realm. In short, they are to descend, burn away his aching heart, rescue him from his dying body, and gather him into their company (leaving his consumed heart and his dead animal flesh behind). A whirling descent (a "perne" is a cone-shaped bobbin; Yeats translates the noun into a verb) is followed by a whirl-ing ascent, as the "me" of the speaker is "gathered" (as to Abraham's bosom) into—and then the problem arises. What does it mean to be gath-ered "into the *artifice* of eternity"? (It is not the same as to be gathered into eternity.) And who is that "me"? Yeats begins to imagine what the conse-quences will be when that gathering has been accomplished. His disembod-ied and "heart-less" *soul* will have joined the choir of the sages, his singing-masters, and will have been taught by them to sing their changeless song, "Holy, holy, holy," before the eternal throne of God. His dying *animal* will have died. With heart consumed, body dead, what is left that can properly be called "me"? Once this disintegration of his ego has occurred, and his soul is in the heaven of the sages, the mosaic, the artifice, that he now be-holds will need to be "corrected": there will then be one additional sage standing within the gold field, the translated-to-heaven W. B. Yeats, appear-ing with the other sages in the cathedral mosaic that visually represents them in eternity. (I take it that "the artifice of eternity" represents the effort to render visible in some art-form the invisibilia of the eternal; its counter-part, "the artifice of time," is the effort to render in art intelligible temporal events.)

Yeats then asks himself whether his soul would in fact like this new sa-cred existence "out of nature." He of course knows it would not: he does not want his soul to live in a single-sex choral group, inhabiting eternity (in reality) and inhabiting (within the mosaic) the artifice by which eternity is religiously represented. His prayer mistakenly assumes that if the dying animal were to be permitted to die, and if the heart were to be "consumed away" by the sages' fire, the "me" that would remain, stripped of heart and body, would be worth saving. But that heart-less and body-less "me" is not, and never can be, the authentic Yeatsian self.

Yeats's vision of joining the company of the sages is what we might call, in the larger Freudian sense, a homosocial and sublimated resolution to the speaker's exclusion—by reason of impotence—from the country of heterosexual intercourse. There are no women in the heaven of the sages. There is no time in the fiery eternity symbolized by the gold background of the mosaic. That this potential identity as pure soul, an eternal inhabitant of God's holy fire, is repellent to Yeats-the-author is revealed by the way the speaker silently turns away from it, diverging strongly from it to imagine, and choose, a destiny entirely different from that religious one. It still remains true for the speaker that "Once out of nature I shall never take / My bodily form from any natural thing," but he refuses to imagine himself, in the future, embodied as a personage in a religious artifact, a sacred mosaic, while finding in a heavenly hymn his replacement for the lost sensual music. Rather, he will be embodied in one of the profane artifacts of time, one serving the court rather than the cathedral; he will take the form of an elaborate golden bird that sings not of divine eternity but of human time—"Of what is past, or passing, or to come."[3] Since the content of his song will be the events of the past, the current moment, or the future, the golden bird belongs to the category of art produced by an artifice devoted to time. The great event of "Sailing to Byzantium" is the speaker's choosing the artifice of time over the artifice of eternity as his domain of future iconic embodiment. The fourth station, in the Emperor's palace, rejects definitively the third one inside the cathedral.

This final choice has, on reflection, become the only possible one for the poet. After his death, what will he become? A singing voice, issuing from the Collected Poems. Is that voice singing solely of God and eternity, as the voices of the sages do? A glance at the Collected Poems refutes that idea; the voice we hear coming from the works of Yeats is that of a chronicler of the past, a commentator on the passing scene, and (in hope) a prophet of the future. At first, to come down from the sublimity of eternity to a mere earthly dwelling (even if a palace) causes in the speaker a self-deprecation and a sense of diminished function, as the little bird sings not to praise God but "to keep a drowsy Emperor awake." However, the poem rises from this temporary irony to take itself seriously at the end, as it evokes the poet's wider social function: to construct a musical form that can record the past, evoke the present, and speculate on the future. The final rhyme—"Byzantium . . . come" reverses, with intent, the orientation of the original (mistaken) desire, expressed at the second station, that "soul clap its hands and sing," aspiring to create a masterpiece of "unageing intellect." Yet the rhyme keeps its sonority; it honors the nobility of the chronicling of humanity in time, even in comparison with the changeless sonority of eternal worship of the divine.

Stations 3 and 4 are mutually exclusive as ultimate destinies: you cannot imagine yourself simultaneously as a sage-singing-in-and-of-eternity (represented in the cathedral of Holy Wisdom by a sacred mosaic) *and* a voice-singing-in-and-of-time (represented in the Emperor's secular palace by a profane golden artifact). The actual content of his own life-work determines the poet's choice of afterlife incarnation. The self-deceiving bitterness of the opening has vanished by the end of the poem. Something has indeed been lost to the human speaker in his reincarnation-within-artifice: the golden bird has no mate, and cannot sing "sensual music." But the bird does have a bodily form (even if artificial), and continues to inhabit a profane heterosexual environment, while he chronicles in song—with an omniscient, almost divine, view—the broad panoramas of time. As he sings to the Emperor, or to the lords and ladies, he will be Hellenic, not Hebraic. As the poem ends, he is back in a place where there is an imminent sensuality in the drowsy Emperor (there is an Empress as well as the Emperor in the worksheets, and "drowsy" is always, in Yeats, a sign of the sensual). The song of the bird is not a "window" to some transcendent "other reality"; it is as opaque as history and the prophecies of history. We live *in* history; we do not "see through" it. The Emperor may suspend his sensuality for a time, kept awake by the bird's singing, but then he will drowse again into sensual sleep. Art, Yeats suggests, is a momentary alternative to sensuality, but not a vehicle of transcendence. The song of the golden bird differs from the ignorant sensual song of the young in that the bird has the historian's knowledge of the past, the journalist's detached view of the passing scene, and the prophet's apprehensive speculative vision; but the golden bird's song is nonetheless, like the song of the young, music of this temporal world, not of a timeless eternity. "I am not (nor was meant to be) a Hebraic sage dwelling in eternity and depicted by artifice in a cathedral mosaic," Yeats feels, "nor are my songs accurately described as weighty 'monuments of unageing intellect'—but I could amuse and instruct an Emperor and his court when I am embodied (in my *Collected Poems*) as a beautiful and expressive secular artifact of hammered gold and gold enamelling." This is a realistic (and classic) position that we can admire, even as we realize that the non-human form of the golden bird may not really be a wholly viable image of afterlife existence for a human being, even in his posthumous virtual form within his collected works.

I return to our original question: does it help in understanding "Sailing to Byzantium" if one thinks about its forms? I have been dwelling on the spatially oriented vectors of its internal form: "Leave X, come to Y, choose either A or B." The first motion of that form is horizontal, as the poem sails, in the first half of the poem, from country to city. But the next motion of the poem goes vertically upward, as it establishes, in III, an invisible "holy" plane of reference situated above the city, in a fiery eternity. The next motion of the poem is vertical again, as, in IV, turning its back on the sages' sacred eternity, it descends to the secular realm of time, where it might seem to come to rest—until the very end, when, with the words "to come," the linear motion of "past, or passing" advances to a gyre progressively opening to the future. One cannot, I am certain, understand the poem properly without taking into account its internal architectonics: the separate regions of each of its four stations, its "wrong" upward divagation to "eternity" and its "right" move downward, back to time, before it extends itself forward into the unknown future.

But there is a second critical question: does it help in understanding "Sailing to Byzantium" if one thinks about its external form? The first external form, the poem's four-part division into "stations," we have already found revelatory of the speaker's spatial "moves" as he meditates his future; the second external form is the Roman numerals themselves, conferring a consequentiality, by interim pauses, on the four "stations" that the same words would not possess as mere stanzas. But the third external form, that of the *ottava rima* stanza in which Yeats chose to cast his material, is also a plainly symbolic one. For Yeats, the *ottava rima* stanza (as we will see in Chapter X) is one that bears connotations of Renaissance Italy (or at least of the poet's idea of Renaissance Italy, derived from his reading and his 1907 trip to Tuscany with Augusta and Robert Gregory). *Ottava rima* (in its non-comic occasions) is stately and ceremonious in motion, suited to the poet's conflicting deliberations about his choice of future incarnation. It also suits, in its grandeur, the matter of the Byzantine Empire, its ceremony and its architecture. It is a stanza spacious enough to contain the heaven of the sages and the palace of the Emperor. However, *ottava rima* is not a symmetrical stanza: its rhyme scheme divides it into a group of six alternately rhyming lines—*ababab*—followed by a couplet, *cc.* Normally, the couplet serves to sum up, or to comment on, the matter that has preceded it. In its first two stations, "Sailing to Byzantium" observes the norm: each ends with a self-contained couplet. But when the true crisis of the painful wound to the ego erupts in part III, the lines can no longer be measured and steady in pace. Agitated by the frustration of the impotent man who has found in the country of sexual coupling no place for himself, no song he can sing, the lines cease to obey the stanza's rhyme-imposed norm of sixain and couplet. The speaker's sentences drive on over line-ends, destroying equanimity of rhythm: the enjambments—"sick with desire / And . . ."; "a dying animal / It knows not"; "gather me / Into"—mimic the urge to escape. And even in the station of final, chosen, secular identity, the anxiety of embodiment impels the single-sentence stanza on to its prophetic gaze. Although the final, inverted rhyme—"Byzantium . . . come"—is resonant, the couplet is not free-standing, but is dependent on its enjambed adjectival lead-in, "set upon a golden bough to sing / To . . ." Knowing the normal composure of serious *ottava rima,* and witnessing how distress and fear force it to depart from its norm, we sense both the desperation of the third station, and the expectant drive toward a visionary future in the fourth.

It is always useful, in thinking about a poem by Yeats, to see whether it is governed by one or more master-tropes. The governing tropes of "Sailing to Byzantium" are symmetry and antithesis. The first half is perfectly symmetrical in length with the second; Yeats makes the symmetry unignorable by his use of identical (if reversed) rhymes at the close of each half. The two halves are also symmetrical in that each presents an antithesis—the first its contrast of profane country to holy city, the second its contrast of asexual eternity to worldly temporality. Each half presents a choice: the protagonist first chooses Byzantium over the country of the young, and later chooses to sing in the Emperor's palace as a golden bird rather than to sing in God's holy fire as a sage (the latter heavenly state embodied below in a cathedral wall-mosaic). The poem is therefore "classical" in feeling, and announces the partial resolution of its antitheses in the ways in which the Emperor's court—in its heterosexuality, its temporal song, and its worldliness—resembles the lost country of the young.

There are other formal decisions on Yeats's part at work in the poem, of course. One is the ornamental intensifying of diction when he represents his own secular aesthetic ("such a form as Grecian *gold*smiths make of hammered *gold* and *gold* enamelling . . . upon a *gold*en bough");[4] another is the grammar of the first station, where the long middle sentence of description is bracketed with two decisive sentences of judgment. But diction, imagery, and grammar are forms that readers can usually perceive by themselves. It is the external and internal shapes assumed by the poem, and the implicit arguments made by the decisive ordering of the stanzas, that need pointing out. The argument of the poem (which will eventually endorse as values— even in the period of impotent old age—the secular, the ironic, and the aesthetic) must begin with the attempted repudiation of the "country" of the young and their "sensual" music; otherwise the defiant flight to the "holy city" would not take on high relief. And naturally the poem must conclude with the description of the "right" choice of embodiment; but prefacing it with a temporarily entertained "wrong" choice makes the "right" one conclusive. The balanced arrangement of stanzas points up the antitheses on which the poem is constructed. And although critics have recognized the initial antitheses between country and city, they have missed the equally fierce antithesis repudiating sacred song in favor of secular music.[5]

Yet however well we see "Sailing to Byzantium" when we consider it by itself, for the fullest sense of it we need to pose it against its 1930 nonclassical complement, "Byzantium" (497–498), which also employs an eight-line stanza, though not *ottava rima*. The composition of this poem was occasioned by Yeats's serious illness ("Malta fever" or brucellosis) in 1929; his death was thought to be imminent. "Byzantium" has no Roman numerals, so we can presume the speaker to be standing in one place; that place, as we gradually discover, is "the Emperor's pavement," next to the harbor where the sea meets the breakwater formed by the Emperor's smithies (in which smiths create the golden artifacts, profane and sacred alike, of Byzantium). The poem is written in eight-line stanzas, but these do not resemble the "square" block of pentameters in the *ottava rima* of "Sailing to Byzantium." In the first place, only five of the eight lines of the "Byzantium" stanza are pentameters; the line lengths are 5-5-5-4-5-3-3-5. And while the reassuringly recurrent rhymes of the *ababab* sixain of the *ottava rima* sustain the reader's sense of dependable form as the stanza progresses, here the rhyme scheme breaks sooner and changes itself more unpredictably, presenting two initial couplets (*aabb*) followed by an embraced-rhyme quatrain (*cddc*). The rhythms, too (unlike the unchanging pentameter of *ottava rima*) change unpredictably. Because the poem opens with a regular pentameter couplet, and is followed by a third pentameter, we expect that steady and easily perceived measure to continue. But then something goes askew: line 4, though it rhymes with line 3, is a foot "too short": it has only four beats, not five. The "missing" beat causes a strong pause:

> The unpurged images of day recede;
> The Emperor's drunken soldiery are abed;
> Night resonance recedes, night-walkers' song
> After great cathedral gong[.]

This careful scene-setting puts us in Byzantium as the gong strikes midnight. The chaotic unprocessed images and sounds of day—its resonance, its sensual music (the night-walkers' song), its male lust and rage (externalized in the drunken soldiery) "recede"—withdraw as if banished by the midnight gong. Above the street floats the dome of the Holy Wisdom, regarding with scorn the inferior human doings of rage ("fury") or lust ("mire") beneath it. In the embraced-rhyme quatrain that follows, huge abstractions ("All that man is") replace the realistic soldiers and their camp-followers:

> A starlit or a moonlit dome disdains
> All that man is,
> All mere complexities,
> The fury and the mire of human veins.

Like the next three stanzas of the five-stanza "Byzantium," this first stanza unfolds in a single unbroken sentence. The speaker watches, as the sights and sounds of day disappear, the rising of the disdainful dome, which dominates the city at the starlit dark of the moon as at the unearthly full. The stage is set: the topic will be human "complexities" arising from the coursing of the blood. To the dome these are "mere" complexities: the dome stands for that which is purged of such complexities, that which harbors within itself ideal images already purged and pure.

A form of self-loathing motivates this opening. Yeats's ever-present reference points, Love and War, the two noble occupations of the heroes of epic and romance, become, in old age, the degenerate forms of themselves that we call lust and rage. The poet wonders whether his emotions have not so coarsened as to make him repellent to himself and to others. In response to a criticism of his late poetry by his friend Lady Dorothy Wellesley, Yeats wrote "The Spur" (1936), an epigram that could stand as epigraph to "Byzantium":

> You think it horrible that lust and rage
> Should dance attention upon my old age;
> They were not such a plague when I was young;
> What else have I to spur me into song?
>
> (591)

In "Byzantium," the poet is spurred into song by the goadings of lust and rage, which he renames mire—the filth of a sty—and blood, symbolic of both sexual arousal and warlike aggression.

The second motivation of the poem, in addition to self-disgust, is yearning—a yearning not so much for death itself as for the knowledge of the afterlife, a glimpse of the world that lies beyond the horizon. The poet wonders, "Whom will I meet there? Will I be purged of mire and blood, and if so, how? Does the spirit persist?" What does a poet become when he is nothing but his *Collected Poems*? It is charming to imagine oneself, once one has become one's poems, as a bird singing to generations of (momentarily) attentive listeners; but what we find in a poet's poems is not a bird but (as Yeats's father once said of Blake) "the man himself, revolting and desiring." Yeats needs to find an image for what he imagines we, his readers, may find him to be, when he is still "alive," in this equivocal sense, within his lifework.

And so he places himself again in Byzantium. In keeping with the fact that the city can be nothing but a projection of what he now is, the population has undergone a startling degeneration: the drowsy Emperor and his lords and ladies have been replaced by their daytime street-equivalents: the Emperor's drunken soldiery and their night-walking prostitutes. These are the unpurged bodily images of rage and lust that resonate through the speaker's days; by night, in the Byzantium of his vision, they recede, like a filthy tide, and permit the desire for purgation to arise, its images projecting their spectral disdain of all complexities of mire and blood. The stanza has not yet identified a speaker: it remains an impersonal description (from the disdainful dome's point of view) with ambitions toward "philosophical" statement.

In the second and third stanzas, we are offered two parallel and tonally complex visions of the afterlife that "float" before the eyes of the speaker.

On the left, we see the mummy that the poet's body will become. On the right, we see a golden bird representing the eventual destiny of his soul:

| Body | Soul |
|---|---|
| Before me floats an image, man or shade, | Miracle, bird, or golden handiwork, |
| Shade more than man, more image than a shade; | More miracle than bird or handiwork, |
| For Hades' bobbin bound in mummy-cloth | Planted on the star-lit golden bough, |
| May unwind the winding path; | Can like the cocks of Hades crow, |
| A mouth that has no moisture and no breath | Or, by the moon embittered, scorn aloud |
| Breathless mouths may summon; | In glory of changeless metal |
| I hail the superhuman; | Common bird or petal |
| I call it death-in-life and life-in-death. | And all complexities of mire or blood. |

We know that these two visions are parallel rather than different because they use the same comparative rhetoric to express the same evaluative perplexity in the speaker: in stanza 2, "What am I seeing—an X, a Y, or a Z?—but it is more Z than Y, more X than Z"; in stanza 3, ["What am I seeing]—A, B, or C: more A than B or C." In each case, a hierarchical comparative choice is made among possibilities: "I am seeing an image (rather than the other possibilities, a man or a shade)"; "I am seeing a miracle (rather than merely a bird or a golden handiwork)." Yeats's first vision is an image of his dead body, its mouth no longer emitting moisture or breath; it has become a mummy (resembling a columnar bobbin wound with grave-bands); it may, the speaker hopes, serve as psychopomp or guide to the putative company of the labyrinthine otherworld. (Yeats may have derived the columnar corpse from Donne's upright shroud-wound death-image reproduced on his memorial in St. Paul's.)

In the stanza 2 vision of the mummy, the eight-line stanza functions differently from the way it had in its first appearance. Now, instead of dividing itself, as it had in stanza 1, into two parts (realistic description of a street scene followed by philosophical abstraction defining the human—"All that man is"), it divides itself into four end-stopped groups of two. The first piece, *aa* (as always, with the two rhyming pentameters, the most stable part of the stanza), sets the stage and defines the vision as an image. The two external bracketing pieces of the stanza (lines 1–2 and 7–8) represent, in turn, description ("Before me floats an image") and response ("I hail [it]"). The two internal pieces (lines 3–4 and 5–6) express the interior hopes of the speaker: the mummy *may* be a clue, its mouth *may* summon the company of other dead. These emotional middle units imitate each other: each presents a longer line followed by a shorter line (5-4, 5-3), causing a pause for speculation at the end of the line following the modal "may":

> For Hades' bobbin bound in mummy-cloth / May unwind the
>      winding path;
> (*pause*)
> A mouth that has no moisture and no breath / Breathless mouths
>      may summon
> (*pause*).

The following unit, however, the hailing, reverses this repeated long/short/ *pause* form, and instead presents a short/long (3-5) statement that broadens as it closes:

> I hail the superhuman; / I call it death-in-life and life-in-death.

The stanza's three counterpointed end-stopped rhythmic possibilities—two equal members (lines 1–2), a long member preceding a shorter one (lines 3–4 and 5–6), and a short member preceding a longer one (lines 7–8) confer on this mummy-stanza its deliberative posing of one specific speculation after another as it confronts the vision before its eyes, finally subsiding to the Coleridgean paradoxes of a specter alive and not alive, dead and not dead.

An entirely different rhythm pervades the stanza of the second apparition, that of the afterlife of the soul. The golden bird which startles the speaker ("Miracle") parallels in its "scorn" the "disdain" expressed by the golden dome. Just as earthly cocks announce dawn, the cocks of Hades (abetted by the cathedral gong) announce midnight; the golden bird can (during the nights where no moon shines) crow like the cocks; or, when the moon appears (with its celestial beauty surpassing any golden handiwork), the bird, in its "glory of changeless metal," is provoked to add words to its crowing, to "scorn aloud" not only the perishable earthly things that resemble it ("common bird or petal") but also all human beings, with their complexities of mire and blood. Here we have no deliberative end-stopped two-line units: instead the stanza is fundamentally unstoppable, although its kernel sentence ("[The] bird can . . . crow, or scorn aloud bird or petal and all complexities") is constantly interrupted by subordinate units of qualification, as the poet thinks his way through the moral attitudes of an artifact.

Let us pause for a moment to summarize: Yeats (as we can call the speaker), seeing the unpurged images recede, is granted a vision of two purged images: what, after death, his body will become (a mummy); and what, after death, his soul will become (a voice). When he reflects on how amazing it is that a living voice—arising from a book—can survive physical death, he decides that although the vision *could* be called a bird, or *could* be called a golden handiwork, its correct name is "miracle." How but by a miracle can we hear voices from ages past speaking from the page? Such voices carry with them, however, the bitterness of a Midas-"miracle": they exist no longer in flesh, but as artifacts of the "changeless metal" of language; eternally fixed, they belong (hammered into form's unity, and no longer vexed by fleshly "complexities" of emotion) to a different order from the human—they are "superhuman" examples of death-in-life and life-in-death.

In order to become the two "purged" afterlife images of himself—dry mummy-body and embittered miracle-voice—Yeats has only to step, as midnight strikes, into the refining fire which consumes unpurged images and enables them to be made—by goldsmiths in the Emperor's smithies— changeless and glorious ones. The supernatural fire, represented in mosaic flames, burns on the Emperor's pavement fronting the shore where (as we learn at the close) the sea breaks against Byzantium. In the fire, human complexity is purged into simplicity; but simplicity, the poet knows, extirpates voice: in "Vacillation" the Heart is "Struck dumb in the simplicity of fire!" The drama of "Byzantium" reaches its climax as the poet faces the fire: will he enter it? The fourth stanza offers the seductive but terrifying invitation of the purging fire, defined in the paradoxes of negative theology: the winding syntax of this part at first euphemizes—by "voluntary" words such as "come" and "leave"—the process of involuntary extinction. But at last—with the word "dying"—the stanza affords no escape from the envisaged anguishing process of purgation, down to its final double "agony":

> At midnight on the Emperor's pavement flit
> Flames that no faggot feeds, nor steel has lit,
> Nor storm disturbs, flames begotten of flame,
> Where blood-begotten spirits come
> And all complexities of fury leave,
> Dying into a dance,
> An agony of trance,
> An agony of flame that cannot singe a sleeve.

This sentence will not let the spirits pause at the end of line 4, where a natural break (as in the preceding three stanzas) "wants" (with the change of rhyme) to occur; the spirits are forced over the line break into their purgation, during which their complexities "leave" them, as the syntax enacts the way in which complexities dwindle and melt as they are consumed in the flame:

> All complexities . . . leave,
>> Dying
>>> into    a dance,
>>>> An agony
>>>> of trance,
>>>> An agony
>>>> of flame
>> that cannot singe a sleeve.

Processes like this agony are what Yeats had left out of "Sailing to Byzantium," where they had been prayed for ("Consume my heart away") but not undergone. Here, in this penultimate stanza of "Byzantium," the speaker, confronting the fire directly, understands what would happen were he to choose to enter it. The mortally ill poet feels wearily the temptation to surrender his complexities and assent even to the flame-convulsion of death. (Although Yeats did not write the poem until he began to recover from his grave illness, the poem is not an aftermath-reflection on a past experience; it enacts, always in the present tense, the speaker in the presence of actual death.)

How—and with what modifications of syntax—can the poem end? Will the speaker repudiate his twin afterlife-visions? Or will he consent to the fiery agony of spiritual purgation, that trance, that dance, which incinerates the "complexities of mire and blood"? At the last, almost-hypnotized moment, the speaker draws back from the step into the fire that would free him from mortal suffering. Turning away from the pavement-fire, he gazes instead out to the sea of life (as the Delphic Oracle had described it) over which he had traveled to come to Byzantium. A flood of other "blood-begotten spirits" like himself are arriving constantly, borne on that sea "of mire and blood" by the dolphins (symbols of resurrection on Roman sarcophagi). The city musters all its resources of art to conquer the spirits begotten by human blood: the smithies of the goldsmiths break the flood, and the flame-patterned marbles, where the spirits dance, break "bitter furies of complexity." But the throngs of unpurged images begetting fresh images (the verb "beget" recalled from "Sailing to Byzantium") continue to arrive without cessation. The speaker's last look is directed toward the sea casting up those images, a sea torn by the desire for resurrection, tormented by the midnight gong of purgation (these adjectives, properly belonging to the throng of arriving spirits, are transferred to the sea as the medium bearing them). Here, an exclamatory mode replaces the former descriptive one, as the poet's language echoes the agitated wildness of "Kubla Khan":

> Astraddle on the dolphin's mire and blood,
> Spirit after spirit! The smithies break the flood,
> The golden smithies of the Emperor!
> Marbles of the dancing floor
> Break bitter furies of complexity,
> Those images that yet
> Fresh images beget,
> That dolphin-torn, that gong-tormented sea.

Although this ultimate stanza of "voice-over" is syntactically divided into the exclamatory and the descriptive, the almost incoherent repetitiveness of the lines binds the two parts together: "Spirit after spirit! . . . The smithies break . . . The golden smithies . . .! Marbles . . . Break . . . Those images . . . images . . . That torn . . . that tormented sea." Yeats produces a cinematic rendition of events-as-they-are-happening, coming almost too fast to be narrated.

The strict formal order observed by "Byzantium" through its first four stanzas—midnight stage-set, body-vision, soul-vision, purgatorial fire—has intimated that a "solution" will be offered at the last to the torn and tormented speaker. However, we see that "Byzantium" closes within, not outside, the Yeatsian complexities. Why, we might ask, does Yeats's version of human life keep changing its focus (though not its elements)?

> All that man is,
> All mere complexities,
> The fury and the mire of human veins.
>
> And all complexities of mire or blood.
>
> Where blood-begotten spirits come
> And all complexities of fury leave[.]
>
> . . . [B]itter furies of complexity[.]

As we scrutinize the successive appearances of the elements above, we can see that man's complexities are first equated with the fury and mire coursing through human veins in the form of blood (blood willing to spill blood as well as the blood of sexual arousal). Then mire's complexities are paralleled to blood's complexities; next, we learn that fury has its complexities too. In short, blood (our animal being) has biological complexities, and the emotional fury throbbing within the blood has complexities, and the mire of lust polluting the blood has complexities of its own as well. The complexities of base emotions collaborate with the complexities of animal vitality itself to render existence insoluble. Life would not seem so insoluble if the riddles of mire, blood, fury, and complexity stayed in one order, in one formulation. Instead, they writhe and twist like Proteus under the hand, presenting us with the choice of either remaining in the unpurged turmoil of the "sea of mire and blood" or else surrendering to the fire. The final stance of the poem in tumult and pain, in a sea torn and tormented, resists the original lure of the neatly divided double vision ("image" and "miracle") of the purged afterlife, and consequently refuses the escape from mortality promised by the deathless flames.[6]

"Byzantium," like the earlier "Sailing to Byzantium," depends for its structure on horizontal and vertical movement; the dominant trope as the poem opens is one of vertical hierarchy. We initially encounter this hierarchy as the "human" horizontal street-motion of "receding" lust and rage is opposed by the vertical and universal "disdain" of the dome. We see hierarchy next in the triple comparative "vertical" rankings, as the poet seeks the most accurate description of the two visions—"shade *more than* man, *more* image *than* a shade; *more* miracle *than* bird or handiwork"; and again, in the image of the bird that looks down in scorn on "common bird or petal." These hierarchical comparisons all have to do with the superiority of the "ideal" over the human. But when the human choice of entering the flame arises, the movement of the poem returns to the horizontal as the speaker directs his gaze to the Emperor's pavement where he stands. The vertical is hinted at in the "flame that cannot singe a sleeve," but the poem is now operating on the horizontal plane, as spirits enter their dying dance amid the flames on the marble pavement. The conflict in the final stanza, too, puts both of the antagonistic forces animating the poem, the ideal and the human, on the same horizontal plane. It can do this because it deflects its interest from the "vertical" after-death products (mummy and golden bird) onto their causes. What causes the mummy is physical death; what causes the golden bird is the labor of the smiths who work the gold in their smithies. The smiths laboring in the smithies are not "in heaven" as the sages in eternity are; they are on the same plane as the sea of human torment, and so the poem ends in a "horizontal" standoff between the breakwater-smithies and the turbulent sea. The speaker refuses, in "Byzantium," to escape either into eternity (by vertical consumption in the flames) or into an "alternative" plane of horizontal artifice (the Emperor's smithies). He remains as he is, a human embodied, even if the body is buffeted by suffering.

"Byzantium" gains by being read together with "Sailing to Byzantium," and vice versa. There are no eternal singing sages in "Byzantium"; and ordinary human "sensual music" has receded with the receding of the street-walkers. The golden bird is not said to "sing," as in "Sailing to Byzantium," but rather to "scorn aloud" common beauty. The spirits being purged do not sing, either, they only dance; and the dance, a form of trance, can tell us nothing of what is past, or passing, or to come. The speaker's face, from the beginning, has been turned resolutely away from nature, fixed on the iconic décor, dome and bird, of the holy city. And although the choices of reincarnation in "Sailing to Byzantium" were daunting—to be a sage in eternity, or to be a voice in a palace—they were at least visible in their embodied artifacts, mosaic and golden bird. But in "Byzantium," when Yeats asks what he will be after death, he sees an embalmed, rather than a reincarnated, self. Its words are its shroud; it may lead us into communication with itself and other dead mouths, but these ghost-mouths, unlike those of the sages, do not sing; they have neither breath nor voice. The hatred of flesh which led to the purgation of common birds with blood in their veins, or common petals with moisture in their bloom, lies behind the double construct of mummy and bird. As soon as real birds and petals come into view, the golden Midas-bird becomes embittered by its own lunar unreality. The speaker of "Byzantium," like the speaker of "Sailing to Byzantium," has decided before the poem opens to repudiate life before it can repudiate him. But the very unsatisfactoriness of mummy and embittered bird as images for the posthumous body and voice propel the poem on. Life will not be held still for posthumous inspection, whether in the form of dome or mummy, bird or trance. Instead, mire and blood heave in flood, dolphins tear the waves, the death-gong sounds its imperative, and new unpurged images constantly replace those that have receded into purgation by fire.

It is illuminating, always, to ask of a Yeats poem what kind of beauty (defining that word as aesthetic gesture) it presents. A different form of beauty is embraced in each of the Byzantium poems, although both present a conflict between something "superhuman" (the eternal sages, the unsingeing flame) and the "merely" human (a temporal song in the Emperor's court, a speaker turning his back on the fire to remain within the complexities of mire and blood). The humor ("To keep a drowsy Emperor awake") and equanimity ("Of what is past, or passing, or to come") of the bird of hammered gold ensure that "Sailing to Byzantium," in spite of its central moment of agony as the ego momentarily disintegrates, ends in the attractive atmosphere of a reconciliatory aesthetic of the beautiful. All is in order in the Emperor's palace. In contrast, the bitterness suffusing "Byzantium" ensures that it remains in the sublime of conflict. In the first poem Yeats is content to become, in his afterlife in literature, the historian of the past, the chronicler of the passing present, and the aspiring prophet of the future. But in "Byzantium" he knows that even in his completed life-work—that miracle—his posthumous voice will be one embittered by the celestial lunar ideal, scorning and even disdaining, through the intrinsic perfection of form, the complexities of life—while still tormentedly contemplating their tumult. We certainly read the agitated "Byzantium" as a painful "corrective" to "Sailing to Byzantium"; yet it is equally possible to read the steady and beautiful ironic pace of the earlier resigned *ottava rima* poem—given pride of place, after all, as the first poem in *The Tower*—as a "corrective" to the desperate clinging to life of "Byzantium."[7]

Both poems are so expertly structured, stanza by stanza, that we would not wish them otherwise. In the first, we advance with the gradually enlightened speaker from station to completed station, ending with his satisfaction in comprehensive temporal song; in the second we stand with the speaker within Byzantium, now gazing at the dome of Hagia Sophia, now hearing its midnight gong, now contemplating successive visions of body and soul, now imagining the fire of purgation, now—refusing purgation—looking backward and outward to the violent sea. It is the mind, not the body, that moves in the single station of "Byzantium": we live within the categories of that mind as it takes the measure of its present and future state. In each poem, the Yeatsian imagination has set itself the task of finding symbols for its present adversity—old age—and has found so many that they have by now entered the minds of readers as if they had always been there: the dying generations, a holy city, a golden dome, a mosaic of sages, a bird of hammered gold, an Emperor's court, a mummy, a hypnotic fire, the marble pavement of the Emperor, the sea of mire and blood. It is only with an effort that we can try to undo in our mind all that the Yeatsian imagination has summoned forth. Suppose Yeats had merely said, "I am old, I am impotent, I fear dying; I can almost see myself as an embalmed corpse; I can almost see myself as an immortal poetic voice; but I am cast down in spirit by perplexity and vexed by physical suffering." We would not remember such sentences; but we remember the superb invention of Byzantium—its heaving waters; its stage-set of inhabitants, dome, bird, and dolphins; its floating visions; its magic flames; its turmoil of the deathbed. And we remember, too, the internal structures of the two Byzantium poems, the first so ordered, the second so convulsively propelled, and the arguments for secular art and for human life, however beset, that are borne home by those arrangements.

## The Poems of the Delphic Oracle

The speaker in the Byzantium poems is a solitary. He may sing—as a golden bird—among the lords and ladies, but he is not one of them. He has refused to become a sage and join the company of the sages in eternity. He cannot enter the purgative fire and join the company of mouths that have no moisture and no breath. It may be in part the wish for company in the afterlife that prompts Yeats's second pair of poems flanking death: these are ones prompted primarily by Greek sources. As we have seen, "Sailing to Byzantium" and "Byzantium" take place in the visionary antechambers of death, as the speakers try to imagine, beyond the crucible of transmutation, some new incarnation. But in the 1931 poem "The Delphic Oracle upon Plotinus" (530–531) and its companion piece of 1938, "News for the Delphic Oracle" (611–612), the speaker has arrived (with some help from the Delphic Oracle) at the actual afterlife that awaits mortals. Plotinus (the third-century founder of Neoplatonic philosophy) is the protagonist of both poems; it is his journey to the afterlife which gives them their focus. The Delphic Oracle (quoted in Porphyry's *Life of Plotinus,* read by Yeats in Stephen MacKenna's translation) had revealed the difficulty of Plotinus's journey through the sea of life to the realm of the Immortals. Addressing Plotinus directly, the oracle said:

> Oft-times as you strove to rise above the bitter waves of this blood-drenched life, above the sickening whirl, toiling in the mid-most of the rushing flood and the unimaginable turmoil, oft-times, from the Ever-Blessed, there was shown to you the Term still close at hand[.] . . . [T]ossed in the welter, you still had vision. . . . But now that you have . . . quitted the tomb that held your lofty soul, you enter at once the heavenly consort: Where fragrant breezes play . . . with the blandishments of

the Loves, and delicious airs, and tranquil sky; where Minos and Rhadamanthus dwell, great brethren of the golden race of mighty Zeus; where dwell the just Aeacus, and Plato, . . . and stately Pythagoras and all else that form the choir of Immortal Love.[8]

Yeats, in his versifying of this passage, is cruel where the Delphic Oracle was kind. He does not allow Plotinus to arrive at the "heavenly consort," or even to glimpse the calm of the afterlife while he is swimming toward it, buffeted by the sea. The poem, in a simple two-part form, offers in its first stanza a picture of mortal existence—turbulent, frustrated, half-blind; in the second stanza, it gives us a contrasting pastoral picture of the realm of the Immortals, known to the Delphic Oracle but not yet attained by Plotinus:

> The Delphic Oracle upon Plotinus
>
> Behold that great Plotinus swim,
> Buffeted by such seas;
> Bland Rhadamanthus beckons him,
> But the Golden Race looks dim,
> Salt blood blocks his eyes.
>
> Scattered on the level grass
> Or winding through the grove
> Plato there and Minos pass,
> There stately Pythagoras
> And all the choir of Love.

The first stanza uses all its *b*'s to bring out the buffetings of the sea; the second shows what Plotinus could see clearly if salt blood were *not* blocking his eyes. Yeats has taken pains, after the obstructions (reversed feet and spondees) of the first stanza, to make the second graciously end in harmonious iambics, "And all the choir of Love." In choosing his stanza form, Yeats alludes to the "folk" aspect of the Delphic Oracle by evoking the ghost of the ballad stanza (*abab*, 4-3-4-3), while modifying that "archaic" form into a more "artificial" and elaborate five-line invention: *abaab*, 4-3-4-4-3. The "extra" "*a*" line prevents the repose that would occur if the fourth line rhymed with the second (as we, hearing the initial ballad-rhythm, expect it to do); therefore the fourth line acts here, in the first stanza, as a retarding obstruction. The ballad stanza beginning would "prefer" (in its traditional length) to have Plotinus arrive in line 4, once he is beckoned (here, as elsewhere, brackets designate a passage confected by me to clarify what the Yeats poem might have done, but did not):

[Behold that great Plotinus swim,
Buffeted by such seas;
Bland Rhadamanthus beckons him,
And bids him take his ease.]

The fact that the inserted "extra" fourth line has four beats rather than three, and continues the "*a*" rhyme rather than presenting the expected "*b*" rhyme, makes us uneasy; but even when the expected "*b*" rhyme arrives in line 5, relieving the prosodic tension, it does not end Plotinus's suffering, but cruelly intensifies it by blinding him in the three stressed syllables with which it opens: "**Salt blood blocks** his eyes."

*good analysis...*

By contrast, when the prolongation of the stanza by the extra "*a*" line recurs in stanza 2, it is untroubling; it merely adds another Immortal, "stately Pythagoras," to the procession. In the country of the gods, there are no more buffetings: the grass is level, there is a shady grove; always at one's ease, one can either recline on the grass or wind through the grove; all the Immortals "pass" in mild succession, effortlessly, as the poem substitutes a meditative pace for its initial turbulent striving. Yeats's response to the "infallible" description given by the Delphic Oracle is to ask whether he himself, if he were Plotinus, would be happy to be consigned to this bland afterlife. The landscape is bland, even Rhadamanthus the judge is bland, the activities (reclining, strolling, passing) are bland, and the society is bland— no women are present. Even the little Erotes of the choir of Love offer, in the Oracle's (translated) words, "blandishments." Yeats rejects the company of these even-toned male Hellenic philosophers just as he had rejected the fiery company of the male Hebraic sages. How could we call a place heaven if it lacked women and children, the young and the old, as well as persons exemplifying the ages in between? And how could we call that place heaven if it omitted sex? And would the appropriate music for a humanly appealing heaven be the bland choruses and sedate iambics of the male "choir of Love"? The sharp structural contrast (as stanza 2 follows stanza 1) between Plotinus's blind mortal struggle and the bland philosophical wanderings that await him ensures that the problem of the afterlife, as it is Delphically enunciated in this poem, remains for Yeats an unresolved one.

Yeats decides, as his life nears its end in 1938, to take up the Oracle's privileged visionary designation, "There," and write a poem in which he would mockingly describe the more agreeable heaven he would design for himself. If the Oracle says "Plato there and Minos pass, / There stately Pythagoras / And all the choir of Love," Yeats the counter-oracle will assert in imitation: "There sighed amid his choir of love / Tall Pythagoras," to assure us that he is reporting—but with fuller information—on the same scene. When he has finished, he rudely entitles his poem "News for the Delphic Oracle." It was published only posthumously (March 1939); Yeats had died on January 28. This late poem is both a celebration of, and a satire on, all mythological imaginings of the afterlife in various cultures. Yeats's otherworld (carefully marked as Paradise by its reprise of the alchemical combination of gold and silver familiar from "The Song of Wandering Aengus" and elsewhere) aims to represent every kind of plenitude.

The main challenge to interpretation posed by "News" lies in the poem's apparent disorder. Yeats assembles what at first appears to be a hodgepodge of personages from the various mythologies of his reading: Celtic, Greek, Christian. He includes—in the poem's Great Chain of Being—gods, human beings, intermediate beings (nymphs and satyrs), and animals (dolphins). He represents in it all the ages of man, from infants (the Holy Innocents) to immortal "codgers," with adolescence (Peleus) in between. And the poem is tolerant of different kinds of sexual activity (solitary, heterosexual, homosexual, masochistic, and inter-species—between Nereid and man, Thetis and Peleus). Indeed, the chief activity of the Yeatsian afterlife is sex (preceded by the characteristic Yeatsian stretching and yawning of drowsy readiness, and accompanied by sighs of love). Being translated to the otherworld is no guarantee of moral status, since those in this Paradise are as fallible as those on earth: love is blind, love is biological, love is predatory. The ruler of this anarchic company is the god of all nature, Pan (his habitat and companions borrowed from the Homeric "Hymn to Pan" and from the Poussin inspiring Yeats).[9] And the music is not the bland unison of the little Loves, but a cacophony, the "intolerable" music of allness. "News for the Delphic Oracle" is the most blasphemous of Yeats's poems: Plato et al. are merely "golden codgers"; Oisin's "fairy bride," Niamh, is an opportunistic "man-picker"; the dolphins make a bumptious arrival, pitching off the spirits who are straddling them; the Holy Innocents rejoice unnaturally as "their wounds open again"; the choir of Love wades out in the bay, proffering laurel crowns to all comers; and the foam is full of fleshy copulating beings, nymphs and satyrs.

"News" is a sequence in three parts or "stations," and we will need to explain, as in the case of "Sailing to Byzantium," why Yeats prefaced his stanzas with Roman numerals.

News for the Delphic Oracle

I

There all the golden codgers lay,
There the silver dew,
And the great water sighed for love,
And the wind sighed too.
Man-picker Niamh leant and sighed
By Oisin on the grass;
There sighed amid his choir of love
Tall Pythagoras.
Plotinus came and looked about,
The salt-flakes on his breast,
And having stretched and yawned awhile
Lay sighing like the rest.

II

Straddling each a dolphin's back
And steadied by a fin,
Those Innocents re-live their death,
Their wounds open again.
The ecstatic waters laugh because
Their cries are sweet and strange,
Through their ancestral patterns dance,
And the brute dolphins plunge
Until, in some cliff-sheltered bay
Where wades the choir of love
Proffering its sacred laurel crowns,
They pitch their burdens off.

III

Slim adolescence that a nymph has stripped,
Peleus on Thetis stares.
Her limbs are delicate as an eyelid,
Love has blinded him with tears;
But Thetis' belly listens.
Down the mountain walls
From where Pan's cavern is
Intolerable music falls.
Foul goat-head, brutal arm appear,
Belly, shoulder, bum,

> Flash fishlike; nymphs and satyrs
> Copulate in the foam.

Yeats took ironic satisfaction in thinking up an otherworld where every-
thing sexual is permitted, where a cornucopial plenitude manifests itself.
But this disorderly accumulation—flung out in a flippant ballad-meter—
in no way resembles Yeats's idea, in "A Prayer for My Daughter," of the
"Horn of Plenty" spilling out its abundance in a ceremonious generational
manner:

> How but in custom and in ceremony
> Are innocence and beauty born?
> Ceremony's a name for the rich horn,
> And custom for the spreading laurel tree.
>
> (406)

In Pan's realm of nature, there are no civilized country-houses, no placidity
of custom and ceremony (though Innocents and beauty and laurel still turn
up). And yet, Yeats's pastoral is inhabited by such unlikely persons that it
cannot be seen as merely a pastoral. There are no named philosophers
in traditional pastoral, and no such heterogeneity of reference. Yeats's after-
life is one in which Nature must incorporate culture, or we would not en-
joy it.

   Once Yeats has imagined his preposterous otherworld (literally pre-
posterous, since within the poem later Celtic personages come into view
before the earlier classical and Christian ones), he dares his readers to un-
derstand the structure of his mythological mockery. At first glance, "News"
gives every external appearance of fine orderliness: there are three equal-in-
length Roman-numeraled parts, each containing three quatrains, so that
each numbered section represents 3 × 3 (a "perfect square" like the 4 × 4
of the "Irish Airman" and the 8 × 8 we shall later discover in "Among
School Children"). Yet for all this appearance of mathematical decorum,
the stanzas are grossly indecorous. Unlike the "perfect" quatrains found
in "Easter 1916"—with "perfect" rhymes (*abab*) and consistent line lengths
(3-3-3-3)—those of "News for the Delphic Oracle" exhibit only the ragged
line lengths and imperfect rhyme of the folk-ballad (4-3-4-3, *abcb*). We are
firmly situated, it seems, in the realm of "low" art. This impression is rein-
forced by the absurdity of the speaker's rhythm and diction, especially as
the sequence opens with its sigh-song of narrative "naïveté" ("And the wind

sighed too"). The artless narrator knows, it appears, only one principal verb for afterlife expression: "And the great water sighed for love, / And the wind sighed too. / Niamh . . . sighed; // There sighed . . . / Pythagoras. / Plotinus . . . // Lay sighing like the rest." (We might recall, from "The Lover's Song" in "The Three Bushes," "For the womb the seed sighs.") What are we to make of this *reductio ad absurdum* of diction? The universal sighing is the very respiration of the animal world, a choral sighing of sex. That the sighs of desire come from codgers makes them unseemly; that Niamh is a deliberate "man-picker" robs the sighs of spontaneity. Because the Innocents are pre-sexual, their cries ought to be innocent, but Yeats gives them a perverse air of masochism by associating the cries with the re-opening of wounds, by calling them "sweet" and "strange," and by allowing them to provoke the ecstatic waters to an erotic laughter. At the same time, the muscular Innocents ("Straddling each a dolphin's back") and the dolphins pitching their burdens off confer an earthy air of circus performance on the scene, while a mercenary atmosphere hovers about the proffering of sacred crowns by the wading Erotes. It is all undignified, sensual, and irrepressible, a "News for the Poet Wordsworth" as well as for the Delphic Oracle. We have indeed traveled far, and seen the children sporting on the shore of that immortal sea that brought us hither, but Wordsworth's elegiac loftiness has been at once violently naturalized into the play of the energetic Innocents, and defamiliarized into ecstatic water-laughter.

The disorder of presentation seems to extend to the whole poem, but as we examine the order of the poem's "stations" we come to understand that Yeats shows, in I, the population of the otherworld; in II, the moment of arrival in the otherworld; and in III, the central activity of this world, copulation. We do not at first deduce Yeats's motive for dwelling on the disparate members of the population, but eventually we see that they are the company he desires to have in the afterlife, and so must represent all the ages of man. The "mature" codgers (Yeats's coevals) and sexually experienced lovers (in the form of Niamh the man-picker) are identified first, preceding the earliest age, the polymorphously sexual infant Innocents. The sequence of the ages of man ends with the tableau of the adolescent Peleus, blinded by love for Thetis, who herself is driven not by love but by biology; her "belly listens" to Pan's "intolerable" music falling from his cavern above.

The Yeatsian landscape does not confirm the original testimony of the Oracle. Yes, we see grass and a shore, but the landscape is neither level nor tranquil: we find a bay, a cliff, mountain walls, and a high cavern. Nor are the inhabitants pursuing dignified activities, such as exchanging philosophical meditations while winding through a grove; instead they plunge into activities ranging from the indecent to the playful to the equivocal. In short, the external prosodic marks of order (equal stanzas, the predictable occurrence of rhymes in lines 2 and 4, the multiplication into 3 × 3 squares) are present to counteract the jumbled *dramatis personae* of the Yeatsian mythological imagination, and to convince us that Yeats does have a plan in mind, that he prefers the lively company here to the sexless breathless mouths and golden bird of his more spectral earlier imaginings.

The Yeatsian imagination, introducing another principle of order, this time a grammatical one, insists on lists of verbs to embody its comic energies. After the initial chorus of repeated sighs joined by Plotinus as he arrives at the shore (as he had not been permitted to do by the Oracle), the verbs include "straddle," "open," "dance," "plunge," "wade," "proffer," "pitch off," "strip," "stare," "blind," "fall," "flash," and (lastly) "copulate"— this final verb drastically clinical, casting off metaphor. At last an internal principle of imaginative order has been asserted: after arriving, "looking about," and resting while being inducted into the atmosphere of love-sighs, all those in the otherworld are constantly engaging in physical activity, chiefly sexual. Another principle of imaginative order can be deduced when we see how the procession of the ages of man (which at first seemed "out of order," with age preceding infancy) displays its actual and intended order as it focuses, at the end, on the moment that keeps humanity in existence: the moment of sexual desire. Yeats displays irony even in this self-portrait of his past, as he shows Peleus as a youth desperately in love, blinded by tears: the folly of love and its imminent heartbreak are caught in the posture of Peleus staring even though blinded. But that virginal male romantic love is immediately demythologized as the evolutionary drive of sex is emphasized in the attitude of Thetis, answering the demand of destiny that she conceive Achilles. Pan, the *genius loci*, sends down his music to compel universal copulation.

The poem has advanced from the opening universal sexual languor through the "perversities" of the masochistic Innocents and the homosexual choir of Erotes, in order to climax in the portrait of the yearning human lover and the knowing Nereid. Both of them obey, in their separate ways, the designer-of-all-nature, Pan, who surrounds their adolescent sexuality with the unmasked copulations of the unbeautiful goat-headed satyrs and the "fishlike" water-nymphs, whose disarticulated body-parts flash in the foam:

> Foul goat-head, brutal arm appear,
> Belly, shoulder, bum,
> Flash fishlike; nymphs and satyrs
> Copulate in the foam.

It might seem that the third of these lines is another trimeter—"Flash **fish**-like; **nymphs** and **satyrs**"—until we recall that in the ballad stanza the third line asks to be given four stresses, and that we must therefore read this line with an initial alliterative spondee: "**Flash fish**-like; **nymphs** and **satyrs**." That heavy rhythm of animal copulation is far from the tripping unstressed syllables of the light, rapid meter that catches the adolescent Peleus in the throes of first love:

> **Slim** adolescence that a **nymph** has **stripped,**
> **Peleus** on **Thetis stares.**
> Her **limbs** are delicate as an **eye**-lid,
> **Love** has **blind**ed him with **tears.**

The old Yeats does not allow this glimpse of innocent yearning to derail his otherworld exploration from its sardonic progress: the final copulations ("belly, shoulder, bum") drastically subvert the blind longing of Peleus, unaware that Thetis's "belly" belongs to Pan.[10] But the foam of the waves remains as emblematic of Peleus's aching sexuality as of the animal sexuality around him: as far back as "The Two Titans," it was the foamy waves of passion that sang their song through the soul of the lover:

> . . . the waves have sung
> Their passion and their restlessness and ruth
> Through his sad soul for ever old and young[.]
> (687)

Like the Byzantium poems, Yeats's pair of "Oracular" poems—the Delphic Oracle's original "divinely inspired" Apollonian vision of the calm realm of the Immortals and Yeats's savage, comic, and grotesque refutation of the idealist view in "News for the Delphic Oracle"—mutually "correct" each other. Yeats's pictorial source, the Poussin painting he believed to represent the marriage of Peleus and Thetis, is, like "The Delphic Oracle upon Plotinus," mythologically coherent, all Greek; but in the capacious and retentive mind of the aging Yeats, Oisin and Plotinus and the Holy Innocents are all at home together. The *topos* of the ages of man is detached from its schematic temporal order to reflect Yeats's triple self-projection; he begins in his present life-moment as a golden codger, tracks his life back to when he was Oisin, goes even further back to infancy, but finally cycles around again to the Oisin position, to himself-as-lover. Content to be caught once more in the sensual music of Pan, he casts himself as the foolish, passionate Peleus. The sense of *déjà vu* about each self-projection is very strong, and accounts for the reactive disenchantment that recurs in each self-presentation. "The Delphic Oracle upon Plotinus," with its calm and soundless grass and groves, is a silent poem conceived in the Neoplatonic region of the Forms, "above the moon," whereas "News for the Delphic Oracle" is a noisy poem, defiantly full of "intolerable" sublunary action and physical sound.

When we look back over Yeats's four poems of the otherworld, we can see that in the last of these, "News," Yeats has abolished all his previous hierarchies. He chooses cacophony of tone and a democratic equality of myth; he disorders the ages of man; and he abolishes as well the received hierarchy of genres: characters from lyric, epic, comedy, farce, and tragedy mix in "News" with an equal absence of dominance, or equal irrelevance. The governing trope of *mélange,* or "allness," has made him abandon the governing tropes of the three previous poems. The governing trope of "Sailing to Byzantium," as we saw, was balanced antithesis. The governing trope of "Byzantium," by contrast, was hierarchy: purged images supersede unpurged ones; a dome disdains all that man is; a golden bird scorns common bird or petal; the vision is shade more than man, more image than a shade; the bird is more miracle than bird or handiwork. The dissolution of hierarchy at the end of "Byzantium"—as images of unstillable begetting and furious conflict disclose the fragility of the system of hierarchical defenses on which the poem rests—returns the reader to the human realm. "The Delphic Oracle upon Plotinus" is governed by the trope of homogeneity: Plotinus will be indistinguishable, in his eventual Elysian blandness, from all the other members of the "Golden Race"—a term in which all individual identity is lost. The Oracle's single index, "There," situates all the inhabitants of Elysium in an identical point of reference, where it is a matter of indifference whether they are stationed in grove or grass. The impersonal voice of the Oracle sees collectively, not individually: all members of the Golden Race are great and stately. The buffeted Plotinus, his vision dimmed by blood and sea-water, is individual only while he swims in the welter of experience; once he is "there" he will become only one among many stately shades. In "News for the Delphic Oracle," however, Yeats rejects balance in favor of disorder, hierarchy in favor of equality, and homogeneity in favor of individuation. In so doing, he risks rejecting music itself: where there are many notes, and all are equal and all individual, both unison and harmony of the conventional sort are sacrificed. But a secret idealism lies within the poem: the conviction that Pan's music of allness—if we could acknowledge it—would awaken in us our deepest desires, which are always sexual ones, and would persuade us to admit our membership in the sighing choir.

From at least the age of thirty, Yeats knew that his poems ultimately belonged not to the realm of ideal wisdom—in spite of the powerful appeal of that region—but to the sublunary world: he had originally intended to entitle his first volume of collected poems (1895) *Under the Moon*.[11] He had to reject, finally, the Byzantine sacred sages and supernatural flames in favor of a secular voice and the torn and tormented sea—and to reject as well the classically reposeful Elysium of the Immortals in favor of the pansexual domain of Pan. As he himself said of his work, "The swords man throughout repudiates the saint."[12] But if all we registered were the similar "outcomes" of these four poems—their adherence to irregular life in spite of the allure of the ideal (of wisdom or disembodiment or philosophical repose)—we would be noting their conclusions without realizing the means by which those conclusions are made persuasive. In each case, forms and structures of every sort are indispensable in conveying not only the choices at stake but also the fashion in which, at this moment, Yeats is conceiving both the ideal and the human. As we become alerted to the evolving journey in each of these poems, we can feel resonating in our mental universe the ceremonious *ottava rima* deliberations of the passage to Byzantium, the jagged edges of dying agony in "Byzantium," the suspense of the quatrains-elongated-into-cinquains of "The Delphic Oracle upon Plotinus," and the jaunty, mocking balladry of "News for the Delphic Oracle." The emotions in each, because they do not resemble each other, must be, and are, mediated by idiosyncratic individual forms, inner and outer. The self-critique that generates each of these poems from the one(s) preceding it puts these texts in what Todorov calls, in *The Poetics of Prose*, a syntagmatic (horizontal) relation to each other, in which the prior text "provokes or modifies" how we see the subsequent text: the relation is that of a "concealed polemic."[13] Yeats's forms, when lifted into visibility, are the armature of that sustained and multi-sided polemic.

Ignoring the forms by which Yeats invents his poems is fatal to interpretation. Even Curtis Bradford, in his early fascinating study of the drafts of the Byzantium poems,[14] does not see what the poems intend as their meaning. He closes his essay by summing up the two poems as follows:

> Both poems are deeply concerned with Unity of Being, and with the achievement of Unity of Being through art. In "Sailing to Byzantium" the protagonist achieves the temporal aspect of Unity of Being by leaving the country of the young, dominated by sensuality, and sailing to Byzantium, symbol of the spiritual life. "Byzantium" explores Unity of Being in its eternal aspect. At the outset of the poem unpurged images of sensuality give way to a serene image of spirituality, the moonlit dome of Hagia Sophia. Death the summoner, personified as a walking mummy, calls the souls of the departed to paradise. The golden bird is again examined, but alone it is not a sufficient symbol of Yeats's paradise. A sufficient symbol is found when the ghosts of the dead swim through the sensual seas on the backs of dolphins, warm-blooded mammals, toward the mosaic pavement where they dance in the purifying flames. We have moved from complexity to ultimate simplicity: sense and spirit have become one inextricable beam; Unity of Being is an ideal valid both in Time and Eternity. (130)

The conflicts of both poems vanish in such a summation; nobody would guess, from this account, that the slide from would-be holy sage to would-be profane bird takes place in the first poem, or that the second poem ends not in "one inextricable beam" of ultimate simplicity but in a violent stand-off between a surge of unpurged images and the golden smithies of the Emperor. As the symbolic plane evolves in its formal aspects from station to station, stanza to stanza, trope to trope, population to population, it propels us from one emotional state to another; and nowhere in the Yeatsian universe, whether in Time or Eternity, does a static "Unity of Being" remain untroubled, even as an ideal. Yeats's forms, as portals to a poem's core, necessarily equal (or in some cases, surpass) the "ideas" on which they confer unforgettable shapes.

In my remaining chapters, I cannot enter into such detail about the poems surveyed. But the principles guiding my inquiry into the poems concerning Byzantium and the Delphic Oracle will lie behind everything that follows, and the reader will I hope remember that governing tropes, forms of geometric and mathematical symmetry, different propositions about beauty, poems that are counterparts to each other, and so on, appear throughout Yeats's work, even if I do not always point out those features. Now, after having seen something of how Yeats works in single poems and paired poems, I want to leap to the site of his greatest poetic ambitions, the poetic sequence, using as my examples two powerful political poems, "Nineteen Hundred and Nineteen" and "Blood and the Moon." They demonstrate how far a great poet can go in being the voice of what is past, or passing, or to come; and they also exemplify how, by means of abstraction, large and recalcitrant events can be brought within the precincts of poetry.

# ᖇ— THE PUZZLE OF SEQUENCE:
## TWO POLITICAL POEMS

Although Yeats's multi-poem sequences are the complex end-point of his lyric experimentation, I want to consider them at this early point to establish the intellectual and emotional accumulation toward which his mature lyrics tend. These sequences, which approach a single phenomenon (civil war) or concept (vacillation) from various angles, replaced in Yeats's ambition the narrative poems of his earlier poetic career. The famous sequences in English before Yeats had linked together poems, such as sonnets, that were identical in shape; but the characteristic Yeatsian sequence—for which my examples here will be "Nineteen Hundred and Nineteen" and "Blood and the Moon"—consists of poems of different shapes linked under one title. The individual members of the sequence are "poems" (as Yeats usually referred to them),[1] but although many of these poems can stand singly as aesthetic units, they take on weight from their presence and placement within the sequence.

What is the imaginative impulse that wants to create a sequence rather than a single poem? And what are the characteristic methods by which such an impulse embodies itself? These methods, as we shall see, may be "magical" in derivation, or they may be motivated by a desire to exemplify a particular genre, rhythm, or stanza form. Sometimes they seem fantastic. The poet's imaginative impulse when constructing a sequence fulfills itself in its act of discovering appropriate form—and by "form" I mean not only the inner and outer shapes of the individual members of the sequence, but also the chosen ordering of the poems from which we derive the implicit argument of the whole. If Yeats's multiple choices of individual form and sequential order are not random (as they certainly are not), can we find plausible ways to describe the phenomenology both of the individual poems and of the sequence as a whole, and can we suggest the aims governing the poet's choices? And can we see the advantage to a poem, especially a political poem, in turning away from the topical and adopting forms of abstraction? Ezra Pound, always one for the topical, was amused by Yeats's inveterate belief that it was the symbol, abstracted from the quotidian, that could hold the quintessence of reality: in *The Pisan Cantos* (#83, 22–26), Pound, in Paris with Yeats, comments on that belief:

> Le Paradis n'est pas artificiel
> and Uncle William dawdling around Notre Dame
> in search of whatever
> > paused to admire the symbol
> with Notre Dame standing inside it[.]

Yeats's symbols for the acts of violence in the two sequences discussed here, and his confidence in those imagined abstractions, needed the implementation of form. For each of my two cases, I will sketch the themes and name the forms of the entire sequence, with the aim of improving our sense of Yeats's formal resources and his imperious management of them.


"Nineteen Hundred and Nineteen" (published in 1928 in *The Tower*) is a long six-part sequence of 130 lines, a work too massive to be understood without study and reflection. It was in part occasioned by the guerilla conflicts in Ireland during 1919 and 1920 between Republicans and the British police, aided by the Black and Tans (an irregular military group, so named from their uniform), composed mostly of men demobilized from the War. (These conflicts anticipated the outbreak of civil war between Republicans and Free Staters in 1922.) But it must be recalled, in order to understand Yeat's concern with violence in "Nineteen Hundred and Nineteen," that the poem was written in the wake of World War I, with its catastrophic rupture of the European status quo.

The formal organization of "Nineteen Hundred and Nineteen" (outlined more fully in the appendix to this chapter) appears to be heterogeneous, mutating spontaneously from part to part. Its six poems, ranging in length from one stanza to six, employ five different rhyme schemes, four distinguishable rhythmic schemes, and three different line lengths; they also represent distinct thematic and prosodic genres. They are voiced differently, too: Yeats writes only once in the first person singular, more frequently in the first person plural, and sometimes in an impersonal voice, narrative or philosophical by turns. How can we explain not only this prosodic and syntactic variety but also the sequential ordering of the poems?

"Nineteen Hundred and Nineteen" was originally entitled "Thoughts upon the Present State of the World" and dated "May, 1921." On April 9, 1921, Yeats commented on his undertaking to Olivia Shakespear, remarking that he had been reading many books, "searching out signs of the whirling gyres of the historical cone as we see it."[2] In a letter to Lady Gregory, he said, "The first poem is rather in the mood of the Anne poem ["Prayer for My Daughter"] but the rest are wilder."[3] As Daniel Albright remarks, "The retitling and redating [of the sequence] may reflect Yeats's sense of the importance of 1919, the year in which . . . the rebel Irish Republican Army was opposed by the Black and Tans."[4] Lady Gregory's journal entry of November 5, 1920, records the atrocity that lies at the heart of Yeats's sequence: Eileen Quinn, a young mother of three, was "shot dead . . . with her child in her arms" by Black and Tan soldiers shooting from a passing lorry.[5] We might at first think that the whole of "Nineteen Hundred and Nineteen" was written to show how that actual event, mentioned in part I, burst in upon the illusions of the past:

> Now days are dragon-ridden, the nightmare
> Rides upon sleep: a drunken soldiery
> Can leave the mother, murdered at her door,
> To crawl in her own blood, and go scot-free.

In "Meditations in Time of Civil War," another political sequence, the comparable topical moment arrives late, in the penultimate poem:

> Somewhere
> A man is killed, or a house burned . . .
>
> Some fourteen days of civil war;
> Last night they trundled down the road
> That dead young soldier in his blood.

Another poet might have made more, in each case, of the local bloodshed and the earlier causes of the present tragedy; Yeats neither begins nor ends with the local event, nor does he treat it in any historical detail.[6] Irish events, though they stimulated "Nineteen Hundred and Nineteen," are not Yeats's principal focus within the sequence; it is the enigma of human violence that is his subject. Why—to leap to the last enigma of "Nineteen Hundred and Nineteen"—would the fourteenth-century high-born Lady Alice Kyteler abase herself to an "evil spirit" (Yeats's words in his note to the poem) such as Robert Artisson, and bring him, by way of erotic offerings, the "red combs" sliced off the heads of her cocks?[7] Why—to return to the first enigma of the sequence—would anyone in ancient Greece become such an "incendiary or bigot" that he would burn religious monuments or melt down artworks for their gold? It is not solely, or even chiefly, political violence that perplexes Yeats in "Nineteen Hundred and Nineteen"; it is rather the recurrent multiform and age-old violence of human beings—even if only the violence of animal sacrifice—that he investigates in the sequence. It is misleading to consider "Nineteen Hundred and Nineteen" only in the context of contemporary Irish conflicts: Yeats himself takes great pains to widen the historical context within the sequence, ranging as far back as ancient Greece (in the burning of the statue of Athena) and ancient Palestine (in the decapitation of John the Baptist after Salome's dance).[8] Although the carnage in Ireland occasioned this sequence, its individual poems are neither comprehended nor exhausted by the events that prompted them.

The originating enigma of "Nineteen Hundred and Nineteen" is the human race's urge to obliterate the very civilizations it has constructed. We might, says Yeats, expect "common things" to be "pitched about" by sublunary change, but surely "ingenious lovely things" (the aesthetic heritage of the West) would be protected by Fate from such violence. Yeats instances, among those lovely things, religious icons such as the olive-wood image of Athena on the Acropolis, and artworks such as the ivory sculptures of Phidias or the inspired Greek simulacra in gold of humble grasshoppers and bees. The sequence begins in the voice of one who values such icons and images:

> There stood
> Amid the ornamental bronze and stone
> An ancient image made of olive wood—
> And gone are Phidias' famous ivories
> And all the golden grasshoppers and bees.

Exactly halfway through its length, this opening poem turns its face away from archaic Greece to comment on present-day Ireland—"Now days are dragon-ridden, the nightmare / Rides upon sleep"—but it ends with a return to ancient Greece and a restatement of its original enigma. The poem is, then, a circular one, ending in the same perplexity with which it began. The initial confidence in the permanence of "ingenious lovely things" is

seen as illusion, and at the close the speaker's language descends to repro-
ducing, in the indirect discourse of its last three lines, the attitudes natural
to the destroyers: contempt ("that stump"), mercenary motives ("traffic
in"), and heedless violence ("break in bits"):

> That country round
> None dared admit, if such a thought were his,
> Incendiary or bigot could be found
> To burn that stump on the Acropolis,
> Or break in bits the famous ivories
> Or traffic in the grasshoppers or bees.

Poems that end where they began—with their emotions unresolved and
their condition as hopeless as it was at the beginning—are a known form
(Yeats was acquainted with Donne's "A Nocturnall on St. Lucie's Day"). But
why would Yeats cast his opening enigma into *ottava rima?*

*Ottava rima* first appears in Yeats's work in the 1928 *Tower;* he continued
to resort to it for the next ten years, through the composition of "The Cir-
cus Animals' Desertion" in 1938. Yeats had used eight-line stanzas earlier,
but not the stately and equable *ottava rima,* which he was to explore with
such versatility. Although "Sailing to Byzantium" was the last composed of
the poems in *The Tower,* its stanza form takes on, by standing first in the vol-
ume, an exemplary function: *ottava rima* (throughout Yeats) stands for Re-
naissance courtly achievement, for culture, for civilization, for "monuments
of unageing intellect," for an achieved artifice (whether of eternity or of
time). The first two stanzas of "Sailing to Byzantium" exhibit the normative
form of *ottava rima* when it is undisturbed: six lines of description or specu-
lation *(ababab),* resolved with a resonant couplet *(cc).* Readers of *The Tower,*
then, encountering the *ottava rima* opening of "Nineteen Hundred and
Nineteen," might reasonably expect another salute to the perpetuity of art,
Hebraic or Hellenic; and the poem's initial praise of ingenious lovely things
is a theme suitable to *ottava rima.* But readers find themselves abandoned, in
the course of the sequence, to enigmas, questions, and outlandish folk leg-
end. And although the first two *ottava rima* stanzas of the opening poem of
"Nineteen Hundred and Nineteen" preserve the normative integrity of
their closing couplets, the last four stanzas, one way or another, break that
stability. The cultural products of civilization are in view, yes, but this
poem's topic is their tragic fate. "He who can read the signs" knows

no work can stand,
Whether health, wealth or peace of mind were spent
On master-work of intellect or hand,
No honour leave its mighty monument[.]

The first part of "Nineteen Hundred and Nineteen" vacillates between creativity and annihilation, free will and determinism. On the one hand, man seems to possess the power not only to create, but also to "read the signs" and, if he is strong enough, to withstand the temptation to "sink unmanned / Into the half-deceit of some intoxicant," even while the free will of the incendiary or the bigot is expending itself on destruction. At another moment, however, the poem will declare that men are but "weasels fighting in a hole," devoid of human reason. And in a third formulation, the poet asserts that the objects of love are not in fact destroyed by violent outside forces, but simply, and intransitively, "vanish" as we look on: "Man is in love and loves what vanishes, / What more is there to say?" These changing speculations within part I of "Nineteen Hundred and Nineteen" are not arranged in any logical or cumulative order: art does not win, reason does not win, animal viciousness does not win, philosophical insight does not win. In this tumult, civilization, in its formal analogue of *ottava rima,* cannot survive further within the sequence; this cultivated stanza form, with its Renaissance aura, never returns after part I.

Yeats's stanzas in this opening poem—all but one—repeat inflexibly a single structure: that of illusion (usually voiced somewhere in the first six lines) and that of illusion disabused (expressed most frequently in the couplet, but sometimes earlier, as in the third stanza, with its biblical warning about cannon unbeaten into ploughshares). (In a poem, such a repeated psychological pattern stands for a determinism irresistible by human will.) For a brief moment, one single stanza, the fifth, resists this fated collapse, announcing (prematurely, as we will discover) a form of comfort: the wise and realistic man is solaced by his "ghostly solitude," which would be marred if he took his superior philosophical knowledge to be a form of triumph. His objectivity in the midst of disaster is disinterested—or so the stanza believes. But as soon as Yeats finds this comfort for his intellect, his emotions rebel, and he denies his pretense that there is "one comfort left."[9]

But is there any comfort to be found?
Man is in love and loves what vanishes,
What more is there to say?

After this admission, there is no more talk of defeating disaster by "ghostly solitude"; instead, the *ottava rima* falls back, in conclusion, into its subjected pattern of illusion disabused, as the Greek ivories are broken and the golden jewelry traded for money. Where can Yeats's sequence go after this apparent philosophic resignation to the depredations of violence? What is he to do with his apprehension that "days are dragon-ridden," that a dragon has been loosed upon his country?

To our surprise, the sequence proceeds, in its single-stanza part II, into an apparently trivial description of an orientalized modern dance, which, by means of its many veils wielded by the batons of "Chinese" (actually Japanese) dancers, creates "a dragon of air." But the poet takes this modern choreography as a symbol ratifying his sense of present "dragon-ridden" history:

> When Loie Fuller's Chinese dancers enwound
> A shining web, a floating ribbon of cloth,
> It seemed that a dragon of air
> Had fallen among dancers, had whirled them round
> Or hurried them off on its own furious path;
> So the Platonic Year
> Whirls out new right and wrong,
> Whirls in the old instead;
> All men are dancers and their tread
> Goes to the barbarous clangour of a gong.

The motion of Loie Fuller's dancers has no sooner been described than it is immediately—within the same single stanza—analogized to the largest motion of the cosmos, the 36,000-year journey of the constellations through the entire zodiac. The scale of space expands to the astronomical, while the index of time flees back to the primitive origins of music (here represented by an Asian "gong" that beats out the deterministic measure that all men are compelled to tread; later, in "Supernatural Songs," primitive music will be made on a "magic drum"; each of these instruments is capable of only a single on/off sound, representing the most basic form of music). Determinism asserts its absolute rule, paradoxically through the apparently spontaneous motion of the whirling dragon-dancers (directed in reality by an unseen choreographic force). Tennyson's "Ring out the old" stands behind Yeats's more sinister variety of change in which new right and wrong are merely exchanged for old right and wrong.

What is the stanza form containing this grim statement? And why does this part of "Nineteen Hundred and Nineteen" consist of a single peculiar and very uneasy stanza? And why will Yeats immediately resort to this stanza again in the next poem, part III of the sequence?[10] Here are the features of this ten-line stanza:

> In *rhyme,* the ten-line stanza divides itself *asymmetrically,* 6-4, with a sestet *(abcabc)* followed immediately (no break) by an embraced-rhyme quatrain *(deed).*
>
> In *logic* and *punctuation,* however, the stanza divides itself *symmetrically* (5-5) into two *equal* parts of five lines each, separated by a semicolon: the first part is about the dance, the second about the Platonic Year.
>
> In *rhythm,* the stanza exhibits yet a third pattern, also *asymmetrical:* the first five lines place a *single* trimeter *between* two pentameter couplets (5-5-3-5-5); the second five lines offer *four* trimeters followed by a single pentameter (3-3-3-3-5).[11]

The stanza is therefore a triply unsettling one: its asymmetrical 6 + 4 rhyme-division does not match its 5 + 5 *logical* division into two equal parts; and the two *logically* analogous equal halves (dancer and year) are *rhythmically* entirely disparate. Graphically, the stanza as a whole begins broadly in pentameters, narrows to a trimeter, broadens again, narrows to trimeters again, and ends in a pentameter: broad, narrow, broad, narrow, broad—a double gyre.

Yeats "defines" this strange stanza for us in the poem for which he invented it, the 1920 "All Souls' Night" (470–474). After telling us first that he wishes to be "wound in mind's pondering / As mummies in the mummy-cloth are wound," he closes the poem by echoing and enlarging that statement:

> Such thought—such thought have I that hold it tight
> Till meditation master all its parts . . .;
> Such thought, that in it bound
> I need no other thing,
> Wound in mind's wandering
> As mummies in the mummy-cloth are wound.[12]

The ten-line stanza created for "All Soul's Night" and reused in "Nineteen Hundred and Nineteen" and "Meditations in Time of Civil War" is the longest single unit in Yeats's mature poetic repertoire. (When the mature Yeats

writes a stanza that is longer than ten lines, such as the eighteen-line stanza
that closes "Nineteen Hundred and Nineteen," he creates it by gathering to-
gether smaller uniform rhyming units, in that case, three sixains.) Because
of its several asymmetries, the ten-line stanza never falls into a "comfort-
able" shape; its syntax strains against its rhymes, its rhymes against its
rhythms. In "Nineteen Hundred and Nineteen" (though not in its other oc-
currences) the ten lines of the stanza invariably compose a single sentence,
a single complex proposal in which several sub-proposals are enwound. We
recall Yeats's statement in "A General Introduction to My Work" of his de-
sire for "a complete coincidence between period and stanza" (E & I, 522–
523). The winding of the syntax through the long sentence is the winding
of Loie Fuller's dancers' veils, or the winding of the constellations through
the circuit of the zodiac, or the winding of the mummy-cloth about the
mummy. The pride of the poet in composing such an expert stanza lies in
having created a texture so dense that it permits the enwinding of the large
with the small, the general with the particular, the symmetrical with the
asymmetrical, the expanding with the contracting. The first half of the
stanza (two solidly rhyming pentameter couplets enclosing a trimeter) of-
fers stateliness: the second half, with its four successive lines in lilting trim-
eter, offers a dance-rhythm stabilized by a final pentameter. By means of
the internally contrastive parts of the stanza, the poet wishes to enclose in
one moment tragedy and joy, discursive weight and lightness of motion.

What can Yeats's purpose be—after the single-stanza part II poem of
Loie Fuller and the Platonic Year—in returning to the very same stanza
form for the next poem of "Nineteen Hundred and Nineteen," the part III
excursus comparing the soul to a swan? Why the emblematic winding
stanza if there are, here, no mummy-bands, no complex veils, and no large-
scale heavenly circuit? It is not until the middle of part III that we find the
new function of this irregular stanza: it is to represent, this time, the wind-
ings of a labyrinth, Yeats's own maze of "art and politics":

> A man in his own secret meditation
> Is lost amid the labyrinth that he has made
> In art or politics.[13]

Yeats's soul—engaged in "art or politics" not only in this poem but during
his entire life—seeks an adequate emblem of its own nature. The central
part III of "Nineteen Hundred and Nineteen"—flanked on the left by parts I
and II (the dragon-ridden present and the dragon of air that is the Platonic
Year) and on the right by the three parts yet to come (IV, V, and VI)—is,

strikingly, the only one among the six poems of the sequence that is written in the first person singular. In it, the Yeatsian "I" speaks out *in propria persona* at the center of the labyrinth he has made of art or politics. The rest of the sequence may be thought of as a series of indices pointing to the "I" hidden among the many impersonal propositions about art and politics that are constantly being proffered and withdrawn. These several propositions, as we see them unfold within the sequence, are irreconcilable on any plane. In these various poems, we are sometimes agents of free will, sometimes helpless creatures of Fate. We are makers of beautiful things; we are destroyers of beautiful things. We live on a human scale; we live on a cosmic scale. We are rememberers; we are forgetters. We are believers; we are mockers. We are creative minds; we are creatures of erotic abjection. We are debased animals; we are the creators of abstract notions of honor and truth. All of these assertions are held in tension within the sequence.

When Yeats decides ("I am satisfied with that") to accept (from the unnamed "mythological poet") the solitary swan as an image for the solitary soul, he frames his central symbol of the labyrinth with two postures of the swan. In the first, the swan represents the joy of potential choice: poised for flight, he is able still to choose "Whether to play, or to ride / Those winds that clamour of approaching night." But in the second posture, the moment of choice has passed: in present-perfect diction, we are told that "The swan has leaped into the desolate heaven." The word "solitary" in the originating "solitary soul" has at this point metamorphosed, via the word "solitude" in the middle stanza (both of them derivatives of *solus*, "alone"), into the Keatsian word "desolate" (from *desolare*, "to abandon," ultimately also from *solus*). (Each of these words contains in its syllable *sol* a graphic pun on *soul*.) The solitary soul has leaped not into the "sky" but into a desolate "heaven," desolate because it is a heaven with no resident God, and because all utopian hopes have shown themselves—in the opening poem—to be illusory. The swan in the desolate heaven is an image vacating life's labyrinth of meaning, forcing Yeats to descend from his grand symbolic swan-sweep to a first-person apocalyptic self-obliteration:

> That image can bring wildness, bring a rage
> To end all things, to end
> What my laborious life imagined, even
> The half-imagined, the half-written page.

Determining on a fierce self-immolation even in the actual moment of this writing, Yeats checks himself and diverges—in keeping with the rhythmical

habit of his asymmetrical stanza—into a trimeter lilt, this time embodying a
Shakespearean song recalling *King Lear:*

> O but we dreamed to mend
> Whatever mischief seemed
> To afflict mankind, but now
> That winds of winter blow
> Learned that we were crack-pated when we dreamed.

The frustrating search for an ethical center to the labyrinth of art and poli-
tics has been forsaken in favor of the tragicomic song of a Shakespearean
fool.

Parts II and III—four labyrinthine stanzas, each a single labyrinthine
sentence—are followed by another single-sentence poem. But in violent
contrast to the intricacy of its predecessors, part IV is a biting trochaic epi-
gram of collective self-mockery, repellently thrusting the high abstractions
"honor" and "truth" up against "the weasel's twist, the weasel's tooth":

> We, who seven years ago
> Talked of honour and of truth,
> Shriek with pleasure if we show
> The weasel's twist, the weasel's tooth.

In part I, the speaker had said of himself and his contemporaries "[We] are
but weasels fighting in a hole"; this recapitulation in part IV is merely the
most visible of many in the poem, repetitions that intensively link the mem-
bers of the sequence to one another, making the whole a sequence rather
than a haphazard gathering of independent poems.[14] The appearance of the
coarse-imaged epigram of the weasels suggests that the conditions of 1919–
1921 (Yeats began the poem on April 9, 1921)—hitherto expressed in the
aristocratic form of the *ottava rima* and the "masterful" form of the labyrin-
thine stanza—have not yet been formulated comprehensively, or even cor-
rectly. The self-irony in part I was chiefly intellectual: "O what fine thought
we had because we thought / That the worst rogues and rascals had died
out"; "We pieced our thoughts into philosophy / And planned to bring the
world under a rule"—with "philosophy" pronounced as if in quotation
marks. Although part I had momentarily lapsed into a bestial self-image
("weasels fighting in a hole"), it departed instantly from that insight into a
lofty self-comfort of believing that the reflective man could read the signs

and could refuse to sink into the deception of an intoxicant. Now, reverting to the image of the weasel, the poem reifies it into physical twist and vicious tooth, trochaically **shriek**ing in **pleas**ure and sonically matching "**We** who" with "**wea**sel's" and "**wea**sel's." The aural effects of part IV are so unpleasant that they put in question all the loftier effects of parts I, II, and III. Part IV's weasels bring the poem to a tone of mordant self-abasement, as their bestiality—uncountered in part IV by any other image—is savagely reiterated. Of all genres, the epigram is the one that most pretends to encapsulate the (debased) essence of its subject.[15] Now that Yeats seems to have repudiated, by this self-hating epigram, the discursive ground of philosophical abstraction, aesthetic mastery, and labyrinthine thought on which he has so far stood during parts I–III, how can he continue his sequence?

He does so, in part V, with a peculiar genre—a first-person-plural exhortation to mockery. This poem is at first consistent with the baseness of weasel-pleasure, as its speaker sardonically recommends, as a form of collective enjoyment, that he and his companions turn to mocking the great, the wise, and the good. But in the fourth stanza the speaker turns on his own practice, mocking his own mockery, denouncing himself and his companions for refusing to bar the door against the ongoing political storm, and using—in the bitter phrase "we / Traffic in mockery"—the low verb "traffic" that was so unthinkable to him in the opening poem, when he could not imagine that anyone could be so mercenary as to "traffic in the grasshoppers or bees":

> Mock mockers after that
> That would not lift a hand maybe
> To help good, wise or great
> To bar that foul storm out, for we
> Traffic in mockery.

Yeats's shamed self-abasement, carried over from part IV's weasels, provides only a partial reason for the existence of this poem in the sequence. The true subject of part V is yet again evanescence, but this time what vanishes is not ivories and golden bees but rather striving human beings—the great who toiled to leave some monument behind, the wise who struggled with aching eyes to understand the documents of the past, the good who attempted to make virtue gay. T. R. Henn and Harold Bloom cite the devastating passage in Shelley (*Prometheus Unbound*, I, 625–628) from which Yeats borrows his categories of great, wise, and good:

The good want power, but to weep barren tears.
The powerful goodness want: worse need for them.
The wise want love; and those who love want wisdom;
And all best things are thus confused to ill.[16]

In each of the first three stanzas of Yeats's part V, the seasonal turn to a "foul storm" with its "levelling wind" (which "shrieks" like the weasels) has undone the work by which the great, the wise, and the good hoped to bar out the storm. "Where are they?" Yeats cries of the vanished strivers, echoing the *ubi sunt* of earlier poets.

What does the form of part V tell us? It is a very peculiar form. It looks like some form of ballad, as we see its rhymes beginning *abab*—but then it adds an extra *b* line. In each of the first three stanzas, the "extra" fifth line serves as commentary, undoing what the first four lines have established: the great toiled, but they never "thought of the levelling wind"; the wise studied, but now merely "gape at the sun"; the good attempted a collective joy in virtue, but "Wind shrieked—and where are they?" The effect is that of climbing up for three or four lines and then rapidly losing, in a single slide, all the ground gained. This might be a plausible stanza form, as I have so far described it, but it is rendered indigestible by its rhythms. Whereas a ballad stanza would be structured 4-3-4-3, following tetrameters with trimeters, this stanza up-ends the process, following trimeters with tetrameters, 3-4-3-4, and then closing with a trimeter, 3. This is a virtually unspeakable rhythm; I cannot think of another such example of "doing the ballad backwards," as one might call it. Yeats may be casting a spell of undoing on the ballad stanza, and complicating it by a fifth-line coda. In any case, there is no ease in the form.[17]

The absolutely undanceable rhythm ironizes the initial convention of the "come-all-ye" and contradicts the repeated folk-derived "Come let us" of each stanza. Yeats's moral position in part V, even in the equivocal reversal of "Mock mockers after that," is laden with self-contempt. The indubitable sympathy for the toils of the great, wise, and good is undone by the recurrence of their defeat. The first-person-plural part V, full of "we's" like its epigrammatic predecessor (IV), refuses high discursive language and (for all the oddity of its invented stanza) similarly refuses, by its "low" ballad-like appearance, Yeats's earlier aristocratic self-presentation, which he conveyed through *ottava rima* or its labyrinthine sequel, forms that imply the lofty complexity of their speaker's thought. If Yeats's earlier choice of "high" forms belied the brutality of his savage subject, human violence, it is also true that neither the whiplash of his "low" epigram nor the spell-casting of his ironic mock-ballad is equal to the theme of the sequence—murderous local and European bloodshed, with not a comfort to be had. The enigmas of violence and evanescence, free will and the agency of fate, still pose themselves, as does the implicit quarrel within the sequence between "civilized" high form and "debased" low form. If neither loftiness nor satire can finally illuminate the origins of human destructiveness, what form can Yeats invent to reveal more accurately the cause of the enigmas he has evoked?

The last of Yeats's attempts at understanding human violence is the three-scene visual fantasy of part VI. In the first of these scenes, a set of horses (most of them riderless and unadorned, but a few still garlanded and with "handsome riders") run past, and, vanquished by the weariness of their repetitive courses, they break and vanish. Yeats's note explains them as apparitions seen by country people: "I have assumed that these horsemen, now that the times worsen, give way to worse" (433). In the second scene, the blind daughters of Herodias, personifying the leveling and labyrinthine wind, whirl in a clamorous "thunder of feet, tumult of images" in which they become objects of desire to bystanders—but should someone dare to touch one of them, their response will be unpredictable: "All turn with amorous cries, or angry cries, / According to the wind." Amorous or angry, depending on the whim of the wind, these dancers incarnate eros or thanatos in turn; they are a violent version of Keats's gnats, "Borne aloft / Or sinking, as the light wind lives or dies," and they represent the mystifying effects of a Fate-wind as blind as its subjects. Both the first and second scenes of Yeats's fantasy—unrestrained horses and clamorous dancers—are merely visible symbols of a hidden turbulence that invisibly and unaccountably generates them.

Behind these screen-images of supernatural incursions into the natural world, Yeats at last reveals the origin of human violence: the sexual satisfaction attending on it, a powerful satisfaction that is always irrational.[18] He borrows his final symbol for that demonic sexual undoing of culture from the chronicles of witchcraft, invoking the tale of the empty-eyed "insolent fiend Robert Artisson," insusceptible in his "insolence" to all the conventions of romance, who has exercised his sexual power over "the love-lorn Lady Kyteler":

> But now wind drops, dust settles; thereupon
> There lurches past, his great eyes without thought

> Under the shadow of stupid straw-pale locks,
> That insolent fiend Robert Artisson
> To whom the love-lorn Lady Kyteler brought
> Bronzed peacock feathers, red combs of her cocks.

Already Robert Artisson has conquered; already the aristocratic woman described with irony as the "love-lorn Lady Kyteler" has brought to him, as a token of her abjection, not only "bronzed peacock feathers," themselves already torn from their original site, but also bloody body-parts, "red combs of her cocks." The outrageous obeisance of high-born lady to low incubus is a symbol, for Yeats, of the drivenness of human desire: it will abase itself before its object, it will commit violence for its object. Robert Artisson "lurches" past, just as the rough beast "slouches" toward Bethlehem; their gait is a mimic version of the monstrous formlessness of their dark-of-the-moon supernatural being. By coupling with the human, they have the power to bring about an unforeseeable new order of things.

What form did Yeats find for his concluding triple vision, which unrolls unbroken from the violent rout of beautiful if wearied horses and riders through the dust and wind, thunder and tumult, of the irrationally angry or amorous daughters of Herodias, to the single malign figure of Robert Artisson corrupting Alice Kyteler? Five lines for the horses, seven lines for the daughters of Herodias, six lines for the repellent liaison; the asymmetry of the lengths is belied by the symmetry of the rhymes (which I separate for clarity): *abcabc defdef ghighi*—or, more accurately, *(abcabc)* × 3. The three sixains succeed each other with no intervening blank space: one vision, three scenes, in a single tripartite pentameter stanza eighteen lines long. The rhymed pentameter sixains are "aristocratic" in genre (because of their Petrarchan ancestry); in this they are kin to the *ottava rima* of part I and the long labyrinthine "metaphysical" stanzas of parts II and III. However, these sixains are presented not as individual "stanzas" of a lyric but as a single, impersonally voiced, ongoing flow. With their supernatural beings riding or whirling or lurching past, these sixains belong in content to the Romance tradition, and stand for the realm of fairy and folk tale, of suggestive but irrational narratives of symbolic people and actions. The horsemen and the daughters of the wind are Romance equivalents of the pagan gods called in Ireland the Sidhe; Lady Kyteler and Robert Artisson arise from narratives of witchcraft. The whole breathes Apocalypse.

What would impel Yeats to end his sequence, which presented at its beginning the "ingenious lovely things" of civilization, with a witch's cauldron of these *dramatis personae*? We are reminded no longer of *Lear* but rather of *Macbeth,* of an uprising of dark impulse: as Yeats says, "Evil gathers head." In giving up, through this final fantasy, the possibility of any rational explanation of human violence and cultural destruction, Yeats rejects any solution that might be thought to lie within the modes so far explored—not only the "civilized" modes of octave and labyrinth, but also the "low" modes of epigram and bespelled ballad. Fantastic images of the supernatural thrown up from the unconscious seem to Yeats to offer a better insight into the enigma of violence than do other poetic modes. It is a daring way to end.[19]

Would "Nineteen Hundred and Nineteen" be a different poem if the order of its component parts were rearranged? One feels immediately that an ending voiced in *ottava rima* discursiveness, or in a reductive folk-form, would carry a very different import from a visionary conclusion in Romance sixains—and one could say the same for any other conjectural order. In short, the order of the sequence contains an implicit argument about its speaker's successive responses to violence. It says that almost any intellectual person, when responding to a tragic contemporary event, begins by resorting to the intellectual tools (seen in part I) of historical analogy and philosophical speculation—or by espousing a resigned determinism such as that evoked by the Platonic Year (seen in part II). Despair at the apparently inevitable "vanishing" of loved things governs part III, with its desire for self-destruction and the destruction of the page under the poet's pen. Sooner or later, however, one's own complicity in the socio-political order is bound to suggest itself, and intellectualizing is put aside (in parts IV and V) in favor of collective self-accusation and an attempt to deny the efficacy, in human affairs, of intellectual and moral will. The only defense against complicity is an admission that, like everyone else, one is driven by implacable irrational impulses, sexual and violent, that are ultimately inexplicable—and such a realization produces part VI. The psychological order determining the succession of parts in "Nineteen Hundred and Nineteen" determines as well the individual forms into which Yeats casts these poems—aristocratic, labyrinthine (collective and personal), epigrammatic, ballad-like, and Romance-derived.

But there is another force determining the forms of the individual parts of the sequence, and that is a "magical" one. Yeats at times liked to guide his poems in "magical" ways; the most evident instance to me, noted in Chapter I, is his implication of the date of the Easter Rising—the 24th day of the 4th month of the year 1916—in the forms of his poem on the event.

In "Nineteen Hundred and Nineteen" a comparable "magical" intent is visible. Part I (which was, in its first printing in *The Dial,* an unnumbered prelude to the rest) is *sui generis.* Part II has two halves, the dance and its analogue in the Platonic year. Part III has three stanzas. Part IV has four lines of four beats each ($4 \times 4$, a perfect square). Part V has stanzas of five lines; and Part VI is written in six-line rhyme-groups. It does not matter, perhaps, whether the reader notices any of these correspondences, but their existence is undeniable, and clearly not random. From its beginnings, Yeats's art had had room for such micro-techniques (as we shall see in the following chapter on his early work), and their appeal—not really distinct from the jigsaw-puzzle aspects of all prosody—never quite faded. Constructing the grand architectonics of "Nineteen Hundred and Nineteen" (and other sequences of comparable virtuosity) requires, of course, an intellectual concentration of a different order of magnitude, but for Yeats all orders, great and small, existed to cooperate in the final forming of the poem.

What do we learn from understanding "Nineteen Hundred and Nineteen" in its formal proceedings as well as in its paraphrasable content? We learn its implicit argument: that, faced with complex historical phenomena, we must guard against resting in our premature intellectualizing impulses (whether "aristocratic" or "labyrinthine") but must also guard against a subsequent resorting to self-debasing judgments or reductive self-categorizations. At the same time, we must admit the likelihood in our responses of such intellectualizing or self-reproachful or over-simplifying reactions. We are brought forcibly face to face with our desire to "make sense" of human behavior, while being confronted with Yeats's final skepticism about such sense-making. We understand, too, that form for Yeats has ideological resonance: that some forms say "stability and order" or "aristocracy" or "Romance," while others say "complexity of thought" or "folk-material" or "essence of something." We learn that the suppression of stanza breaks (and therefore of stanza-essence) denotes the refusal to grant successive scenes discrete reality, implying, by this flowing of one cursive and disturbing "vision" of disorder into another, that they are all versions of one thing, fully revealed only in the last scene. We learn that stable forms (such as *ottava rima*) can be destabilized to significant effect; that forms possessing several competing inner structures (such as the ten-line "labyrinthine" stanza) change shape as they are considered under different categories—rhythmically, or logically, or by rhyme-pattern; that reversed forms (as in the upside-down ballad) are disturbing; that tragedy and joy (as in the "labyrinthine" stanza) can coexist in a stanza's asymmetrical and contrastive rhythms. We of course also see—as we do in all of Yeats's work—the usefulness of the other resources of poetry: symbol, analogy, irony, narrative suspense, distinct imaginative planes, and varied *dramatis personae*. We come to appreciate, above all, a powerful attempt by the poet to ingest his country's tragic contemporary moment whole, to analogize it to comparable moments of the human past, and to project his exploration of the abstract enigma of violence into a set of chosen symbolic forms, prosodic as well as thematic. An understanding of Yeats's decisions concerning form and arrangement keeps us from acquiescing in a merely biographical and historical interpretation of "Nineteen Hundred and Nineteen," and invites us instead to consider the sequence as the product of a versatile formal imagination seeking "befitting emblems of adversity" ("Meditations in Time of Civil War"). If they did not have befitting form, they would not be befitting emblems.

Does Yeats, we wonder, return to the poetic methods that we have seen here when he is constructing his other sequences? The short answer (as we would expect) is that he finds a new set of methods for each sequence. It might seem that "Meditations in Time of Civil War" (1922) is imitating "Nineteen Hundred and Nineteen" (1921): after all, both sequences open with an *ottava rima* poem, and "Meditations" contains a three-stanza poem ("My House") in the ten-line "labyrinthine" stanza used in parts II and III of "Nineteen Hundred and Nineteen"; "Meditations" exhibits ballad-like measures in parts V and VI, and ends, like "Nineteen Hundred and Nineteen," with a tripartite visionary scheme.[20] Nonetheless, the total impression left by "Meditations" is not at all like the one left by the earlier sequence. "Nineteen Hundred and Nineteen" has, for instance, no subtitles prefacing its "stations." Who would have imagined, reading the running subtitles of "Meditations"—"Ancestral Houses," "My House," "My Table," "My Descendants," "The Road at My Door," "The Stare's Nest at My Window," and "I See Phantoms, etc."—that such topics could direct a poem on civil war? Where is the war? And even though part VI of "Meditations" returns to the mode of tripartite vision seen in the close of "Nineteen Hundred and Nineteen," it does so in an entirely different prosodic form—five eight-line double-quatrain stanzas (*ababcdcd*) composed in vague "wavering" hexameters as "Monstrous familiar images swim to the mind's eye." In short, the two sequences remain imaginatively and prosodically distinct (and "Meditations" has none of the numerical play of "Nineteen Hundred and Nineteen"). By concentrating in "Meditations" on the domestic place and objects around which the civil war rages, Yeats finds a new focus for a political poem, different from the cosmic range of "Nineteen Hundred and Nineteen."

We can see Yeats turning to entirely different methods in his later sequences. "Supernatural Songs" will be discussed in Chapter XII below; here I will offer evidence of his invention of structures in "Blood and the Moon" (480–482), a four-part sequence in the second of Yeats's volumes named from his tower, *The Winding Stair*. "Blood and the Moon" was occasioned by the 1927 assassination of Kevin O'Higgins, vice-president of the Free State government and a man whom Yeats considered a friend. "I am now at a new Tower series, partially driven to it by this murder," Yeats wrote to Olivia Shakespear (*L*, 727). Foster remarks that Higgins was killed not so much for his policies in 1927 as by his having "ordered seventy-seven executions of his ex-comrades during the civil war," when he was in the Free State cabinet (Foster, II, 343). As earlier executions brought about later assassination, an unstoppable circuit of blood-shedding seemed to have become an established fact in Ireland.

Yeats's sequence opposes the terrene stain of blood to the moon's unstainable celestial light—but its way to that opposition is a winding one. Foster considers the sequence "an uneven performance, obscure and declamatory by turns," though he adds that it is "replete with wonderful phrases" (Foster, II, 346). I believe there is more to be said for "Blood and the Moon" if one comes to understand its strange and at first inexplicable structure, which consists of the following parts:

I. a slender twelve-line block of three trimeter *abba* quatrains without stanza breaks;
II. an eighteen-line segment consisting of six irregularly long-lined *aaa* tercet stanzas;
III. a square douzain (twelve-line verse-block) consisting of three *abba* pentameter quatrains; and
IV. a second douzain identical in form with III.

Why the tall trimeter-block as an opening? Why the straggling uneven tercets in the middle, separated by stanza breaks (the only stanza breaks of the poem)? Why two identical pentameter blocks at the end? And why do the two closing pentameter douzains have the same *abba* rhyme-pattern as the trimeter part I?

I confess to being long baffled by this structure. And yet (as it turns out, and as I was slow to see), Yeats himself has explained it as he goes. The tall part I is "*this* tower"; part II's six-tercet climb through history is "*this* winding gyring, spiring treadmill of a stair, . . . my ancestral stair"; and the prosodically identical parts III and IV (identically square in appearance on the page) represent two ways of looking at "the dusty, glittering windows" of the tower. One can see the windows as transparently "glittering" as they permit the light of the moon to fall on the tower floor (III); or one can focus on their "dusty" inside surface on which doomed butterflies, unable to fly out, "cling" (IV). (We have already seen these two ways of looking through or at a surface in "Sailing to Byzantium," as the poet confronts the sage-mosaic.)

Yeats chooses, in "Blood and the Moon" (as in no other sequence), a graphic, pictorial method of arrangement. In the first "station" of the sequence he will show us, from the outside, the tall shape of the tower he has restored; then, in the second station (part II) he will laboriously climb its stair, stopping from time to time; and finally, in the third and fourth stations in the upper chamber of the tower (parts III and IV), he will contemplate its windows. (He is tempted to rise to the upper ruined battlement, but he breaks off before he does so, and the battlement does not generate any pictorial equivalent of itself.) The underlying symbolic unit of the poem is clearly three-ness: *three* quatrains in I, six (that is, two times *three*) stanzas of *three* lines each in II, *three* quatrains in III, *three* quatrains in IV. These threes stand, I believe, for the three architectural features of Yeats's location depicted in the sequence: tower, stair, and windows. (In school, Yeats found geometry easy.)

The laborious actual "rise" of the tower in stone is long past, as is the "rise" of the race that built it; therefore Yeats's symbolic tower-of-words lifts itself rapidly before us in a tall, slender verse. With the vertical effort of its medieval construction now over, the tower has taken on its secondary, intellectual, function as an emblem: this "decided-upon" status is denoted by the "forethought" of the *abba* non-linear choice of rhyme-form (repeated in parts III and IV). The tower's former defensive use prompts Yeats's choice in the first station of the martial trimeter over his original tetrameter (which would be too wide and would make the image of the tower on the page too squat);[21] but the tower is a ruin, "half dead at the top," and so the poet's additive song ("rhyme upon rhyme") becomes a "mockery," as he makes a "mock" word-tower arise on a virtual, not a real, plane. The whole poem— tower, stair, and windows—is the powerful "emblem" the poet has set up: it "mocks" (is the image of) the physical tower, stair, and windows, and "mocks" (repudiates) the nation-state which is, like the tower, already "half dead at the top."

Although part I began in the first draft as a verbless noun-list of the fea-

tures of the tower and its surroundings, Yeats converted the passage to an
authoritative, performative speech-act, "Blessed be this place":

> Blessed be this place,
> More blessed still this tower;
> A bloody, arrogant power
> Rose out of the race
> Uttering, mastering it,
> Rose like these walls from these
> Storm beaten cottages—
> In mockery I have set
> A powerful emblem up,
> And sing it rhyme upon rhyme
> In mockery of a time
> Half dead at the top.

Although this opening part introduces two of the central nouns of the se-
quence—"blood" and "power"—the relative "weightlessness" of this trimeter
tower denotes its purely virtual existence, its construction out of rhymes,
not stones. It is the only "song" of the sequence: Yeats "sing[s]" it.

A real effort, however, is necessary as the poet subsequently climbs the
winding stair within the tower to arrive at a high vantage-point. The six dis-
tinct and unwieldy tercets (two threes, of course) exert a gravitational drag,
stair-portion by stair-portion, as the elderly Yeats mounts one step at a time,
line by line, pausing after each three steps, finding the climb physically tir-
ing. (The tercet-lines are based loosely on the hexameter, the measure used
to mimic stilt-walking in "High Talk"; see Chapter VI.) As Yeats enters upon
the gyre-stair of history, he recalls past towers (two real ones in Alexandria
and Babylon, and other emblematical ones, Shelley's "thought's crowned
powers" in *Prometheus Unbound*). Still ascending, he pauses to declare (in an-
other performative utterance) the symbolic status of this stair, what he has
ordained that it should represent:

> I declare this tower is my symbol; I declare
> This winding, gyring, spiring treadmill of a stair is my ancestral stair;
> That Goldsmith and the Dean, Berkeley and Burke have traveled
>     there.[22]

The strain of climbing the stair generates more outrageously lengthy lines
as the poet summons to mind his predecessors Swift, Goldsmith, Burke,

and Berkeley, describing the last of these, Berkeley, in a stanza the like of which Yeats had never before written, and which is inexplicable except as an equivalent to physical exertion: step, step, step, as in "this pra**gmat**ical, pre-**pos**terous **pig**" and **"so solid seem"**:

> And God-appointed Berkeley that proved all things a dream,
> That this pragmatical, preposterous pig of a world, its farrow that so
>    solid seem,
> Must vanish on the instant if the mind but change its theme.

In the next, and last, tercet, the poet reaches the top of his tower-stair. He pauses at that point to summarize, in a newly "high" diction, the views and principles bequeathed to him by his mental "ancestors," citing their achievements in the order in which he had mentioned them earlier, Swift and Goldsmith in the first line of the tercet, then, each with his own line, Burke and Berkeley:

> *Saeva Indignatio* and the labourer's hire,
> The strength that gives our blood and state magnanimity of its own
>    desire;
> Everything that is not God consumed with intellectual fire.

Now that the stair has been climbed, and the poet has arrived at the last inhabited (therefore windowed) room, what does he see? That "seven centuries" of the bloody slaughter of innocents on this terrain have left no stain on the unearthly moon, that it remains wholly untouched by human affairs. For all the efforts of executioners to cast blood upon it, it has maintained its purity. And yet it is blood that saturates this first douzain, as though the poet, having absorbed the "Odour of blood on the ancestral stair," cannot forget that he, like Swift, owns a human "blood-sodden breast." As he contemplates the "arrowy shaft" of light aimed by the unclouded moon at the tower floor, he rages with anger at the thought that the moon remains perpetually and serenely uncontaminated. (Although the *abba* quatrain-rhyme ensures the greatest possible distance between the "moon" that ends line 1 and the "stain" that ends line 4, the fact that they rhyme, even if inexactly, suggests that they are here conceptually inextricable, as are purity and contamination. By contrast, when Yeats rhymes the two words again in part IV, as the inner rhymes of the last quatrain of the poem, he reverses the order in which they rhyme: "stain: moon," just as he had reversed "come: Byzantium" to "Byzantium: come" at the end of "Sailing to Byzantium." Such reversals represent, I believe, the doing and undoing of a poetic "spell.")

The poet refers to the blood-stained floor on which he stands by the distal deictic "there," as though denying his own connection with it. He will not group himself with the past assassins by saying "here." The first ten lines of the douzain are themselves blood-saturated:

> The purity of the unclouded moon
> Has flung its arrowy shaft upon the floor.
> Seven centuries have passed and it is pure,
> The blood of innocence has left no stain.
> There, on blood-saturated ground, have stood
> Soldier, assassin, executioner,
> Whether for daily pittance or in blind fear
> Or out of abstract hatred, and shed blood,
> But could not cast a single jet thereon.
> Odour of blood on the ancestral stair!

Four "blood's" in ten lines: the pure moon is still steadily shining, no matter how many "blood's" the poet casts up at it like gouts of gore, no matter how many varieties of shedders of blood ("soldier, assassin, executioner") he enumerates, no matter how many motives for blood-shedding ("daily pittance . . . blind fear . . . abstract hatred") he can summon, no matter how many centuries have passed—seven—in which innocent blood has been shed. The douzain is extraordinary in its mimicry of hurled blots of blood, all of them ineffectual.

Even if we have shed no blood ourselves, the "blood-saturated" ground of the earth repels us from its very surface, and (resisting the fact that we cannot leave the earth), we submit ourselves to "some intoxicant" to make ourselves drunkenly think that we can choose a purer destiny than our mortal one. The tenth line of the douzain leads to a fantasy that one can join the moon in its purity:

> Odour of blood on the ancestral stair!
> And we that have shed none must gather there
> And clamour in drunken frenzy for the moon.[23]

Yeats's part III douzain, as he gazes at the moon, expresses two sorts of disgust—a disgust for ancestral violence (the bloody stair, like the bloody floor, is "there," not "here"), and a disgust for man's "drunken" desire to evade his own condition. These revulsions drive the poem to its final rage against the corrupt, even "lunatic" human frenzy of longing for the ideal realm of the moon.

So far, nothing in "Blood and the Moon" has suggested, against the horrors of blood-slaughter mocked by an unattainable moon-purity, an alternate way of viewing the human condition. Wrenched by admitting that even his own ancestral stair reeks of blood, the poet looks a second time at a window—one of those through which he had seen, and clamored for, the moon. (This second look explains why parts III and IV are prosodically identical: the window-frames are the same size, or the poems represent two different ways of looking at the same window.) This time, the poet does not look *through* the window to the inaccessible and uncontaminated moon; he looks instead *at* the window, stopping his gaze at the inside of the glass pane.[24] All the windows in the tower, glittering on the outside with lunar light, are, he sees, covered on the dusty inside with multicolored butterflies, butterflies with wings like tortoise-shell, wings like peacock-feathers, butterflies who, unable to escape, cling dying to the pane:

> Upon the dusty, glittering windows cling,
> And seem to cling upon the moonlit skies,
> Tortoiseshell butterflies, peacock butterflies,
> A couple of night-moths are on the wing.
> Is every modern nation like the tower,
> Half dead at the top?

The poet's change in vision-focus, from the lunar absolute to the trapped butterflies, brings into view the pathos of life, rather than its violence. With pathos comes pity, with pity comes fellow-feeling, with fellow-feeling comes resignation to the ineluctable difference between the mortal and the incorruptible. The moon, remote and pure and dead, is as it is; human beings are as they are, ever subject to the greed for power that leads to the shedding of blood. Earth-creatures cannot aspire to moon-purity, moon-wisdom. Yeats closes in deep acknowledgment of that true "vision of reality," using for his final conclusions Aristotelian abstractions carefully worded so as to distinguish definite from indefinite article: "the property . . . a something . . . everything . . . a property":

> No matter what I said,
> For wisdom is the property of the dead,
> A something incompatible with life; and power,

> Like everything that has the stain of blood,
> A property of the living; but no stain
> Can come upon the visage of the moon
> When it has looked in glory from a cloud.[25]

By the final quatrain, as we pass from "blood" to "stain" to "moon," we see that Yeats is ready to bless, and not to clamor for, the moon. He is remembering Shelley's "Ode to a Skylark," as it compares the song of the lark to the exalted moment when "from one lonely cloud / The moon rains out her beams, and heaven is overflowed." Yeats's moon looks in glory from a cloud, and the poet, having acquired at last the gift of pity in lieu of the torment of rage, is no longer futilely compelled to cast blood at it.

"Blood and the Moon" has become an "abstract" political poem (one might say) because it has abstracted the topical events of O'Higgins's executions and his consequent assassination into a confrontation between the stained and the pure, blood and the moon. The sequence would not have made its philosophical abstractions ("wisdom," "power," "a property") and its historical abstractions ("soldier, assassin, executioner") so humanly credible if it had not been grounded in its solid graphic representations: Yeats's lithe virtual tower, its exhausting real stair, its two windows. These locate the poet firmly in space as he contends with the opposition of blood and moon; and by miming the swift rise of the tower, the difficult, intermittently pausing ascent up the winding stair, and the flanking views of the windows, Yeats gradually gives us the whole tower and himself moving within it. The poet's last question—"Is every modern nation like the tower, / Half dead at the top?" takes us up beyond the windowed room to the ruined battlement, and makes us wonder if that region, like the tower, the stair, and the windows, will also shape itself into an emblematic lesson. But instead of looking for an answer, Yeats dismisses his question: "No matter what I said." He dismisses it because the poem is dissolving into resignation to the human and admiration for the celestial. The moon does not (as, say, in Whitman) "look down" on the human scene; it remains within its own region, as it looks in glory from a cloud.

"Nineteen Hundred and Nineteen" and "Blood and the Moon" attest to Yeats's extraordinary capacity to confront a contemporary event, generalize it into abstraction, and deploy his reflections on it through a number of poems and symbolic forms into a meaningful sequential order. Each of the great sequences, similarly scrutinized, would reveal other Yeatsian strategies for investigating multiple aspects of complex events or concepts. I have merely wanted to claim here that Yeats's formal choices in his sequences are not made at random, but are motivated; that we can explain Yeats's choices and deduce his presumed intentions as he decided to cast his material into these forms and not others. With a sense of Yeats's care in inventing adequate emblematic forms for individual poems (such as the single poems considered in Chapter I), paired poems (such as the Byzantium and Oracle poems considered in Chapter II), and the sequences described here, we can go on to a more systematic study of Yeatsian forms, beginning, in the following chapter, with some techniques and shapes that the poet discovered early and then reused in more mature poems.

# APPENDIX: Schematic Summary of "Nineteen Hundred and Nineteen"

I: "Many ingenious lovely things are gone"

| | | |
|---|---|---|
| Rhyme form: | *abababcc* | |
| Feet in line: | 5 throughout (pentameter) | *(ottava rima)* |
| Rhythm: | iambic | |
| Stanza-length: | 8 lines | |
| Length of poem: | 6 stanzas | |
| Voice(s): | "We" | |

II: "When Loie Fuller's Chinese dancers enwound"

| | |
|---|---|
| Rhyme form: | *abcabcdeed* |
| Feet in line: | 5535533335 |
| Rhythm: | iambic |
| Stanza-length: | 10 lines |
| Length of poem: | 1 stanza |
| Voice(s): | impersonal |

III: "Some moralist or mythological poet" (same stanza form as in II)

| | |
|---|---|
| Rhyme form: | *abcabcdeed* |
| Feet in line: | 5535533335 |
| Rhythm: | iambic |
| Stanza-length: | 10 lines |
| Length of poem: | 3 stanzas |
| Voice(s): | "I," impersonal, "We" |

IV: "We, who seven years ago": (4 × 4, a perfect square)

| | |
|---|---|
| Rhyme form: | *abab* |
| Feet in line: | 4 throughout (tetrameter) |
| Rhythm: | trochaic |
| Stanza-length: | 4 lines |
| Length of poem: | one quatrain-stanza |
| Voice(s): | "We" |

## V: "Come let us mock at the great"

| | |
|---|---|
| Rhyme form: | *ababb* |
| Feet in line: | 34343 |
| Rhythm: | iambic (with trochaic substitutions) |
| Stanza-length: | 5 lines |
| Length of poem: | 4 stanzas |
| Voice(s): | "We" |

## VI: "Violence upon the roads: violence of horses"

| | |
|---|---|
| Rhyme form: | *abcabc* (× 3) |
| Feet in line: | 5 |
| Rhythm: | iambic (with dactylic and trochaic substitutions) |
| Stanza-length: | 18 lines |
| Length of poem: | 1 stanza |
| Voice(s): | impersonal |

### "NINETEEN HUNDRED AND NINETEEN": SUMMARY

| | |
|---|---|
| Number of poems: | 6 |
| Number of rhyme forms: | 5 (II and III have the same rhyme form) |
| Number of rhythms: | 4 (iambic, iambic/trochaic, iambic/dactylic/trochaic, trochaic) |
| Number of line lengths: | 3 (trimeter, tetrameter, pentameter) |
| Number of stanzas: | 1 (II, IV, and VI) |
| | 3 (III) |
| | 4 (V) |
| | 6 (I) |
| Stanza-lengths: | 4 lines (IV) |
| | 5 lines (V) |
| | 8 lines (I) |
| | 10 lines (II, III) |
| | 18 lines [3 x 6] (VI) |

## IV

# ✑ "Magical" Techniques
## in the Early Poems

The Yeats most of us know, reread, and quote is the Yeats of the accomplished years following *Responsibilities* (1914). But the groundwork of the adult triumph was laid in Yeats's twenties, thirties, and forties, in a series of technical investigations into the possibilities of rhyme, meter, stanza form, and lexical and phonetic resemblance. Though a good deal has been written about Yeats's early themes, there has been little systematic study of his technical work in the first part of his publishing life. I can give in this chapter only a few instances of his most interesting technical forays, but these examples will suggest how important the mastery of such forms was to him, early and late.[1]

Because the thematic material in the early poems is frequently thin or repetitive (even to readers familiar with the poet's esoteric interests), we can best understand Yeats's poetic originality in some of these poems as of a technical, more than an imaginative, order. I will not take up the slightest poems, even though their technical interest is often considerable; instead, I want to glance at poems of more lasting worth.

I need to begin by sketching out some of Yeats's paths into technical investigation. An evident one is by way of rhyme, and Yeats would ultimately, as Marjorie Perloff has shown,[2] work hard all his life to establish a meaningful relation of sameness or difference between words that rhyme—as, in "Sailing to Byzantium," he rhymes *young* with *song*, or *soul* with *animal*. In earlier years, he was less concerned with a semantic relation between rhyming words than with the relation of their respective lengths. He learned to avoid exclusively monosyllabic rhyme-strings such as those in the 1886 "The Indian upon God"—*trees/knees, pace/chase, speak/weak, sky/eye, talk/stalk, tide/wide, eyes/skies, he/me, say/gay, night/light.* Even in such a list, however, we can see that the rhyme *sky/eye*, in itself of no particular interest, gains visibility when it is repeated in the reversed plural *eyes/skies*; and, though Yeats eventually repudiated consistently monosyllabic strings, he continued to find as many as he could of rhymes such as $\bar{i}/sk\bar{i}$, in which one rhyme-word consists of the basic rhyme-sound while the other has prefaced the rhyme-sound with an additional consonant or two, showing how rhymes are "built." A sampling of Yeats's usages in this respect might include *old/cold, air/hair, out/trout, are/star, on/shone, ear/deer.* Sometimes, when no monosyllabic word representing the rhyme-sound exists in English (as we have no word *eep* or *eap*), the rhyme is made, as before, by adding an extra prefacing consonant to a word already beginning with a consonant, as in *leap/sleep, light/flight.* The rule of thumb for such rhymes is that one must begin with the simplest available morpheme and build another rhyming word upon it.

With respect to monosyllabic rhymes, although Yeats often rhymed monosyllables with the same spelling of the rhyme-sound (such as *hob* and *bob*), he liked very much to rhyme those spelled dissimilarly (such as *fire* and *choir*). In the latter case, the more divergent the spellings, the better. Anyone can rhyme *tears* and *fears,* but it takes a sense of visual amusement to rhyme *tears* and *weirs,* or *goes* and *knows.* There are times when Yeats wants consciously to rhyme words that are chiefly similarly spelled, associating this sort of "perfect" rhyming with either primitive religion ("The Indian upon God") or mental simplicity; "The Ballad of Moll Magee" for the most part uses rhymes spelled alike *(say/day, me/see),* so that one tends to notice nonce exceptions such as *byre/fire.* Yeats was well aware (as we shall see in "The Arrow") of the graphic appearance of his rhymes as well as their aural consonance.

What Yeats began working on after he had explored monosyllabic rhyme and other isometric forms (such as a disyllable rhyming with a disyllable—*island/highland*) was asymmetrical rhyme, in which the two rhyming words are not of the same syllabic length. This technique of asymmetry, when brought to perfection, became a characteristic marker of his mature style, as we can see from the rhymes of "Sailing to Byzantium"—*unless/dress/magnificence, wall/soul/animal, thing/enamelling/sing,* and of course the repeated *come/Byzantium.* The middle and late poems derive their colloquiality in part from that sort of rhyming, especially in moments when the latter syllables of the longer rhyme word become very light: *absurdity/me, caricature/more.*

At first, Yeats's asymmetrical rhymes are relatively uninteresting, as in *sea/melody.* Soon, however, he invents the trick of rhyming a long proper name like *Knocknarea* with *away,* or *Lissadell* with *hill,* or *Mocharabuiee* with *sea;* and he becomes aware of the differing effects of having the long rhyme-word precede the short one, and vice versa: *Lissadell/hill* is a distinctly different poetic coupling from *hill/Lissadell*—the former hints at tension, the latter, closure. (These early perceptions of the effect of reversal are not lost; they are remembered in *come/Byzantium; Byzantium/come*.) Yeats also begins to rhyme polysyllabic words such as *bitterness* and *commonness,* a decision that will lead to unprecedented serious quadrisyllabic rhymes such as *fantastical* and *impossible* in "The Tower." He also risks using asymmetrical slant rhymes such as *school/beautiful* or *enough/love*. He becomes curious about what the French call *rime riche,* in which a word is made to rhyme with itself (present in "The Grey Rock," "He Wishes for the Cloths of Heaven," and later in "Beautiful Lofty Things"). Together with the interest in *rime riche* goes an investigation of internal or "extra" rhyme, in which end-rhymes are linked with a rhyme-word "buried" somewhere inside the line (as in "He Wishes for the Cloths of Heaven").

It would probably be true to say that Yeats's chief technical inventiveness, all along, lay in his rhythmic practice, but because we have no universally accepted notation for rhythmic effects, and because his attempts in this line are so various, I leave the rhythmic field aside here, in frustration at the absence of adequate notation. Stanza form is more amenable to comment; and, because stanza form is inseparable, in Yeats, from its contrapuntal relation with sense units or syntactic units, his experiments in stanza form can be discussed adequately only with respect to particular instances.

This brings me to my first example of Yeats's work with technique, the 1899 poem "He Wishes for the Cloths of Heaven," an eight-line experiment in *rime riche* and internal rhyme:

> Had I the heavens' embroidered cloths,
> Enwrought with golden and silver light,
> The blue and the dim and the dark cloths
> Of night and light and the half-light,
> I would spread the cloths under your feet:
> But I, being poor, have only my dreams;
> I have spread my dreams under your feet;
> Tread softly because you tread on my dreams.
>
> (176)

Here, as elsewhere in *The Wind Among the Reeds,* Yeats has departed from his earlier iambic habit in order to explore dactylic and anapestic feet; this poem emphasizes a dactylic rhythm ("**blue** and the **dim** and the **dark cloths**") in its first, counterfactual, unit (lines 1–5), but an anapestic and iambic one in its second, narrative part (lines 6–8). The yearning intensity of the counterfactual is borne by the ictus of the dactyl "**Had** I the"; the proud humility of the narrative is translated by the poem's progress into the gentleness of a partially anapestic meter: "I have **spread,**" etc.

It would seem that Yeats thought, when he had finished this poem, that he had made something very beautiful. When we ask ourselves what aesthetic effect he was working toward, we see first of all the excessively foregrounded rhyme-words, three of which—*cloths, light,* and *dreams*—are repeated within lines as well. We also see the internal rhymes *night/light* and *spread/tread,* the assonance of *being/feet/dreams* and of *embroidered/enwrought,* and the alliteration of *had/heaven/half.* In fact, the only significant word that dwells phonetically unattached to others in the poem is the word *poor;* Yeats thus makes it stand out unmoored, unmated, unwanted, awkward. Being poor, says the protagonist of the title, he wishes. His wishes are fantasies of possession, as he dreams he has the fabric of the sky itself—the cloud-cloths, star-embroidered, rich in the golden and silver lights of sun and moon—available to him for a courtier's gesture. The poem works by a substitution: when, in line 6, the speaker says "I have only my dreams," we mentally amass under the single category "dreams" all those longings he has already told us about—the whole "Had I . . . I would" dream of the first five lines, with its gorgeous ennobling of the sky so as to make it worthy of the beloved. No non-lover (the poem wants us to think) would have the motivation to elaborate in this way the elemental presence of sun, moon, and stars.

"He Wishes for the Cloths of Heaven" is a good place to observe how Yeats has begun to define his stanza forms. Though defined by its rhymes *(ababcdcd)* as two quatrains, the poem is printed as a single octave, indicating that for Yeats the notion of a "stanza" is not determined by rhymes alone. The eight lines here are printed as one stanza rather than two because there is no syntactic stop at the end of the first quatrain; the first sense-unit extends through line 5. This sort of non-fit between sense-unit and rhyme-unit is one that Yeats exploited to the utmost (in spite of his equal fondness for the coincidence of stanza and period). Ultimately he reached in some poems (for example, "The Tower," part III) a height of "perversity" in which the last place he would put a sense-break was at the point of rhyme-break.

In "He Wishes for the Cloths of Heaven" the conspicuously asymmetrical shape—a five-line, long-breathed curve of the counterfactual followed by three one-line statements of the lover's state ("I . . . have only my dreams," "I have spread my dreams," "you tread on my dreams")—works by its evident singularity and irregularity against the static, even monotonous, round of the *rime riche*. We could say that the *rime riche* stands for the lover's fidelity, while the irregular syntactic bursts stand for his hope, inadequacy, and nervousness. It is the emotional suggestiveness of these formal properties that gives them their intimate interest for Yeats. He would continue, all his life, to counterpoint sense-units against rhyme-units so that neither would become too predictable; a notable case in point is the ingenious variety of sense-units played against the *ottava rima* of "Among School Children," a contrapuntal variety which confers on the poem its air of spontaneous musing, inner hesitation, recalcitrance, and emotionality. In a later poem, the lady of "The Three Bushes" tells her lover that she hopes to hear "if we should kiss / A contrapuntal serpent hiss," and this contrapuntal principle of aesthetic tension, visible as early as "He Wishes for the Cloths of Heaven," was never forsaken by Yeats.

While working closely on all sorts of structural forms—meters, rhymes, and stanza shapes—Yeats began almost at once to subvert that formality in many ingenious ways. His use of subtraction is one of his least-noticed elaborations. Though it may seem paradoxical to call subtraction a form of elaboration, it too is a way of emphasizing something, and becomes a part of the Yeatsian stanzaic artifice as it calls attention to what is missing. This device is evident and formally satisfying in "The Lover Mourns for the Loss of Love," in which (I supply the proper names that Yeats omits in the interest of universality and abstraction) Yeats-the-lover, addressing Maud-the-beloved, recounts how his fidelity to her has caused him to lose the love of his mistress (Olivia Shakespear):

> Pale brows, still hands and dim hair,    *a*
> I had a beautiful friend    *b*
> And dreamed that the old despair    *a*
> Would end in love in the end:    *b*
> She looked in my heart one day    *c*
> And saw your image was there;    *a*
> She has gone weeping away.    *c*
> [..........................................]    [*a*]
> (152)

The first quatrain of this poem *(abab)* imposes itself solidly as it closes with a colon after the strong closing rhyme-word *end* of line 4 (duplicated

internally in the same line). We expect a second quatrain as conclusive as
the first, and we seem to be finding it: *cac*—but then the poem vanishes. We
have read *day/there/away*, but then a blank occurs instead of a rhyme word
to match *there*. For symmetry of rhyme-units, the poem would seem to
"need" an eighth line such as "And I lack your love and her care." But the
lover's double lack—his beloved woman unpossessed, his kind lover un-
loved—is expressed powerfully by the total absence of an eighth line. We
notice that the poem is nonetheless formally complete, since the end-word
of the second line of quatrain two, *there*, matches the *a* rhymes *(hair/de-
spair)* of the first quatrain, leaving no line unrhymed.

Yeats never forgets what he has once invented, and a comparable omis-
sion of an expected closing line turns up memorably (if at first invisibly) at
the very end of "The Tower." Part III of "The Tower" rhymes in trimeter
quatrains, *abab*, but the last "quatrain" has only three lines, as can be seen
from this excerpting of the close:

| | |
|---|---|
| Now I shall make my soul, | *a* |
| Compelling it to study | *b* |
| In a learned school | *a* |
| Till the wreck of body, | _____*b*_____ |
| Slow decay of blood, | *a* |
| Testy delirium | *b* |
| Or dull decrepitude, | *a* |
| Or what worse evil come— | _____*b*_____ |
| The death of friends, or death | *a* |
| Of every brilliant eye | *b* |
| That made a catch in the breath— | *a* |
| Seem but the clouds of the sky | _____*b*_____ |
| When the horizon fades, | *a* |
| Or a bird's sleepy cry | *b* |
| Among the deepening shades. | *a* |
| [...............................] | [*b*] |
| (416) | |

We notice in this late passage many persistences from early Yeats—the
rhyme *eye/sky* of the vowel/consonant(s)-vowel sort, and the monosyllabic
same-spelled rhymes *death/breath* and *fades/shades*. But we also find the
slant rhymes so common in later Yeats, as well as the rhyme *delirium/come*,
reminiscent of the poet's youthful experiments in asymmetrical rhyme. As

the shades deepen and the horizon fades, the last line vanishes with breath itself, and where we expected a conclusion we find a blank. As he had done in "The Lover Mourns for the Loss of Love," Yeats anchors the second-line rhyme-word of the last "deficient" quatrain *(cry)* to rhymes of the preceding quatrain *(eye, sky)*, so that the poem sounds formally complete even though stanzaically it remains incomplete, as the bird's sleepy cry subsides in silence.

There are other "missing" lines in early Yeats, as in "Peace," where a missing line "exists" in order to show that Time has begun to destroy the most beautiful of living forms. And in "The Fascination of What's Difficult," as we shall see in Chapter VI, the missing fourteenth line of the "sonnet" leaves infinite space for what will happen once the speaker "find[s] the stable and pull[s] out the bolt." Yeats will also find a use for "absent" lines in the poem prefacing *Responsibilities:* "Pardon, old fathers." Although the poem is constructed in pentameter sixains, rhyming *abcabc*, the fourth (and last) "sixain" falls short by two lines, and is cast in a different rhyme scheme from the one that prevails in the preceding sixains. It is in his "insufficient" closing *abab* quatrain that Yeats deplores his own insufficiency: instead of the poem's possessing the "proper" 24 lines of four sixains, he has written only 22 lines, and has truncated what should have been his final sixain:

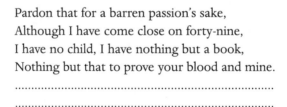

Pardon that for a barren passion's sake,
Although I have come close on forty-nine,
I have no child, I have nothing but a book,
Nothing but that to prove your blood and mine.
...................................................................
...................................................................

I cannot leave the topic of "missing" lines without citing the most famous instance, the line Yeats deleted from his epitaph at the end of "Under Ben Bulben." As we know from a letter *(L, 913)* and the drafts, the epitaph consisted originally of four lines, of which Yeats ultimately dropped the first:

Draw rein; draw breath.
Cast a cold eye
On life, on death.
Horseman, pass by!

The dimeters of this quatrain, combined into tetrameters, would make a couplet analogous to those composing the rest of the poem:

> Draw rein; draw breath. Cast a cold eye
> On life, on death. Horseman, pass by!

These lines are formally complete, whether considered as a true dimeter quatrain (as envisaged by the poet) or as an internally rhymed variant of the normal tetrameter couplet used in "Under Ben Bulben." When Yeats decides to delete the first dimeter, he makes his inscription formally incomplete from both points of view, and thus further emphasizes the discrepancy of nonce dimeters occurring in a tetrameter poem. The deletion makes us read the epitaph (italicized by Yeats) as a quatrain that falls silent after its third line:

> *Cast a cold eye*　　　*a*
> *On life, on death.*　　*b*
> *Horseman, pass by!*　*a*
> [.........................]　[*b*]

The original opening line, "Draw rein; draw breath," had placed Yeats's epitaph in the *Siste viator* tradition, and it is likely (given Yeats's debt in "Byzantium" to Coleridge's self-composed epitaph) that Yeats had in mind the Christian formulations of Coleridge, from whom he borrowed the rhyme *death/breath,* as well as the passer-by and the exclamation point:

> Stop, Christian passer-by!—Stop, child of God . . .
> O, lift one thought in prayer for S.T.C.;
> That he who many a year with toil of breath
> Found death in life, may here find life in death![3]

By deleting the opening line of his original epitaph, and commanding the (mounted) passer-by to pass by (rather than to draw rein to stop and draw breath to pray), Yeats repudiates the Christian communion implored in piety by Coleridge, and substitutes for it a modernist and skeptical haughtiness, together with a modernist asymmetry of form. At the same time, as Warwick Gould reminds me, we may suspect a debt, noted by H. J. Oliver in the Arden *Timon of Athens,* to Timon's epitaph:

*Here lie I, Timon, who alive, all living men did hate.*
*Pass by and curse thy fill, but pass and stay not here thy gait.*[4]

Another "missing" line, noticed by editors, occurs in "Under Ben Bulben," which, as published, exhibits a "missing" line between lines 55 and 56. As the poem stands, line 55 (ending in "ease") remains unrhymed:

> Quattrocento put in paint
> On backgrounds for a God or Saint
> Gardens where a soul's at ease;
> Where everything that meets the eye,
> Flowers and grass and cloudless sky,
> Resemble forms that are or seem
> When sleepers wake and yet still dream.
>
> (639)

During the composition of the poem, as James Pethica shows,[5] Yeats had written a line that gives "ease" its rhyme, with an allusion to Coventry Patmore:

> Quattrocento put in paint
> On backgrounds for a God or Saint
> Gardens where a soul's at ease;
> The soul's perfection is from peace[.]

Whether Yeats deleted the line because it seemed superfluous to explain why a soul would be at ease in a heavenly garden (as I suspect), or whether he and others overlooked its absence in the typescript submitted for publication (an unlikely event), the poem proceeds smoothly in its published version because of the repeated "where" linking the lines: "Gardens where a soul's at ease; / Where everything that meets the eye," etc. Yeats was willing to let a poem go into print with a line missing, as we know from "The Municipal Gallery Revisited," in which one of the *ottava rima* stanzas lacks its third "*b*" line:

> My medieval knees lack health until they bend,
> But in that woman, in that household where
> Honour had lived so long, all lacking found.

Childless I thought, 'My children may find here
Deep-rooted things,' but never foresaw its end,
And now that end has come I have not wept;
No fox can foul the lair the badger swept—[.]

Yeats had already written a complete eight-line stanza in this place. Its first three lines are the same as in the final version, but it then reads:

Childless, I thought, 'my children may learn here
What deep roots are,' and never foresaw the end
Of all that scholarly generations had held dear;
But now that end has come I have not wept;
No fox can foul the lair the badger swept[.]
(603)

Yeats was so meticulous in his creation and refinement of forms that he would rather disfigure a form by omission than pad it with superfluity or irrelevance (those "scholarly generations").

In addition to "missing" lines, there are also "extra" lines in Yeats's poetry, occurring in the early work in both "The Moods" (1893) and "The Old Men Admiring Themselves in the Water" (1902). "The Moods" is an interesting and ambiguous halfway-house between poems with "missing" lines and poems with "extra" lines:

| | |
|---|---|
| Time drops in decay | *a* |
| Like a candle burnt out, | *b* |
| And the mountains and woods | *c* |
| Have their day, have their day; | *a* |
| What one in the rout | *b* |
| Of the fire-born moods | _____*c*_____ |
| Has fallen away? | *a* |

In terms of rhyme, this short poem is indubitably (as I indicate above) a sestet with one "extra" line—*decay, out, woods / day, rout, moods / away.* However, the poem also exhibits itself—in terms of its syntactic sense-units—as a poem composed in quatrains (as I indicate by the horizontal line below), rhyming *abcabca*[-]. The second quatrain remains "incomplete" after the manner of our former "missing" lines:

> Time drops in decay
> Like a candle burnt out,
> And the mountains and woods
> Have their day, have their day; _____
> What one in the rout
> Of the fire-born moods
> Has fallen away?
> [..........................]

The first quatrain declares the transience of both Time and nature; the second retorts with a question that celebrates, by contrast, the immortality of the fire-born (therefore eternal) moods.[6] (Yeats: "The mysterious instinct that has made [the artist] an artist . . . teaches him to discover immortal moods in mortal desires.")[7] We finish "The Moods" without being sure whether we should describe it formally as a sestet with an "extra" appended line, denoting the persistence of the moods even after the sestet (the unit of time) has been completed, *or* as an octave with a "missing" line, denoting the "absent" (but self-evident) rhyming answer to the final question [for instance (if absurdly), "They remain alway"].

The other early poem that may be seen as practicing the addition of an "extra" line is a nine-line piece of chinoiserie consisting of three three-line sentences:

### The Old Men Admiring Themselves in the Water

| | |
|---|---|
| I heard the old, old men say, | *a* |
| 'Everything alters, | *b* |
| And one by one we drop away.' | *a* |
| They had hands like claws and their knees | *c* |
| Were twisted like the old thorn trees | *c* |
| By the waters. | *b* |
| I heard the old, old men say, | *a* |
| 'All that's beautiful drifts away | *a* |
| Like the waters.' | *b* |

(208)

What makes us hesitate to call this simply a nine-line poem in (syntactic) tercets is its structural hint of an alternate stanza form, that of reprise: lines 1–6 seem to compose one "stanza," and then the poem recommences with a repetition of the opening of the poem ("I heard the old, old men say"). One is tempted at first to see the poem as a "deficient" two-stanza poem:

| | |
|---|---|
| I heard . . . say, | I heard . . . say, |
| "Everything alters, | "All . . . drifts away |
| And . . . away." | Like the waters." |
| They had . . . knees | [......................... |
| Were twisted . . . trees | ......................... |
| By the waters | .........................] |

However, one could also see "The Old Men" as a single-stanza poem (lines 1–6) to which has been added a refrain (the last three lines) echoing its beginning. I believe that both of these descriptions are insufficient. What really happens in the poem is that the narrator, after hearing the old men's declaration of universal transience (lines 1–3) is prompted to reflect on their physical deformities (lines 4–6). Then the narrator hears them speak again: this time, in what I see as the "extra" lines of the poem, the old men reflect on a special sort of transience—the transience of beauty. The narrator does not comment on their second statement. But his implicit comment is afforded by the title: "These ugly old men, with their claw-like hands and their twisted knees, are talking about *themselves* in referring to the beautiful that passes: they are admiring *themselves* in the water." That is why I regard lines 7–9 not merely as a reprise but as an *addition* to lines 1–6: lines 7–9 introduce a new item (the beautiful), and they can be understood only by our "supplying" to them the title, which tells us that the beautiful to which the old men refer is themselves. This cunning use of a title as the last word is another instance of Yeats's interest in the reformulation of genre: here, he turns what is formally the first "word," the title, into the last "word" (expressed in lines 7–9), as he illustrates the persistence of physical vanity, even into old age.

The device of the "extra" line or lines also turns up, as we would now expect, in late Yeats, notably in the two additional lines appended to "Crazy Jane on the Mountain" (1938). The poem seems to be one of structural reprise, as lines 11–12, "'Last night I lay on the mountain' / (Said Crazy Jane)," match lines 1–2, "'I am tired of cursing the Bishop,' / (Said Crazy Jane)." In that case, the reprise-unit should conform, in length, to the first, ten-line, unit, thereby making a poem of twenty lines. But the poem actually has twenty-two lines: to the two ten-line units, an "extra" couplet has been added as a coda. I print the poem in two columns in order to show its structure, although in fact it runs through its twenty-two lines without a break:

I am tired of cursing the Bishop,    Last night I lay on the mountain
(Said Crazy Jane)    (Said Crazy Jane)
Nine books or nine hats    There in a two-horsed carriage
Would not make him a man.    That on two wheels ran
I have found something worse    Great-bladdered Emer sat,
To meditate on.    Her violent man
A King had some beautiful cousins,    Cuchulain sat at her side;
But where are they gone?    Thereupon,
Battered to death in a cellar,    Propped upon my two knees,
And he stuck to his throne.    I kissed a stone;
    I lay stretched out in the dirt
    And I cried tears down.

(628)

Throughout its entire twenty-two lines, the poem rhymes, in slant fashion, on some vowel coupled with *n*: *Jane/man/on/gone/throne/Jane/ran/ man/thereupon/stone/down*. Because the expected rhyme keeps arriving (generally in a monosyllable, so as to be appropriate to Jane's "simple" ballad status), we may not notice the poem's structural asymmetry; and because the twenty-two lines of "Crazy Jane on the Mountain" are printed as a single block, the proportions of the poem at first remain obscure. On reflection, after noting the reprise-effect, we see that the first ten lines of Crazy Jane's speech concern current events (the murder of the Czar and his family, cousins to the King of England); the following twelve present, as a substitute preferable to modern violence, Crazy Jane's vision of two Celtic heroes: that "violent man" Cuchulain and his consort Emer of mythological physical endurance, her bladder-capacity legendary. Inescapably, one feels that the last two "extra" lines, appended to the second ten-line unit, function as an intensive "second ending." In a ritual of thanksgiving for her vision, Jane kisses a stone, thereby ending her second ten-line unit; but the meditation on murder with which the poem had begun returns to her mind, and causes her thanksgiving to turn unexpectedly to desolation:

I lay stretched out in the dirt
And I cried tears down.

Part of the effect of that turn to desolation is missed if we are not aware that the last two lines "exceed" the ten lines that would, if the poem had retained symmetry, create in Crazy Jane's vision in her reprise-unit a redeeming equal match "canceling" her preceding lament. (And we miss the "stuck" quality of Jane's meditation and vision, which explains her return to desolation, if we do not note her inability to rhyme on any sound but "n.")

In other cases, too, Yeats used profitably the uncertainty conferred on a poem by ambiguous relations among its sense-units. The most famous example of such ambiguity of relation in the early verse is the song "Who Goes with Fergus?" from *The Countess Kathleen*. The poem is composed of two six-line stanzas rhyming *abcabc*. In the first sixain, the syntactic units—a three-line question *(abc)* and a three-line set of injunctions *(abc)*—exactly match the rhyme division, suggesting the ease of abandoning erotic hopes and fears to go live with Fergus, a king who has abdicated his throne:

| | |
|---|---|
| Who will go drive with Fergus now | *a* |
| And pierce the deep wood's woven shade | *b* |
| And dance upon the level shore? | *c* |
| Young man, lift up your russet brow, | *a* |
| And lift your tender eyelids maid, | *b* |
| And brood on hopes and fear no more. | *c* |

But in the second stanza the sense-break comes after two lines, not three. This puts rhyme and sense at odds, or at least places them in a disturbing asymmetrical relation to each other, creating a "false quatrain"—tightly connected by anaphora and syntactic parallelism—out of the last four lines:

| | |
|---|---|
| And no more turn aside and brood | *a* |
| Upon love's bitter mystery; | *b* |
| For Fergus rules the brazen cars, | *c* |
| And rules the shadows of the wood, | *a* |
| And the white breast of the dim sea | *b* |
| And all dishevelled wandering stars. | *c* |

(125–126)

In the most complex move of the poem, the paired semiotic correspondences between lines in stanza 1 and lines in stanza 2 come out "wrong," leaving one piece unmatched, a piece "left over":

| | | |
|---|---|---|
| Who will drive with Fergus | = | Fergus rules . . . cars |
| Wood's woven shade | = | shadows of the wood |
| level shore | = | white breast of . . . dim sea |
| ? | = | dishevelled wandering stars |

There is nothing in stanza 1, or so it seems, to match the last line of the second stanza, "And all dishevelled wandering stars." The stars draw their very effect from their excessiveness, their "extra-ness" in the absence of any corresponding material. The word "dishevelled," like the word "breast" used of the sea, makes the stars seem female, increasing the erotic attractiveness of Fergus's world. Because lines 3, 4, and 5 of stanza 2 have echoed in exact order lines 1, 2, and 3 of stanza 1, we expect line 6, in its turn, to match something (preferably line 4 of stanza 1) to keep the order going. But the stars match nothing, surprising us by their fine excess. We see then that the *total* poem has the form of a chiasmus:

| Question | Negative Injunction | Negative Injunction | Conclusion |
|---|---|---|---|
| Fergus | Brood no more | No more brood | Fergus |

The interior chiasmus ("And brood on hopes and fear no more / And no more turn aside and brood") is the "hinge" connecting the two sixains. Going off with Fergus is the alternative, for man and maid alike, to brooding on love's bitter mystery. Yeats suggests, I think, that Fergus is himself an erotic power, ruling the masculine brazen cars and the feminine breast of the sea.

In Fergus's world, earth and sky—the woven shadows of the wood and the dishevelled wandering stars—are made to share so many common letters and phonemes (**shad**ows/-**shevelled, woven/wood/wand**ering) that they unite to create the expansiveness and continuity of a realm without visible boundaries. The lovers have exchanged love's bitter "mystery" (the one polysyllabic rhyme-word in the poem, and therefore foregrounded) for an increasing expanse from wood to seashore to wayward and straying stars. The "expansion" beyond the matched lines of horizontal movement to the vertical realm of the unmatched stars gives the "extra" line 6 a quasi-infinite dimension. We are left unsure whether we have read a poem of two six-line stanzas, or a triple twelve-line chiasmus; a poem in doubled tercet-units of rhyme, or a poem insisting by its syntax on a quatrain-unit; a symmetrical poem in which lines are matched in rhyme, or an asymmetrical poem with a "leftover" line at the end.

A comparable counterpoint of syntactical and stanzaic form can be seen in "The Everlasting Voices" (1895), an eight-line poem which at first, because of the semicolon after line 4, looks as though it were written in two irregularly rhyming quatrains—*abac/baca*—that voice a series of injunctions. Nonetheless, the poem is equally well represented formally by a scheme which shows it to consist of a regularly rhyming inner sestet *(bacbac)* flanked fore and aft by a refrain *(a)*—"O sweet everlasting Voices, be still." The alternate rhyme scheme thus becomes *a/bacbac/a*:

| | |
|---|---|
| O sweet everlasting Voices, be still: | *a* |
| Go to the guards of the heavenly fold | *b* |
| And bid them wander obeying your will, | *a* |
| Flame under flame, till time be no more; | *c* |
| Have you not heard that our hearts are old, | *b* |
| That you call in birds, in wind on the hill, | *a* |
| In shaken boughs, in tide on the shore? | *c* |
| O sweet everlasting Voices, be still. | *a* |

The return of the initial refrain means that the haunting Voices will never cease, that the poem "begins over again" at its end and cannot reach its apocalyptic hope.

The "ambiguous" stanzas in this and other poems—are they sestets? are they octaves? are they quatrains?—are congruent with the frequently ambiguous rhythms of the early poetry. Yeats often aims at a "floating" formal undecidability of rhythm coincident with his attempt to reproduce meditative hovering. The odd alexandrines, pentameters (often in dactylic or anapestic rhythms), and even trimeters of the early poetry will be seen to have their descendants in the later verse—but there they are less wavering, more pointed, more sure of their inextricability from theme.

At the other extreme from hovering sensitivity, undecidability, lack, and ambiguity stand full power and command. The early poetry occasionally does possess that perfection, attained in at least one case, I believe, because Yeats derived confident will from his accomplished formal intent. The most beautiful example in the early verse of a poem employing what I think of as "magical" means is "The Song of Wandering Aengus," a poem deriving from the Irish *aisling* lyric, in which the speaker is vouchsafed a vision of a female embodying the national spirit. Aengus, we are told, is the Irish Apollo, the god of poetry; and although he is here shown as a human quester, he is also the chosen consort of a beckoning goddess, and his last words are words of powerful determination: "I will find out where she has gone / And kiss her lips and take her hands." Here is the poem (composed in *abcb* quatrains grouped into eight-line stanzas). I give its "magical" words and syllables in bold:

### The Song of **Wand**ering Aengus

I went **out** to the hazel **wood,**
Because a **fire** was in my **head,**
And cut and peeled a hazel **wand,**
And hooked a berry to a **thread;**
And **when** white **moth**s **w**ere on the **wing,**
And **moth**-like stars were flickeri**ng out,**
I dropped the berry in a stream
And caught a little **silver** tr**out.**

When I had laid it on the **floor**
I went to blow the **fire** aflame,
But something rustled on the **floor,**
And some one **called me by my name**:
It had become a glimmeri**ng** girl
With **apple** blossom in her h**air**
Who **called me by my name** and ran
And faded through the brighteni**ng air.**

Though I am **old** with **wand**ering
Through hollow lands and hilly lands,
I **will** find out where she has gone,
And kiss her lips and take her hands;
And walk among long d**apple**d grass,
And pluck **till** time and times are done
The **silver apples** of the moon,
The **gold**en **apples** of the sun.

(149–150)

Although "The Song of Wandering Aengus" is composed in alternately rhymed *quatrains*, it is printed in *octaves*, three of them, and we must ask why the quatrains were run together in this fashion. The underlying story is simple: Aengus, using as bait a berry hooked by a thread to a hazel wand, catches a trout that turns into a girl, who after calling him by name, vanishes, leaving Aengus resolved to pursue her. But the way Yeats uses language in this poem suggests that he believes that language has powers of its own which are independent of the story it tells. It is not an accident, I think, that the first thing **wand**-ering Aengus does is to cut a **wand,** or that his **head** finds a **thread.** Such pairings assert that magical, non-rational, non-etymological relations between words are as important to Yeats as logical, semantic, or etymological connections. Other magical links are made in the rhyme-words and elsewhere: just as the word **head** is contained in **thread,** so **out** is contained in **trout, air** in **hair, time** in **times, though** in **through,** and the phrase **hollow lands and hilly lands** contains **low lands and hi[gh] lands.** These linked words are made even more salient when they are foregrounded in various ways—**though** and **through,** for instance, by being placed in the same initial position in successive lines, and others by being placed in a rhyme-position.

Other word relations in the poem are no less arbitrary. **Moths** on the **wing** on earth are mysterious mirrors to **moth**-like stars in the sky. The erotic **fire** in Aengus's head is replicated by the literal **fire** he blows aflame. The *rime riche* of **floor** and **floor,** and the repetition of **called me by my name,** are used, I think, to keep the setting and action constant while magical transformation occurs creepingly in the nouns and pronouns. We can see the metamorphosis happening before us in Aengus's narration:

> [I] caught a little silver **trout.**
>
> When I had laid **it** on the floor
> I went to blow the fire aflame;
> But **something** rustled on the floor,
> And **some one** called me by my name;
> **It** had become a glimmering **girl**
> With apple blossom in her hair
> Who called me by my name and ran
> And faded through the brightening air.

The wander**ing** hero of the title, when moths were on the **wing** and stars were flicker**ing,** finds a glimmer**ing** girl who fades through the brighten**ing** air and makes him old with wander**ing.** These irrational -**ing** repetitions (along with **wand**ering and **wand**) connect the title—"The Song of Wandering Aengus"—to the stanzas. Similar "magical" links cause the peculiar conclusiveness of the ending. Of course, as we read "the **silver apples** of the moon, / The golden **apples** of the sun," we notice the semantic reprise of **"silver"** trout and **"apple**-blossom" in the girl's hair, but it is only by inspection that we realize how the conclusiveness is also caused by the foreshadowing power of **"old"** for "**golden**" and "**dappled**" for **"apples."**[8] The **"out"** words, too—"I went **out** . . . when stars were . . . **out** . . . and caught a **trout** . . . I will find **out**"—are non-rational "magic" manifestations in the narrative. The very fabric of "The Song of Wandering Aengus" suggests a reduplicative spell-casting, full as it is of anaphora and the repetition of phrases, lines, and sounds. This sort of "self-generating" poetry is meant to mimic absolute command—a magus's command of entirely mastered experience, or a god's command over fate. We understand, as we come to the end, why the poem is presented as three octaves rather than as six quatrains. The structure enacts the phases of the narrative: a stanza for the trout, a stanza for the girl, and a stanza for the quest.

In addition to perfectly mastered experience and language, this performative poem promises, and gives, a paradise—the end of the quest foretold in Aengus's determination that he *will* (not "shall") attain the glimmering girl. Although many of the satisfactions of the prophesied paradise are foreshadowed, we are, I think, surprised by the appearance of "the golden apples of the sun." The silver trout had been caught at twilight and brought home at evening; the silver apples of the moon therefore seem proper to the fish and to the glimmering girl it became—but the golden apples of the sun burst surprisingly upon this nocturne. They have been forecast (we can see in retrospect) by the dawn scene of "brightening" air into which the girl paradoxically "fades" in her escape—"[She] ran / And faded through the brightening air." Aengus knows that though she was silver and glimmering on this earth she will become golden, in the brightening sun, in some Blakean eternity. (The word "brightening" is one of the class of verbs, such as "redden" or "wane," having positive or negative infinite extension in time.) We feel, at the end of "The Song of Wandering Aengus," an alchemical foretaste of the gold of the Byzantium poems.

The forms of beauty we have been examining are subtle ones—variations in the length of rhyme words, overlapping stanzaic and syntactic forms, missing or extra lines, *rime riche,* incantational replication, magical and irrational word-links, and so on. They do not by any means represent Yeats's entire technical repertoire in the early work. But they do show him in possession of various deliberate forms of beauty, the result of tenacious experimental work. After looking closely at the early verse, we are ready to believe Yeats's remark in "Adam's Curse" about the intense labor required to articulate sweet sounds together. Many of the lines of the early poetry still show the seams, in their elaborate artifice, of the poet's sedulous stitching and unstitching. It is in the later poetry that the verse that seems but a moment's thought becomes sovereign. In his later writing, Yeats profited from his early exhaustive trials of the possibilities of musical language. Like Sidney in the Psalter and Herbert in *The Temple,* he left almost no metrical or stanzaic stone unturned.

The incantatory power of reduplicative language (learned in part from Swinburne but not abused) served Yeats as an index of magically intended writing throughout his life. We hear it in the repetitions of "The Gyres":

> The gyres! The gyres! Old Rocky Face, look forth;
> Things thought too long can be no longer thought,
> For beauty dies of beauty, worth of worth. . . .
>
> (564)

Repetition, by spell-casting, is the guarantee of revolution; transformative or revolutionary spells must be repetitive first, and then—with their unexpected glow of golden apples or resurrective disinterments from broken sepulchers—revolutionary. The history of Yeats's style reveals how much, in the long run, the late manner is a result of his early poetic successes, which made the visual and auditory presence of individual words, rhymes, stanza schemes, and syntactic parallels take on an almost palpable shape and solidity.

I close with one last example. In the phenomenally extensive charts of language in Yeats's brain, words differing from each other by only one letter (or two) held adjacent places on some great linguistic wheel. To make rhymes in one poem come only from that special subset was, to Yeats's mind, to construct a designated and magically aimed message, sure to find its target, an arrow of the soul. Here is "The Arrow":

> I thought of your beauty, and this arrow,
> Made out of a wild thought, is in my marrow.
> There's no man may look upon her, no man,
> As when newly grown to be a woman,
> Tall and noble but with face and bosom
> Delicate in colour as apple blossom.
> This beauty's kinder, yet for a reason
> I could weep that the old is out of season.
>
> (199)

"The Arrow" is not one of the better poems of *In the Seven Woods*, and it allows itself a little latitude by permitting the second *s* in *blossom*. But it tells us that Yeats made strong subliminal associations between *bosom* and *blossom*, *no man* and *woman;* that *marrow* is the place for a wounding thought-*arrow;* and that the un*reason*ableness of *season*al change struck him as the *trea-sonableness* of *season*al change struck Frost. Poetic thinking proceeds not only by propositions and images, as we sometimes think, but also by such lexical and phonemic slippages and linkages. We cannot read Yeats at all without recalling this axiom of poetic composition.

## V

# ⌒ Tales, Feelings, Farewells:
# Three Stages of the Yeatsian Ballad

Yeats wrote ballads for over fifty years. They play a strong role in his work both early (in his nation-building phase) and late (in his old-age search for the "primitive"); they appear much less frequently in the middle years of his career, when he was intent on exploring more complex lyric forms. Because Yeats's poetry defines "the ballad" widely, so will I,[1] apologizing here for the length of this chapter, since any attempt to look at fifty years of poetic evolution is bound to take time. The innumerable decisions—on poem length, stanza form, rhythmic variation, archaic or modern diction, demotic or fine language, rhyme words, personae, the construction of sequences, and so on—that Yeats had to make in writing his ballads need to be taken into account in asking what sort of poet he was and what sort of poems he wanted to write, where he succeeded and where he failed. It may sometimes be wearying, for critic and reader alike, to subject a single poetic form, in all its variety, to description and analysis; but it is the only way to see what the poet-as-poet spent his days doing, and to explain the ventures of his aesthetic within that single form. It seems to me that we owe it to the poet to work at understanding his poems with at least some of the intensity and ingenuity he expended in writing them. A chapter such as this one on the ballad can, if it seems long, be dipped into intermittently (which is, after all, the manner in which poems are written over a lifetime). Because the insoluble question of how to write a modern ballad was a genuine problem for Yeats from first to last, his long-term investigations and revisions of the genre hold a unique place in the history of his career. Like nothing else, they illuminate his enormous tenacity and his unremitting inventiveness.

Ballad-poetry is so frequent in the *Collected Poems* that I can here merely sketch its extent and variety, first in single poems, then in Yeats's ballad sequences, and finally in the poems of his last years. Like his nineteenth-century predecessors from Scott and Wordsworth to Keats, Yeats stretched the scope of the ballad while retaining (if also often defying) many of the conventions that identify it: its narrative plot; its quatrain stanza (sometimes accompanied by a refrain, sometimes extended to six lines); its simplicity of means; its focus on a dramatic moment; its use of conversation; its impersonality; and its expression of a collective voice. As a young poet, Yeats began, naturally enough, with the common ballad stanza written in lines of alternate tetrameter and trimeter (4-3-4-3, Common Meter)[2] in which only the second and fourth lines rhyme *(abcb)*. Later, Yeats moved away from ballads determined by narrative content alone toward ones with more lyric and metaphysical themes, while inventing complex varieties of the ballad stanza.[3] Eventually, he experimented with attaching lyric songs to an overarching ballad story (as in the sequence "The Three Bushes"), or (as we have seen in the late free-standing ballad "Crazy Jane on the Mountain") he eliminated stanza breaks and rhymed his ballad throughout in a single *b*-rhyme sound (making a desolating effect like a piper's drone).

Yeats's ballad writing followed on that of the "Young Ireland" poets, but differed from theirs in that his ballads were consciously worked, not hastily written; they were not topical "street-ballads" but rather aligned themselves with the ballads of such literary figures as Scott and Wordsworth.

## The Single Ballad, 1888–1921

If we look at Yeats's early ballads, we can see that some (such as the 1888 "Ballad of Father O'Hart") are conventional in unfolding a narrative content of changing events. But the 1889 "Ballad of Moll Magee" (94–96) emphasizes, as it takes up the Wordsworthian theme of the forsaken woman, the feelings of the speaker rather than a plot. "Moll Magee" reveals the distraught mind of a repudiated wife who tells a piteous tale: she has inadvertently smothered her baby and has in consequence been driven from the house by her husband:

> I lay upon my baby;
> Ye little children dear,
> I looked on my cold baby
> When the morn grew frosty and clear.
>
> A weary woman sleeps so hard!
> My man grew red and pale,
> And gave me money and bade me go
> To my own place, Kinsale.
>
> He drove me out and shut the door,
> And gave his curse to me;

> I went away in silence,
> No neighbour could I see.

Moll may resemble a Wordsworthian character, but her poem lacks one of the chief characteristics of Wordsworth's lyrical ballads, the dependence of the plot on a psychological change in the speaker or observer ("We Are Seven," "An Anecdote for Fathers"). Here we see no such alteration: throughout, Moll Magee remains unchanged in mind (a fact symbolized by the near-identity between her first utterance and her last). Here is the first:

> Come round me, little childer;
> There, don't fling stones at me
> Because I mutter as I go;
> But pity Moll Magee.

And here is her last:

> So now, ye little childer,
> Ye won't fling stones at me;
> But gather with your shinin' looks
> And pity Moll Magee.

By its economy of speech and the bareness of its circumstance, "The Ballad of Moll Magee" shows its indebtedness to the Border ballads. But Yeats's early ballad-content remains within one branch of the Wordsworthian tradition, in that his protagonists are, for the most part, poor, overworked, or old. That he created ballads about priests (Father Gilligan, Father O'Hart) suggests that he wanted to reach the Catholic readers of Ireland, to include them in the national literature he hoped to create—a generous if aesthetically unproductive impulse. Yeats's early ballads remain within common spheres of reference, and do not predict his drive toward originality in the form.

By 1897, in *The Wind Among the Reeds,* the Yeatsian ballad begins to be distinguishable from the ballad of his predecessors, as occult matter begins to infiltrate Yeats's verse. Although "The Blessed" (166–168) is voiced by speakers with Irish names (Cumhal the king and Dathi the hermit), and although its hermit refers in Christian terms to "God's mother," the same hermit, at the close, advises the king of the revelatory potential of drunkenness for occult vision of a Rosicrucian sort. The promise of visionary ecstasy brings a dactylic lilt to the 4-3-4-3 *abab* ballad stanza:[4]

'I see the blessedest soul in the world
And he nods a drunken head.

'O blessedness comes in the night and the day
And whither the wise heart knows;
And one has seen in the redness of wine
The Incorruptible Rose[.]'

A few years later, in *The Green Helmet* (1910), conventional ballad personae such as Moll Magee have vanished (for the time being). The steersman who speaks the ballad "His Dream" (253–254) possesses an educated voice and uses occult symbols. In a slight metrical modification (4-4-4-3) of the *abab* ballad stanza, the steersman retells his dream, in which he bore in his boat a shrouded form whose name, the shore-onlookers cry, is "Death":

Though I'd my finger on my lip,
What could I but take up the song?
And running crowd and gaudy ship
Cried out the whole night long,

Crying amid the glittering sea,
Naming it with ecstatic breath,
Because it had such dignity,
By the sweet name of Death.

The ballad, in this dream-guise, becomes a Symbolist poem in which narrative content has been reduced to a minimum. Yet something of the collective anonymity of the ballad persists, since the speaker's voice is framed by a collective utterance from the crowd, who usurp the poet's privilege of naming the body borne by his ship. Thus Yeats attaches to the lyric atmosphere of "His Dream" the collective emphasis proper to a ballad; but the poem's surreal Symbolist images are alien to the more rugged ballad tradition, and Yeats would soon turn away from the Symbolist ballad as he did from the plot-centered ballad.

Now Yeats begins to experiment with the topical ballad based on current events, where he will find distinct success, in part because his work in the theater had liberated him into genuinely colloquial diction. *Responsibilities* (1914) contains several topical ballads concerning the Hugh Lane controversy (which arose from the refusal of the Municipality of Dublin to build a gallery to house Lane's collection of paintings).[5] "September 1913"

(289–290)—originally entitled "Romance in Ireland (On reading much of the correspondence against the Art Gallery)"—is written in Long Meter (4-4-4-4), and it doubles the ballad quatrain to make an eight-line stanza *(ababcdcd)*. Nonetheless, it is marked unmistakably as a poem belonging to the ballad tradition by its refrain, "Romantic Ireland's dead and gone, / It's with O'Leary in the grave." But instead of appending an impersonally voiced refrain to the completed ballad stanza (as is usual), Yeats incorporates the refrain (by means of its rhyme-words) into the body of the stanza as an inseparable part of the lyric speaker's own outburst:

> Was it for this the wild geese spread
> The great wing upon every tide;
> For this that all that blood was shed,
> For this Edward Fitzgerald died,
> And Robert Emmet and Wolfe Tone,
> All that delirium of the brave?
> Romantic Ireland's dead and gone,
> It's with O'Leary in the grave.[6]

In this scornful ballad, the doomed heroes of 1798 represent the "true" Irish collective. Yeats sets himself against the narrowly mercantile Catholic middle class of his own time, who are viewed as a foreign "you" by the alienated Anglo-Irish poet:

> What need you, being come to sense,
> But fumble in a greasy till
> And add the halfpence to the pence
> And prayer to shivering prayer, until
> You have dried the marrow from the bone?

In choosing to cast the matter of "September 1913" into ballad form, Yeats implies that the most venerable literary genre of "Romantic Ireland" is the ballad, resuscitated by the poet as the native song in which to insert a roll call of vanished heroes (comparable to the later drumroll of names ending "Easter 1916"). The poet sees himself as the speaker for a better collective. Although Yeats never abandons the identification of the ballad with Irish resistance (see his last ballad, "The Black Tower," discussed later in this chapter), he does not restrict his ballads to political topics. And although he will sometimes put aside his "lowly" speakers, the appeal of the "low" per-

sona is resuscitated in his later years in such protagonists as Crazy Jane and
Old Tom.

In time, Yeats begins to create his own form of ballad stanzas. In the
1914 "Beggar to Beggar Cried" (299–300), he incorporates the refrain into
the stanza itself, as he did in "September 1913"; but whereas in "September
1913" the refrain rhymes with the lines preceding it, in this beggar-poem
Yeats puts the refrain—in "low" diction, unrhymed and italicized—in the
penultimate line-position:

> 'Time to put off the world and go somewhere
> And find my health again in the sea air,'
> *Beggar to beggar cried, being frenzy-struck,*
> 'And make my soul before my pate is bare.'

Yeats then goes so far as to insert *two* unrhymed refrains in a single bal-
lad in "Running to Paradise" (300–301), where the "personal" refrain ("For
[And] I am running to Paradise") is displaced upward to the middle of the
stanza, while the "collective" one, printed in italics, occupies the normal
closing position *("And there the king is but as the beggar")*. The effect of the
separate positioning of two refrains can be felt as one scans the opening
stanzas:

> As I came over Windy Gap
> They threw a halfpenny into my cap,
> For I am running to Paradise;
> And all that I need do is to wish
> And somebody puts his hand in the dish
> To throw me a bit of salted fish:
> *And there the king is but as the beggar.*
>
> My brother Mourteen is worn out
> With skelping his big brawling lout,
> And I am running to Paradise;
> A poor life, do what he can,
> And though he keep a dog and a gun,
> A serving-maid and a serving-man:
> *And there the king is but as the beggar.*

The expanded seven-line stanza in long meter (4-4-4-4) of "Running to Para-
dise" is separated by its first unrhymed refrain into an anterior couplet and a

posterior tercet; the "collective" refrain then closes the poem *(aabcccd)*. The impetus of the running is suggested by the growth from couplet to tercet of the rhymes, while the refrains furnish the pauses of self-explanation (where the speaker is going, and why a beggar especially would want to go there). Such a poem displays Yeats's free inventiveness within the general category of ballad-form, as he here suits the often anapestic metrical movement of the stanzas to his restless peasant, who refuses to be bought or bound even by the putative formal imperatives of the ballad stanza.

As Yeats's middle ballad-style reaches a new sophistication of content, he decides to try presentation not in stanzas but in a single block, since a poem can move more intently when there is no white space or refrain to interrupt it. Although we find in the 1914 poem "The Dolls" (319) many familiar characteristics of the ballad ("low" diction, three-beat Half Meter, and the *abab* quatrain as the unit of composition), the coincidence of sentence and independent stanza no longer obtains; the syntax can run on as it pleases, and the trimeter beat displaces the alternating rhythms of the standard ballad quatrain, 4-3-4-3. In "The Dolls" a doll-maker is disgusted by biological being, and, like his dolls, feels revulsion at the displacement of art by nature. A living baby has been born in the doll-maker's house, where hitherto only "generations" of dolls have been produced. Although the indignant dolls on the shelves indict both the doll-maker and his wife as begetters of this hated new occupant, the husband takes no responsibility for the infant, and the wife abjectly apologizes to her husband for the "accident" of its birth. In the three-part "plot" (advanced by each new speaker and speech-act), those commenting on the new baby are "a doll" (who "bawls" for one line), then "the oldest of all the dolls" (who "screams" for a little more than five lines) and finally "the doll-maker's wife" (who "murmurs" for two lines):

> A doll in the doll-maker's house
> Looks at the cradle and bawls:
> 'That is an insult to us.'
> But the oldest of all the dolls,
> Who had seen, being kept for show,
> Generations of his sort
> Out-screams the whole shelf: 'Although
> There's not a man can report
> Evil of this place,
> The man and the woman bring
> Hither, to our disgrace

A noisy and filthy thing.'
Hearing him groan and stretch
The doll-maker's wife is aware
Her husband has heard the wretch,
And crouched by the arm of his chair,
She murmurs into his ear,
Head upon shoulder leant:
'My dear, my dear, O dear,
It was an accident.'

This satiric trimeter ballad suggests, with the wife's apology, that the doll-maker sides with his dolls, preferring the work of his hands to the "noisy and filthy" evidence of his sexual life.[7]

By 1916 (when Yeats is fifty-one), he can make the ballad quatrain serve almost any purpose. The *abcb* quatrain comes to seem less a self-contained unit than a base upon which interesting things can be built. Yeats's most original and beautiful addition to the ballad quatrain is the asymmetrical couplet that he appends to it in "The Wild Swans at Coole" (322–323). We hear, as we begin to read the poem, a ballad quatrain (4-3-4-3) rhyming *abcb*, but this familiar form encloses not a narrative content but a distinctly lyric one:

The woods are in their autumn beauty,
The woodland paths are dry,
Under the October twilight the water
Mirrors a still sky[.]

It is a ravishing surprise when, seeing that the punctuation following "sky" is *not* a period but a semicolon, we find our eye and ear drawn into a long and luxurious full pentameter which, by enjambment, overspills itself in wonder into a conclusive trimeter:

Upon the brimming water among the stones
Are nine and fifty swans.

The closing couplet, with its asymmetrical rhyming lines, is somehow deeply solacing, as the "ballad" stanza—overbrimming both its quatrain-base and its tetrameter-trimeter metric—extends itself into completion. Yeats's newly invented stanza is able to be both exultantly emphatic (noting of the swans "the bell-beat of their wings above my head") and commonplace ("And now my heart is sore"). It is as though the antagonism of "The Dolls" (between the biologically produced "primitive" baby and the wooden dolls of "developed" artifice) has been imaginatively solved in this hybrid stanza, part folkform, part lyric artifice.

More such efforts to combine high and low, not all of them successful, now drive Yeats's experimentation with the ballad. In seeking to bring high and low to a common focus, he sometimes presses the low too far. In the ballad "Under the Round Tower" (331–332), for instance, Billy Byrne, sleeping on his great-grandfather's battered tomb at the monastic site of Glendalough, has a dream of the sun and the moon as king and queen dancing and singing in the round tower there, eventually spiraling up all the way to the top of the winding stair. The poem is a Long Meter ballad quatrain with an appended couplet (4-4-4-4-4-4, *abcbdd*) which must obey the added condition that lines 1 and 3 of each stanza must end in a trochee.[8] It is brought strongly into the ballad tradition by the lowly beggar-speaker whom it quotes; but he, though now penniless, is (according to the narrator of the ballad) a descendant of the noble family of "O'Byrnes and Byrnes" buried at Glendalough. Yeats, seeking here as in "The Song of Wandering Aengus" a conjunction of high and low, imposes the rough diction of the ballad-lexicon on the gold-and-silver alchemical symbol of perfect sexual union. The "high" union of sun and moon is expressed in "low" language, since "bellowed" and "pranced" are the only words Billy Byrne can find to describe the ritual acts of the "heavenly bodies" as they sing and dance in symbolic representation of the energy and joy of sexual intercourse: Billy "stretched his bones and fell in a dream / Of sun and moon that a good hour / Bellowed and pranced in the round tower."

The dance of sun and moon climaxes in their ascent to the top of the tower, as Billy dreams

> Of golden king and silver lady,
> Bellowing up and bellowing round,
> Till toes mastered a sweet measure,
> Mouth mastered a sweet sound,
> Prancing round and prancing up
> Until they pranced upon the top.

What does Yeats expect to gain by such a "low" ballad-reduction of occult alchemical symbolism sexually enacted by royal personages? (There was no such reduction in diction in the alchemical ending of "The Song of Wandering Aengus.") He does achieve an account of sexual intercourse which paradoxically combines (in verse as in life; Yeats was recently married) the physical prancing and bellowing remarked by Billy Byrne with a feeling of cosmic exaltation as earthly bodies become "celestial" solar and lunar ones. Billy Byrne is one of the ballad-framed Yeatsian Irish visionaries and aphorists of whom the most famous is Crazy Jane; yet Yeats's self-defense against "high" visionary language through Billy's grossly primitive account of "bellowing" and "prancing" seems more aggressive than convincing. Since the grotesque vocabulary of Billy Byrne is by itself manifestly inadequate as a vehicle for the "high" dance of sun and moon, Yeats supplements it (not very successfully) by a "high" web of semantic and syntactic repetition which, beginning in a loose weave, becomes tighter and tighter until the dance of sun and moon climaxes in the stanza I have quoted above, after which it loosens once again. These repetitions constitute the "lyrical" aspect of the poem, offsetting its "low" ballad diction and the quasi-refrain "On great-grandfather's battered tomb" which closes the first and last stanzas. "Under the Round Tower," in its uneasy amalgam of ballad bellowing and astrological dance-repetition, never really accomplishes its hope to fuse the popular and the cosmic.

Yeats's two ballads on the Easter Rising, "Sixteen Dead Men" and "The Rose Tree" (held from publication, along with "Easter 1916," until the 1921 volume *Michael Robartes and the Dancer*), represent Yeats's attempts to think himself into the position of the dead patriots without revealing the mixed personal feelings he candidly exposes in "Easter 1916." Both ballads extend the stanza to six lines, *abcbdb,* and each embodies a dialogue, the first between two sides of Yeats himself ("we" and "you") and the second (a less complicated one) between the rebels Padraic Pearse and James Connolly, which ends in the realization that given the insuffiency of words "too lightly spoken," the only "water" to restore the Rose Tree of liberty is "our own red blood." The dialogue-form permits two opinions about the Rising to occupy each poem, but "The Rose Tree," although it "debates" whether liberty can be restored by words or only by the shedding of blood, is more a tribute to Pearse's mysticism of blood-sacrifice than a real debate.

"Sixteen Dead Men," however, with its tragic and macabre title, is a worthy piece of ballad-writing, in which a grisly nobility is not compromised by the folk-diction that Yeats employs. The poem is plainspoken without being "low," and it is technically interesting: in each stanza at least one surprising rhyme occurs, even though Yeats confines himself almost exclusively to monosyllables for his end-words. Yeats's ingenuity can be appreciated by the thought-experiment of abstracting the poem to a writing exercise: "Write a ballad about the Easter Rising in three six-line stanzas for which the rhymes will be *shot, not, pot; overcome, dumb, thumb;* and *alone, Tone, bone.*" Of course Yeats did not compose "Sixteen Dead Men" "backwards" in this way, but as he conceived and filled out his stanzas he reached far to find "common" but (in this context) unexpected rhyme-words. As he sought to avoid the clichés already enveloping the executed patriots, he visualized a literal afterlife gathering of the sixteen dead men, still "loitering," as ghosts are wont to do, around the place where they died. Having set the cauldron of rebellion boiling, they linger (or rather, as newly homeless men, "loiter") to keep it active by stirring it. The speaker of the ballad, converted to revolution, is disavowing the past perennial Irish political debates in favor of urgency of response to the executions:

> O but we talked at large before
> The sixteen men were shot,
> But who can talk of give and take,
> What should be and what not
> While those dead men are loitering there
> To stir the boiling pot?

The second stanza brings the vividness of this dance of death—corpses clustering to stir a boiling pot—into close focus by naming Pearse and MacDonagh, and depicting their gruesome bodily condition. Here, the speaker rebukes a "you" who still argues (logically, as Yeats himself had done) in favor of waiting to see what Parliament will do when the War of 1914 is concluded:

> You say that we should still the land
> Till Germany's overcome;
> But who is there to argue that
> Now Pearse is deaf and dumb?
> And is their logic to outweigh
> MacDonagh's bony thumb?

Imagining, luridly, his fellow-poets stripped of bodily senses and of flesh, Yeats animates their corpses, now reduced to skeletons, as silent witnesses to the absurdity of adducing logic in the presence of violence. The speaker's horror and pain—the emotions that generated his image of the poet Pearse deprived of ear and voice and the poet MacDonagh's writing thumb denuded to bone—are held at bay, almost silenced, by the bare words found for those images. But the skeletons deserve better than this macabre evocation, and, relenting, Yeats not only "cures" Pearse's "deafness" and "dumbness" but also grants the sixteen dead men an apotheosis. In his last sight of them, they have found the company of elder Irish revolutionaries and are gladly conversing with them, not voice to voice as in former "give and take" but—as Yeats hews to the truth of bodily disappearance—"bone to bone":

> How could you dream they'd listen
> That have an ear alone
> For those new comrades they have found,
> Lord Edward and Wolfe Tone,
> Or meddle with our give and take
> That converse bone to bone?

There is a dignity in this last vision that owes something to Lycidas's encountering, after his resurrection from drowning, those "solemn saints and sweet societies" that greet him "and wipe the tears forever from his eyes." "Sixteen Dead Men" finds, brilliantly, that equilibrium of "high" and "low" to which Yeats thought the ballad-form might at last bring him. High and low continue to cohabit successfully in the memorable ballad sequences to come, which are novel in pressing the ballad as far as it will go in the direction of lyric.

## Ballad Sequences, 1926–1936

With the founding of the Cuala Press by Yeats's sisters in 1902, Yeats became able to print his own new works in limited editions and to add to them works by other, chiefly Irish, writers. From 1906 on, the Cuala Press also printed broadsides bearing a single popular song or a lyric, some bearing illustrations by Jack Yeats (the poet's brother), which were hand-colored at the Press. The salience of ballads in the closing years of Yeats's life arises from his late part in this enterprise, as he edited for the Press two series of monthly broadsides (the first, in 1935, with F. R. Higgins; the second, in 1937, with Dorothy Wellesley). Yeats cherished to the end of his life the hope that some of his works might pass into the mouths of the people; works with such potential, he thought, were his simpler lyrics, his marching songs, and above all, his ballads. But he could not resist, in his latter days, the temptation to compose not single ballads meant to be sung but ballad sequences—long, sometimes obscure, and occasionally bawdy—all of them unlikely to be taken to the public heart.

It is in the four sequences "A Man Young and Old" (1926–1927), "A Woman Young and Old" (1927–1928), "Words for Music Perhaps" (1929–1932), and "The Three Bushes" (1936) that Yeats, using ballad conventions, most fully dedicates himself to creating lyrics rather than narratives. Let me give a sample or two of Yeats's inventiveness within each of them.

"A Man Young and Old," the earliest of these sequences, is written entirely in ballad form, except for its closing poem, which is an irregularly metered long-line chorus translated from *Oedipus at Colonus*.[9] Although all ten short ballad poems within the sequence are composed in Common Meter (4-3-4-3), only two of the ten (VII and VIII) are constituted by ballad quatrains *(abcb);* the other eight are cast in sixains (4-3-4-3-4-3) which are based on the ballad quatrain, and rhyme *abcbdb.* The individual poems in "A Man Young and Old," in spite of their circumscription within the ballad-atmosphere of the total sequence, are certainly better described as lyrics than as ballads. Of these, the single most "lyrical" one in diction and plot is the two-stanza poem "The Death of the Hare." It displays an unsettling construction, in which two apparently unrelated acts in the first stanza—the hunting down of a hare by a pack of hounds, and the lover's compliment to his lady—are, in the second stanza, suddenly and painfully joined. There the lover realizes—recalling the "wildness" which his beloved seems to have lost but which she may at any instant re-exhibit—that she will be hunted down by society just as the hare is hunted by the "yelling pack":

> I have pointed out the yelling pack,
> The hare leap to the wood,
> And when I pass a compliment
> Rejoiced as lover should
> At the drooping of an eye,
> At the mantling of the blood.
>
> Then suddenly my heart is wrung
> By her distracted air

> And I remember wildness lost
> And after, swept from there,
> Am set down standing in the wood
> At the death of the hare.
>
> (453)

("But even at the starting pose, all sleek and new, / I saw the wildness in her," says Yeats of the young Maud Gonne in "A Bronze Head.") Yeats in "The Death of the Hare" subordinates his minimal narrative elements (such as "I remember wildness lost") to the contrast between the lover's rejoicing and the wringing of his heart.

As "A Man Young and Old" advances, the language turns demotic, bearing out the personal "transfiguration" announced by the lover in the first poem of the sequence—that he has been transformed, by his lady's rejection, into a "lout, / Maundering here, and maundering there, / [Empty] of thought" (451). The poems become ballads about psychic alteration, even extending to Wordsworthian delusion (see "The Mad Mother"), as the lover becomes a wandering beggar accompanied by "the friends of his youth" Madge and Peter, who, like the lover, have been driven mad in old age by love and pride: Madge thinks that the stone she carries at her breast is a child, and Peter thinks himself the "King of the Peacocks" (456).

In "His Wildness" (the ballad that prefaces the closing Sophoclean chorus) Yeats makes a move that could scarcely take place in a conventional ballad, as the speaker metamorphoses, via peacock and stone, into a metaphysical amalgam of himself and his dead friends. The lover asks to be translated to the sky by a self-propelled apotheosis ("O bid me mount and sail up there / Amid the cloudy wrack"), but if he were to attain that altitude the lover would not be exalted into a hero or a saint, but would remain an ordinary man singing (like Madge) a lullaby to a stone, accompanied (like Peter) by the cry of a peacock:

> Were I but there and none to hear
> I'd have a peacock cry,
> For that is natural to a man
> That lives in memory,
> Being all alone I'd nurse a stone
> And sing it lullaby.[10]
>
> (458–459)

Yeats's interest in inserting within a "low" ballad-frame such lyrical and "metamorphosed" content continues strongly in "The Three Bushes."

For final publication in 1933, Yeats chose to end all three of the sequences of 1926–1932 with a translation of a classical Greek fragment: for "A Man Young and Old," *The Tower*'s chorus from *Oedipus at Colonus;* for "Words for Music Perhaps," his paraphrase "The Delphic Oracle upon Plotinus"; and for "A Woman Young and Old," a chorus from the *Antigone.* This decision was a deliberate one on Yeats's part, reaffirmed to his publisher in a 1933 letter concerning the proofs for *The Winding Stair.* Yeats writes:

> Please leave the section called "Words for Music Perhaps" as I have arranged every poem with its number. It is a [?series] of poems related [?one] to an other & leads up to a quotation from the Delphic oracle, as the two other series "A Man Young & Old," and "A Woman Young & Old" lead up to quotations from Sophocles. The poems in "Words for Music Perhaps" describe first wild loves, then the normal love of boy & girl, then follow poems about love but not love poems, then poems of impersonal ecstasy, & all have certain themes in common. (#5923)

Why was Yeats, in 1933, unwilling to preserve at the close the folk-form of "A Man Young and Old" as he had when he ended it in 1928, with a ballad recalling "Stories of the bed of straw / Or the bed of down" (lines confirming his perennial wish to include—as he says in "The Municipal Gallery Revisited"—both "the noble and the beggar-man")? And why could he not leave alone his original shape for "A Woman Young and Old"? (As David Clark reports, "'From the Antigone' was not part of 'A Woman Young and Old' until the typescript of *The Winding Stair* . . . which was sent to the publisher on 13 March 1928.")[11] Yeats had not previously thought of putting translations from Sophocles at the ends of these two ballad sequences. The idea seems to have come to him, Clark suggests, when he decided, in preparing the copy for the *Collected Poems* of 1933, to use what had been a freestanding poem ("The Delphic Oracle upon Plotinus") to close the sequence "Words for Music Perhaps."[12] The wish to place these three "low" ballad sequences within a grander tradition by appending "noble" classical fragments to them hints at some uncertainty on the older Yeats's part concerning the aesthetic status of the ballad form standing alone. Perhaps Yeats thought that audiences would discount poems phrased so simply as his ballads, but would be called to attention when the authority of the Delphic

Oracle itself was summoned to stamp *Finis* for the one sequence, and the authority of Sophocles for the other two. (He felt no such need to append any classical buttressing to his later ballad sequence, "The Three Bushes," which appeared in volume form for the first time in the Cuala Press *New Poems* of 1938.)

Yeats's 1933 letter to his publisher on "Words for Music Perhaps" describes the sequence as an amalgam of genres, first presenting poems of unusual "wild love," then poems of archetypal young love, then meditations on love, then "poems of impersonal ecstasy," and finally a fragment from the classical tradition. By this point, as the letter confirms, a Yeatsian ballad sequence could embrace almost any lyric subgenre and any subjective attitude. Extended emotional scope characterizes not only the sequence Yeats describes in the letter but also "A Man Young and Old" (as we have seen) and "A Woman Young and Old."

"A Woman Young and Old" (1927–1928), with its eleven poems, matches exactly in length "A Man Young and Old" but diverges from it thematically, tonally, and formally. While "A Man" (in its final form) ends with a degree of hope, as Plotinus (though still buffeted by the sea) is beckoned to the "bland" harmony of philosophical groves, "A Woman," in its final form, concludes tragically, as "Oedipus' child / Descends into the loveless dust" (540). Also, "A Woman"—though it begins with ballad stanzas in poems I and II—wanders much further away from the ballad than does "A Man," departing from the ballad stanza (or some variant thereof) in almost half of its units—five of the eleven poems.[13] I will not take up these non-balladic poems here, but the fact of their presence needs to be mentioned in order to show how singular, and how unconstrained by ballad-unity, "A Woman Young and Old" is seen to be when contrasted with "A Man Young and Old," even though the two sequences, as Yeats's letters attest, evolved together.[14] Yeats had found such personal freedom in the display of genres that the presence of ballads in a sequence did not now exclude the appearance, within the same sequence, of more complex lyric forms.

As an example of Yeats's use of the ballad stanza for a "metaphysical lyric," I cite poem IX of "A Woman Young and Old"—"What lively lad most pleasured me" (538)—which anticipates the successful blended tonality, "aristocratic" and "demotic" at once, of much of the later ballad sequence "The Three Bushes" (1936). Built on the distinction between the love of the body and the love of the soul, "What lively lad" uses the simplest possible words to establish its ground, as terms of the body ("pleasure/pleasured," "body/ bodily," "touch," and the punning "breast"/"beast") are set against terms of the soul ("soul," "naked," "close and cling," and "delight"). Such terms, because they are supported by other words that stay comfortably within ballad-diction—"lie" and "love," "lad" and "laugh," "clothes," and "bird"—remain in harmony with the "ballad atmosphere" created by the poem's 4-3-4-3-4-3 *abcbdb* six-line variant of the ballad quatrain. There is even a remnant of conventional ballad-dialogue in the question and answer that inaugurate the lyric, following from an implied question by an interlocutor ("What lively lad most pleasured you?"); and there exists a skeleton of ballad love-plot in the frustration (during earthly life) of sexual intercourse between the female speaker and her beloved. Yet the whole import of the poem is not narrative, not conversational, not folk-oriented, but rather psychological. It centers around a particular form of "misery"—the frustration of the passionate love of a soul unable to have a sexual relation with the person she loves, and who loves her. (In the 1915 poem "Presences" [358], thinking of himself and Maud Gonne, Yeats had called such a relation "that monstrous thing / Returned and yet unrequited love.")

So, in "What lively lad," against the flow of ballad conventions, Yeats places counter-currents: the emphasis on the soul (so unballad-like); the exclusively lyric focus on emotional "misery" in life rewarded by "delight" after death; and the woman's gnomic and even occult statement that the lover who embraces the soul after death has a reward specifiable only in the language of negative theology: "He it has found shall find therein / What none other knows." The power of such disembodied love can never—says the woman as she closes her ballad—be extinguished by any "bird of day" (such as the lark that disturbs the Romeo-and-Juliet lovers in the aubade "Parting"). Here is Yeats's ballad, which for convenience I call "metaphysical" since it treats of a love transcending the physical and maintained in the eternal:

What lively lad most pleasured me
Of all that with me lay?
I answer that I gave my soul
And loved in misery,
But had great pleasure with a lad
That I loved bodily.

Flinging from his arms I laughed
To think his passion such
He fancied that I gave a soul

Did but our bodies touch,
And laughed upon his breast to think
Beast gave beast as much.

I gave what other women gave
That stepped out of their clothes,
But when this soul, its body off,
Naked to naked goes,
He it has found shall find therein
What none other knows,

And give his own and take his own
And rule in his own right;
And though it loved in misery
Close and cling so tight,
There's not a bird of day that dare
Extinguish that delight.

The balance between ballad and lyric is entirely tilted, in "What lively lad," toward the lyric: rather than a narrative's being unfolded, a special set of frustrated emotions is being defined. But the simple and "low" diction, with its recognizable affinities to ballad-speech, determines our placing this poem in the ballad-genre rather than in the general set of lyrics written in Common Meter (a set that would include, for instance, the poems of Emily Dickinson, which, while in Common Meter, do not for the most part hark back to elements of the narrative ballad, but rather find their affinities within the hymn-tradition). It was a challenge to Yeats to represent what the ballad would sound like if it talked of heaven. But he affirms here, as he did at the close of "Sixteen Dead Men," that human beings do not change their nature just because they have been relocated from earth to heaven. "When this soul, its body off, / Naked to naked goes," love does not desire union any less. Intercourse in heaven (drawn by Yeats from the same Swedenborgian idea of "the intercourse of angels" that he would invoke in "Ribh at the Tomb of Baile and Aillinn") can be accommodated within "ordinary language," as the lover will "give his own and take his own / And rule in his own right," experiencing the delight—now confirmed as eternal—that lovers take in each other. The final triumph of a presumed "low" genre in Yeats is its confident transcription of the goings-on in heaven, whether present ("Sixteen Dead Men") or future ("What lively lad").

Thinking about women old as well as women young, Yeats invents an old woman, "Crazy Jane," as the central personage in the well-known sequence "Words for Music Perhaps." Yeats's adoption of the persona of an old woman allows him to be brazen in old-age expression of the body's desires, sometimes impersonally but also (when Jane speaks of herself and Jack the Journeyman) personally. Although the Crazy Jane poems (including the late addition "Crazy Jane on the Mountain" and the unpublished "Crazy Jane on the King")[15] belong in general to the ballad tradition, they too reveal Yeats experimenting with ballad form. One of Jane's lyrics, for instance ("Crazy Jane Grown Old Looks at the Dancers"), recalls the ballad form only in its refrain: this tetrameter poem in three seven-line stanzas rhyming *abacacb* incorporates a mid-stanza refrain, *"Love is like the lion's tooth"* (which, as the drafts astonishingly betray, began life as the comparably alliterative *"Love is like the lily flower"*). Many of the poems in "Words for Music Perhaps" are hybrids of this sort, combining some aspect of the ballad—a persona such as "Old Tom the Lunatic"; or a refrain; or a quotation from an early Irish folk song as in "'I am of Ireland'"—with some aspect of the Yeatsian intellectual lyric.

In the twenty-fourth poem of "Words for Music Perhaps," for instance, it is solely the title—"Old Tom Again"—that links this metaphysical poem (a lyric of "impersonal ecstasy") with the ballad tradition. "Old Tom," earlier labeled a lunatic, has now put aside folk-speech and has suddenly acquired epigrammatic power and intellectual concentration in his splendid Long Meter sixain. It is composed of two tercets resembling each other in form (*aba* and *cbc*) and linked together by their mutual middle *"b"* rhyme, for reasons that will take some time to understand:

> Things out of perfection sail,
> And all their swelling canvas wear,
> Nor shall the self-begotten fail
> Though fantastic men suppose
> Building-yard and stormy shore,
> Winding-sheet and swaddling-clothes.
>
> (530)

Old Tom here defiantly asserts his confidence in the perpetuity or immortality of "self-begotten" souls. To the ordinary eye, these souls depart like ships from the "building yard," sail with "swelling canvas," and then are wrecked in a storm. Or, as Yeats drops the nautical metaphor in favor of human terms, the souls—to the literal eye—grow out of their swaddling clothes, live their life, and after death are wound in their shroud. Although these linear soul-journeys, nautical and actual, come to grief, they are followed, Old Tom declares, by a return to perfection, a completing of the circle and a restoration into life again. It is only out-of-touch "fantastic men" (doubters of such invisible spiritual roundings in and out of perfection) who suppose that the visible and ever-tragic earthly life is the only reality. The self-begotten, with their internal perfection perpetually renewed, can never be said to "fail." Yeats puts all this, amazingly, in six epigrammatic lines.

Such a poem, metaphorically hybridizing ships and human life, asserts "perfection" as the origin and end of all things: they sail out of perfection and—after some period of earthly existence—they sail back into perfection again. If to common eyes they appear to end in "failure"—storm-wreck or winding-sheet—they will nonetheless issue again from perfection, taking on (as the poem ends) new swaddling-clothes. "Fantastic men" may believe, deludedly, that origins and ends are indisputably linear points, but Yeats, convinced of the impossibility of spiritual annihilation for the "self-begotten," sees origins and ends as simply way-stations out of and back into perfection, the evolved soul's natural home. The power of the poem lies in the confident "swelling" crescendo of its first three lines, and the unsettlingly rapid zigzag of the final two—from shipyard out to stormy shore, shroud back to cradle. The poem disdains to explain its concept of "self-begetting," just as it disdains to explain why it calls sober realists "fantastic" or why it condemns their supposition that birth and death are facts. "Impersonal ecstasy" need not defend itself; its strength lies in monumental asseveration, not in "some sort of evidence" ("To a Wealthy Man"). Yeats's desire to connect a poem of such intellectual and occult sophistication to the ballad tradition by putting it ostensibly into the mouth of "Old Tom" suggests his ambitions for the carrying-capacity of the ballad form. The intellectual concepts here are borne entirely by metaphor and synecdoche (which symbolize—in contrast to simile—direct vision). If "Old Tom" spoke in similes, the poem would be greatly weakened.

I return to the matter of this poem's peculiar verse-form. The proclamation of "Old Tom Again" is undermined to a certain extent, we might think, by the rhyme scheme Yeats chooses for the poem. He understandably sets old Tom's fierce assertions to a march beat; but why the unsettling *abacbc* rhyme scheme? The ear—expecting a monosyllabic *b* rhyme-word in the fourth line (*sail, wear, fail,* [*-air*])—is disturbed by encountering a disyllabic end-word presenting the sound *-ose (suppose)*. The next line, which ought to re-establish some sort of rhyme-pattern, does in fact do so, but, since the rhyme for *wear* is the slant rhyme *shore*, the ear is still not sure whether a pattern is emerging. It is not until the ear reaches final closure in *clothes*, linked to *suppose*, that one can conclude that *shore* was put in place to rhyme with *wear*.

The poem also defies expectation by its strange disjunctiveness of diction as it passes from couplet to couplet. In the first two lines, the abstract words "things" and "perfection" are followed by the literal marine-words "sail" and "canvas"; the next two lines insert such unexplained concepts as "the self-begotten" and "fantastic men"; and the last two lines consist merely of four nouns. (I count "stormy shore" as a modified noun equal in semantic status to the other three.) The first two of the closing four nouns ("building-yard" and "stormy shore") deal with ships, the second two ("winding-sheet" and "swaddling-clothes") with human beings. The four nouns combine as an impregnable chiasmus, with the two "death-terms" in the middle and the two "birth-terms" as the outer brackets: "building-yard : stormy shore :: winding-sheet : swaddling-clothes." This chiasmus replicates the circular voyage proclaimed by Old Tom—birth to death, death to birth.

In "Old Tom Again" there is no attempt at logical persuasion, and the syntactic couplet-organization of the themes does not dovetail with the tercet-organization *(aba cbc)* of the rhyme. All these initially confusing traits of the poem appear to "contradict" its other, affirming, aspects—sturdy tetrameters, a strict, intellectually organized chiasmus, and apodictic statement. If Old Tom were speaking from heaven's "perfection," he could offer pure and untroubled vision in which there would appear no unsettling factors: his sixain might rhyme in firm parallel tercets *abcabc* (as does poem XXIII of "Words for Music Perhaps") or, even more firmly, in a quatrain-plus-couplet, *ababcc* (as does poem XIV). However, because Tom must speak from earth, in an expression of faith rather than of evidence, his visionary poem (which would appear "lunatic" to realists) embodies itself less conclusively, using two dissimilar tercets linked only by their common *b*-rhyme. Pieces such as "Old Tom Again" represent Yeats's most ambitious "metaphysical" exertion within the ballad atmosphere of "Words for Music Perhaps."

But the most "metaphysical" of Yeats's ballad sequences is indubitably "The Three Bushes," in which Yeats decides to append to the overarching ballad (which gives the sequence its title) several internal and purely lyric "songs," spoken by the *dramatis personae* of the ballad, utterances that arise from crucial "philosophical" nodes within the ballad story. Yeats began the ballad retelling the story of lady and lover by taking over elements from a short medievalizing ballad by Dorothy Wellesley that he had begun to revise (so he believed) on her behalf.[16] Wellesley's poem had set the situation: a high-born lady, who wishes to preserve her chastity, sends her chambermaid in her place to the bed of her pleading lover. Yeats's opening ballad, written in sixains *(abcbcb)*, tells its story (as ballads often do) chiefly through conversation: of its eleven stanzas (each bearing the same free-standing refrain, *"O my dear, O my dear"*), only the last four are purely narrative. I quote stanzas 3 and 4:

> 'I love a man in secret,
> Dear chambermaid,' said she.
> 'I know that I must drop down dead
> If he stop loving me,
> Yet what could I but drop down dead
> If I lost my chastity?'
> > *O my dear, O my dear.*

> 'So you must lie beside him
> And let him think me there,
> And maybe we are all the same
> Where no candles are,
> And maybe we are all the same
> That strip the body bare.'
> > *O my dear, O my dear.*

For a year the lady's scheme of nightly sexual substitution succeeds, and the poems of her deceived suitor, nourished on "love," grow in power. On the anniversary of his first lovemaking, the lover, racing to return to his lady, is killed when his horse stumbles. The lady immediately dies of grief ("for she / Loved him with her soul"), and the ballad then contrives its double ending. In the first ending, the chambermaid plants two rose bushes commemorating the lovers:

> The chambermaid lived long, and took
> Their graves into her charge,
> And there two bushes planted
> That when they had grown large

> Seemed sprung from but a single root
> So did their roses merge.
> *O my dear, O my dear.*

In the second ending—which takes place after the chambermaid's own death—the understanding priest to whom the chambermaid had confessed her tale buries her next to lover and lady, setting a rose bush on her grave as well: "And now none living can / When they have plucked a rose there / Know where its roots began." These two endings smooth out the sexual and moral tensions of the situation, letting it fade back—as its fictional epigraph, pointing to a Latin source, intends *("An incident from the 'Historia mei Temporis' of the Abbé Michel de Bourdeille")*—into the safely distanced period of the *Roman de la Rose*. But, as we shall see, the songs appended to the sequence reawaken those philosophical tensions. If I dwell on Yeats's chosen meters for the songs in what is to follow, it is because they bear meanings important to the sequence, meanings that have generally been overlooked.

Yeats gives occasional comic overtones to the opening ballad: the lady grows jealous "if the chambermaid / Looked half asleep all day," and the actually deceived (but never disillusioned) lover meets an abrupt alliterating accidental death ("He dropped upon his head and died"); lines like these take the tale, as it is first presented in folk form, out of the realm of the tragic ballad retelling a death. Yet the triangular story—prolonging itself in Yeats's imagination as an erotic link to Dorothy Wellesley—leads to a new kind of sequence-structure, as the poet begins to append to the ballad-tale various first-person lyrics for the ballad characters to sing (for which the impetus comes, probably, from the songs inserted by Shakespeare into his plays). Although the initial governing ballad is already phrased in simple and largely monosyllabic words, some of the songs reduce language yet further, reaching their minimalist quintessence in the last of the "insertable" lyrics, "The Chambermaid's Second Song," which reflects the chambermaid's impassive submission, night after night, to a deceitful sexual conjunction devoid of emotional dimension. Like the chambermaid's first song, her second song is in dimeter; it is a sixain sentence-fragment, in which the thrice-employed monorhyme *worm* effectively makes refrain indistinguishable from stanza:

> From pleasure of the bed,
> Dull as a worm,
> His rod and its butting head

> Limp as a worm,
> His spirit that has fled
> Blind as a worm.

In spite of the contemptuous adjectives applied by the chambermaid to the lover's "rod and its butting head,"[17] the dactylic thrust of that phrase physically governs the plunging rhythm of the refrain: "**Dull** as a / **Limp** as a / **Blind** as a / **worm**." The chambermaid, the dactyls tell us, has not forgotten her sexual encounter with the lover. Although a residue of physical memory lingers in the metrical pulse of the chambermaid's second song, there is no sentimental aftermath: the chilly minimalism of language and meter enacts the emotional absence of her participation.

Yeats differentiates the three characters of "The Three Bushes" by the songs they sing. The chambermaid, in her first dimeter dixain, had had a moment of motherly relenting in her "cold breast," saying of the lover, "God's love has hidden him out of all harm." But she ends that first song with tight-lipped satisfaction, saying, "Pleasure has made him / Weak as a worm," the phrase that is picked up and repeated, with further denigrating adjectives, throughout her second song, as we have seen. Surprisingly (at first glance), the lady's lover (who resembles Peleus, blindly in love, in "News for the Delphic Oracle") also sings his song—his only one—in dimeter (because, as the meter crucially implies, it is in fact the chambermaid, not the lady, he has lain with). Thinking he has achieved union with his beloved, he proclaims, in the content of his song, aspiration ending in fulfillment, a triple harmonic parallelism of mind, body, and the life of nature. The yearning iambs and anapests of the first three lines of the lover's song sink into achieved iambs in his closing seven words; only at the last moment does the song's *aabccb* rhyme scheme tie the knot of *sighs* and *thighs*, connecting the first tercet of a generalized present tense to the "now" of the actual present tense of the second tercet with its nightfall and diffused "rest":

> Bird **sighs** for the **air**,
> Thought for **I** know not **where**,
> For the **womb** the seed **sighs**.
> Now **sinks** the same **rest**
> On **mind**, on **nest**,
> On straining thighs.

Although the lover's song matches the chambermaid's second song ("From pleasure of the bed") in its dimeter "width" and its sixain length, it differs from her second poem in three ways: in its diversified rhyme scheme (against her reductive monorhyme *worm*); in type of metrical feet, his longing anapests and satisfied iambs against her dactyls reminiscent of the sexual thrust; and in conception, his inclusion of "thought" and "mind" against her relentless reiteration of the physical. It is pleasing that (since they have been a sexual couple) their songs should in some respects match; it is right that (because there has been no meeting of minds accompanying the meeting of bodies, and because the compliant maid is aware while the deceived lover is deluded) they should also diverge.

How will Yeats prosodically differentiate the lady from the chambermaid and the lover? At first it seems that he does not differentiate her at all, since her first song is in the same dimeter as their three. But when we understand that in this song she is characterizing herself as "No better than a beast / Upon all fours," we see that her dimeters express her moral humiliation in being enslaved by her sexual feelings, a state in which she is no better than her about-to-be-deceived lover and her sexually subservient chambermaid.

We are not, of course, to read this sequence literally: the lady is not a "real" person who has betrayed her lover and subjugated her chambermaid; rather, we are reading a fairy-tale parable of the soul's attempt to liberate itself from the power of sexual desire. Once again, the choice of a female persona enables Yeats to write as he could not *in propria persona;* and we must recall, in understanding Yeats's quarrel with himself as he invents these late female personae, that Crazy Jane is as defiantly sexual as the Lady is defiantly chaste. When we come to another Yeatsian female persona, the moon, in the "Supernatural Songs," we see that she alternately approaches toward and retreats from her lover, the sun; if she were to obliterate herself in him, she could no longer sing her "sweet cry," "I am I, am I," but if she sequestered herself from him, it is implied, she would lose her light. In all these instances, Yeats plays with submission to the sexual and resistance to it.

In "The Three Bushes," when the lady's first song opens, she feels abased by her body's sexual longing, and sings in her reductive dimeters:

> I am in love
> And that is my shame.
> What hurts the soul
> My soul adores,
> No better than a beast
> Upon all fours.

Why would Yeats choose dimeter as the form of speech suitable to the sensual body? It is the most short-breathed form of metrical language, especially in its minimal four-syllable line ("I am in love") which we see predominating in the lady's last quatrain above. Dimeter—even in the lover's anapestic lines—is a necessarily barren, almost unadorned, meter: "For the womb the seed sighs." Both lover and chambermaid must remain permanently imprisoned in dimeter sexual diminishment; only the lady can escape it. She escapes it because she stands for consciousness, "the soul," larger and more various than the body, which she, if only partially, repudiates.

"The Lady's Second Song"—as, having devised her scheme of substitution, she abandons the shaming dimeters of the sexual body—is cast in the conventional ballad-alternation of tetrameter and trimeter (with an occasional substitution of a trimeter for a tetrameter). And the stanzas end with a liturgical refrain from the litany, *"The Lord have mercy upon us,"* through which the lady is made to speak impersonally for all.[18] The lady is no longer shrunken to the dimeters of abjection, but she is still, in this second of her three songs, someone who has yet to undergo full usurpation of body by soul. Her verb of instruction to herself is proleptic—*must learn;* the future is phrased in an *if*-hypothesis; and the prayer-refrain, "[May] *The Lord have mercy upon us,"* puts the lady still within an optative circumstance, in which she thinks she may be able to preserve, through her chambermaid's "limbs," the love expressed by touch while nurturing in herself a love proper to the soul:

> Soul must learn a love that is
> Proper to my breast,
> Limbs a love in common
> With every noble beast.
> If soul may look and body touch
> Which is the more blest?
> > *The Lord have mercy upon us.*

Of course, the chambermaid's "limbs" learn no sort of love at all, as we have learned from her songs. The lady's envisaged compromise here, in which she and the chambermaid split "love" into two things, each called "a love," is not really conceivable, any more than the reserving of sight to the soul and touch to the body.

By the time of her third song, the Lady, having resolved on chastity and saved her soul's independence, speaks in self-possessed tetrameters, in non-balladic couplet-certainties. Since she has commanded the chambermaid's substitutive role, and has ensured her own absence from the lover's bed, she can speak, as commentator on sexual conjunction by others, in a line twice as long as the self-loathing dimeter eked out by the humiliated body. She now describes the union of her lover and her maid in the habitual present tense; the sexual substitution planned for the present and the foreseeable future is as good as done. Her song—a single indivisible sentence (voiced in two equal six-line clauses)—derives its "either neither" of indistinguishable conjunction from "The Phoenix and Turtle"; and the love that is "split" here is that within the deceived lover's heart. The lady addresses the chambermaid:

> When you and my true lover meet
> And he plays tunes between your feet,[19]
> Speak no evil of the soul,
> Nor think that body is the whole,
> For I that am his daylight lady
> Know worse evil of the body;
> But in honour split his love
> Till either neither have enough,
> That I may hear if we should kiss
> A contrapuntal serpent hiss
> You, should hand explore a thigh,
> All the labouring heavens sigh.

Yeats wittily rhymes *lady* with *body* in this poem of the perplexity of the one with the other; like Crazy Jane, he rhymes *soul* with *whole;* anticipating what the lover will sing, he rhymes *thigh* with *sigh*. The desire of the lady that both she and the chambermaid shall sense ghostly echoes of the experience forbidden to each—she, as she chastely kisses her lover, to hear the serpent's hiss of sensuality; the chambermaid, as she endures the lover's caress, to hear a sigh of heavenly creation—offers an instance of Yeats's continual intention that the "partial mind" should complete itself, that body and soul, low and high, should reach some sort of mutual understanding. At least the lady is no longer demanding that the chambermaid feel "love." But one may feel that spiritual independence, obtained by forgoing bodily desire, is bought at too high a price.

Neither "A Man Young and Old" nor "A Woman Young and Old" has a clear plot that could be retold in an overarching ballad such as the one that

literally prefaces and narratively encloses the songs of "The Three Bushes."
Yeats seems to have conceived—once Dorothy Wellesley had shown him
her ballad—a series of lyrics which engage both female and male experi-
ence, but which would forbid, to any of the ballad-personae, a satisfactory
conjunction of sexuality and love. Although the conventional ballad qua-
train in Common Meter had been Yeats's base-unit for most of "A Man
Young and Old" and a good part of "A Woman Young and Old," he chose to
keep it in abeyance after the opening ballad of "The Three Bushes," resort-
ing, as we have seen, to dimeter and tetrameter for most of the songs. The
ordinary ballad meter is restored only in the sixains of "The Lady's Second
Song," with its mournful generalizing trimeter refrain:

> What sort of man is coming
> To lie between your feet?
> What matter, we are but women.
> Wash; make your body sweet;
> I have cupboards of dried fragrance,
> I can strew the sheet.
> *The Lord have mercy upon us.*

Yeats's four ballad sequences affirm their connection to the traditional
English ballad, but they continually adjust that tradition toward reflection.
The ballad sequences sometimes have "Irish" ingredients ("Words for Music
Perhaps"), while at other times their Irish dimension is obscure ("The Three
Bushes"). They do not betray the desire for religious and national inclusive-
ness that prompted the "priest-ballads" of Yeats's youth; they prefer the ren-
dering of personal emotion to the unveiling of a plot or the enunciating of
nationalist sentiment. These sequences represent Yeats's utmost effort to
bring the ballad under the vault of the lyric tradition. Yet they remained for
him ballads, attached to the pole of oral literature and folk tradition. With
regret, Yeats wrote to Dorothy Wellesley (March 29, 1937, #6888), "I have
several ballads poignant things I believe, more poignant than anything I
have written. They have now come to an end I think & I must go back to
the poems of civilisation."

## Late Ballads, 1938–1939

In Yeats's old age, the ballad form sometimes coarsens, as he dreams of
writing songs that will be sung in the streets (while in another part of his

mind he knows how dubious a hope that is). It is not for Manion the Roaring Tinker (of "Three Songs to the One Burden," 1939) that Yeats will be remembered as a poet. Nonetheless, Yeats himself probably admired the *sprezzatura* (in the much-revised "Three Marching Songs," 1938) of "Grandfather sang it under the gallows," in which an old man condemned to be hanged had, according to the refrain, succeeded in replacing his stolen tambourine by plucking down the moon from the heavens. The 4-4-4-4-3-3 stanza has a "kick" at its anapestic penultimate trimeter line; the subsequent four-line refrain (4-3-3-4) shows "Grandfather" getting the better of the robbers:

> 'Money is good and a girl might be better,
> No matter what happens and who takes the fall,
> But a good strong cause'—the rope gave a jerk there,
> No more sang he, for his throat was too small;
> But he kicked before he died,
> He did it out of pride.
>
> *Robbers had taken his old tambourine*
> *But he took down the moon*
> *And rattled out a tune;*
> *Robbers had taken his old tambourine.*

This is Yeats in less than good voice, for all his metrical care (the three-beat line of Grandfather's kick begins with a propulsive anapest: "But he **kicked** be**fore** he **died**"). As such a poem tells us, Yeats is still investigating the poetic potential of the ballad form. Amazingly enough, Grandfather's unsatisfyingly truculent gallows-song prepared the structural ground for Yeats's last poem, the great ballad "The Black Tower" (635–666). Drafts of "The Black Tower" appear on the reverse (in one instance) and on the same page (in another) of drafts of the "Three Marching Songs"—earlier called "Three Revolutionary Songs."[20] The verse-form of "The Black Tower" is very close to that of the ballad of Grandfather on the gallows, except that "The Black Tower" *(ababcc)* opens with a "perfect" tetrameter quatrain, *abab* (instead of "Grandfather's" imperfect *abcb*). Although the meter of "The Black Tower" is iambic, not dactylic/anapestic as in the initial quatrain of "Grandfather," its many trochaic substitutions in initial feet give the rhythm a downbeat suitable to military resolve. Its "oath-bound men" are firmly masculine, but they are not, like Grandfather on the gallows, obstreperous.

As "The Black Tower" opens, a group of starving soldiers, long be-
sieged in their tower, are responding to the envoy from their banner-bearing
enemies. He has come to demand their surrender, but, speaking Yeats's last
words as a poet, the soldiers deny the envoy's taunt that their king is dead
and forgotten. Whether he is dead or not (the soldiers reply), they refuse to
yield; they stand bound to their feudal oath. The unusual four-line refrain
(with tetrameters embracing trimeters, as in "Grandfather's" refrain) dark-
ens progressively from faint moonlight to the increasing blackness of the
tomb. The refrain sings of the dead buried upright on a mountain, their
bones shaking (in real or apparent motion) in response to the roaring of the
shore-wind:

### The Black Tower

Say that the men of the old black tower,
Though they but feed as the goatherd feeds,
Their money spent, their wine gone sour,
Lack nothing that a soldier needs,
That all are oath-bound men:
Those banners come not in.

*There in the tomb stand the dead upright,*
*But winds come up from the shore:*
*They shake when the winds roar,*
*Old bones upon the mountain shake.*

Those banners come to bribe or threaten,
Or whisper that a man's a fool
Who, when his own right king's forgotten,
Cares what king sets up his rule.
If he died long ago
Why do you dread us so?

*There in the tomb drops the faint moonlight,*
*But wind comes up from the shore:*
*They shake when the winds roar,*
*Old bones upon the mountain shake.*

The tower's old cook that must climb and clamber
Catching small birds in the dew of the morn
When we hale men lie stretched in slumber

Swears that he hears the king's great horn.
But he's a lying hound:
Stand we on guard oath-bound!

*There in the tomb the dark grows blacker,*
*But wind comes up from the shore,*
*They shake when the winds roar,*
*Old bones upon the mountain shake.*

Various interpretations have been offered of the archaic soldiers in the tower and the banner-bearing besiegers outside. Mrs. Yeats told A. Norman Jeffares that this was a poem "on the subject of political propaganda," implying that the besiegers are those who want poets to become scribes for their tendentious beliefs.[21] Others have seen the oath-bound remnant in the tower as the defeated Anglo-Irish refusing to bow to the new nationalist Catholic state. Foster (II, 648) thinks that Yeats was recalling *The Masque of Finn*, "a play he had seen at Padraic Pearse's school thirty years before"— since even at that time Yeats had referred the masque to his personal life, writing to Lady Gregory that "the waiting old men of the defeated clan seemed so like ourselves."[22] These conjectures, however, do not explain why the tower should be a black one. If the line "There in the tomb the dark grows blacker" confirms that the Black Tower bears the color of death, then Yeats may see, in the besieged men, his own state as he lies dying, refusing to surrender to death even though he is already within its precinct and under its power.[23]

"The Black Tower" needs to be interpreted in conjunction with Yeats's other deathbed poem, "Cuchulain Comforted." This poem (discussed more fully among Yeats's rare verse-forms in Chapter XIII) is a poem of concession and purgation; in it, Cuchulain is invited by a troop of "bird-like things" to abandon his former warrior-values and to accede to weakness, cowardice, and the communal sewing of linen shrouds. (Such an after-death counter-phase to the life actually lived is called in *A Vision* "The Shiftings.") The afterlife (formally represented in "Cuchulain Comforted" by Yeats's use of Dante's *terza rima*) requires, for the completion of Cuchulain's soul, that his defiance, warrior-skill, and individuality be forgone. Yeats had always believed in the necessity of completing his partial mind—of living, at least in imagination, a life which opposes one's actual life. The poet had to adopt the mask of the anti-self (as he put it) as well as to live by the creative will of the self. At the moment of death Yeats writes two antithetical poems because he finds himself unable to choose between a meek Cuchulain-mask and a powerful Tower-will. If "Cuchulain Comforted" is the poem of the hero Cuchulain's anti-self as it assents to quiet, even feminized, group life, then "The Black Tower" is the poem of the heroic creative will—the poem of self-assertion, force, and tenacity.

One moving aspect of "The Black Tower" is that it—like "Cuchulain Comforted"—is a poem of group life, not of individuality. In an army, men live communally and perform communal actions. This is not a poem affirming that the soul is self-begotten, self-delighting, and that its own sweet will is Heaven's will. On his deathbed, Yeats longs to imagine a company of which he can be part—and that company will be either the bird-like singing shades of the purgatorial "Cuchulain Comforted" or the oath-bound men of the life-force in "The Black Tower." If we ask whether, in life, Yeats had known of an oath-bound remnant of soldiers defending, in defeat, a last outpost under siege, we think immediately of the Easter Rising and the General Post Office in Dublin where its soldiers made a last stand. If we remember that the group of poems now known as "Three Marching Songs" (from which Yeats derived his stanza for "The Black Tower") was once provisionally entitled "Three Revolutionary Songs," we can hardly doubt a reference to the outnumbered holders of the General Post Office in Yeats's defiant ballad of the defeated but embattled men in the Black Tower. After all, Yeats had just finished writing his last play, *The Death of Cuchulain,* which ends with a song that asks "What stood in the Post Office / With Pearse and Connolly?"

When, in connection with "The Black Tower," we think back to Yeats's earlier poem "In Memory of Eva Gore-Booth and Con Markiewicz" (discussed with other tetrameter poems in Chapter VIII), we recall that although Yeats at first displays a derisive attitude toward the political activities of the Gore-Booth sisters, he ends by imploring Con and Eva to be his firm-spoken commanders in an incendiary campaign to burn up time: "Arise, and bid me strike a match / And strike another till time catch; . . . / Bid me strike a match and blow." The final envisaged act of the Gore-Booth elegy is, then, a communal one, to be accomplished by the sisters and the poet acting together. It is to a comparable communal ethos that Yeats turns at the moment of his own death, both in "Cuchulain Comforted" and in "The Black Tower." When he chose to cast his last poem into ballad form, it would have been clear to him that the form would evoke his earlier ballads about the Easter Rising: "Easter 1916," "Sixteen Dead Men," and "The Rose Tree."[24]

"The Black Tower" departs from the chronological narrative organization that is characteristic of the ballad. The poem poises itself at a single crucial moment—the one during which the men under siege, confronting the envoy from their enemies' camp outside the tower, repudiate his demand that they surrender. And the ballad begins not with a narrative but with a command, as the entrapped soldiers instruct the enemy-messenger to carry back two statements: "Say to your king that these men in the tower lack nothing; and say that they are oath-bound." These two commanded statements are of different sorts: the first is anti-materialist and hyperbolic ("Without money, without wine, they nonetheless lack nothing"); the second is historical and ethical ("They are bound by an oath of fealty taken in the past"). The result of those two facts (the soldiers' spiritual self-sustenance and their feudal loyalty) is a third fact: that the banners of the besieging army will not be allowed to enter, whether to give physical relief or to exact political allegiance—or, more likely, to massacre those within.

The first stanza of "The Black Tower," opening *in medias res,* is deliberately perplexing, spoken *by* an unidentified person or persons *to* an unidentified person or persons, and followed by a mysterious refrain concerning unidentified dead men buried upright in "the" tomb on an unidentified mountain. The rest of the ballad is spoken in a collective first person by the besieged men, first as they ventriloquize the insinuating offer of the besiegers, and next as they address the besiegers directly: "If [our king] died long ago / Why do you dread us so?" The ballad includes a dismissive rejection of their own cook's claim that their king is alive: "He's a lying hound." (The old cook ventures out briefly at dawn to "climb and clamber," trying to catch "small birds" that the men in the tower may eat, the rest of their food supply having been consumed.) The soldiers have no money left with which to buy food, even if there were a way to do so; they have no water supply within the tower; and they have been so long besieged that their wine has gone sour. They will not live much longer, in spite of their defiant boast to the enemy that they are still "hale men." Therefore "the dark grows blacker," and the blackness can only deepen into extinction.

Such a "ballad" is a single freeze-frame, immortalizing one moment out of a much longer implied epic tale. The longer story would narrate the earlier attack on the true king's army by the forces of the usurper; the retreat of the king's men to their last redoubt; the absence of their king for a prolonged time while they wait in their fortress to be rescued; and finally the intimidating appearance of the victorious enemy troops, with their envoy, at the very wall of their tower. Yeats's ballad-moment contains, by implication, all of those events. Yeats believes—if we are to infer his inner state from these last words—that he will not, this time, be rescued from the assault of his old enemy, death; and tragic joy is not a response he can call up here. It is not an inner gaiety that the men in the Black Tower call on; it is the ethical force of their oath. They will not comfort themselves with the false hope for the king's return offered by one of their own, nor will they succumb to the bribes and threats of their enemies outside.[25]

In making his ballad into a freeze-frame, voicing a single defiant collective message at the moment before certain death, Yeats wrests the innate narrativity of the ballad as far as it can go in the direction of instantaneity. He retains the simplicity of vocabulary proper to the archaizing ballad, but by emphasizing in the second and third stanzas the inimical forces (whether of outer threat or of self-delusion) that might shake the men's fortitude, he keeps before us those frailties (of body in the first instance, of soul in the second) that undermine resolve. The "otherworldly" refrain is a proleptic burial of these steadfast men. And all of this takes place in a single present-tense glimpse—the threat, the bribes, the hunger and thirst, the lying cook, the fortitude, the blackening dark, entombment.

Yeats has successfully rid himself here of various missteps that marred, in whole or in part, other ballads: token Catholicism (the "priest" ballads), faux naïveté (Moll Magee), unseemly coarseness (the Roaring Tinker), sentimental nationalism ("The Rose Tree"), and the intrusive occult (Billy Byrne at Glendalough). "The Black Tower" is Yeats's purest ballad on political themes, perhaps because among them it reaches the highest degree of abstraction—it is the least specific, most archaic, and most ghostly.

No other modern poet was so determined as Yeats to make the ballad a substantial and lifelong part of his *oeuvre*. Nobody—to give Yeats credit—was so willing to fail at reviving the ballad-genre. To him, the ballad represented not only the strongest modern link to oral literature but also his own indispensable connection to the Young Ireland poets he had read in his youth, and to those "Fenian rhymes" he had heard from the servants in his grandfather's house in Sligo. Ballads in English (to supplement those in Irish) had after all been called for, in urgent terms, by Yeats's predecessor-poet Thomas Davis, in his "Essay on Irish Songs":

But whatever may be done by translation and editing for the songs of the Irish-speaking race, those of our English-speaking countrymen are to be written. . . . Buy a ballad in any street in Ireland, from the metropolis to the village, and you will find in it, perhaps, some humour, some tenderness, and some sweetness of sound; but you will certainly find bombast, or slander, or coarseness, united in all cases with false rhythm, false rhyme, conceited imagery, black paper, and blotted printing. A high class of ballads would do immense good—the present race demean and mislead the People as much as they stimulate them; for the sale of these ballads is immense.[26]

To forsake the ballad would have been, for Yeats, to forsake the oral past of poetry, the legacy of ballads in Irish, past Irish verse in English, and his own childhood past as well. And though we can see in Yeats's earliest ballads the influence of British poets, from the anonymous authors of the Border Ballads through Scott and Wordsworth to Rossetti, Morris, and Wilde, we tend to forget those influences as Yeats gradually turns the form into something more characteristically Yeatsian—less occupied with the poor than Wordsworth, less decorative than Rossetti and Morris, more inward than the songs of Young Ireland, bleaker (at the end) than the more melodramatic Wilde, and determined (as some other writers were not) to incorporate the matter of Ireland, past and present.

The importance of balladry to Yeats is not to be doubted. As he wrote in letter #7036:

I am setting out on a great task a hundred Irish songs new & old for
Macmillan one half probably, modern, some from the broadsides. . . .
The Irish-race—our scattered 20 million—is held together by songs but
we must get the young men who go to the American universities as well
as those in factories & farms.

In compiling the 1935 Broadsides for the Cuala Press, Yeats and Higgins wrote in their preface, "Anglo-Irish Ballads":

There is a possibility that the simple metres based on lines of three and
four accents, eight or six syllables, all that constitute what Mr G. M.
Young calls the fundamental 'sing-song of the language,' come to the
poet's tongue with their appropriate tunes.

And in 1936 Yeats wrote to Dorothy Wellesley (#6644), describing his plan to write a ballad on Parnell:

I do not want Broadsides to be archaic. They contain such poems for unaccompanied singers which we want to hear sung. I plan quite deliberately that about one fourth should reflect the modern mind where most subtle.

Yeats hoped that his own ballads and songs would actually be sung. Having finished the Parnell poem, he wrote, "I have lately written a song in defense of Parnell . . . a drinking song to a popular tune & will have it sung from the Abbey stage at Xmas" (#6717). Later, he added: "I shall not be happy until I hear that it is sung by Irish undergraduates at Oxford under Gilbert Murrays nose" (#6731).

The ballads are not, perhaps, the first poems by Yeats that an anthologist of modern poetry would choose to represent him by; and with few exceptions (notably "Easter 1916") they have not passed into folk-memory as Yeats wistfully hoped they might. But they are for Yeats the robust and earthy magnetic pole that opposes (and sometimes incorporates) the equally strong metaphysical pole representing the "complexities of mire and blood." The spindle of Yeatsian necessity needed both poles to keep it in motion.

## VI

# ⌒ TROUBLING THE TRADITION: YEATS AT SONNETS

It is no surprise that Yeats wrote sonnets; he was, after all, a poet intensely interested in all verse possibilities. However, the sonnet invites particular attention because it is one of the two formats (the ballad is the other) that stayed steadily with him all his life. (In Yeats's hands, each of these forms migrated, in its social character, toward the other; he was capable of giving, in "The Three Bushes," a metaphysical sophistication to the folk ballad, and in "High Talk," a spoken folk force to the courtly sonnet structure.) Yeats chose the sonnet form for some of his most famous poems—among them "At the Abbey Theatre," "While I, from that reed-throated whisperer," "Leda and the Swan," and "Meru," to name only those that are recognizably fourteen-line pentameter poems with a sonnet structure, if not always with conventional rhyme-patterns.

What the sonnet meant to Yeats, historically speaking, was verse consciously aware of itself as written, not oral; verse from a European court tradition; verse knowing itself to be artifice, and often speaking about its own art; verse (although of Italian origin) associated with the essential English lyric tradition, from Wyatt and Surrey through Shakespeare, Milton, Wordsworth, and Keats. Precisely because of its centrality to English literature, the sonnet compelled from Yeats both his literary allegiance and his nationalist disobedience. When we wonder why Yeats wrote so few "proper" sonnets, we can find the answer, I think, in his distinctive mixture of that allegiance and that disobedience. My topic here is what Yeats did with the sonnet: why he took it up, how he modernized it, and how—although he was writing in English—he made it Irish. I believe that certain poems of his are better understood if we consider them as sonnets, even if they appear to be odd or "defective" ones. (I will be defining "sonnet" in a special way here, in order to include some poems of twelve or thirteen lines, for reasons I will give as I proceed.)

The sonnet came to Yeats in two basic versions: the two-part Petrarchan form (octave and sestet) and the four-part Shakespearean form. The Petrarchan sonnet, because of its two-part verse structure, falls easily into such dialectical structures as question and answer, or one view versus another view. The Shakespearean sonnet, with its four parts—three alternately rhymed quatrains and a couplet—is capable of teasingly complex logical structures. Yeats, with his attachment to antinomies, was naturally drawn to the Petrarchan opposition of parts; yet with his at least equal attraction to multiple perspectives, he was interested by the possibilities of the fourfold structure. Unable to leave either alone, he ended up writing both.

Yeats composed a Petrarchan sonnet at nineteen, and published one at twenty-one, but it was not until he was forty-seven that he wrote his first full Shakespearean sonnet ("At the Abbey Theatre"). Yeats's long avoidance of the true Shakespearean sonnet—while suggesting his love for it by writing numerous poems in blocks of three Shakespearean quatrains—was, I suspect, sustained by his nationalist wish to seem independent of English forms, and especially of court-forms from the Elizabethan era, when the plantation of Ireland by English settlers was being accomplished, and the extirpation of indigenous Irish culture was begun.

## First and Last Sonnets

Yeats's first extant sonnet ("Behold the man") was never published,[1] but soon enough, in 1886, he put into print a sonnet called "Remembrance"—like his first, a Petrarchan one. His last sonnet, "High Talk," was published posthumously. In spite of the half-century presence of the sonnet form in his work, it was a structure he used sparingly. He never undertook a sonnet sequence; instead, in his sequences (such as "Nineteen Hundred and Nineteen" or "Supernatural Songs") he assembled verse-structures of many different types. It was not the sonnet's capacity for linkage that interested him; he saw it as a short free-standing form. It appealed to Yeats, with its two or more potentially contrastive parts, as formally embodying—as a more linear structure could not—that quarrel with ourselves out of which, he said, we make poetry.

I begin this chapter by exhibiting the startling contrast between Yeats's first published sonnet and his last. I do this to point out not only the extended life-span of the form in his work but also the conspicuous changes it underwent. The 1886 Petrarchan "Remembrance" is a meditative sonnet with almost no thought-content: summed up, it says, "Remembering thee [thrice repeated], during the hours of this night, I muse, while the light fades, and the evening star rises; just now, my soul rose up and touched it":

Remembering thee, I search out these faint flowers
Of rhyme; remembering thee, this crescent night
While o'er the buds, and o'er the grass-blades, bright
And clinging with the dew of odorous showers,
With purple sandals sweep the grave-eyed hours—
Remembering thee, I muse, while fades in flight
The honey-hearted leisure of the light,
And hanging o'er the hush of willow bowers,

Of ceaseless loneliness and high regret
Sings the young wistful spirit of a star
Enfolden in the shadows of the East,
And silence holding revelry and feast;
Just now my soul rose up and touched it, far
In space, made equal with a sigh, we met.

(704–705)

The young poet attempts to give a "Shakespearean" effect in the last two lines by separating them grammatically (as a past-tense clause) from the preceding twelve present-tense lines. This languorous sonnet tells us that although it observes the Italian form in sentiment and in rhyme, its internal structure comes closer to that of the Shakespearean sonnet, offering a closing thought-couplet preceded by three "remembering thee" clusters of thought—the first concerned with the "faint flowers" of rhyme, the second with the passage of "the grave-eyed hours" of time, and the third with the young star that sings "of ceaseless loneliness and high regret." It is as if a poet tempted by the four-part English sonnet were refusing visible homage to it by "concealing" a Shakespearean structure of thought under a veil of Petrarchan rhyme—just as Shakespeare himself had often "concealed" a two-part Petrarchan thought-structure within his four-part prosodic template.

After reading this dreamy early sonnet, what a shock it is (and not altogether a welcome one) to see what the sonnet has become in Yeats's hands by 1938. "High Talk," his last sonnet (spoken by a persona named Malachi), is a fourteen-line poem, yes; a white space separates it into octave and sestet, yes; but it is anomalously composed in rough hexameters. (Each hexameter line perhaps punningly attempts to make up, by its "extra" metrical foot, for some of the deficiency in height that Malachi reports of his modern fifteen-foot stilts compared with the twenty-foot stilts of his grandfather.) In one of Yeats's "magical" controls, the lines (except for 6, 7, and 14) display fifteen syllables, because Malachi has fifteen-foot stilts. "High Talk" is made formally unconventional not only by its hexameters but also by its rhyming couplets (*aa, bb,* etc.), a verse-form that in late Yeats signifies a reductive and "primitive" moment.

This "wild" late sonnet is declaimed in tones very far from the muted ones of *fin-de-siècle* murmuring that arise from the 1886 "Remembrance." Yet "High Talk" belongs thematically to the conventional sonnet-tradition because its topic is its own aesthetic: it defends, in the despairing and exultant language of the Yeatsian end-days, a consciously elevated, "stilted" art. Yeats draws its ironic title from Shelley's "hopes of high talk with the departed dead" in "Ode to Intellectual Beauty"; Malachi has lost such hopes since, as he says, "whatever I learned has run wild."[2] Malachi Stilt-Jack is a populist avatar of the tenth-century high king Malachi (commemorated in Moore's "Let Erin remember") who "wore the collar of gold / That he won from the proud [Danish] invader." Yeats's Malachi speaks an apocalyptic demotic in his primitively rhyming couplets, their hexameter a retrospective echo of high, "stilted," epic style. (Yeats's first letter, to his sister, says, "I am getting stilts.")[3]

The octave of "High Talk" takes place indoors in a village. The last inheritor of tradition, the artisan Malachi, chisels and planes in solitude the wood for new stilts to replace the taller ones of his grandfather, which have been stolen. While working, Malachi imagines that when he has finished, he will replace the "poor shows" of circus parades (with their obedient and caged animals) by stalking freely through the village on his completed stilts to gratify—he says in self-derision—children and women looking for diversion. No adult male audience is mentioned:

> Processions that lack high stilts have nothing that catches the eye.
> What if my great-granddad had a pair that were twenty foot high,
> And mine were but fifteen foot, no modern stalks upon higher,
> Some rogue of the world stole them to patch up a fence or a fire.
> Because piebald ponies, led bears, caged lions, make but poor shows,
> Because children demand daddy-long-legs upon his timber toes,
> Because women in the upper storeys demand a face at the pane,
> That patching old heels they may shriek, I take to chisel and plane.

The sestet of the sonnet, surprisingly, moves not into the imagined parade down village streets but into wild nature. Announcing that his stilts and his persona have been metaphors, Malachi finds himself, in his sestet, outside society altogether; he is beside the sea at the break of dawn, in the company of unloosed creatures—a barnacle goose and those sea-waves called in legend the horses of Mannanan:

> Malachi Stilt-Jack am I, whatever I learned has run wild,
> From collar to collar, from stilt to stilt, from father to child.
> All metaphor, Malachi, stilts and all. A barnacle goose
> Far up in the stretches of night; night splits and the dawn breaks
>     loose;
> I, through the terrible novelty of light, stalk on, stalk on;
> Those great sea-horses bare their teeth and laugh at the dawn.
>
> (622–623)

"Wildness" had long attracted Yeats. As far back as 1901, he had written to William Sharp, "I have an advantage over you in having a very fierce nation to write for. . . . It is like riding a wild horse. If one's hands fumble or one's knees loosen one is thrown" (*CL*, III, 125). The "wild" style that would match that of a "fierce nation" was not yet invented by the Yeats of the 1886 "Remembrance," but "High Talk" exhibits that style "run wild," recalling the Irish Pegasus who was to be let loose at the end of "The Fascination of What's Difficult."

To take the measure of Yeats's evolution in this genre, we might compare Malachi's grotesque late aubade to the youthful trochaic tetrameter aubade called "A Dawn-Song," which follows the sonnet "Remembrance" in the *Variorum Poems*:

> Wake, *ma cushla*, sleepy-headed;
> Trembles as a bell of glass
> All heaven's floor, with vapours bedded—
> And along the mountains pass,
> With their mushrooms lightly threaded
> On their swaying blades of grass,
> Lads and lasses, two and two,
> Gathering mushrooms in the dew.
>
> (705)

The genre of this aubade is pastoral (it is in the line of Milton's tetrameter "L'Allegro"); the genre of Malachi's aubade is apocalyptic. There are no erotic lads and lasses in "High Talk," and by its end, "heaven's floor" is inhabited by the vigorous barnacle goose while the horses of the sea bare their teeth. These savage inhabitants would burst open any normal English sonnet or aubade, while the extravagance of Malachi Stilt-Jack not only tolerates but invites them.

Yeats, with the example of Sidney and Shakespeare before him, feels himself within his rights in placing into the sonnet consideration of his aesthetic and his audience; but rhetorical elevation, "high talk," has in Malachi's populist translation become the elevation of great-granddad's stilts, and the audience for poetry (once the Shakespearean "eyes of all posterity") has been reconceived in trivial terms, as children desiring a giant father-image and frustrated women seeking titillation from a voyeur at their window. Yet tradition—from Malachi's collar of gold to Malachi's collar, from Astrophel's borrowed Italian stilts of language to Malachi's home-made ones, from Petrarch-father-of-the-sonnet to Yeats-child-of-the-genre—links this sonnet to its Renaissance predecessors. "High Talk," in its formal enactment of the etymology of "tradition"—"a handing across"—goes so far as almost to obliterate, through its bridged pairs of line 10, the hexameter's normal medial caesura: "From collar to collar, from stilt to stilt, from father to child." The caesura "ought" to occur between "stilt" and "to"; the difficulty of placing one there makes the words group themselves semantically (in groups of two) rather than metrically, forcibly calling the reader's attention to the visible handing-over.

Yeats follows sonnet tradition in "baring the device," exposing the artificial nature of his construct: "All metaphor, Malachi, stilts and all." Yet the metaphor cunningly survives its apparent repudiation; "I stalk on," says the speaker two lines later, and it is his internalized stilts that make him able to "stalk," one-two, one-two, the measure marked by the sound of the stilts, dividing the hexameter line into four parts (as we include a pause at the medial caesura and at the line-end): "Far **up** | in the **stretch**es | of **night** | *pause* | night **splits** | and the **dawn** | breaks **loose** | *pause*." The exultation of the sea-horses—teeth bared, laughing—makes them kin to that "beast" (as Yeats wrote when introducing his play *The Resurrection*) "that I associated with laughing, ecstatic destruction." "High Talk," by means of its forms "run wild," voices Yeats's view that the "high" rhetoric of the sonnet tradition had collapsed with the rest of European culture in the interwar period. We understand Yeats's cultural commentary here only if we see Malachi's apocalyptic images, his primitive couplets, his aberrant prosody, and his exultant despair as the formal ruination of the courtly European sonnet by a new primitivism.

## Apprenticeship

During the half-century between the 1886 sentimental conventionality of "Remembrance" and the 1938 grotesque stylistic populism of "High Talk," Yeats engaged in a lengthy investigation of the formal possibilities of various aspects of the genre: the sonnet's constituent parts—octaves and sestets, quatrains, tercets, and couplets; monosyllabic versus polysyllabic rhymes; and construction in pentameter and hexameter. Some of this investigation may appear purely technical, but technique was never, for Yeats, without conceptual meaning. Thus, when we find him in his twenties (1892) truncating a Petrarchan sonnet by Ronsard ("Quand vous serez bien vieille") into an English pentameter douzain under the title "When You are Old," we immediately ask what he had in mind in writing this douzain, and later, many more. Did he not like sonnets? We know that he did. Did he think Ronsard untranslatable in sonnet form? We know he did not, because the later sonnet "At the Abbey Theatre," adapted from Ronsard's "Tyard, on me blasmoit," has the proper fourteen lines. Why, then, in "translating" "When You are Old," does Yeats prefer a douzain—three Petrarchan quatrains employing different embraced rhymes (with the inner rhymes indented in the first printing)—to a full sonnet; and why does he depart, in his version, from Ronsard's thematic material? Here is Yeats:[4]

> When you are old and gray and full of sleep,
>> And nodding by the fire, take down this book
>> And slowly read and dream of the soft look
> Your eyes had once, and of their shadows deep.
>
> How many loved your moments of glad grace,
>> And loved your beauty with love false or true,
>> But one man loved the pilgrim soul in you,
> And loved the sorrows of your changing face.
>
> And bending down beside the glowing bars
>> Murmur, a little sad, 'From us fled Love.
>> He paced upon the mountains far above,
> And hid his face amid a crowd of stars.'
>
> (120–121)

Yeats's model, "Quand vous serez bien vieille,"[5] exhibits a characteristic Petrarchan break at the beginning of the sestet, in this case, a break in pronouns. The octave is a prophecy with "vous" in the subject-position; but the first two lines of the sestet, while still implicitly addressing the beloved "vous," chillingly introduce a first-person grammatical subject—the speaker, when he will be dead and buried:

> Je serai sous la terre, et, fantôme sans os,
> Sous les ombres myrteux je prendrai mon repos.

And though the poem returns to "vous" in its closing command ("Vivez, si m'en croyez," etc.), the hollow first-person authorial *voix d'outretombe* has exercised a powerful interruptive effect. Yeats, reworking Ronsard, eliminates that first-person rupture and writes a small continuous exhortation in "You": "When you are old, take down this book, and read, and dream, and murmur 'From us fled Love.'" He thereby preserves homogeneity of mood and referent at the expense of the French poem's tension between the narrative of the mistress's living future and the poet's somber vision of his own rest in the grave. Yeats's "translation" offers a single mourning parabola of narration, climaxing in its central third-person description of the "one man" who "loved the pilgrim soul in you."[6] The creation of a coherent emotional "atmosphere," rising, climaxing, and falling, as in "Remembrance," continues to be Yeats's aim in the nineties. The true inner quarrel of the binary Petrarchan sonnet is too much for him, as are the conflicting perspectives of the four-part Shakespearean sonnet. He therefore continues with the more manageably unifiable pentameter douzain, a form to which he returns (with variable rhyming) all his life, down to the year before his death. (The last douzain in pentameter, as we shall see in Chapter XII, is the couplet-rhymed "Whence had they come" in the 1935 *Supernatural Songs;* but Yeats later, in 1938, composed a douzain in unrhymed hexameter, "Beautiful Lofty Things," to be discussed when I take up Yeats's rare forms in Chapter XIII.)

In the same month (October 1891) in which he wrote his Ronsardian embraced-rhyme douzain "When You are Old," Yeats composed his first Shakespearean douzain, "The Sorrow of Love." I reproduce it here as it first appeared in *The Countess Kathleen* (1892), where it was addressed to the beloved and consisted of three end-stopped Shakespearean quatrains in alternating rhyme, with alternate lines indented.[7] Like "When You are Old," "The Sorrow of Love" is founded on a parabolic structure: we see a visually and aurally pleasing natural scene which conceals "earth's old and weary cry"; then there occurs the troubling of the speaker's boyish soul by a girl with "red mournful lips"; after his acquaintance with erotic love, the speaker, no longer innocent, finds the elements of the natural scene transformed. They now reveal life's underlying tragedy, and are "shaken with earth's old and weary cry" as they metamorphose from natural facts into symbols of the wounded heart:

> The quarrel of the sparrows in the eaves,
>     The full round moon and the star-laden sky,
> And the loud song of the ever-singing leaves
>     Had hid away earth's old and weary cry.
>
> And then you came with those red mournful lips,
>     And with you came the whole of the world's tears,
> And all the sorrows of her labouring ships,
>     And all [the]⁸ burden of her myriad years.
>
> And now the sparrows warring in the eaves,
>     The crumbling moon, the white stars in the sky,
> And the loud chanting of the unquiet leaves,
>     Are shaken with earth's old and weary cry.
>
>                              (119–120)

Unity of movement is achieved in this douzain, as in "When You are Old," by the elimination of any real psychological conflict; the writer (in contrast to the youthful speaker of whom he writes) knows from the beginning the tragedy which the young man, instructed by frustrated love, comes to discover permeating and transforming the formerly neutral, and sometimes even joyous, scenery. (The homogeneity of tone is conferred by Yeats-the-writer, obeying his "nineties" aesthetic of the unbroken note; if the changed feelings of the young man were governing the poem, there would have been a more painful break in tonality.)

In Yeats's hands, the sonnet—whether Petrarchan or Shakespearean in its quatrain-rhyme—is for a long time compressed into twelve lines, three quatrains, of a continuously evolving parabolic arc, with a homogeneity of effect in which the end, though it may intellectually (as here) contradict the beginning, formally mirrors it. No couplet is allowed to add its concise mood-sharpening bite at the end. "I like," said Yeats in a lost letter quoted by its recipient, Lafcadio Hearn, "to close so short a poem with a single unbroken mood" (*CL*, III, 101).

Although the binary structure of the Italian sonnet—a form which usually presents at least two perspectives on its subject—eventually begins to creep into Yeats's sonnet-work, it does so at first in the unthreatening form of a complementary reciprocity between two people. Yeats's first overtly Irish sonnet, "The Harp of Aengus" (an unrhymed sonnet, structurally Petrarchan in its two parts), splits into octave and sestet in order to accommodate the dual agency of Edain and Aengus as together they make a strung harp (their story is repeated in the 1903 "Baile and Aillinn"). First, Edain, using her lover's hair, weaves seven harp-strings; later, after she has been malevolently transformed (by Midhir's wife) into a fly, Aengus makes a harp-frame out of "Druid apple-wood" to awaken the strings:

> Edain came out of Midhir's hill, and lay
> Beside young Aengus in his tower of glass,
> Where time is drowned in odour-laden winds
> And Druid moons, and murmuring of boughs,
> And sleepy boughs, and boughs where apples made
> Of opal and ruby and pale chrysolite
> Awake unsleeping fires; and wove seven strings,
> Sweet with all music, out of his long hair,
> Because her hands had been made wild by love.
> When Midhir's wife had changed her to a fly,
> He made a harp with Druid apple-wood
> That she among her winds might know he wept;
> And from that hour he has watched over none
> But faithful lovers.

Edain is the agent in the "octave" (lines 1–9); the (conventional) spillover of line 8 into line 9 enacts her being made "wild by love" as she weaves her harp-strings. Aengus is the agent in the "sestet" (lines 10–14), carving a harp-frame for the strings in order to communicate with Edain after he has lost her. Her metamorphosis out of the human realm separates in time the two actions within the sonnet—weaving by her, carving by him. Here, no prolonged connection can occur between lovers on earth; they must endure successivity, not interpenetration, of agency. Because the actions of Edain and Aengus remain complementary and not antagonistic, the true conflict-potential of the Petrarchan division into parts remains unused. Nonetheless, in this narrative sonnet[9] Yeats has at least moved away from meditative immobility, and has introduced an Irish myth of aesthetic creation into a tradition which, in its continental and English manifestations, had been more hospitable to classical and Christian myth than to local folk material. Yeats marks his Irish sonnet as anomalous with respect to the European tradition not only by its abandonment of rhyme[10] and its use of folk material but also by its closing dimeter line, which leaves the rest of the fourteenth line open for Aengus to continue, into an indefinite expanding future, his ministry to "faithful lovers."[11]

Finally, at the age of thirty-seven, in "The Folly of Being Comforted" (reproduced here with its first, 1902, phrasing and punctuation), Yeats approaches, but does not reach, the conflict that he will find indispensable to the true sonnet. In this fourteen-line poem (written in rhymed couplets resembling those of "Adam's Curse," published later in the same year), Yeats constructs, to mimic conversation, an architectonic structure that is neither Petrarchan nor Shakespearean, dividing the poem into two sixains and a couplet. In the first six lines, a well-meaning friend assures the lover that his love-folly will surely wane (and he become wise) with the waning of his beloved's beauty; in the next six lines, the lover rebuts the friend by asserting the beloved's ever-increasing beauty; and in the closing couplet, the lover turns away from his interlocutor and instead addresses his own heart, crying out that the specious offered comfort cannot outlast his next glimpse of his beloved's face. Being comforted, ceasing to believe in the permanence of love, would be the true "folly":

> One that is ever kind said yesterday:
> 'Your well-beloved's hair has a thread of grey,
> And there are little creases about her eyes;
> Time can but make it easier to be wise,
> Though now it's hard, till trouble is at an end;
> And so be patient; be wise and patient friend.'
> But heart there is no comfort, not a grain;
> Time can but make her beauty over again
> Because of that great nobleness of hers;
> The fire that stirs about her when she stirs
> Burns but more clearly. O she had not these ways
> When all the wild summer was in her gaze;
> O heart O heart if she would but turn her head,
> You would know the folly of being comforted.
>
> (199–200)

The debate here does not take place within the lover himself, but rather between the persuading friend and the rebutting lover. The lover has never been persuaded at all: "But heart there is no comfort, not a grain." Given the absence of an internal quarrel, a division of the heart itself into warring factions, "The Folly of Being Comforted," for all its fourteen lines, lacks the antithetical perspectives of a true sonnet. At this point, although Yeats remains attracted to the brevity and concision of the quatorzain, he is not yet willing to face and reproduce the emotional contradictions within the speaker that the multiple parts of a sonnet exist to make formally evident.

## True Sonnets

The poems I have looked at so far represent Yeats's apprenticeship to the potential of the sonnet structure. We come now to his maturity. Yeats's first "real" sonnet—that is, one which follows the Petrarchan and Shakespearean principle of volatility of feeling and tone—is the title poem (dated August 1902) for his 1903 volume *In the Seven Woods*. Though unrhymed, it has the complexity of a persistent Yeatsian inner quarrel—his long-standing dispute between the pastoral and the apocalyptic—which we have already seen exemplified in the early versus the late aubade (and which is also lurking in the proposed division of poems into the categories "Arcadian" and "Irish" in his first volume, *The Wanderings of Oisin*). At first, the sonnet called "In the Seven Woods" seems to be setting up a homogeneous atmosphere resembling the ones found in Yeats's earlier "parabolic" douzains, "When You are Old" and "The Sorrow of Love": scene, interruption, tonal return. The first twelve lines of "In the Seven Woods" indeed trace an evolving parabola from pigeons and bees to pigeons and bees, but the homogeneity of that progress is interrupted in the middle by a bitter contrasting glance (here italicized). That glance is enclosed—as a negative climax berating English archaeological vandalism and the Irish celebrations of the coronation of Edward VII—within the two pastoral hums:

> I have heard the pigeons of the Seven Woods
> Make their faint thunder, and the garden bees
> Hum in the lime tree flowers; *and put away*
> *The unavailing outcries and the old bitterness*
> *That empty the heart. I have forgot awhile*
> *Tara uprooted, and new commonness*
> *Upon the throne and crying about the streets*

> And hanging its paper flowers from post to post,
> Because it is alone of all things happy.
> I am contented, for I know that Quiet
> Wanders laughing and eating her wild heart
> Among pigeons and bees . . .

If the poem ended there, at line 12, Yeats would be repeating the douzain-structure that he had already extracted from the sonnet form—a structure that answered his aesthetic needs for rise, climax, and fall, one that emphasized closure and reaffirmation. But because of the disturbance caused by "Tara uprooted, and new commonness / Upon the throne," he must press his art beyond a pastoral douzain. He therefore adds a disturbing sonnet-close, in which an apocalyptic personage supervenes upon pastoral allegory:

> I am contented, for I know that Quiet
> Wanders laughing and eating her wild heart
> Among pigeons and bees, while the Great Archer,
> Who but awaits His hour to shoot, still hangs
> A cloudy quiver over Parc-na-Lee.
> (198)

Besides the Marvellian garden-personification of Quiet (here Hibernicized via Dante's "Ego Dominus Tuus" into something wild and heart-consuming),[12] there is an additional mythological inhabitant of the Coole woods—a "Great Archer, / Who but awaits His hour to shoot." This unspecified executioner, who dominates this title poem of *In the Seven Woods* (a volume subtitled "Being Poems chiefly of the Irish Heroic Age"), belongs to that congeries of beings who inhabit Yeats's apocalyptic poems and await their "hour." As the Archer "awaits His hour," he owns the same words—deriving from the Messianic phrase of Jesus, "My hour is not yet come"—as the Rough Beast, whose "hour [has] come round at last" and the Secret Rose, of whom the poet says, "surely thine hour has come."

Yeats said of the sonnet "In the Seven Woods" that it was "much more likely to please Irish people than any [poem] I have done" (*CL*, III, 94). Its single-sentence five-line "sestet" is the first in Yeats to employ the declarative phrase "I know." "I am contented, for I know," begins the sestet, looking forward to two greater sestets—"The darkness drops again, but now I know" ("The Second Coming") and "Hermits upon Mount Meru or Everest . . . / know" ("Meru"). These declarations recall an even more famous sestet about knowledge, in which the acquisition of knowledge is put as a question: "Did she put on his knowledge with his power?" ("Leda and the Swan," discussed below). We can see from these instances of sestets pursuing a final sort of knowledge that Yeats has by now fully internalized the need to present, in the octave of a sonnet, a genuine problem, to which (in these cases) a sestet will reply that something has (or may have) at last become intelligible or known. Embittered by the "uprooting" of Tara and Dublin's craven celebrations, the poet resolves his bitterness by lengthening his perspective: when the Great Archer at last looses an arrow from his cloudy quiver, Tara will be restored and Ireland will become independent.

Yeats's inner quarrel between his wish to preserve his aesthetic quiet among pigeons and bees and his reactive ideological bitterness—the disequilibrium that so disturbed his writing life—has been staged here as an inner sonnet-quarrel between pastoral and apocalypse. We think, as we first read "In the Seven Woods," that the poet has found aesthetic solace when he returns, in line 12, to the pigeons and bees; but that Arcadian climax leads to a further, more dangerous, "Irish" apocalyptic climax, that of the Great Archer. As an archetype of Apocalypse, living in a specific part of the seven woods of Coole Park, the Archer can *be* Irish even if unnamed as such. The Archer has a Miltonic function (to avenge those slaughtered heroes whose bones are being disturbed in the Tara excavation), but his allegorical being is esoteric, and peculiar to Yeats's form of occult nationalism. Wild Quiet and the Great Archer, taken together, represent Yeats's perennially divided Muse. But despite the architectonic satisfactions of "In the Seven Woods," the poem is still evading, in its abandon of rhyme, the issue of rhymed sonnet-structures, and what such rhymed units can be made to mean for Yeats as he inherits them from Petrarch and Shakespeare and bends them to his own uses.

When, six years later, Yeats writes "No Second Troy," he has become aware of the defect within his earlier Shakespearean douzain "The Sorrow of Love": that it did not reflect the actual inner momentum of the Shakespearean sonnet, which is a continually evolving meditation eventually reformulated or countered by a concise and often epigrammatic couplet. Yet he continues to avoid, in "No Second Troy," writing a full Shakespearean imitation. What will Yeats do to make "No Second Troy" exemplify, though it remains a douzain, the inner conflict of a Shakespearean sonnet? And how will he give its traditional matter—love, that staple of sonnets—some Yeatsian individuality?

The structure of "No Second Troy" is determined by its syntactic ordering into four questions reflecting on the congruence, or lack of congruence, between a person's outer deeds and that same person's inner being. The first five lines question Maud Gonne's *doing;* the next five lines question her *being;* a single line then asks whether her *doing* was a necessary consequence of her *being;* and a single closing question justifies her *doing* from the nature of her *being.* Although Yeats printed the douzain as a solid block, I separate it here (to clarify its four-part syntactic structure) into its four successive questions:

> Why should I blame her that she filled my days
> With misery, or that she would of late
> Have taught to ignorant men most violent ways,
> Or hurled the little streets upon the great,
> Had they but courage equal to desire?
>
> What could have made her peaceful with a mind
> That nobleness made simple as a fire,
> With beauty like a tightened bow, a kind
> That is not natural in an age like this,
> Being high and solitary and most stern?
>
> Why, what could she have done being what she is?
>
> Was there another Troy for her to burn?
>
> (256)

Even though there are only three *formal* units here—the three Shakespearean quatrains—the syntax refuses to obey that prosodic scheme and sets itself up as a counter-force, declaring that the poem, like a Shakespearean sonnet, actually consists of four logical units: its four questions. Question 1 is the first "quatrain," expressing the poet's discomfort with Maud Gonne's apparently petty actions; question 2, corresponding to the second quatrain of a Shakespearean sonnet, opposes to her petty actions the nobility of her nature; question 3 (line 11) performs the function of the Shakespearean third quatrain, summing up the two previous ones that have sketched Gonne's doing against her being, revealing in its central clash of verbals the nugget of the poem's existential conflict between deeds and inward being— "Why, what could she have *done, being* what she was?"; and question 4 (line 12) performs the function of a countering Shakespearean couplet, saying that in a heroic age Gonne would have played a role like that of Helen, a role in which her doing would be commensurate with her being; but in our unheroic context, deeds will be debased, since there is no second Troy to be placed *en jeu*. Dublin is no Troy; its quarrels are not epic ones. The gyre, in its historical spiral, has once again cast up the archetype of noble Beauty, but has not located it in a commensurate historical moment. The tension between worldly doing and Platonic being, existence and essence, was for Yeats another version of the conflict between the real and the ideal, and the felt intensity of the poem springs from these irreconcilable pulls in himself, as he strove to estimate Maud Gonne aright by holding within a single poem her reality and his justice. These three quatrains have a wiry Shakespearean strength in their overlapping formal and syntactic structures, but the poem's exclusively interrogative syntax and its (recognizable) Irish heroine prevent its being a mere imitation of Renaissance English form. Yeats is on his way, we can see, toward the four-part English sonnet, confident that he can adopt it (as he eventually will) without disloyalty to Ireland.

I want to spend a moment on another Yeatsian sonnet-experiment, a thirteen-line poem called "The Fascination of What's Difficult" (1910). Yeats's prose draft in the *Memoirs* of September 1909 says:

> Subject: To complain of the fascination of what's difficult. It spoils spontaneity and pleasure and it wastes time. Repeat the line ending 'difficult' three times, and rhyme on bolt, exult, colt, jolt. One could use the thought of the wild-winged and unbroken colt must drag a cart of stones out of pride because it's difficult, and end by denouncing drama, accounts, public contests—all that's merely difficult. (*Memoirs*, 229)

Because Yeats's rhyme-recipe outlined here, if followed, would produce seven individual lines ending in the sound "*-olt*," it seems that what Yeats first had in mind was a fourteen-line poem in which every other line would end in "*-olt*." The actual poem, however, uses *difficult* only once, not thrice, as a rhyme-word. Nonetheless, of the four words that rhyme with *difficult* in the actual poem—*colt, jolt, dolt*, and *bolt*—three come from Yeats's original list. In the event, the poem ends up with thirteen lines rather than its first-envisaged fourteen, and we must, to understand Yeats's intent, understand his choice of truncated length.

"The Fascination of What's Difficult" is a poem of frustration and conflict. The country's divine Pegasus, a winged colt (art is young in Ireland, not yet grown), is longing to fly, yet is made by day into a cart horse and is tethered by night in a stable, while the poet, his destined rider, struggling to bring the Abbey Theatre into being, occupies himself with "theatre business, management of men":

> The fascination of what's difficult
> Has dried the sap out of my veins, and rent
> Spontaneous joy and natural content
> Out of my heart. There's something ails our colt
> That must, as if it had not holy blood
> Nor on Olympus leaped from cloud to cloud,
> Shiver under the lash, strain, sweat and jolt
> As though it dragged road-metal. My curse on plays
> That have to be set up in fifty ways,
> On the day's war with every knave and dolt,
> Theatre business, management of men.
> I swear before the dawn comes round again
> I'll find the stable and pull out the bolt.
>
> (260)

Though it falls short by one line, "The Fascination of What's Difficult" feels like a sonnet, not least because it begins with a perfect Petrarchan *abba* embraced quatrain-rhyme—*difficult, rent, content, colt*. But Yeats "cheats" on the Petrarchan demand by letting the final *a* line of quatrain 1 do double duty, serving (notionally) also as the initial *a* line of "quatrain" 2: [*colt*] *blood, cloud, jolt*. He also eases the Petrarchan scheme by introducing a new inner rhyme in the second "quatrain" instead of repeating within it the *"-ent"* rhyme from quatrain 1. These two indulgences give us a seven-line narrative Petrarchan "octave" that reads like this: *difficult, rent, content, colt,* [*colt*] *blood, cloud, jolt*. The octave does a characteristically Yeatsian spill (this time an indignant one) into the next half-line, as it ends its account of the metamorphosis of Pegasus into a cart-horse. And though the sestet of "The Fascination of What's Difficult" rhymes in conventional Petrarchan fashion *(plays, ways, dolt, men, again, bolt)*, Yeats disobeys traditional rules in maintaining the octave rhyme-sound *"-olt"* into the sestet, making it echo throughout the poem as it unites phonetically the two parts of the "sonnet." In spite of its Petrarchan rhyme-scheme, the sestet of "The Fascination of What's Difficult," which replaces narration with performative speech-acts ("My curse on . . . / I swear"), exhibits an intellectual structure resembling that of a Shakespearean "sestet"—a quatrain followed by a couplet. The first four lines of the sestet continue the sustained complaint of the poem, but the syntactically free-standing last two, in a sudden reversal, swear to break free of all managerial constraints.

In a casual reading, one might overlook both the implied sonnet-structure of "The Fascination of What's Difficult" and its absent fourteenth line, and might think that its originality lies in its Irish theme, its sudden performative curse, and its insertion of words like "road-metal" and "theatre business" into a piece that also contains Pegasus. And of course these features—a quotidian subject-matter, a closing burst from narrative into performative speech, and mixed factual and mythological diction—do form part of its originality as lyric utterance. Yet it would be a pity to miss altogether its defiance of the continental sonnet tradition (where Pegasus had sometimes found a home) as it asserts that the European Pegasus, rejuvenated, is now stabled in Ireland. The poem can be seen as Yeats's analogue to Whitman's nationalist boast about the Muse, "She's here, installed amid the kitchenware!" ("Song of the Exposition"). Yeats's rhyming would not be seen as transgressive, either, if we did not bring the sonnet template to mind. By the "missing" fourteenth line (recognizable, too, only by applying the sonnet template) Yeats intends to represent, I think, the airborne escape out the unbolted stable door of poet and Pegasus together. If we do not recognize the poem as a sonnet *manqué,* we miss the fine wit of the close, the "whoosh" of non-verbal air after the thirteenth line. (We have already seen such "missing" lines elsewhere, notably in the last part of "The Tower" and in Yeats's self-epitaph.)

Although the famous 1910 Coole Park poem now called "Upon a House Shaken by the Land Agitation"[13] is in fact a Shakespearean douzain like "No Second Troy" (and is placed next to the parabolic douzain "These Are the Clouds"), it, too, feels like a sonnet, in part because of its preoccupation with the "ruins of time," an immemorial sonnet-topic. Yeats's diary entry of August 7, 1910, comments: "I wrote this poem on hearing the result of reduction of rent made by the courts. . . . This house has enriched my soul out of measure because here life moves within restraint through gracious forms" (*NC*, 93). The poem is a protest against Irish willingness to starve out, by the new land law, the architectural, governmental, and literary legacy—the eagle-gaze and eagle-thoughts and eagle-wings—of the Protestant Ascendancy:

> How should the world be luckier if this house,
> Where passion and precision have been one
> Time out of mind, became too ruinous

To breed the lidless eye that loves the sun?
And the sweet laughing eagle thoughts that grow
Where wings have memory of wings and all
That comes of the best knit to the best? Although
Mean roof-trees were the sturdier for its fall,
How should their luck run high enough to reach
The gifts that govern men, and after these
To gradual Time's last gift, a written speech
Wrought of high laughter, loveliness, and ease?

(264)

The poem (as it stands in its 1912 final version) is composed of three ques-
tions. Because the first of these is coterminous with the initial quatrain, the
poem exhibits a fully Shakespearean beginning: a pentameter *abab* quatrain,
syntactically self-enclosed. Such an opening (together with the block-like
appearance of the poem on the page) makes the reader expect that a sonnet
has begun to unfold. The second question needs only three lines, and corre-
sponds structurally to the second quatrain of a regular Shakespearean son-
net. The third question, like the first, has a Shakespearean quatrain (lines 9–
12) all to itself, though it is prefaced by an important two-line concession
(lines 7–8). The two especially resonant questions, then, the first and the
last, occur as full alternating-rhyme quatrains, and one almost feels, fin-
ishing the poem with those quatrains in the ear, that one has read a four-
part Shakespearean argument: Question, Question, Concession, Question.

There is far greater complexity in this douzain than in the comparably
interrogative douzain "No Second Troy." Because a question has been put
by the speaker—"How should the world be luckier if this house fell into
ruin?"[14]—we are inclined to look for an answer. And the speaker's later con-
cession, preceding quatrain 3, suggests that he has already heard a provoca-
tive statement from an unseen interlocutor, who has generated the poet's
response by saying "The world *would* be luckier if this house fell, because
mean roof-trees would be the sturdier for its fall." The speaker's closing
quatrain, with its reservations about the future potential of the mean roof-
trees, is best heard as a rebuttal to the full argument of his implied interloc-
utor, who has said (we deduce) not only that the mean roof-trees would be-
come economically sturdier but also that their inhabitants would (given the
ruin of the Anglo-Irish hegemony) become self-governing and educated,
freed from dependency and backwardness. But (Yeats-the-speaker replies in
rebuttal), will the people of the mean roof-trees ever be able to govern

themselves as well as they have been governed? And will their writing, once they become literate, ever attain the status of literature?

Yeats, it seems, composes his poem largely as a rebuttal to the implied words of his populist (Catholic) interlocutor, who has asserted, before the poem began, that it would be luckier for the world if the new rent legislation passed, whatever its effect on great houses. Provoked, Yeats opens with a peremptory demand for a justification of that opinion: "*How* should the world be luckier in that case?" We read "Upon a House" better when we hear in it the concessions the poet makes as he considers the populist argument. He admits the possibility of his invisible opponent's claims—yes, with the departure of the Anglo-Irish "big house" and its inhabitants, the poor might well be economically better-off, and might take the reins of government, and might even perhaps become literate. But Yeats cannot in honesty forbear to defend his own culture by means of Platonic comparatives. There is, after all, he feels, something more important to a culture than the abating of poverty, something more desirable in government than the civil strife that will follow the extinction of the Anglo-Irish, something more aesthetic than mass propaganda for the newly literate. Will the luck of those made sturdier by the fall of Coole run high enough to reach civilized negotiation instead of civil war, and will they master that art of intimacy with language and its ironies sufficiently to write something different from their current coarse propaganda? In the short run, Yeats's misgivings were not unfounded. There *was* a civil war; popular nationalist literature *was* aesthetically crude. This "sonnet" would be less intellectually tense if the speaker had not so evidently incorporated the position of his opponent within his own questions; that very incorporation was a symbol of his own inner quarrel between his Anglo-Irish culture and his nationalist hopes.

Yeats makes the last two lines of this douzain "read like" an epigrammatic Shakespearean couplet by starting up in them a new theme—that of fluent and self-observing literature as "gradual Time's last gift." Even the near-rhyme of "speech" with "ease" helps to create the illusion that the poem ends with a Shakespearean couplet. "Upon a House Shaken by the Land Agitation" sounds Shakespearean, too, because of its use of one of Shakespeare's most common figures of speech, the figure of reduplication, which, as so often in Shakespeare's sonnets, stands for plenitude. Yeats carries out reduplication here not only by repetition of words (*wings, wings; best, best; gifts, gift; laughing, laughing*) but also by alliteration and assonance (*passion* and *precision; laughter, loveliness; gifts, govern, gradual, gift; written, wrought*) and by all the words assonating on long "e": *breed, sweet, eagle, mean, trees, reach, these, speech, ease.* The "wrought" nature of the language is Shakespearean in its deliberate evocation of courtly stateliness; as we conclude these lines, we almost have the impression of having read a Shakespearean sonnet, even if we have not. The principle of contradiction has been fully presented in the poem, since one part of Yeats's nationalism wanted Ireland free of England while another part, at this stage, hoped to find in the new state the perpetuation-by-incorporation of Anglo-Irish culture. The only way in which "Upon a House Shaken by the Land Agitation" is *not* a Shakespearean sonnet is by its remaining within the douzain-template. Yeats is still, we see, avoiding a full imitation of Shakespearean form. If he had written his Coole poem in true fourteen-line Shakespearean form, he might have been seen as sending—in this controversial poem—a sign of allegiance to English culture, and to be proposing questions more rhetorical than (as they actually were) genuine. Forgoing a formal "match" between Coole and English Renaissance form, Yeats will be an Irish douzain-writer, not an English sonneteer. It may also be that he, like Keats, disliked the effect of the terminal couplet.

When we do finally come, in Yeats's mature work, to a real sonnet in Shakespearean form, "At the Abbey Theatre" (264–265)—Yeats's pentameter adaptation, done in Paris in 1911, of Ronsard's Alexandrine Petrarchan sonnet "Tyard, on me blasmoit, à mon commencement"[15]—the poem, paradoxically, does not in fact feel Shakespearean, at least not in structure. Addressing Douglas Hyde of the Gaelic League under his Irish *nom de plume* meaning "Little Pleasant Branch," and sardonically calling him "most popular of men," Yeats complains of the fickleness of the Abbey audience. He exasperatedly asks "Dear Craoibhin Aobhin" (pronounced "Creeveen Eeveen") how to control the Abbey audiences, so irritating in their inconsistency, hating sublimity one day, hating commonness the next:

> Dear Craoibhin Aobhin, look into our case.
> When we are high and airy hundreds say
> That if we hold that flight they'll leave the place,
> While those same hundreds mock another day
> Because we have made our art of common things,
> So bitterly, you'd dream they longed to look
> All their lives through into some drift of wings.
> You've dandled them and fed them from the book
> And know them to the bone; impart to us—
> We'll keep the secret—a new trick to please.

> Is there a bridle for this Proteus
> That turns and changes like his draughty seas?
> Or is there none, most popular of men,
> But when they mock us, that we mock again?

This poem is, externally speaking, a Shakespearean sonnet, with its length and its rhymes all in order. But its first and second quatrains are enjambed; and its thought-structure, reflected in the number of lines occupied by each sentence—1, 6, 3, 2, 2—is closer to the expostulatory rhythms of drama than to the measured "written speech" of the Shakespearean sonnet. Yeats's poem, full of aplomb and satirical energy, is far more colloquial than the usual Shakespearean sonnet (not least because Yeats has in mind, as he had in "The Fascination of What's Difficult," Ben Jonson's "Ode to Himselfe," in which the poet advises himself, because of the audience's "indicting and arraigning," to quit the stage).[16] Still, Yeats has visibly turned Ronsard's Petrarchan-rhymed hexameters into Shakespearean-rhymed pentameters in homage to Shakespeare the *Globe* playwright, ancestor to Yeats himself in the Irish playhouse. At last, by an end-run through France, Yeats has been able to bestow the external form of the Shakespearean sonnet on an Irish poem.

In 1914, at the age of forty-nine, Yeats hybridizes a sonnet,[17] appending a Petrarchan/Miltonic sestet to a Shakespearean octave in the "closing rhymes" (as he later named them)[18] for the volume *Responsibilities*. In this one-sentence poem Yeats cites his Syrinx-Muse, his friends, and Lady Gregory as consolations against the notoriety that now hounds his life and writings. "Notoriety" was in fact Yeats's first title for this sonnet:[19]

> While I, from that reed-throated whisperer
> Who comes at need, although not now as once
> A clear articulation in the air,
> But inwardly, surmise companions
> Beyond the fling of the dull ass's hoof
> —Ben Jonson's phrase[20]—and find when June is come
> At Kyle-na-no under that ancient roof
> A sterner conscience and a friendlier home,
> I can forgive even that wrong of wrongs,
> Those undreamt accidents that have made me
> —Seeing that Fame has perished this long while,
> Being but a part of ancient ceremony—

> Notorious, till all my priceless things
> Are but a post the passing dogs defile.
>
> (320–321)

"While I, from that reed-throated whisperer," though beginning with Shake-spearean rhymes and invoking Jonson, has Milton as unseen presider over its public orientation, its enjambed quatrains, the complex nested syntax of its athletically sinewed single sentence, its irregular Petrarchan sestet, and its insertion into its lines of a third-person non-classical proper name ("Ben Jonson") as well as a local name ("Kyle-na-no").[21] As in Milton, too, there appear phrases alien to the Shakespearean sonnet, such as "the dull ass's hoof" (borrowed from Jonson) and "a post the passing dogs defile." This defiantly public poem aims its catapult of subordinate clauses and interpolated absolutes against the illiterate asses and dogs of publicity. As it climbs inexorably to its penultimate-line climax in the word "Notorious," it uses language as a weapon, one unwieldable by those subhuman beings who can only bray and bark, kick and piss. The sheer derisive power of rhetoric, flaunted here by Yeats as by Milton in the face of enemies, reveals how Yeats has fortified the Shakespearean sonnet form by hybridizing it with the tone of its Miltonic cousin. And the poem's lexical violence defines, by contrast, what the obverse of such scornful linguistic moments might be, when language would be reabsorbed into its proper use, defined here as that "ancient ceremony" rewarded by the goddess Fama, Yeats's Latin divinity comparable to Milton's Greek "all-judging Jove." We need to register Yeats's adoption of the mixed rhyme-scheme here before we can admire his muscular wrenching of the initially Shakespearean form to his denunciatory "Miltonic" intent.

Yeats extended the sonnet in one famous instance—"The Second Coming" (1919)—by writing two successive octaves before arriving at the sestet. Lest this be thought a capricious notion peculiar to me, this way of seeing the poem has also been proposed by Seamus Deane:

> Yeats's own presence comes into the poem at the strategic moment
> when the first eight lines of what could have been a sonnet like "Leda
> and the Swan" are resumed, not into a sestet, but into a full sonnet. We
> not only have a sonnet and a half, we have an aborted sonnet that is then
> reborn as a full one, as the poem itself comes for the second time,
> brought to its full formal strength by the sudden intervention of the poet
> who now reveals himself to be the speaker.[22]

Why does Yeats write "The Second Coming" in blank verse, and why does the first octave come to a halt, unable to proceed immediately to a sestet? Why must the poem start over, adding another octave to itself before it can reach its sestet-conclusion? These are complicated questions, and I can suggest only brief answers here. The short answer to the question of blank verse is that for Yeats in 1919, during the period of *A Vision,* blank verse (discussed below in Chapter IX) is the medium of instruction (as in "The Phases of the Moon" and "Ego Dominus Tuus"); by using it, he emphasizes the didactic nature of "The Second Coming." What is it that "saves" the poet from his halt at line 8 and enables him to write the rest of the poem (or—since "the rest" consists of an octave and a sestet—to write an alternate sonnet)? The poem was saved by the poet's decision to cease being an impersonal prophet and write as an individual, to speak in the first person. And why must this sonnet be an expanded one? Because it foretells a monstrous birth, for one thing, and is one of Yeats's several experiments, of which "High Talk" is another, in making the sonnet monstrous. "Leda and the Swan," to which I will turn after investigating "The Second Coming," is yet another "monstrous" form.

"The Second Coming," in the drafts as well as in the final version, tries to write itself first without an identified speaker or a first-person "I." It rehearses an impersonal symbolic narrative that employs successive unrelated metaphors of falcon, center, tide, and ceremony:

> Turning and turning in the widening gyre
> The falcon cannot hear the falconer;
> Things fall apart; the centre cannot hold;
> Mere anarchy is loosed upon the world,
> The blood-dimmed tide is loosed, and everywhere
> The ceremony of innocence is drowned;
> The best lack all conviction, while the worst
> Are full of passionate intensity.

"Turning and turning in the widening gyre / The falcon cannot hear the falconer." But no sooner is this visual metaphor conceived than it breaks down into helpless abstractions: "Things fall apart"; "The centre cannot hold"; "Mere anarchy is loosed upon the world"; "The best lack all conviction." Though metaphor attempts to reclaim its place as an explanatory strategy in the words "tide" and "ceremony," it is defeated once again by its slide from concreteness ("the *blood*-dimmed *tide*") to abstraction ("the *cere-*

*mony of innocence*"). The metaphors clash in their heterogeneous notation. In the drafts, we can see Yeats tending toward topical instances from the Russian revolution, the French revolution, and perhaps the Irish troubles as well;[23] then, desiring a diction that would cover many such examples, he decides not to be historically specific, a decision that led him to his opening generalizations. The octave comes to an end, and the poem itself has not found a center, a coherent point of vantage. Is there some mediating strategy which would be composed not of allegorical tropes (falcon or tide), nor of historical presences (Marie Antoinette in the drafts), nor of abstract propositions ("Things fall apart")? The poem reproduces this hiatus in composition by a blank space, after which it begins again.

Yeats finds that he must, in honesty, express his poem in the first person, rejecting prophetic philosophical universals in favor of an entirely different means of generalizing. To this end, he pursues a personal myth—his myth of supernaturally driven historical change producing an incarnate signal of the new (Helen in the classical era, Christ in the Christian one). The convulsion represented by the supernatural birth must be one applicable to France in 1789, Russia in 1917, or Ireland in 1919. When "The Second Coming" begins its second octave, it has dropped its former impersonal declamatory mode for a more naked one, that of first-person agitation:

> Surely some revelation is at hand;
> Surely the Second Coming is at hand.
> The Second Coming! Hardly are those words out
> When a vast image out of *Spiritus Mundi*
> Troubles my sight: somewhere in sands of the desert
> A shape with lion body and the head of a man,
> A gaze blank and pitiless as the sun,
> Is moving its slow thighs, while all about it
> Reel shadows of the indignant desert birds.

No longer a remote Gibbonian analyst, the speaker is now a desperate witness, listening to his own over-protesting words: "Surely some revelation is at hand; / Surely the Second Coming is at hand. / The Second Coming!" Exclamation brings its own credulous phrase, "the Second Coming," into embodiment; and behold, in place of the transcendent *parousia* of Christ, a menacing mythological sphinx-shape appears, arises, and moves with dread intent, disturbing its indignant bird-beholders who spill over, in an equally indignant *volta,* through the ninth line. Belief has now not only been rewarded by image, it has been infused with doctrine: "Now I know" says the first-person speaker of this "second" decisive sonnet as he begins his curtailed "sestet." He does know one thing—that he is not seeing the glorious Second Coming of Christ but a reprise, in grotesque form, of the birth of a new energy at Bethlehem. Some unspecified agency, the speaker says, has set a cradle rocking again in the East, vexing the Christian double millennium into nightmare; but the speaker does *not* know something else—the essential nature of the beast which he has seen only in its external shape as it rouses itself from the Egyptian sands:

> The darkness drops again; but now I know
> That twenty centuries of stony sleep
> Were vexed to nightmare by a rocking cradle,
> And what rough beast, its hour come round at last,
> Slouches towards Bethlehem to be born?
>
> (401–402)

The fractured syntax of this supposedly "enlightened" five-line "sestet," which irregularly joins (as objects of "know") a noun clause of statement with a non-coordinate independent question, acts out the anxiety of the speaker: "I know / *That* twenty centuries . . . were vexed . . ., / *And what* rough beast . . . / Slouches?"

The gross structure of "The Second Coming," then, presents a first, impersonal, and metaphorically disturbed octave of abstract narration, followed by a second self-referential octave of alarmed but fascinated myth as the speaker listens to, and then illustrates, his own phrase "the Second Coming." He concludes with a first-person "sestet" of doctrinal enlightenment and existential menace. Within this three-part "Petrarchan" compositional structure—octave, octave, sestet—can we perhaps ascertain Petrarchan thought-structures to confirm our sense that the poem is an extended sonnet? The opening octave, though it at first appears to be organized in couplets (produced by the slant rhymes of *gyre* and *falconer, world* and *hold*), is at a more fundamental level constructed in a series of half-lines, separated by medial breaks, in which the "left" half represents the dissolution of form, and the "right" half represents the threatened world order:

| **Chaos** | **Order** |
|---|---|
| Turning and turning | in the widening gyre |
| The falcon cannot hear | the falconer |
| Things fall apart | the centre cannot hold |

Mere anarchy is loosed               upon the world
The blood-dimmed tide is loosed     and everywhere
The ceremony of innocence is drowned

                           The best

lack all conviction, while
the worst are full of passionate intensity.

The reader, encountering these lines, is forced to "look" left and right, left and right, enacting the distracted gaze of the speaker. The opening octave sequesters itself from the rest of the poem by this syntactic half-line gesture of conspectus.

The second octave, on the other hand, is phrased in full lines because the speaker's would-be worldwide prophecy has been replaced by the single image of first-person revelation:

> Surely some revelation is at hand;
> Surely the Second Coming is at hand.

And the full line continues to be the norm for the rest of the poem, which wants to resemble, in its concluding fourteen lines, a Petrarchan sonnet in which the mythological octave of the Rough Beast is able to generate a philosophical sestet opening with "I know." However, the historical conclusion which follows the introductory sestet-clause "now I know" cannot carry on serenely to the end, as we have already seen; it is disturbed by the speaker's mythological turn in the final two lines, where image blots out doctrine, and apprehension erases prophetic confidence. By showing us a poem in which normal sonnet convention (where a sestet immediately follows an octave) is upset by the poem's demanding the appearance of a second octave before the sestet can be written, Yeats gives us the impression that his poem has "free will," that it "cannot" follow its opening octave to an immediate sestet of confident philosophical conclusion. The poem rebels, in an almost "Irish" way, against English Enlightenment models of a progressive philosophy of history.

This "monstrous" sonnet, "The Second Coming," is followed by an equally interesting experiment in 1923, "Leda and the Swan." Once again (as he had in "While I, from that reed-throated wanderer") Yeats composes a hybrid Shakespearean-Petrarchan sonnet, its parts "mismatched" on this occasion to represent the engendering (by Zeus on Leda) of the half-divine, half-human Helen. Yeats emphasizes the several parts of the sonnet by separating them with white space:

A sudden blow: the great wings beating still
Above the staggering girl, her thighs caressed
By the dark webs, her nape caught in his bill,
He holds her helpless breast upon his breast.

How can those terrified vague fingers push
The feathered glory from her loosening thighs?
And how can body, laid in that white rush,
But feel the strange heart beating where it lies?

A shudder in the loins engenders there
The broken wall, the burning roof and tower
And Agamemnon dead.
                                        Being so caught up,
So mastered by the brute blood of the air,
Did she put on his knowledge with his power
Before the indifferent beak could let her drop?

                                                                    (441)

"Leda and the Swan" is Shakespearean in the alternately rhymed quatrains of its octave *(abab cdcd)*, Petrarchan in its sestet *(efgefg)*. Like "The Second Coming," "Leda and the Swan" structures itself at first in half-lines, then in whole lines. The half-lines represent the two participants in Helen's conception, and the speaker is uncertain whether he should ratify the absolute right of Zeus to set destiny going in a new direction or should sympathize with Leda's initial terror. Ascribing parts (italicized in the schema below) to the two participants, the speaker goes back and forth from the swan-god-lover to the hapless "girl," until the two protagonists join in a mutual single-line climax:[24]

| **Leda** | | **Zeus** |
|---|---|---|
| | A sudden blow: | |
| | | The great wings beating still |
| above the staggering girl. | | |
| *her* thighs caressed | | by the dark webs |
| *her* nape caught | | in *his* bill, |
| | | he holds |
| *her* helpless breast | upon | *his* breast |
| | How can | |

those terrified vague fingers   push          the feathered glory
from *her* loosening thighs?

                      And how can

body,                    laid             in that white rush,
but feel                               the strange heart beating

                where it lies?
      A shudder in the loins engenders there . . .

These two Shakespearean quatrains are respectively narrative and empathetic, and both project Leda's view of what is happening. The first quatrain sketches the elements of the scene, and the second poses two rhetorical questions, best seen as reflecting Leda's own thoughts, of which the first justifies her physical submission and the second justifies her acquiescence in pleasure. She has been not only held but (as only she could phrase it) "caressed," not only terrified but seduced; her thighs are not loosened, as in forcible rape, but are "loosening" (as only she could feel it) of their own free will, because she has now felt the heart of her strange lover beating (in contrast to the earlier shocking blow from the beating of his wings). (The sestet will sum up this distinction between resistance and consent by contrasting its phrase of rapture, "caught up," to the octave's phrase of assault, "caught.")

As the octave proceeds, we follow, in a series of nouns, Leda's gradual perceptions of her assailant: first, she experiences a blow from unascribed-to-a-person wings and webs, with both nouns prefaced by the definite article, "the great wings," "the dark webs"; next, she perceives her capturer as male ("*his* bill"). He and she, though still separated by the gendered pronominal adjectives "his" and "hers," are brought closer as they are made to share a single noun, when *her* (human) *breast* is held upon *his* (avian) *breast*. As Leda comes to understand that this is no ordinary swan, his noun-substance as she perceives it becomes newly identified as "glory" (and even though separated from her by the definite article, the sensually felt adjectival "feathered" makes "the glory" soft to Leda's perception); next he is pure penetrating motion, "rush" (separated from her by the distal deictic adjective "that," but seen through her eyes as "white"); and finally he is her lover, as she is excused from resistance by finding the beating heart within the white rush where she lies. Even before the moment of climax, Yeats suppresses Leda's former emphatic perception of separate gendered possessive adjectives, *his* and *her* (his bill, her breast, and so on); we hear of "the" undifferentiated loins, of a single place, "there" (where male and female meet), where the engendering takes place. One cannot separate the shudder of orgasm from the engendering in the womb: during the moment of that "shudder that made them one" (as Yeats calls it in "Solomon and Sheba"), Zeus and Leda are indivisible.

The sonnet, having united Zeus and Leda, now has to enact their disjunction. We see, for a moment, the swan-lover-god in one three-part epithet, as Leda, knowing him in all three of his aspects for the first time, understands that she has been caught up and mastered by the "brute [animal] blood [human] of the air [divine]." Zeus has approached Leda in order to engender Helen, to enable (by having Leda "put on" his power) his next millennial plan—the Trojan War and its sequelae in the death of Agamemnon and others (or, to put it otherwise, the matter of Homer and the tragedies). Although he has had to let Leda assume his generative power, Zeus does not want Leda to descry his plan: if she does, he loses his uniqueness as sole knower of the future. Yet, was it possible, wonders the speaker (who has now entered the poem *in propria persona,* no longer "channeling" Leda's perceptions but introducing, from his own historical knowledge, the acts and consequences of the Trojan War), for Leda to enter into physical oneness with all three aspects—swan, lover, god—of Zeus and *not* gain some access to his mind? "Did nothing pass before her in the air?" asks a manuscript draft (in the Latin *nonne* form that presumes a positive answer).[25] It is certain that Leda, in conceiving Helen, put on Zeus's power; did she not put on his knowledge too, before the "indifferent beak"—as Zeus hastens to detach himself from swanhood and resume his normal invisible state— could let her drop? Putting on Zeus's knowledge would be for Leda the assumption of an intellectual power to match the biological power that she has certainly "put on"; and the question posed in the draft suggests that Zeus could not have it all his own way. Descending to the human, he gives the human access to the divine.

But is there any evidence in the poem as it stands to suggest that Leda put on Zeus's knowledge before he could let her drop? While the Shakespearean quatrains of the octave develop the story of the conception of Helen, the Petrarchan sestet is preoccupied with the historical after-effects of that conception. Conflict in this sonnet derives from Yeats's ambivalence with respect to the question of free will. Yes, we are helplessly caught by destiny; but we are also caught up by it and join ourselves to it. No, we cannot know the future; but cannot we sometimes attain, as Milton and Blake thought, to "something like prophetic strain"? Yeats breaks off the story of

Leda to interpolate, in lines 10–11, *before* he completes her story, what Leda *would* have seen *had* she put on Zeus's knowledge—"The broken wall, the burning roof and tower / And Agamemnon dead." That is, Yeats makes *us* have the prophetic vision *before* our last glance at Leda (lines 11b–14, "Being so caught up," etc.). We cannot deny, as we finish reading the sonnet, our Yeats-given knowledge of the future catastrophe of Troy, and so we are forced—as we return in line 11 to Leda's story—to bring along that knowledge with us, unable to forget it as we finish the poem. This persuades us, I believe, that Leda had the vision too (just as Yeats, writing "A Bronze Head," thought that Maud Gonne, his Helen, had had a prophetic vision of her future life: "I saw the wildness in her and I thought / A vision of terror that it must live through / Had shattered her soul"). And because Yeats had long identified Helen and Maud, "Leda and the Swan" is for him and his readers an Irish poem, asking how cultural destruction-bearers like Helen and Maud arrive at their destiny. "Leda and the Swan," like "No Second Troy," allows Yeats to excuse in Maud a course of action different, in its violence, from any he would have found possible for himself.

If his myths of historical change engendered in Yeats the unnatural births and hybrid forms of the sonnets "The Second Coming" and "Leda and the Swan," he could, when he decided to examine turbulence from a more distant vantage, return to the Shakespearean sonnet. Because we have already explored his last "outrageous" sonnet, "High Talk," I close with his penultimate use of the sonnet form in the great valediction "Meru," which is Shakespearean in rhyme, Petrarchan in internal structure. This triumphant example of having the best of both sonnet-worlds, written in 1933–1934 when Yeats was almost seventy, is not Irish in any visible sense. Yet its central line, "Egypt and Greece, good-bye, and good-bye, Rome!" would be taken, by any Irish reader, as a farewell not only to the empires of Egypt, Greece, and Rome, but also to the British Empire. Yeats had defended the achievements of that Empire in "Upon a House Shaken by the Land Agitation," and had wanted to see its glories and monuments, civic and literary, preserved. Now, having accepted the bitter fact that no civilization can sustain itself indefinitely, because human thought is always bent on demystifying the "manifold illusion" that sustains any organization of life, he is ready to say "a gay good-night" to all successive cultures, including his own. How, actually, he asks, is culture successively created and destroyed?

> Civilization is hooped together, brought
> Under a rule, under the semblance of peace

By manifold illusion; but man's life is thought,
And he, despite his terror, cannot cease
Ravening through century after century,
Ravening, raging, and uprooting that he may come
Into the desolation of reality:
Egypt and Greece, good-bye, and good-bye, Rome!

Against the almost artless sweep of that chiastic mid-sonnet farewell utter-
ing two "goodbyes" with empires bracketing them, Yeats constructs, pre-
ceding the farewell and following it, two buttressing structures. The first, al-
ready cited, is the history of "man"; the second is the history of "hermits":[26]

Hermits upon Mount Meru or Everest,
Caverned in night under the drifted snow,
Or where that snow and winter's dreadful blast
Beat down upon their naked bodies, know
That day brings round the night, that before dawn
His glory and his monuments are gone.

(563)

"Man" lives in society, and is ceaselessly, through his restless thought, build-
ing and destroying culture; "hermits" have forsworn society, and live in a
naked and detached solitude where their sole activity is to "know." In "Lapis
Lazuli" (1936), Yeats would write "All things fall and are built again, / And
those that build them again are gay," but here he is concerned not with man
as builder but with man in his function as destroyer, a function he had ear-
lier condemned when Coole Park was threatened. By now, however, Yeats
has come to realize that he himself is not only a builder but also a destroyer,
that thinking itself always propels the dissolution of past cultural syntheses,
his own Anglo-Irish synthesis included: "Things thought too long can be no
longer thought," as he would write in "The Gyres" (1936). The only people
able to remain aloof from participation in cultural creation and destruction
are those who, like the Hindu hermits on Everest or its mythological coun-
terpart, Mount Meru,[27] have the detachment to see that all cultural systems
are equally illusory and transient. The hermits' perfect imperviousness—
even under the worst assaults of nature on their naked bodies—is the re-
ward of their esoteric knowledge.

How does Yeats's sonnet enact the restlessness of man and the immobil-
ity of the monks, each given a single sentence on either side of the grand

gesture of farewell? The "hooping together" processes of civilization are mimicked by Yeats's syntactically back-stitching picture of the progress of its illusions:

> Civilization is hooped together
> brought
> under a rule
> under the semblance
> of peace
> by manifold illusion.

By a syllable-pun, man-ifold illusion seems man-made; but man is deceiving himself—he cannot live by the coerced and coercing semblances of any civilization. After the adversative "but," the rest of the octave is undeviatingly and fiercely linear; the life of thought has no time for the rules and constraints of "civilized" stasis. Man (despite his terror) cannot cease destroying illusion in his search for truth. He goes unstoppably and grimly forward:

> Ravening
> through century
> after century,
> Ravening,
> raging,
> and uprooting
> that he may come
> into the desolation of reality.

Although the advance of the ravening destruction is linear, Yeats inserts one back-loop here (by means of the second "Ravening") in order, I think, to connect this passage to the back-loops of the "hooped" construction of "civilization" in the first quatrain. Milton's "hard r's" have been borrowed for man's headlong campaign of ravening, raging, and (up)rooting; in the pursuit of reality, grinding thought cannot be reined back from its devouring. The enjambment between the first two Shakespearean quatrains is an exhibitionistic one, splitting verb and complement over the line break: "[Man] cannot cease / Ravening." The Shakespearean shape of self-contained quatrains is arrantly violated, just as man's thought transgresses the rules of culture. The resulting Keatsian "desolation" means that the little towns of civilization have always had to be deserted by their folk, who will follow yet another "mysterious priest" of thought to the next stage of cognitive "ravening."

The hermits, on the other hand, live in a sentence which is entirely static. Its kernel-phrase, "Hermits know," presents a verb of state, not a verb of action. The hermits know what the Shakespearean couplet says: "That day brings round the night, that before dawn / [Man's] glory and his monuments are gone." The dynastic word "monuments"—not only because it is conspicuously Shakespearean (and Horatian and Ovidian) but also because (in the atmosphere of "man" and "man-ifold") it almost reads as "mon-u-*men*-ts"—is the right word for the cultural achievements known by the hermits to be ephemeral. Yeats now knows that there are no such perdurable things as "monuments of unageing intellect." The philosophical equanimity of the hermits is twice tested: as Yeats first imagines them, they are somewhat protected from the weather as they shelter in a cavern; but he immediately revises that imagining and puts them outside, naked, at the full mercy of the Himalayan winter. The long chiastic arc "Hermits . . . snow . . . snow . . . bodies" mimics their prolonged exposure to the elements, and gives the postponed climactic predicate, "know," its full ascetic value. The enjambment between the third Shakespearean quatrain and the final couplet—a mild one between verb and object, "know / That"—violates, like the earlier "destructive" enjambment "cease / Ravening," the usual pre-couplet end-stop of the Shakespearean sonnet; but here in the ascetic sestet the constraints of culture are indifferently ignored rather than, as in the octave, disrupted by violent incessant thinking.

There is more to be said about all these "sonnets." They could equally well (in a different book from this one) be considered under their several thematic concerns, their generic affiliations, the volumes where they appear, and so on (I will in fact be reconsidering "Meru" when I discuss in Chapter XII the sequence "Supernatural Songs," of which it is the conclusion). Here I have merely wished to insert some of Yeats's experiments into the history of the sonnet in English, and to show how Yeats renewed the form, not least by making his sonnets "Irish" through myth, allusion, and implication, and "hybrid" by structure and rhyme. How much of what I have said about these poems could be said without reference to the sonnet tradition? A good deal, of course—everything, for instance, that I have mentioned in summarizing general topics, attitudes, and tones. But what I have said about the inventive architectonics of these pieces rests, I think, on our perceiving them *as* sonnets—or as sonnets *manqués,* sonnets tightened to douzains, monstrous sonnets, hybrid sonnets, transgressive sonnets, unrhymed sonnets, and so on. And what we perceive of their originality often depends on our knowing how Yeats arouses conventional sonnet expectations and then plays havoc with them by offering a sonnet in ranting hexameters, or a Shakespearean sonnet that is violently enjambed, or a centaur-like fusion of the Shakespearean and the Petrarchan forms, or a pastoral sonnet that turns apocalyptic.

Yeats would have wanted us to notice such things, because they are part of our intuited shock as we read these poems, even if we cannot at first say what it is that is shocking us. They are part of his way of saying, to his English readers, "I am not writing the English sonnet as you know it. Even though I know it more intimately than you, it is for me a site of experiment, whereas for you it is a site of cultural memory." Since he deliberately introduced Irish themes into his sonnets—from the god Aengus to Malachi's collar of gold, from the Abbey Theatre to Coole, from Maud Gonne to Douglas Hyde—it is clear that he wanted at least some of these poems to "feel" Irish, not English. That desire must have been one of Yeats's motives for shaking up the form; other motives, chiefly expressive emotional ones, of course also sponsored his innovations.

Critics sometimes ask whether Yeats was the last of the Victorians or the first of the Modernists. In his sonnet practice, certainly, he left no aspect unscrutinized in his modernizing of the genre. Like all the best Modernists, he disturbed forms without entirely abandoning them. And since the principal historical function of poems is to enable the production of more poems, we have Yeats's exhilarating experimentation to thank, in part, for the continuing survival of the sonnet in British, Irish, and American verse.

## VII

## ∽— The Nationalist Measure:
## Trimeter-Quatrain Poems

In Yeats's poems, trimeter lines appear by themselves in many stanza forms—as the second and fourth lines of the ballad stanza, for example. In this chapter I examine only entire poems (or segments of sequences) written in trimeter,[1] and, within this class, only the subset of seventeen poems that exhibit "perfect" quatrain rhyme, *abab*.[2] First attempted in 1913 with "To a Friend Whose Work Has Come to Nothing," *abab* trimeter-quatrain form acquired for Yeats, I believe, an independent nationalist meaning, first with respect to "aristocratic" women, and then also with respect to "heroic" or "noble" men. The most famous of such poems is "Easter 1916"; other well-known ones are "The Fisherman" and part III of "The Tower," Yeats's poetic last will and testament. (The appendix to this chapter gives a complete list of the seventeen trimeter-quatrain poems, with their respective sub-forms—number of stanzas, types of rhymes, and so forth.)

Why did Yeats shape one group of his poems in trimeter quatrains rhyming *abab*? In casting "raw material" into metrical form, he certainly did not (as this book exists to show) decide on forms at random. In the preceding chapters I have tried to explain what some traditional forms meant to him, and how he renewed them. Now I turn to the trimeter quatrain, to see what it is possible to say about how Yeats used this form, and what sort of material invited or required it.

Iambic trimeter poems in alternately rhymed *abab* quatrains (henceforth, for brevity, "*abab* trimeters" or "trimeter quatrains") have no distinguished history in English verse before Yeats. Hundreds of ballads, hymns, and lyrics exist in the form of alternating tetrameter and trimeter ("God rest ye merry gentlemen / Let nothing you dismay"), but rhyming iambic trimeter is rare.[3] When, as a girl, I first read a poem in sustained trimeter, I found it thrilling; I had never before encountered this striking rhythm. Yet it was not in Yeats that I saw it, but in "The Poet" by Cecil Day-Lewis (whose book for young people, the 1944 *Poetry for You,* had led me to his verse). I reproduce below the trimeter passage that so swept my young self away, noting the number of syllables in each line. Twice, a trochaic foot has been substituted in the initial position for the metrically expected iamb; and once—in line 5—a trochee appears in the final foot:

For now imagination—     (7)
My royal, impulsive swan,     (7)
In raking flight—I can see her—     (8)
Comes down as it were upon     (7)
A lake in whirled snow-floss     (6)
And flurry of spray, like a skier     (9)
Checking. Again I feel     (6)
The wounded waters heal.     (6)
Never before did she cross     (7)
My heart with such exaltation.[4]     (8)

Later, with a sense of betrayal, I discovered that Day-Lewis was merely copying Yeats—imitating a rhythm (and borrowing the swan-symbol) that Yeats had made unmistakably his own. There is a lilt and swing in these lines that comes not only from three reversed feet (trochees in place of iambs in lines 5, 7, and 9) but also from the occasional anapests and dactyls and feminine endings that create (in seven of the ten lines above) "extra" syllables beyond the required six. If one were to rewrite the passage in strict iambic trimeter, six syllables per line, and with no reversed feet, it would lose its impetus:

[For now I feel my soul
Is like a royal swan,
In raking flight I see
Her slowly sink upon
A lake beside the floss
Of snow, and by a tree
She checks her flight. I feel
The wounded waters heal.
In youth she did not cross
My life in such a role.]

Such a paraphrase (while of course ruining the sense) deletes the rhythmic urgency of the poem. Cecil Day-Lewis had clearly captured Yeats's dashing syllabic and metrical ways of enlivening the iambic trimeter line. I'll have more to say about Yeats's practice in detail as we look at the *abab* trimeters below and the subjects they take up.

Yeats's first poems in *abab* trimeter honor women whom the poet admired or women linked to them: Lady Gregory; Maud Gonne's daughter, Iseult; Maud herself; Olivia Shakespear; and Yeats's wife, George. The trimeter-quatrain form first appears in "To a Friend Whose Work Has Come to Nothing," a poem concerning aristocratic honor, in which the friend in question is Lady Gregory. Augusta Gregory had seen the apparent failure of her prolonged effort to bring her nephew Hugh Lane's paintings to Dublin, and found herself slandered in the public press. The natural act when attacked is to defend oneself, but Yeats in this poem counsels silence. One who is "honour bred" cannot compete against the shameless lies of those who not only have no honor but are not even ashamed when they are exposed as liars. In characterizing Gregory, Yeats links, by the word "bred," the quasi-parenthetical phrase "being honour *bred*" to the later, more salient, remark that Gregory is *"bred* to a harder thing / Than Triumph."* He urges her, in the face of slander, to "be secret," and advises her to choose to play her lyre—like the mad King Goll of an earlier poem—in the wilderness.[5] Here is the poem, in which I have starred the lines with "extra" syllables and have also noted the occurrence of reversed feet:

| | |
|---|---|
| Now all the truth is out, | (6) |
| Be secret and take defeat | (7)* |
| From any brazen throat, | (6) |
| For how can you compete, | (6) |
| Being honour bred, with one | (7)* |
| Who, were it proved he lies, | (6) (reversed first foot) |
| Were neither shamed in his own | (7)* |
| Nor in his neighbours' eyes? | (6) (reversed first foot) |
| Bred to a harder thing | (6) (reversed first foot) |
| Than Triumph, turn away | (6) |
| And like a laughing string | (6) |
| Whereon mad fingers play | (6) |
| Amid a place of stone, | (6) |
| Be secret and exult, | (6) |
| Because of all things known | (6) |
| That is most difficult. | (6) (reversed first foot) |

(290–291)

Yeats has added an extra syllable in three lines and has reversed the sensitive first foot in four others, so that seven of the sixteen lines depart from the minimal six-syllable iambic metrical scheme, and are thereby made mobile and lively. Yeats does not, in this four-quatrain, two-sentence poem, separate each quatrain from the next by a stanza break, as we might have expected. We might at least have thought to find a stanza break after the second quatrain, where the first sentence ends in its question mark, but no: the poem runs on to its close without a break (as we saw "An Irish Airman" do as well). The four quatrains, then, make up one sixteen-line "stanza," and we must ask why the poem is arranged in this way. The verse derives its rapidity in part from the absence of any pause between the end of quatrain 1 and the beginning of quatrain 2: "For how can you compete, / Being honour bred." A comparable enjambment links quatrains 3 and 4: "Whereon mad fingers play / Amid a place of stone." The counterpoint visible here of sense-units (two) against quatrains (four) against number of stanzas (one) is among Yeats's most significant discoveries for the future. Counterpoint creates many competing structures, each with its own geometry. The poem consists of a single stanza not only because it consists of a single speech-act (the adjuration "Be secret and take defeat . . . turn away . . . Be secret and exult") but also because it rounds upon itself in a long chiasmus from line 2 to line 14: "Be secret and take defeat . . . Being honour bred . . . Bred to a harder thing . . . Be secret and exult." This single and total chiasmic arc gives this lyric its solidity of structure, and intends to imply—as chiasmus always does in its mannered pre-arrangement of syntax—considered forethought behind Yeats's advice to his friend.

Yeats could have written this poem with a different rhyme scheme—for example, interlinked rhymes (such as those used by Day-Lewis in "The Poet") instead of rhymed quatrains. In 1910, for instance, Yeats had cast the trimeters of "A Friend's Illness" (a poem about Lady Gregory that recalls the close of George Herbert's "Virtue")[6] into interlinked rhymes which create a seven-line caudated sixain (*aabccbc*). The closing dimeter in the "extra" coda-line represents the "supernatural" quality in the soul that makes it outweigh the whole world:

> Sickness brought me this
> Thought in that scale of his:
> Why should I be dismayed
> Though flame had burned the whole
> World, as it were a coal,
> Now I have seen it weighed
> Against a soul?
> (267)

With that example of Yeatsian interlinked rhyme in mind, let us try "To a Friend" in non-quatrain rhymes:

> [Now all the truth is out,
> Do not yourself compete
> Being honour bred, with one
> Who, were it proved he lies,
> From such a brazen throat,
> Were shamed nor in his own
> Nor in his neighbor's eyes:
> Be secret and take defeat.]

Voiced in such randomly appearing rhymes, the speech-act of the poem seems uncertain: nothing is said ringingly because the rhymes, not gathered into quatrains, are not expectable or conclusive.

Let us try "To a Friend" in yet another possible verse-structure, rhymed couplets:

> [Now all the truth is out
> From every brazen throat,
> Be secret and take defeat,
> For how can you compete,
> Being honour bred, with one
> Who were not shamed in his own
> Nor in his neighbours' eyes,
> Were it once proved he lies?]

The couplet form, we see, brings itself to an epigrammatic halt at the end of each two lines, as the thread is, so to speak, bitten off. The trimeter couplet is too aphoristic and short (unlike the longer heroic couplet) to mimic conversational intimacy, the advice of one friend to another. By contrast, Yeats's *abab* trimeter quatrains—made lively by extra syllables and reversed feet—can be both intimate and conclusive, shapely and yet—when enjambed into a long stanza—unobtrusive. From 1913 on, Yeats settles on the trimeter quatrain as a useful form. But he has not yet attached to it an implied and sustained content.

Trimeter quatrains next appear in the single-stanza lament "To a Child Dancing in the Wind" (published with "To a Friend" in *Responsibilities*). The twelve-line poem is addressed to Iseult Gonne, Maud's adolescent daughter.

At this time in her life, the poet says to Iseult, she may freely dance on the shore because her heart, unlike his older one, is not burdened by the disappointments and tragedies of the nationalist endeavor. Yeats experiments here with making irregular sense-units, not ones larger than the individual quatrain, as in "To a Friend," but smaller. "To a Child," though it possesses only three quatrains, exhibits five sense-units, ranging in length from a single line to five lines. Unforeseen stops within quatrains produce an effect of rhythmic spontaneity in the utterance, and serve to disguise the regular quatrain-pattern. Although the poem appears on the page as one long stanza, I illustrate its counterpointed structure here by inserting spaces between its five sense-components and placing an underline to mark the close of each quatrain:

> Dance there upon the shore;    (1 line)
>
> What need have you to care
> For wind or water's roar?    (2 lines)
>
> <u>And tumble out your hair</u>
> That the salt drops have wet;    (2 lines)
>
> Being young you have not known
> The fool's triumph, nor yet
> <u>Love lost as soon as won,</u>
> Nor the best labourer dead
> And all the sheaves to bind.    (5 lines)
>
> What need have you to dread
> The monstrous crying of wind?    (2 lines)
>                    (312)

Several features prevent us from hearing "To a Child" as a poem in regular quatrains: the irregular length of the sense-units (1, 2, 2, 5, 2); the rhythmic disturbances occasioned by pyrrhics and spondees; the occasional slant rhymes that make quatrain-units slightly harder to recognize ("known/won"; "bind/wind"); and the skips of the poet from one sort of speech-act to another (permission, question, permission, statement, question). While keeping his quatrains intact as rhyme-units, Yeats is taking pains to fragment them by many means, hoping to make his utterance appear "casual" and "unpremeditated," suitable to his subject, a young girl dancing spontaneously.

The thematic congruence of "To a Child" with "To a Friend Whose Work Has Come to Nothing" appears in the "lyric center" of "To a Child," in which Yeats is lamenting what the old have had to endure: "The fool's triumph" (which Lady Gregory, "Bred to a harder thing / Than Triumph," has had to bear); and "the best labourer dead / And all the sheaves to bind"—a reference to Gregory's nephew Hugh Lane, drowned at sea before the Municipal Gallery could be approved. Both "To a Friend" and "To a Child," then, are associated with Gregory, as is a third poem in seven trimeter quatrains, "Friends" (315–316), which praises under that title Augusta Gregory, Olivia Shakespear, and Maud Gonne. Like "To a Friend," "Friends" combines its quatrains into a single stanza that links the three women under the single category, "friends." Of its two sentences, Gregory and Shakespear share the first (sixteen lines), while Maud Gonne alone possesses the second, with twelve lines all to herself. The trimeter-quatrain form now includes not only Lady Gregory, but also Iseult and Maud Gonne and Olivia Shakespear; it has become a container for content about admired women.

To these four "aristocratic" females, *The Wild Swans at Coole* adds a fifth, Yeats's wife. "On Woman" (345–346) draws George Yeats (under the figure of the Queen of Sheba) into the sphere of the *abab* trimeter quatrain. In the nine-quatrain second stanza of "On Woman," Yeats praises sexual relations both in general and in particular, and yearns, if he is to be reincarnated, to know the passion of love again. The seventh quatrain of the nine is "defective," having only three lines: the poet hopes, in the afterlife,

> To find what once I had
> And know what once I have known,
> Until I am driven mad.

Because the solitary unrhymed end-word *known* has echoes nearby in the rhyme-words of the preceding quatrain *(moon, again)*, and also of those in a subsequent quatrain *(one, Solomon)*, it does not register as phonetically unanchored. Nonetheless, the "wrongness" of this defective quatrain may hint at something "wrong" in the poet's life-situation itself. (The poem at this point has dropped its focus on George Yeats, and has "defected" to reminiscence of Yeats's passion for Maud Gonne.)

The first stanza of "On Woman" praises woman's compliance of mind, but the second stanza spends its opening energy on the pleasure of sex, expressed in the three initial disyllabic words—"Harshness," "Pleasure," and "Shudder"—that rhythmically are reversed initial feet:

> Harshness of their desire
> That made them stretch and yawn,
> Pleasure that comes with sleep,
> Shudder that made them one.

Yet the rest of the second stanza—its more powerful half—is about neither female compliance nor the shudder of sex, but rather about insomniac sufferings, the consequence of Yeats's unrequited love for Maud Gonne. He prays—in order that he may have and know her once more—for reincarnation:

> Until I am driven mad,
> Sleep driven from my bed,
> By tenderness and care,
> Pity, an aching head,
> Gnashing of teeth, despair.

The reversed initial feet here in the disyllabic "Pity" and "Gnashing" of course "undo" the earlier marital climax in "Pleasure" and "Shudder." We may feel, at the end of this poem, that George Hyde-Lees, left stranded halfway through the poem, has not actually been successfully integrated into the charmed group of female figures inhabiting Yeats's trimeter quatrains.

In June of 1914, disheartened by the political climate of Dublin, Yeats composed his first trimeter poem honoring not a woman but a male figure, his ideal nationalist native, a generic Connemara fisherman. "The Fisherman" (347–348) distinguishes its solitary and rural protagonist, to his advantage, from the base Dublin crowd. The first stanza of the poem—six quatrains—glances briefly at the fisherman himself before devoting most of its space to a slashing attack on the contemporary urban crowd, among whom Yeats sees none but the craven and the insolent, drunken knaves and common wits, who are engaged in "the beating down of the wise," resulting in "great Art beaten down." The contemptuous energy of this satiric passage risks dominating the poem, as Yeats lists

> The craven man in his seat,
> The insolent unreproved,
> And no knave brought to book
> Who has won a drunken cheer,

> The witty man and his joke
> Aimed at the commonest ear.

This rhythmic and linguistic aggressivity is opposed to the tranquillity of the first eight lines of the poem, in which we were introduced to the figure of a transparently idealized "wise and simple" fisherman, who is situated far away from the despised urban characters, and who is dangerously removed as well—by the predominatingly iambic "naïveté" of his second quatrain—from the emotional crisis which animates Yeats's subsequent passage of denigration. Yeats begins with simple iambic predominance:

> It's long since I began
> To call up to the eyes
> This wise and simple man.

Will the poem founder, we ask ourselves, by characterizing the base urban populace more vividly than the simple unlettered fisherman?

The reason "The Fisherman" does not founder is that it springs from a moment in which Yeats has found the courage to face his persistent (and aesthetically debilitating) tendency to idealize his "own race":

> All day I'd looked in the face
> What I had hoped 'twould be
> To write for my own race
> And the reality.

"To write for my own race"—one can hear in the spondee *(own race)* the poet's proprietary yearning for a blood-link to a literate and appreciative national "family." Given the unsatisfactoriness of the urban audience ("The living men that I hate"), we might expect Yeats to say, "I'll write for a subset of my own race, for the wise and simple rustic peasants"—or, as he was later to call them, "the indomitable Irishry." Such a regressive choice—one that tempted many nationalist writers—is both embraced and resisted in Yeats's poem. It is embraced as the poet—directly provoked by his "scorn" of the Dublin crowd—begins, in the first of the poem's two stanzas, to imagine a suitable man of the people, dressed in such a way that he becomes part of the landscape as he goes "To a *grey* place on a hill / In *grey* Connemara clothes" (italics mine). The second stanza (two-thirds the length of its predecessor) reprises the idealized picture of the fisherman in lines which (to our relief) become more rhythmically alive with a reversed foot and internal spondees, as the fisherman climbs a hill and casts his line into the stream. We see (I print the stresses in bold):

> a **man** . . .
> **Climb**ing **up** to a **place**
> Where **stone** is **dark** under **froth,**
> And the **down-turn** of his **wrist**
> When the **flies drop** in the **stream.**

Even this turn to physical gesture, however, would not adequately strengthen the simple figure of the fisherman against the vivacity of the base town. The poem is saved conceptually only by the two-line passage that follows, which characterizes the fisherman, astonishingly, as

> A man who does not exist,
> A man who is but a dream.

Yeats candidly admits—even bitterly asserts—that his idealized fisherman is entirely absent from actuality. But by adding that it is a matter of responsibility to imagine him into being—since dreams are also hopes, and in dreams begins responsibility—Yeats sets before the arrogant and cynical town a powerful countervalue, that of the nonexistent (but not for that reason to be forsaken) "fit audience" named by Milton. The fisherman belongs to the ultimate aristocracy—that of the Platonic Forms, those heartbreaking because unattainable "Presences" (as Yeats later named them) "that passion, piety, or affection knows / And that all heavenly glory symbolize" ("Among School Children"). However, because the fisherman is unlettered, he is an incomplete symbol for a positive nationalist future. (This deficiency will be remedied by the insistence, in Yeats's last will at the end of "The Tower," on learning and art as national values.)

What does one write for that forever-to-be-absent, but always-to-be-imagined audience? What poetic does one embrace when writing for a Platonic Form? A bold prophecy—"I shall have written him one poem"—quickly tempered by doubt—"maybe"—introduces Yeats's two desiderata for the right sort of poem. It must be passionate (at least as passionate, in a positive way, as one's negative hatred of the craven and the insolent); and it must be "cold." Satire is never "cold" enough to be objective: Yeats's picture of the Dublin crowd is really a cartoon, as caricatures must be. However, the ultimate aim of poetry is not caricature, but "accuracy with respect to the structure of reality" (Stevens).[7] Caricature, stemming from anger, may be one of the temporarily useful strategies of poetry *en passant*, but the "cold" and truthful representation of Irish reality (however complex) is what Yeats here vows to create. A "cold" poem would be as endangered by nationalist sentimentality as by satiric anger. Only by conceding the nonexistence of the ideal is the real made a possible object for an artist; yet the ideal must be kept in view in order to judge the real. Yeats's desire in *A Vision*—"To hold in a single thought reality and justice"—finds its poetic expression here at the close of "The Fisherman."

It was not until the uprising of 1916 shocked Yeats into a meditation on male heroic action that he could include warriors in his nationalist measure. "Easter 1916" (written in 1916 but held back from trade publication until 1921) brings Yeats's enjambed quatrains into the public arena, as he explores the appeal and psychic danger of heroic action. In his youth, Yeats had tended to distinguish his ego-ideal from the usual ones recommended to males by Western culture—those of the aggressive warrior or the public statesman (Achilles, Pericles). His heroes had been the passive Oisin or Fergus, those who abandon, at least for a time, the strenuous Fenian life, either to be carried off by a fairy mistress or to abdicate from the cares of the crown. Yeats's fisherman is a pastoral descendant of those figures. But the events of 1916 forced Yeats into an unwilling admiration of those nationalists whose tactics of violence he had consistently repudiated. Before 1916 he had become estranged from his activist friends, unable, when he met them on the street, to do anything more than utter— in the cardinal offense for a poet—"polite meaningless words." Once the rebels of 1916 had been transformed, by being executed, into founding heroes of Irish independence, Yeats had to puzzle out their role, admit them to his nationalist aristocracy, and adapt his female- or rural-oriented trimeter quatrains to a more public male-dominated genre, that of the political poem.

As I mentioned in Chapter I, Yeats chose his stanza-lengths (16; 24; 16; 24) and 4-line rhyme-unit in "Easter 1916" in symbolic commemoration of the date of the Easter Rising—the 24th day of the 4th month of 1916. But why were these emblematic stanzas composed in trimeters? Such a poem could equally well have been written, one might think, in tetrameter quatrains (while keeping the calendrically dictated stanza-lengths of 16 and 24 lines). Thus recast, the opening stanza of "Easter 1916" might read as follows (with apologies to Yeats):

[I have met them at close of every day,
Coming abroad with vivid faces
From counter or desk among ancient grey
Eighteenth-century Dublin houses.
I have passed with a civil nod of the head,
Or brief polite meaningless words,
Or have lingered awhile and civilly said
Yet other polite meaningless words,
And thought before I had fully done
Of a mocking tale or a bitter gibe
To please a more welcome companion
Around the fire at the lamplit club,
Being certain that both they and I
But lived where the motley of fools is worn;
All that is changed, changed utterly,
Among us a terrible beauty is born.]

If we ask ourselves how this pastiche "sounds different" from "Easter 1916," we recognize the contrast between the rapidity and intensity of the trimeter quick-march of "Easter 1916" and the more sedulous and deliberate step of such tetrameters. In essence, every trimeter line has a musical "rest" at the end, a pause which is not really a pause, but which approximates the caesura in the English hexameter.[8] "Easter 1916" is easily rescripted as a poem in hexameters:

[I have met them at close of day // coming with vivid faces
From counter or desk among grey // eighteenth-century houses.]

It is in "Easter 1916" that we most clearly recognize the trimeter as half of an "epic" hexameter, as a meter therefore suited, by its literary descent, to "noble" or "epic" material. Rhymed trimeter quatrains are, however, "tighter" in construction than normal hexameters, since the rhymes at the end of lines 1 and 3 of each quatrain (here, *day* and *grey*) would not exist in the ordinary hexameter couplet (which has a rhyming word only at the end of each six-beat line). Hexameters are "speeded up" by being printed as trimeters. Yet the trimeters are strengthened by retaining the ghost of the epic hexameter, a prosodic reminiscence.

The nervous "half-lines" of "Easter 1916" are nowhere seen to better advantage than in its anomalous third stanza, a pastoral, animated by verbs, that praises, in one- or two-line glimpses, the rapidity of natural change. We are back in the world of the fisherman:

> A shadow of cloud on the stream
> Changes minute by minute;
> A horse-hoof slides on the brim,
> And a horse plashes within it;
> The long-legged moor-hens dive,
> And hens to moor-cocks call;
> Minute by minute they live:
> The stone's in the midst of all.

Swiftness of motion suits Yeats for all the lists in "Easter 1916," not only for the inventory of natural creatures just quoted but also for the four-member deictic list (in the second stanza) of "that woman" and "this man" and "this other" and "this other man," each of whom has to be outlined in a thumbnail sketch explicit enough to enable us to attach the appropriate name to three of them when we come to the drumroll at the end: "MacDonagh and MacBride / And Connolly and Pearse." Tetrameters (or, worse, pentameters) would drag the enumeration of the natural creatures or the human characters out to tedious length. Let us do the pastoral creatures in "Wordsworthian" pentameters:

> [A horse hoof quiet-sliding on the brim,
> The horse himself there plashing in the stream,
> The moor-hens, long-legg'd as they slowly dive,
> The moor-cocks, hearkening to the crying hens,
> All live in time as minutes pass them by,
> And in their midst we find the silent stone.]

No impression of "changing minute by minute" could survive in the stately breadth of such pentameters. Trimeter is Yeats's "lively" or "quick" form.

As we have seen in "The Fisherman" and "Easter 1916," Yeats began to admit men to the "aristocratic" nationalist company of earlier trimeter-quatrain poems. He also added a further nationalist woman to the female pantheon—"that woman," Constance Markiewicz. The next persons to be brought into the realm of the trimeter *abab* quatrain are two "noble" siblings, Mabel Beardsley and her brother, the artist Aubrey Beardsley. Mabel Beardsley, ill with cancer and visited kindly and regularly by Yeats, is the subject of the seven-part *Wild Swans* sequence (362–367) called "Upon a Dying Lady" (not, we should note, "Upon a Dying Woman"; Yeats emphasizes Mabel's aristocracy of soul). Two of its seven parts—"Her Race" (V) and "Her Friends Bring Her a Christmas Tree" (VII)—are written in "perfect" *abab* quatrains; two slightly irregular other parts, II and IV, might be included with them.⁹ "Her Race" (365)—the first of the *abab* sections—describes, in a single three-quatrain sentence, Mabel's lofty impenitence and her resemblance in "valour" to her dead brother, Aubrey. The technical interest of "Her Race" lies in its studied alternation of feminine and masculine rhymes, chosen in tribute, I think, to Mabel and Aubrey, since the poem mentions them both. In the second of these two *abab* sections—VII, the closing poem, a three-quatrain, two-sentence address to death (366–367)—the poet asks the "great enemy" to pardon Mabel's friends for decorating a Christmas tree for her, and to grant her a little more time to live, in spite of her gallant gaiety which might be resented by Death:

> Give her a little grace,
> What if a laughing eye
> Have looked into your face?
> It is about to die.

Yeats lightens his trimeters here by confining himself chiefly to monosyllables. Of the sixty words of poem VII, only ten are polysyllabic, and nine of those have only two syllables; Mabel's verse is almost as frail as she.

What else did the trimeter alternately rhymed quatrain mean to Yeats, in addition to its link, in his mind, to gallant women, revolutionary nationalist men, and nationalist Platonic Forms such as the fisherman? We know that he prized this sort of quatrain, taken singly, for its epigrammatic quality, as we can see by looking briefly forward to a four-line epigram called "Youth and Age" (434) in *The Tower* (1928). In a significant shift, the initial trochees in lines 1–2 (used when the poet himself is the subject of the verb) subside into initial iambs in lines 3–4 (when the servile world possesses the agency). The quatrain thus is made to exemplify rhythmically the speaker's truculent youth followed by his "flattered" age:

> **Much** did I rage when young,
> **Being** by the world oppressed,
> But **now** with flattering tongue
> It **speeds** the parting guest.

The later epigram "Spilt Milk" also depends on the tension of the free-standing *abab* trimeter quatrain.

The epigrammatic possibilities of the trimeter quatrain were in fact never absent from Yeats's mind, and he calls on them in a single-stanza, two-sentence, three-quatrain epigram called "Death" (476). It commemorates yet another nationalist hero—The O'Rahilly, who was assassinated in 1927. The epigram, sometimes coarse in substance, is a genre basically aristocratic in attitude; and Yeats, in the first quatrain (chiastic, and thereby doubly epigrammatic) of the elegy "Death," elevates man by distinguishing human emotional awareness before death from the state of beasts, who are unaware of their approaching end:

> Nor dread nor hope attend
> A dying animal;
> A man awaits his end
> Dreading and hoping all[.]

The poem "violates" the unity of its next quatrain by splitting it into two sentences. A period concludes a two-line vatic utterance about man:

> Many times he died,
> Many times rose again.

The two following lines, which complete that quatrain, are absorbed into a five-line exemplum exhibiting the heroism of the "great man" about to be murdered, who, far from exhibiting the alternating dread and hope that attend ordinary men at such a moment, derides the death he sees before him:

> A great man in his pride
> Confronting murderous men
> Casts derision upon
> Supersession of breath;
> He knows death to the bone—

The final line—"Man has created death"—also "violates" the unity of the quatrain in which it occurs. It departs unexpectedly from the preceding narrative of the "great man" in order to pronounce a philosophical paradox: that since no one has experienced death and lived to tell the tale, "death" is merely a man-made concept. ("Death's not an event in life, it's not lived through," wrote Robert Lowell in a late sonnet, paraphrasing Wittgenstein.)

Given that the first six lines of the twelve-line "Death" describe the ordinary man's dread and hope, and the last six the great man's derision of death, why did Yeats not divide the poem into two stanzas? I think the poem is printed as a single stanza because the great man's aristocratic scorn can be adequately valued only as it surpasses the ordinary man's fluctuating "dread and hope." And the emotional reactions of *both* the ordinary *and* the extraordinary man must be evaluated against the absence of conscious emotions in dying animals. The three distinct categories—animals, ordinary men, and great men—mutually define each other, and therefore belong in the same single-stanza epigram. Moreover, if we look more closely, we can see that after five lines about the "great" man, Yeats returns in the last line to "man" in general—not the specific "a man" ("any man, except a great one") with whom he had begun, but "man" in the sense of "mankind," the race of men. As a culture, we have "created death"—elaborated the concepts, rituals, and myths attendant on the word. It means only what we choose to ascribe to it. The "great" man perhaps understands this truth, since "He knows death to the bone." He can therefore, unlike his fellowmen, scorn death as mere "supersession of breath"—the suppression of a purely biological function, unimportant by contrast to fortitude of spirit.

How does Yeats use the trimeter after employing it to embrace his triple nationalist pantheon of "aristocratic" women, noble men (eventually including Mohini Chatterjee, in the poem called by his name—a name that is, as Deirdre Toomey remarked, itself a perfect trimeter), and Platonic Forms? At the age of sixty, choosing the trimeter quatrain for his own last testament (as he closes "The Tower," 414–416), Yeats daringly makes this terse prosodic measure, with its lingering overtones of the persons earlier commemorated within it, an autobiographical form. He begins by imagining his heirs:

> It is time that I wrote my will;
> I choose upstanding men
> That climb the streams until
> The fountain leap, and at dawn
> Drop their cast at the side
> Of dripping stone.

Yeats explains the return of the fisherman (here in plural form) by asserting that in his youth he was one of those athletic youths, "Being of that metal made / Till it was broken by / This sedentary trade." It is assumed here that the young fly-fishers will somehow follow their testator's trajectory of study, and that they too will become acquainted with "learned Italian things / And the proud stones of Greece, / Poet's imaginings / And memories of love."

As we scan Yeats's trimeter will to its end, we see that it consists of nineteen quatrains, but that its last quatrain is defective: it lacks a fourth line. The "missing" line, like the comparable "missing" line in Yeats's three-line (once four-line) self-epitaph, stands on the page for the cessation of the speaker's breath, the death of his voice. The will is composed in four stanzas of different lengths, which exhibit two anomalies: the first stanza breaks off after the first line of the thirteenth quatrain, and, as I have said, the last stanza lacks one line at the close. The anomalous break between stanzas 1 and 2 helps to make the truncated and brief second stanza—which departs from the rhetoric of will-making to speak about the jackdaw's nest in Yeats's tower—an odd and unsettling one. It consists of only seven lines, since its "first" line has been appropriated by stanza 1. (The equally brief third stanza, by contrast, consists of two regular quatrains and is entirely self-contained and stable.) The strange second stanza on the jackdaw departs from the bequest-substance of the will in much the same way as, in "Easter 1916," the anomalous third stanza of the changing natural creatures departs from the historical matter of the rest of the poem. These stanzas, in both "Easter 1916" and "The Tower," are pastoral escape-hatches, in which "animals" who neither dread nor hope, but exist solely in instinctual motion (including perhaps "the rider" in "Easter 1916"), show us the life we might live were we not compelled by consciousness to go beyond animal existence. In the twelfth quatrain of Yeats's will, we have just heard how "Man" creates for himself "a superhuman / Mirror-resembling dream." Yeats then gives a humble natural analogue to man's formidable construction of art, in the anomalous seven-line second stanza (which begins with a sentence-fragment):[10] man makes his mirror-dream just as, by a comparable instinct, the jackdaws chatter and make nests:

> As at the loophole there
> The daws chatter and scream,
> And drop twigs layer upon layer.
> When they have mounted up,

> The mother bird will rest
> On their hollow top
> And so warm her wild nest.

It is by surprises such as this unexpected parallel between "poet's imag-inings" and intentionless instinctual behavior that Yeats makes his last will "cold" as well as "passionate." We may be more than animals, but we are also animals; and what the mother bird does—brood and sit—when the twigs have mounted up is what the artist does when he has accumulated learning and memories. The poet, by such an analogy—made conspicuous by its isolation in a single truncated stanza—bequeaths to his successors not only the spiritual values of faith and pride, but also the instinctual values of warmth and generative power.

A look at Yeats's closing trimeter quatrains in "The Tower" enables us to see his resolution of the deep oscillation, in his final testament, between a "high" polysyllabic language of metaphysical intellectuality and a "low" monosyllabic language of earthy simplicity. Most of the end-words in this part of the poem are monosyllabic, even when the poet is speaking of Plato and Plotinus:

> I mock Plotinus' thought
> And cry in Plato's teeth,
> Death and life were not
> Till man made up the whole,
> Made lock, stock and barrel
> Out of his bitter soul.

Trimeter quatrains are at their most ringing when they offer forceful speech-acts (such as mocking and crying out) framed by sharp-chiseled, largely monosyllabic, end-words such as "teeth" and "whole." Although from time to time we see Yeats departing from such terse end-appearances to murmur in reverie of a *"Translunar Paradise"* or a *"superhuman / Mirror-resembling dream,"* we conclude from the vigorous monosyllables above that it is a strong, plain-speaking man with a strong will who has been declaring his legacies in this final testament.

But now the effortful will-making must subside gradually into the si-lence of the last moments of life, and the trimeter quatrains must adjust ac-cordingly. Yeats changes the direction of his poem as the outer-directed speech-act of bequest—"I leave"—gives way, once all the bequests are done, to the inner-directed resolve, "Now shall I make my soul." As Yeats contemplates what he may have to face in the future, he composes an unforgettable passage, hierarchically ordered, that compiles a rising list of end-life disasters that begins—begins!—with "the wreck of body." After the body is wrecked, what worse thing can happen, the reader asks, except death itself? But Yeats's relentless ascending list of losses presses on:

> Now shall I make my soul,
> Compelling it to study
> In a learned school
> Till the wreck of body,
> Slow decay of blood,
> Testy delirium
> Or dull decrepitude,
> Or what worse evil come—

Yeats's genius for specificity of language carries this list. After the wreck of the body comes impotence ("slow decay of blood," in which the Latin root of "decay" means "to fall down"); then irritable forgetfulness ("delirium" means "to stray from the proper furrow"); then absence of mental capacity in "dull decrepitude" (the Latin root of "decrepitude" means "to crack or break"). We can see that Yeats—after his earlier sharp monosyllables—is here, to great effect, summoning powerful quadrisyllabic "learned" words: *delirium, decrepitude*. It is horrifying that after this catalogue Yeats can muse, "Or what worse evil come." What could possibly be worse than decay, delirium, and decrepitude? He answers, with a fourth alliterating *"d,"* "The death of friends"—those friends, female and male, honored so often in earlier trimeter-quatrain poems that they now slip effortlessly into his memory and ours:

> Or what worse evil come—
> The death of friends, or death
> Of every brilliant eye
> That made a catch in the breath—

Even beyond the death of friends, there is the worst evil, the unimaginable chief one—the "death / Of every brilliant eye / That made a catch in the breath." Maud Gonne had not yet died, nor had some of Yeats's other lovers; but he could imagine a later time of old age in which not one woman—

among those whose beauty had aroused him aesthetically and sexually—remained alive. The heavy vowels in the end-words of Yeats's inventory of evils seem like the dull sounds of clods of earth falling into a grave: *study, body, blood, delirium, decrepitude, come.*

Of course there is a recovery of sound at the end of the passage, in "the hour / When the swan must fix his eye / Upon a fading gleam." Eventually, in the elegiac but "cold" ending of the poem, all the dreadful evils

> Seem but the clouds of the sky
> When the horizon fades,
> Or a bird's sleepy cry
> Among the deepening shades.

By using two progressive verbs—"to fade" (of the horizon) and "to deepen" (of the shades), both of them implying a gradual decline of the seeable—Yeats shows us his sight, and the light, dimming before our eyes. Finally, through the unobtrusively "missing" last line (concealed by making the "*b*" rhyme of the last, defective "quatrain" accord with the "*b*" rhymes of the preceding quatrain), he lets his body die and his voice fall silent.

Each of the last two stanzas of the poem—the two-quatrain summary last will ("I leave both faith and pride / To young upstanding men") and the "four"-quatrain stoic soul-making—is a single sentence, and each displays the unsettling counterpoint in which sense-unit and quatrain-unit do not coincide. In the summary bequest of faith and pride, the sense-units consist of five and three lines; by contrast, in the passage on soul-making and the evils of life's end-stage, the ever-enjambed quatrains do not permit separate sense-units. The brilliant late rhyme-words are, at first, not exact but slant; but nonetheless they are (while the poet's intellect is still unharmed) concordant in being either monosyllabic ("soul" and "school") or disyllabic ("study" and "body"). However, with the decay of sexual energy and of mind itself, the rhymes become visibly discordant not only in syllable-count but also in semantic category: "blood" and "decrepitude"; "delirium" and "come." But then, as the poem readies itself to subside into silence, the rhymes, reflecting the cleared, if fading, consciousness of the last moments, suddenly become not only semantically concordant but also entirely monosyllabic, and perfectly consonant in sound: "death" and "breath"; "eye" and "sky" and "cry"; "fades" and "shades."

The trimeter alternately rhymed quatrain has become in Yeats's hands, by the time of "The Tower," a wonderfully expressive medium joining him

and his friends. Of course he used other meters as well for his national-
ist "Olympians"—*ottava rima* in the late elegies "Coole Park, 1929" and
"Coole Park and Ballylee, 1931"; unrhymed hexameters in "Beautiful Lofty
Things." But he chose the trimeter quatrain for his own last will, and that
fact alone suggests the importance, to the poet, of this form that he had so
renovated, with its elevated aura stemming from its relation to epic hexam-
eter, and its subject matter moving from the aristocratic ideal that Yeats
welcomed when he found it in women to the more recalcitrant subject, for
him, of violent action on the part of men. The fact that he could also em-
body in the trimeter quatrain the Platonic form of the fisherman who does
not exist means that the conceptual reach of this form became, for him,
very wide. That he could, in his last use of the form, let it serve as the vehi-
cle of his own voice making his will and making his soul proves that it was a
form as intimate to him as any that he used. Because Yeats "invented" the
trimeter quatrain as a major form in English verse, it is more closely identi-
fied with him, and with Ireland, than the ready-made inherited forms that
he embraced—the tetrameter couplet, blank verse, the ballad, the hexame-
ter, the *ottava rima* stanza, the sonnet, the douzain, rhyme royal. Through
the passion and ingenuity with which he used it, the trimeter *abab* quatrain
became Yeats's nationalist vehicle *par excellence,* and the poems he chose to
cast in it need to be recognized as a group defining, for Yeats, modern Irish
forms of nobility.

# APPENDIX: List of Yeats's *abab* Trimeter-Quatrain Poems

Yeats's seventeen poems or sequence-segments written between 1912 and 1932 in *abab* (mostly iambic) trimeter quatrains are the following. They are listed in the order of placement in the *Variorum Poems,* but with dates of composition (if known, and if occurring in a different year from first printing) or first printing added.

Key:

[*abab* × a number] = number of run-on quatrains before stanza break
(*abab* indicates the presence of quatrain-structure, not the actual rhymes, which, in run-on quatrains, are normally labelled *ababcdcd,* etc.)

+ = a stanza break, followed by the next stanza

(m) = masculine rhyme

(f) = feminine rhyme
("m and 4f", e.g., means a poem in which all rhymes are masculine except for 4 rhymes which are feminine)

When a fractional number follows *abab* (e.g., *abab* × 11 1/4), it denotes that there is a stanza break following the first line of the twelfth quatrain.

A starred quatrain is one that is missing a line ("On Woman," "Upon a Dying Lady" II, and "The Tower" III).

The poem's first printed title, if different from that in *CP,* is given in brackets.

If a poem was printed (e.g., in a Cuala Press volume or in a journal) before its publication in a trade volume, I name the place of earlier publication, using the conventional abbreviations for Yeats's volumes (e.g., *GH* means *The Green Helmet*).

*RESPONSIBILITIES* (1913)

"To a Friend Whose Work has Come To Nothing" [*abab* × 4] (m) [*Poems Written in Discouragement,* 1913]

"To a Child Dancing [on the Shore] in the Wind" [*abab* × 3] (m) [*Poetry,* Dec. 1912]

"Friends" [*abab* × 7] (m) [1911; *GH,* 1912]

"The Dolls" [*abab* × 5] (m) [1914]

## The Wild Swans at Coole (1917)

"On Woman" [abab × 2] + [abab × 6] + [aba]* + [abab × 2] (m and 4 f) [1914; *Poetry*, Feb. 1916]

"The Fisherman" [abab × 6] + [abab × 4] (m) [1914; *Poetry*, Feb. 1916]

"Upon a Dying Lady" [1912–1914; *The Little Review*, Aug. 1917]
    II      [abab × 3, *the second quatrain defective by one line] (mfmfmfmfmfm)
    IV    [abab × 2, the last b-rhyme-word the same as the first] (m)
    V     [abab × 3] (fmfm)
    VII   [abab × 3] (m)

## Michael Robartes and the Dancer (1921)

"Easter 1916" [abab × 4] + [abab × 6] + [abab × 4] + [abab × 6] (m and 4 f) [1916; *New Statesman*, Oct. 1920]

## The Tower (1928)

"The Tower" III [abab × 11 1/4] + [abab × 1 3/4] + [abab × 2] + [abab × 3 3/4]* (m and 8 f) [1925; *New Republic*, June 1927]

"Youth and Age" [abab] (m) [*The Cat and the Moon*, 1924]

## The Winding Stair (1933)

"Death" [abab × 3] (m) [1927; *The Winding Stair*, 1929]

"Spilt Milk" [abab] (m) [1930; *Words for Music Perhaps*, 1932]

"Mohini Chatterjee" [abab × 2 3/4] + [abab × 4 1/4] (m) [*Packet for EP*, 1929]

"Quarrel in Old Age" [abab × 4] (m + 2 f) [1931; *Words for Music Perhaps*, 1932]

## VIII

## ⌒ MARCHES AND THE EXAMINATION
## OF CONSCIENCE: THE TETRAMETER LINE

The four-beat line, appearing without an intermixture of lines of dif-
fering length, occurs early in Yeats. Some of its first manifestations—faint
and wavering rhythms of Paterian impressionism, and Swinburnian dance-
rhythms with heady alliteration—did not prove lasting. But other versions
of the tetrameter—iambic, trochaic, or a mixture of these two rhythms—
appeared in Yeats's poems for years. The line, intermediate in length be-
tween the rapid trimeter and the ceremonious pentameter, proved adapt-
able to many rhyme-units and to stanzas of different lengths. The number
of Yeats's tetrameter poems precludes offering a complete list of them, as
one can for his sonnets, trimeter quatrains, blank verse, and *ottava rima* po-
ems. The central examples I take up in this chapter will, I hope, justify my
title; Yeats's tetrameters can be used sternly or decisively or interrogatively,
but also musically, gently, and epigrammatically. There is very little they
cannot do.

Yeats used the tetrameter line in any number of stanza forms. He
shapes it, for instance, into couplets in both "Under Ben Bulben" and "The
Man and the Echo," but to very different rhythmic effect. In "Under Ben
Bulben," after some commanding initial trochees, the couplets *(aa)* become
predominantly iambic:

> Under bare Ben Bulben's head
> In Drumcliff churchyard Yeats is laid,
> An ancestor was rector there
> Long years ago; a church stands near[.]
>
> (640)

By contrast, in "The Man and the Echo" incisive and insistent trochaic cou-
plets predominate:

> Did that play of mine send out
> Certain men the English shot?
>
> (632)

The tetrameter line can also be used to create attractive quatrain-forms. In his elegy for the Gore-Booth sisters, Yeats shapes the line into embraced quatrains, *abba* (the "In Memoriam" stanza):

> The light of evening, Lissadell,
> Great windows open to the south,
> Two girls in silk kimonos, both
> Beautiful, one a gazelle.
>
> (475)

In "Lapis Lazuli" he once again uses the tetrameter line for rhymed quatrains, but this time they are rhymed alternately, *abab*, bringing the stanza close in feeling to the ballad:

> Two Chinamen, behind them a third,
> Are carved in lapis lazuli,
> Over them flies a long-legged bird
> A symbol of longevity[.]
>
> (566)

These (as Wallace Stevens would say) are only indications. Between 1866 (with Book I of "The Wanderings of Oisin") and 1938, Yeats wrote some eighty poems using the four-beat line, without any consistent adherence to a single rhyme-form or stanza-unit. He groups the tetrameter line not only into couplets and quatrains, but also into cinquains, sixains, septets, octaves, and stanzas longer than octaves, of which the longest ("The Players Ask for a Blessing," 1902) runs to twenty lines of uninterrupted interwoven rhymes. Before looking at whole poems, it is useful to examine the nature of this line, in part by comparing it with its flanking lines in the prosodic spectrum (trimeter on the left, pentameter on the right), in part by seeing how it is modified by the rhyme-units and stanza-units into which it is gathered, in part by a comparative glance at the rhyme-units (such as the ballad stanza) in which it alternates with trimeter.

What do we notice first about the external form of a poem—the length of its line, the rhythm of its line, its terminal rhymes, the rhyme-units into which lines are grouped, or the shape of its stanza? When rhythm is emphasized, as in the emphatic trochaic opening of "Under Ben Bulben," that insistent ictus may strike us first. And when the poem is written in couplets, as "Under Ben Bulben" is, the rhyme-unit, too, is thrust at us immediately, complete by the second line. In fact, we would hear the opening of "Ben Bulben" very differently if it did not call us to almost military attention with its insistent first-line trochees, its instantly apparent couplet-form, and its strong monosyllabic rhyme of *head* and *laid*. Let us suppose that the opening lines began with iambs rather than trochees, were arranged not in couplets but in *abab* quatrains, and had some feminine rhymes:

> [Beside Ben Bulben, in tale long storied,
> And where an ancient church stands near,
> In Drumcliff churchyard Yeats is buried;
> An ancestor was rector there.]

Such an iambic alternately rhymed quatrain, although in tetrameter like Yeats's original lines, would hardly demand instant alertness. Unlike couplets, quatrains do not declare themselves right away. When we read, for instance, the gentle first two lines of the Gore-Booth elegy, "The light of evening, Lissadell, / Great windows open to the south," the quatrain stanza form of the poem has not yet been established, and we are invited into the poem rather than summoned to obey it.

We can try to determine, looking at some of the four-beat poems, why Yeats cast certain imaginative materials into this line, and why, in each particular case, he chose the specific rhythmic form, rhyme-unit form, and stanza form for the poem in question. We need first to have a sense of the tetrameter quatrain (Yeats's most common grouping of the four-beat line, 4-4-4-4) by distinguishing it from its two chief competitors among Yeats's poems, the ballad stanza (4-3-4-3) and the trimeter quatrain (3-3-3-3). The ballad stanza has a musical "rest" after every other line, a natural voice-pause useful for paced storytelling:

> The old priest Peter Gilligan
> Was weary night and day; [*rest*]
> For half his flock were in their beds,
> Or under green sods lay. [*rest*]
> (132)

To show the difference of effect between the tetrameter quatrain and the ballad stanza, let us try the experiment of converting the first into the second. Here is the 1922 poem "The Wheel," which interprets all human restlessness as a desire for death. It reads, in its original iambic *abab* tetrameter:

> Through winter-time we call on spring,
> And through the spring on summer call,
> And when abounding hedges ring
> Declare that winter's best of all;
> And after that there's nothing good
> Because the spring-time has not come—
> Nor know that what disturbs our blood
> Is but its longing for the tomb.[1]
>
> (434)

"The Wheel" argues that our spirit's propulsive yearning, its discontent in every condition, is in truth a longing for the ultimate quiescence of the tomb. Imagine the effect on this poem's momentum if it were forced into ballad rhythm, with a pause at the end of every other line:

> [Through winter-time we call on spring,
> In spring on summer call, [*rest*]
> And when abounding hedges ring,
> Find winter best of all; [*rest*]
> And after that there's nothing good
> For spring-time has not come— [*rest*]
> Nor know that what disturbs our blood
> Is longing for the tomb.]

Yeats, we conclude, found the four-beat line suitable for driving ongoing processes, ones that don't naturally suffer a hiatus. In the service of that momentum, Yeats has also suppressed the white space that would "normally" separate the two differently rhymed quatrains of "The Wheel"; he wants to emphasize the fact that the poem is a single uninterrupted ongoing sentence.

Just as the ballad stanza supplies a pause in every *other* line to facilitate storytelling, the trimeter quatrain (used most tellingly by Yeats in "Easter 1916") has a pause at the end of *each* line, a built-in unsounded "fourth beat" which suggests an invisible but implicit march-step: left, right, left, [*right*]:

> I write it out in a verse— [*step*]
> MacDonagh and MacBride [*step*]
> And Connolly and Pearse [*step*]
> Now and in time to be, [*step*]
> Wherever green is worn, [*step*]
> Are changed, changed utterly: [*step*]
> A terrible beauty is born.
> (394)

The march-step calls us to order, keeps us in file, and shortens the breath-line. Imagine this passage rewritten in the sing-song rhythm of the ballad stanza, and see how its military force abates:

> [I write it out in a verse: [*rest*]
> MacDonagh and his friend MacBride
> And Connolly and Pearse [*rest*]
> Now and in every time to be,
> Wherever green is worn, [*rest*]
> Are changed in substance utterly,
> A terrible beauty is born. [*rest*]]

Going a step further, imagine the original trimeter passage from "Easter 1916" amplified into four-beat lines, and see how it loses its kinetic martial tension in favor of narrative exposition:

> [I write it out in bardic verse,
> MacDonagh and the bold MacBride
> And soldiers Connolly and Pearse
> Now and in every time to be,
> Wherever green's by patriots worn,
> Are changed forever, utterly,
> A terrible beauty is newly born.]

In both of the original cases above—driving tetrameter for "The Wheel" and peremptory martial trimeter for "Easter 1916"—Yeats's choice of meter has a distinct imaginative and mimetic advantage.

The four-beat line occupies a position between the shorter song-forms (dimeter, trimeter, ballad) and the long-breathed pentameter. Historically speaking, tetrameter can become a song ("Where the bee sucks, there suck I") or a light form of inventory ("L'Allegro"); it can also serve as a march-rhythm ("The glories of our blood and state") as it does in Yeats ("Arise and bid me strike a match"). It can, in its more unemphatic forms, direct an apparently artless narrative ("In Memory of Alfred Pollexfen"). There is always something lyric about the tetrameter, and often something expository. It can pass seamlessly, within a given poem (see "In Memory of Eva Gore-Booth"), from its lyric aspect to its expository or martial one. Yeats delighted in its varieties.

In looking at a few of Yeats's shorter tetrameter poems, investigating what (besides momentum, lyric feeling, and expository sense) the four-beat line brings out in each case, I will be treating the line as embedded in a stanza form which also, more often than not, bears symbolic meaning for Yeats. And the line is necessarily embedded as well in the poem's internal structural evolution, which tracks its emotional development.

## Early Tetrameter Poems

The best-known, and most beautiful, example of tetrameter among Yeats's early poems is "The Song of Wandering Aengus" (1897), already discussed in some detail in Chapter IV. The poem is a myth of origin, which answers the question, "Why must Aengus forever wander; what is he restlessly seeking?" Aengus sings of his vision of a magical girl, who vanishes as soon as he sees her; he pursues her ever after, hoping to find her at last. Here, the additive quatrains (two to a stanza) and their multiple connections in "and" act out the inevitability of the three linked stages of Aengus's poem: desire-vision-pursuit. Aengus's original burning erotic yearning, his fishing in the stream of the enchanted hazel wood, the metamorphosis of the trout that he catches into a "glimmering girl," and the consequences for his life all follow a fated course. I repeat here, to illustrate these qualities, the first stanza and the closing lines:

> I went out to the hazel wood
> Because a fire was in my head,
> And cut and peeled a hazel wand,
> And hooked a berry to a thread;
> And when white moths were on the wing,

And moth-like stars were flickering out,
I dropped the berry in a stream
And caught a little silver trout.

. . . . .

I will find out where she has gone,
And kiss her lips and take her hands;
And walk among long dappled grass,
And pluck till time and times are done
The silver apples of the moon,
The golden apples of the sun.

(149–150)

The enchained paratactic form of the opening stanza ("I went out . . . / *And* cut *and* peeled . . . / *And* hooked . . . / *And* caught") is still in play at the end: "I will find out . . . / *And* kiss her lips *and* take her hands; / *And* walk . . . / *And* pluck till time and times are done / The silver apples of the moon / The golden apples of the sun." We learn from this inflexibly additive structure of concatenation, matching the tetrameter momentum, that the impress taken from a first love forever determines the way our future is shaped. We might ask why the determining passionate event—the first sight of the beloved, the "glimmering girl"—is delayed until the halfway point of the poem. The first half of the poem, we find, is occupied by that rationalizing chain of prefiguration that we construct after the fact, once we have been smitten by a crucial encounter. In poetry, such convergent prefigurings, prefacing the charmed vision, create an atmosphere of purposive magic: the symbolic *fire* in *wand*ering Aengus's head leads him to the *hazel*wood with its *hazel wand,* which leads to the berry, which leads to the fish, which leads to the real *fire* on the hearth, which leads to the girl who calls the speaker "by [his] name," that name revealed at the beginning, in the title.

The quatrains of "The Song of Wandering Aengus" are "imperfect" ones: that is, they rhyme *abcb* rather than *abab*. In this they resemble the basic ballad quatrain, giving the poem an air of folk-verse appropriate to the story it tells. In spite of its rhyme-units being quatrains, the poem is arranged in stanzas of eight lines. This strategy keeps the links of enchainment close; it also reduces the graphic look of the poem, as we saw earlier, from what would have been six separate quatrains to three schematic stanza-phases: prefiguration, incarnation, aspiration. The expanding shape of this pattern—announced in the increasingly lucent "brightening" and continued in the future-tense verbs of the close—enacts not only Aengus's yearning hope for a rediscovery of his beloved but also the ever-widening terrain of his wandering, "through hollow lands and hilly lands." Reading "The Song of Wandering Aengus," we understand Yeats's intention to create an abstract and stylized version of the enchained, uncheckable, enlarging, and idealizing aspects of falling in love—together with the frustration of its perpetually postponed conclusion. All aspects here work ardently together: the primitive "and"-linkage of the sequential events, the ballad-like rhyme scheme, the three octaves of unfolding erotic desire, the hope suggested by *brightening* (countered by the terminal elusiveness embodied in *faded*), and, above all, the steady unshakable ongoing momentum of the four-beat lines.

Although a second early four-beat poem, "Who Goes with Fergus?" (1892)—also treated more fully in Chapter IV—raises the same hope of otherworldly adventure as "Aengus," it is very different both in mood (one is urged to reject love's "bitter mystery") and in formal shape (two *abcabc* sixains). Yet this poem too relies on a paratactic syntax and the propulsive force of the tetrameter to frame its invitation to the young to leave the frustrating erotic world for the better otherworld of Fergus, the king who has abdicated his throne. At the close, however, Yeats departs from the horizontal tetrameter propulsion governing the poem to that point, and allows the line to "go vertical" with its gaze at the stars:

> Who will go drive with Fergus now,
> And pierce the deep wood's woven shade,
> And dance upon the level shore?
> . . . . .
> For Fergus rules the brazen cars,
> And rules the shadows of the wood,
> And the white breast of the dim sea,
> And all dishevelled wandering stars.
>
> (125–126)

The vertical moment rises beyond chariots and woods and sea to the unknown, the unordered, the yet-to-be charted stars. Yeats here plays the ongoing momentum of the tetrameter—begun by a strong initial beat, "**Who** will go drive"—against its more temperate expository form in his closing reprise ("For Fergus rules . . . sea"). But in the close he allows the tetrameter to resume its driving force with the unexpected lift skyward, thereby demonstrating his understanding of the energetic—but interruptible—potential of the line.

Remembering (perhaps from "L'Allegro") the suitability of the tetrameter couplet for making an inventory, list, or catalogue, Yeats calls on it in "He Remembers Forgotten Beauty" (1896), for the lover's enumeration of items representing "the loveliness / That has long faded from the world":

> The jewelled crowns that kings have hurled
> In shadowy pools, when armies fled;
> The love-tales wrought with silken thread
> By dreaming ladies upon cloth
> That has made fat the murderous moth;
> The roses that of old time were
> Woven by ladies in their hair . . .²
>
> (155–156)

Unlike Milton, who contains his inventory-items within their couplets ("To hear the lark begin his flight, / And singing, startle the dull night"), Yeats, in the case of the first item here, divides the two-line meaning between two couplets ("hurled" does not rhyme with "fled"); in the second, he enlarges his description of the item beyond the couplet-frame ("thread," "cloth," "moth"); only in the third ("were," "hair") does he make item and couplet coincide as they "ought" to do. The lovely potential "neatness" of tetrameter couplets, so salient in "L'Allegro" (a characteristic that Yeats will make good use of in "The Man and the Echo"), is here consistently avoided, not only by the non-coincidence of item and rhyme-unit but also by enjambment within and over items in the list. In spite of such deliberate counterpointing of sense to rhyme-unit, however, the iambs of "He Remembers Forgotten Beauty," in their "dream-heavy" regularity, fall back into a lulling habitual tetrameter beat that even Yeats's reversed or spondaic feet, irregularities of inventory, and frequent enjambment cannot overcome:

> For that pale breast and lingering hand
> Come from a more dream-heavy land,
> A more dream-heavy hour than this;
> And when you sigh from kiss to kiss
> I hear white Beauty sighing, too,
> For hours when all must fade like dew.
>
> (156)

Drowsy with dreams, this early tetrameter sings its lists in a single tone, a repetitive music.

## The Middle Tetrameter

It was not until his middle period, when social concerns entered his poetry as an overt subject, and the writing of plays energized his syntax and diction, that Yeats (influenced by Swift's fluent tetrameter practice) infused into his tetrameters satiric drive and wit. When it came to politics, Yeats found the hard-driving pulse of the four-beat line useful, and he began to revel in its polemic potential when it is shaped into forcibly enjambed quatrains that omit, for the most part, white space between rhyme-units. In the rapid "perfect" quatrains (abab) of "To a Wealthy Man Who Promised a Second Subscription to the Dublin Municipal Gallery If It Were Proved the People Wanted Pictures" (dated by Yeats 1912),[3] Yeats takes advantage of the relative swiftness of the enjambed four-beat line (when it uses hypotactic rather than paratactic syntax) to make a quick scan of commendable aesthetic production over time. Greece provides the Western world with a matrix of logic, law, and art; Plautus writes his Latin plays centuries before Christ; a Renaissance prince, Duke Ercole of Ferrara, offers his own copy of Plautus to his "mummers" so that they might, by imitating Roman comedy, begin a vernacular theater; Castiglione reports a comparable patronage of the arts in Urbino by Guidobaldo da Montefeltro; and Yeats comments that these patrons looked to nourish Italian logic, law, and art not only from the indigenous example of classical Rome (as Romulus and Remus were suckled by a "Roman" wolf), but that the Italian warlord-patrons also became cultivated "By sucking at the dugs of Greece." The poet urges these ancient and Renaissance models on the "wealthy man" who has said that he will fund a gallery for the pictures in the Lane bequest only if it can be "proved" that the people of Dublin "want pictures."

Yeats divides his poem—we don't at first know why—into two grossly unequal parts, the first of twenty-eight lines, the second of only eight. Before the poem launches itself into its historical narrative about the Italian patronage-system, it offers an eight-line single-sentence derisive "modern" prelude about the wealthy man, which might, we think on our first reading, have been printed as a detached stanza about the wealthy man's miserliness, to match the closing eight-line coda urging the wealthy man to give, to patronize the arts of today. The first sentence of the poem, describing the

Irish patron's truculent and hectoring demand, uses its enjambed four-beat lines to mimic that pitiful adding of "Paudeen's" pence to "Biddy's" half-pence which will (according to the wealthy man) supposedly summon his withheld guineas. The successive strata of monetary contributions, little and big, are mimicked, piece by piece, in Yeats's syntax—"You will not give again / Until enough [pence and halfpennies] / have lain / To be . . . 'evidence' / Before you'll put your guineas down":

> To a Wealthy Man Who Promised a Second Subscription
> to the Dublin Municipal Gallery If It Were
> Proved the People Wanted Pictures
>
> You gave, but will not give again
> Until enough of Paudeen's pence
> By Biddy's halfpennies have lain
> To be 'some sort of evidence',
> Before you'll put your guineas down,
> That things it were a pride to give
> Are what the blind and ignorant town
> Imagines best to make it thrive.

After this contemporary sketch of withheld support, the remaining twenty lines of the first stanza hurtle through history. Their continually run-on lines, their suppression of white space between quatrains, and their sentences flagrantly overflowing the rhyme-units are all formal indices of the "magnificence"—the overflowing generosity—that Yeats ascribes to Renaissance patrons. At a headlong pace, the poem unscrolls its proper nouns—Duke Ercole, Plautus, Guidobaldo, Urbino, Cosimo, Michelozzo, the San Marco Library, Italy, Greece. The bit-players in this cinematic scanning of past munificence are the ignorant populace: the "onion sellers" in the Ferrara marketplace, the shepherds around Urbino, the rancorous crowds of Florentines who drove Cosimo de' Medici into exile. (These anonymous members of the populace are the counterparts of the contemporary "blind and ignorant" "Paudeen" and "Biddy" of the opening lines, who, according to the wealthy man, had shown no "evidence" of wanting pictures.)

The historical chronicle in this stanza reveals Yeats's tendency to make sense-units "grow" as the poem grows: here, the five lines concerning Duke Ercole are followed by the six lines describing Guidobaldo, themselves exceeded by the nine lines devoted to Cosimo (I mark with underlining the formal divisions between quatrains):

> What cared Duke Ercole, that bid
> His mummers to the market-place,
> What th'onion-sellers thought or did
> <u>So that his Plautus set the pace</u>
> For the Italian comedies?
> And Guidobaldo, when he made
> That grammar school of courtesies
> <u>Where wit and beauty learned their trade</u>
> Upon Urbino's windy hill,
> Had sent no runners to and fro
> That he might learn the shepherds' will.
> <u>And when they drove out Cosimo,</u>
> Indifferent how the rancour ran,
> He gave the hours they had set free
> To Michelozzo's latest plan
> <u>For the San Marco Library,</u>
> Whence turbulent Italy should draw
> Delight in Art whose end is peace,
> In logic and in natural law
> By sucking at the dugs of Greece.

Each of the three patrons—Duke Ercole of Ferrara, Guidobaldo da Montefeltro, and Cosimo de' Medici—appears in energetic action in a single, self-contained, and syntactically complex hypotactic sentence. These three sentences are therefore to be viewed as offering parallel exempla, as simultaneous ventures of that historical Renaissance moment in which civic sponsorship of the classics of Greece and Rome brought "turbulent Italy" to a "delight in Art whose end is peace." We now understand—as we did not at first—why the wealthy man must inhabit the *same* stanza as the Renaissance nobles: his mean-spirited condition for his donation is the negative parallel to the open-handedness of the Italian patrons. The wealthy man is forced to "live" in the same opening stanza as the Renaissance lords; he is to be shamed by being brought into "their" stanza, "shown up" by the vignettes of his more generous predecessors.

The shape of "To a Wealthy Man," then, is a dialectic rather than a linear one. The poem sets forth two opposite options for the rich man ("will not give" and "Give!") flanking a triple set of historical models:

> A:  Your current (bad) choice ("will not give")
>      *vs.* those whose (good) choice was to give
>      Ercole . . . Guidobaldo . . . Cosimo
> B:  Your future (good) choice ("Give!")

Yeats, ever conscious of structure, ends his poem with a separate two-quatrain coda of contemporary exhortation, an end-frame corresponding exactly in length to the two-quatrain contemporary opening-frame:

> Your open hand but shows our loss,
> For he [Cosimo] knew better how to live.
> Let Paudeens play at pitch and toss,
> Look up in the sun's eye and give
> What the exultant heart calls good
> That some new day may breed the best
> Because you gave, not what they would,
> But the right twigs for an eagle's nest!
>
> (287–288)

Let the pence and the halfpennies of the people continue to be spent on gaming in the street, says Yeats; what is necessary is that the guineas of the wealthy man should provide the "twigs" for the nest—the Lane Gallery—that will eventually produce the young eagles of Irish art. The desired accretive piling of twig upon twig is not unlike the enumeration of Renaissance cultural exempla carried out by the four-beat lines, which never relax from their heaping of examples, extending over rhyme-units to display them. For such purposefully assembled architectural "twigs," an "imperfectly" rhymed quatrain would hardly be proper: for this construction, one that recommends the perfecting of culture, the individual quatrain-bricks must be perfect too.[4] And because the poem concerns the public issue of the Lane bequest (much discussed in the newspapers at the time), the poet—though he does not conceal his learning, and freely mentions historical examples—chooses, for the diction of his poem (and especially for its rhymes), a colloquial set of words: "down" and "town," "made" and "trade," "hill" and "will," "draw" and "law," "live" and "give." These are newspaper-level words, and the poem is an opinion-piece, its pointed satiric emphasis and its brief exempla obeying the laws of forceful journalism as well as the laws of poetry.

A wholly different use of the tetrameter in Yeats's middle period is the strange and neglected 1916 elegy in iambic/trochaic couplets, "In Memory of Alfred Pollexfen." It is a purely "private" poem, a family poem, mourning the burial the day before of "a humorous, unambitious man," Yeats's uncle Alfred. In his fifties Alfred left the indifferent city of Liverpool where he was "a nobody in a great throng," and came home to his wife and children in Sligo, where people had known him and his family since he was born. Alfred was the youngest of the seven Pollexfen brothers, the youngest in fact of the twelve Pollexfen children; his elder brother George, already dead, is buried with their parents in the Sligo tomb where Alfred too will lie. But where is a third brother, John the sea-captain of Liverpool, dead as well, but buried away from Sligo? These are the relatively unpromising materials out of which Yeats constructs his 39-line, single-stanza elegy in mixed iambic and trochaic tetrameter couplets. "In Memory of Alfred Pollexfen" is, in diction and syntax, the simplest of Yeats's elegies, although like "To a Wealthy Man" it displays the tendency of Yeats's sense-units to grow longer as a poem progresses. The gradual lengthening, we notice, is here strangely and briefly interrupted in the middle and dropped at the close: the sentences occupy 5, 7, 8, (2, 1,) 12, and 4 lines, respectively. The last sentence (of 4 lines) is clearly a coda, but what are we to make of the strange hiatus in which a *two*-line sentence and a *one*-line sentence interrupt the previous advance in sentence-length of 5, 7, and 8 before a subsequent sentence can progress to 12 lines? These one- and two-line sentences call attention to themselves for more reasons than their anomaly in length, as we shall see.

We recognize with some perplexity that more than half the poem has gone by before we find a word about its subject, Alfred Pollexfen. At the burial, Yeats's mind has drifted back, first, to the time, twenty-five years ago, of the death of his grandparents William and Elizabeth Pollexfen; next, to the time, five years ago, of the death of his melancholy uncle George (a Mason and an astrologer); and finally, to the unspecified time—actually sixteen years earlier—of the death of his restless (and also melancholy) sailor-uncle, John:

> Five-and-twenty years have gone
> Since old William Pollexfen
> Laid his strong bones down in death
> By his wife Elizabeth

> In the grey stone tomb he made.
> And after twenty years they laid
> In that tomb by him and her
> His son George, the astrologer;
> And Masons drove from miles away
> To scatter the Acacia spray
> Upon a melancholy man
> Who had ended where his breath began.
> Many a son and daughter lies
> Far from the customary skies,
> The Mall and Eades's grammar school,
> In London or in Liverpool;
> But where is laid the sailor John
> That so many lands had known,
> Quiet lands or unquiet seas
> Where the Indians trade or Japanese?

As we examine the opening of "In Memory of Alfred Pollexfen" (still awaiting the appearance of its subject) we see that, although the elegy rhymes in couplets, the basic sense-unit for the first half of the poem is the quatrain, composed of enjambed couplets. Quatrains (more or less) follow serenely on through line 20: the actual sense-division is 5; 3; 4; 4; 4. Then something odd occurs: we encounter a "defective" quatrain composed of those two anomalous sentences we have already noted, a two-line one followed by a one-line one. The "defectiveness" of this three-line "quatrain" causes the poem to have 39 lines instead of its "correct" 40:

> He never found his rest ashore,
> Moping for one voyage more.
> Where have they laid the sailor John?

The "missing line," the "fourth" line of this "quatrain," stands in for the missing John. We do not at first sense its lack because the first rhyme-word of the next quatrain, *son*, rhymes with *John*. As we have seen, Yeats uses the same strategy in other poems ("The Tower," part III and "On Woman," for instance) to keep us from realizing that other three-line "quatrains" are comparably "defective." Had Yeats reduced the defective "quatrain" to a couplet (the rhyme-unit of the elegy), its "defectiveness" would have been less visible; but instead he made the anomaly even more salient by having the "extra" third line (following the rhyme *ashore* / *more*) reiterate the lament for John already voiced: "But where is laid the sailor John . . . / Where have they laid the sailor John?" The "flaw" of the defective quatrain, the pained bafflement attached to the missing body, is so poignant that it threatens to deflect interest from Alfred (as yet unmentioned), to whom the pathos of the elegy (we assume from the title) should more properly be attached.

The second half of the poem, Alfred's half (as we might call it), abandons the first half's individual quatrain-tombstones dedicated to the already-dead in favor of run-on quatrains more suitable to the recently living Alfred. Yeats's unambitious uncle, capable of contentment in the family's Liverpool firm, but also subject to homesickness for Sligo and his family, is at last permitted entry into his unassuming (but not simple) poem. A single twelve-line sentence (largely iambic, to suit mild Alfred) sums up Alfred's Sligo burial and the homeward-turning course of his last decade of life. The former fixed quatrain-tombstones melt into reminiscence, and the rhymes become unemphatic:

> And yesterday the youngest son,
> A humorous, unambitious man,
> Was buried near the astrologer,
> Yesterday in the tenth year
> Since he who had been contented long,
> A nobody in a great throng,
> Decided he would journey home,
> Now that his fiftieth year had come,
> And 'Mr. Alfred' be again
> Upon the lips of common men
> Who carried in their memory
> His childhood and his family.

I come now to the central oddity of the poem: although its title represents it as an elegy for one person, it is in fact an elegy for six. Five of these Pollexfens are explicitly mentioned: William and Elizabeth Pollexfen, Yeats's maternal grandparents; George (Yeats's father's schoolfellow, the uncle Yeats knew best) buried beside them; John, buried elsewhere, forever absent; Alfred, joining his parents and brother George in the tomb.[5] But a sixth Pollexfen is hidden here, as she is hidden in "A Prayer for my Daughter": Susan Mary Pollexfen Yeats, Yeats's mother and the sister of the buried uncles.

Susan, who died on the third of January, 1900, was buried not in the family tomb in Sligo with her parents and siblings, but in London.[6] With the death of Alfred in 1916, Yeats in Sligo feels anew the death of his mother, buried abroad. Her unnamed presence-in-absence generates, I believe, the strange coda to the poem, which recalls that at every Pollexfen death, women heard the lament of "a visionary white sea-bird"—in Irish, the Banshee, or "white" ("ban" in Irish) fairy ("Sidhe," pronounced "Shee"). (The Sidhe are, in Irish belief, adult gods and goddesses, not "fairies" in the diminutive sense.) In letters sent at the time of George Pollexfen's death, Yeats strictly associates the Banshee with his mother and her people. In *Autobiographies* (55) he writes that after the death of his little brother Robert, "I heard people telling that my mother and the servant had heard the banshee crying the night before he died." To Edward Gordon Craig he writes on September 28, 1910, after the death of George Pollexfen, "An old uncle, a fine astrologer, has just died here after being wailed over by my mother's Banshee"; and a day later, to Annie Horniman, he says, "The Banshee, that follows my mother's people cried over him. It was heard both by the nurse & my sister [Lily]" (#1433, #1435). Yeats, in commemorating Alfred Pollexfen, now joins that company of mourning women; but he does so by making his poem accompany the cry of his mother's Banshee, represented as "a visionary white sea-bird":

> At all these death-beds women heard
> A visionary white sea-bird
> Lamenting that a man should die;
> And with that cry I have raised my cry.
> (360–361)

"By marriage with a Pollexfen we have given a tongue to the sea cliffs," said Yeats's father of the Yeatses who, of themselves, he said, had "ideas and no passions."[7] Yeats here silently includes his Pollexfen mother in the family elegy, as he becomes the verbal echo of the cry of her visionary white ("ban") sea-bird / Sidhe-bird / Banshee.

Why did Yeats cast his elegy for Alfred Pollexfen—for the several dead Pollexfens—into such "simple" tetrameter verse? His other elegies prefer more complex forms; even the tetrameter Gore-Booth elegy at least uses the complex *abba* rhyme, while here Yeats rhymes in the most primitive of forms, the couplet. Augusta Gregory is elegized (in the two Coole Park poems) in *ottava rima*, as is Parnell ("Parnell's Funeral"), as are the friends who are commemorated in "The Municipal Gallery Revisited";[8] Robert Gregory is elegized in the seventeenth-century octave-stanza that Yeats borrowed from Cowley; the "Olympians" (in "Beautiful Lofty Things") appear in epic hexameters, and Maud Gonne (in the proleptic elegy "A Bronze Head") in rhyme royal. The Pollexfens were not artists or writers, but merchant-traders; their commemoration (Yeats must have thought) should match their simplicity, even their naïveté. The poet therefore places among his lines things the Pollexfens themselves might have said. They might have spoken of "seas / Where the Indians trade or Japanese"; they might cry, re-peating themselves, "Where have they laid the sailor John?" They might boast that "Masons drove from miles away / To scatter the Acacia spray" at George's funeral; they might refer familiarly to such Sligo sites as "The Mall" and "Eades's grammar school." As we see Yeats ventriloquizing the Pollexfens in "artless" tetrameter couplets (while maintaining his authorial presence not only as he delays Alfred's appearance but also as he conceals his mother in the coda), we see to what extent these tetrameters—open, disarming, almost childlike in their rhythms and diction—are reminiscent of the sweetness of the tetrameters of "The Song of Wandering Aengus," while remaining—as those of "Aengus" do not—within contemporaneity of reference and domesticity of language. This poem, composed by the great-est modern Irish poet, exemplifies, in deference to his "humorous, unambi-tious" uncle, the art that conceals art. The poem becomes strangely affect-ing because of the unwonted modesty of its presentation.

## Late Tetrameter Poems

"In Memory of Alfred Pollexfen" makes us aware of the potential mild-ness of the tetrameter. If we had only the more outspoken and peremptory Yeatsian examples of that meter in mind ("To a Wealthy Man," "The Man and the Echo"), we might have judged such an energetic and even martial line unsuitable for elegizing two women, Eva Gore-Booth (who died in 1926) and her sister Constance Gore-Booth Markiewicz (who died in 1927). "In Memory of Eva Gore-Booth and Con Markiewicz" (475–476), dated by Yeats October 1927, was brought into being, evidently, by Con's death. The elegy of the Gore-Booth sisters resorts in turn to several capacities of the tetrameter: the mild, the sardonic, and the martial, using the first to draw the quiet domestic portrait with which the poem begins, the second to den-igrate the sisters' politics, the third to burnish the apocalyptic end of the poem. As I mentioned earlier, Yeats chooses for this "aristocratic" elegy the tetrameter embraced-rhyme *abba* quatrain that was used (in stanzaic form) by Tennyson throughout *In Memoriam* (the poet's elegy for his dearest friend, Arthur Hallam). Yeats seems to have had the *In Memoriam* quatrain in mind as soon as he began to write the Gore-Booth elegy; the drafts show him immediately adopting the embraced-rhyme form.[9] In the event he decides, while keeping the rhyme-scheme, not to produce discrete four-line Tennysonian stanzas with it, but to create a sequence of two Roman-numeraled unequal parts, the 20-line Part I and the 12-line Part II. (As I explained in Chapter II with respect to "Sailing to Byzantium," Yeats affixed Roman numerals to the parts of poems to make each portion represent a different place or position of the speaker—a "station," as I have called it, taking the word from Keats's praise of Milton's "stationing" of characters in a visual field.) The first page of the extant drafts displays, besides the Tennysonian stanza form, the two questions that stimulated the poem: how did it come about that the exquisite beginning of the sisters' youth was followed by the tragedy and the inconsequence of their adult lives, and were they responsible for that decline? The first cluster of words on the draft page announces the tragedy (apparently exculpating the sisters, and blaming "Ireland"), while the second cluster evokes the remembered beauty of Yeats's first visit to Lissadell, the Gore-Booth house:

> But Ireland is a hag & seems
> What she touches with her breath
> . . . ~~but~~ pardoned drags out weary years
>
> Sunlight upon sea & hill
> A table spread
> A table & window to the south[10]
>
> > (*WS*, 3)

As we know, the finished poem reverses the draft order, and begins not in denunciation but in the sweet liquid measures of idyll, a montage of commas:

> The light of evening, Lissadell,
> Great windows open to the south,
> Two girls in silk kimonos, both
> Beautiful, one a gazelle.

Although this opening is self-contained, with its syntactic unit (a sentence-fragment) coinciding with the lines of the quatrain, increasingly the sentences—charged, as they are, with fateful unfolding events—overrun and disregard their quatrains. The poem—I am for the moment setting aside one couplet, to be considered later—interrupts its own opening scene (with its gentle euphonious tetrameters) and utters a scornful, intellectually dismissive, and sexually tinged repudiation of the women's political endeavors (its harshness rendered by hard *c*'s, *d*'s, and *g*'s):

> The older is condemned to death,
> Pardoned, drags out lonely years
> Conspiring among the ignorant.
> I know not what the younger dreams—
> Some vague Utopia—and she seems,
> When withered old and skeleton-gaunt,
> An image of such politics.

Yeats's acerbity seems to have been provoked (as the latter part of the sequence confirms) by his guilt at his own passivity while others of his generation, among them the sisters, took action against British rule. (Constance, imprisoned and condemned to death for her part in the Easter Rising, was subsequently pardoned because she was a woman. After a year's incarceration, she was released and subsequently continued her political activism; Eva became a suffragist.)

How, the poet wonders, can one account for such a tragic end after such a promising beginning? In the drafts, Yeats attempts (but ultimately rejects) two unexciting preliminary versions of a two-line explanatory and exculpatory image of seasonal succession: spring turns to summer and then to autumn. The first of these rejected versions ascribes the waning of the season to temporal attrition, as summer "wears" on to autumn:

> But the spring to summer wears
> That bring [*sic*] round October breath.
>
> (*WS*, 5)

The second rejected attempt makes the summer leafage "disappear" under the breath of a softer version of the Shelleyan autumnal wind:

> The summer foliage disappears
> Under the October breath.
>
> (*WS*, 5)

Yeats drops the second line concerning the October breath (though some sort of line ending in "-eath" will be necessary here to supply a rhyme for "The older is condemned to death"). But he keeps, through several more drafts (*WS*, 11, 15, 16), the line "But the spring to summer wears," never arriving at a complementary line with an end-word rhyming with *death*. Even as the poem went into several successive typescripts, an entire line remained missing. When, at the very last minute (in a paste-down inserted in the publisher's mock-up for the first edition of *The Winding Stair*) Yeats solves the crucial problem of the explanatory and exculpatory lines, it is with a new inspiration, drawn from Milton's "Lycidas." Yeats now summons words not of attrition or fading, but of unexpected violence:

> But a raving autumn shears
> Blossom from the summer's wreath.
> (WS, 16n)

Upon the lyrical sisters at Lissadell, vengeful Atropos wields her shears; in the line following the ravages of autumn, we encounter with almost posthumous pain the formerly intact blossoms in summer's garland. In lieu of his former rhyme, *breath*, for *death*, Yeats invents *wreath*, an entwined circlet of flowers. *Shears*, in Yeats a powerful verb, had been a noun in his source, "Lycidas":

> But the fair guerdon when we hope to find,
> And think to burst out into sudden blaze,
> Comes the blind Fury with the abhorrèd shears,
> And slits the thin-spun life.

By echoing, but transforming, his predecessor—as Milton's *blind fury* becomes a *raving autumn*; his *slits* (verb) becomes *shears* (verb); his *shears* (noun) becomes *shears* (verb); and his *blaze, blossoms*—Yeats makes his new lines both distinctly allusive and notably original. The "blame" for the tragedy of the sisters is, by these last-minute lines, ascribed to the madness of a raving fate, and the sisters are exempted from judgment. We notice how Yeats, counteracting the lulling iambic music of the poem's opening at Lissadell, has forced the tetrameter here to a savage trochaic beat, and has invented a clashing spondaic enjambment as the accented *shears* roves over the line-end to cut the accented *blossom:*

> But a raving autumn shears
> Blossom from the summer's wreath.
>
> (WS, 16, nn5/6)

Although Yeats inserted the image of youthful beauty as a wreath of blossoms only after the poem was set in type, I believe he must have had it subliminally or projectively in mind from the time he began to compose the poem, since in each of its two Roman-numeraled parts, the poem itself generates a wreath, a circlet: this is its crucial structural feature (and accounts for Yeats's decision not to observe quatrain stanza breaks). At the close of the 20-line part I, memory doubles back on life as the last lines join themselves to the opening ones, creating a "wreath," by repeating the initial portrait of the sisters: "Two girls in silk kimonos, both / Beautiful, one a gazelle":

> Many a time I think to seek
> One or the other out and speak
> Of that old Georgian mansion, mix
> Pictures of the mind, recall
> That table and the talk of youth,
> Two girls in silk kimonos, both
> Beautiful, one a gazelle.

Similarly, in the 12-line part II, the final line, "Bid me strike a match and blow," joins itself to the earlier "Arise and bid me strike a match," as a second, apocalyptic, "wreath" avenges the destruction of the first, innocent, one.[11]

Although Yeats was led by Tennyson's elegiac example to the *In Memoriam* quatrain, he has to make something of his own out of that "perfect square" of four by four—the four-foot line shaped chiastically, *abba*, into four lines of embraced rhyme. What can this elegy tell us about what Yeats did with his Tennysonian inheritance? We notice, after the stilled verbless tableau with which the poem opens (a painting presented through nouns—*light, Lissadell, windows, girls*), how the violence of the Miltonic shears (mutating from noun to verb) tears the tableau apart, generating the quick sketches of the later life of the sisters, in which ten years are condensed into a few words. In the close of part I ("Many a time"), we see the peaking of Yeatsian enjambment (here more persistent than in Tennyson) as line after line ends in an active verb propelling desire: the poet has wanted to *seek out* ("one or the other"), *speak of* ("that mansion"), *mix* ("pictures of the mind"), *recall* ("that table and the talk of youth"). The four-beat lines here unspool over line-ends, arriving quickly at the terminal completion of the first stanza's wreath. (I will say more below about Yeats's revision of the *In Memoriam* quatrain.)

So far, during part I, Yeats has spoken of the sisters in the third person—"two girls," "the older," "the younger." But now, as he begins part II, sheer will to atone for that never-ventured visit to the Gore-Booths while they were alive presses him to encounter the sisters directly, even if to do so he has to cross over to a different "station," the realm of the dead. That "crossing over to another place" (as in "Sailing to Byzantium") generates Yeats's use of Roman numerals to identify "In Memory" as a sequence rather than a two-stanza lyric. By leaving his original station and moving to their realm of shadows, Yeats becomes able to address the shades of the sisters directly in the second person, raising considerably the temperature of the poem. There is still, perhaps, a tinge of condescension in his tone: now, he says, the sisters have learned what he has always known—"the folly of a fight / With a common wrong or right." In the drafts he had begun somewhat patronizingly:

> Learn dear shadows in the grave
> ~~Instructed now beyond the grave~~
> All the folly of a fight
> That ~~such [?as/?&]yo[u] should~~ never fight.
>
> (*WS*, 7)

But in the finished poem, Yeats's tone is no longer one *de haut en bas;* rather, he has taken on, in lieu of his former antagonistic personal attitude, the stance of an aphorist, enunciating truisms of proverbial wisdom:

> Dear shadows, now you know it all,
> All the folly of a fight
> With a common wrong or right.
> The innocent and the beautiful
> Have no enemy but time.

Then, in the most startling turn of the poem, Yeats reverses his previous scorn and admits that to accomplish his own future he needs to seek help from the sisters, whom he envies for their orientation to action (as he will envy the soldiers in "The Road at My Door" from "Meditations in Time of Civil War"). The sisters are the ones with incendiary experience; he, the poet at his "sedentary trade," would have no idea how to set off an ordinary explosion, much less one that would burn up time, that real enemy of innocents such as the beautiful girls at Lissadell:

> Arise and bid me strike a match
> And strike another till timve catch;
> Should the conflagration climb,
> Run till all the sages know.[12]

The sisters will be the military leaders in this cosmic expedition; the poet cannot strike the match until they bid him do so. If they command him, and join him, the three of them together will carry off the metaphysical act to surpass all others, the fiery apocalyptic victory over time foretold in the book of Revelation. In the next, and equally surprising, reversal of his inculpation of the sisters, the poet—at first so distant in his third-person treatment of the Gore-Booths, and more recently their pleading subordinate begging them to issue the incendiary order—now makes common cause with them as his equals, changing from his sympathetic, then pleading, second-person address to a gripping first-person plural that inculpates (in strong trochaic beats) *both* himself and them:

> We the great gazebo built,
> They [the sages] convicted us of guilt;
> Bid me strike a match and blow.

Between the first enclosing "wreath" of the poem (which is completed by the echo-close of part I) and the inception of the second wreath in the sixth line of part II ("Arise and bid me strike a match") Yeats inserts his detached aphorisms of moral commentary, more general and philosophical than either of the "wreaths." The shape of the poem thus becomes a three-part one: wreath, aphorisms, wreath. We need to explain, then, why Yeats constructed it in *two* numbered parts rather than a more "logical" three. Expanded, the representation of the binary shape of the poem looks like the diagram below. We see that part I is occupied by the active worldly life historically led by the sisters, while part II takes place on the imaginative plane of an afterlife sage-realm where the sisters, now shades, dwell:

Part I, stationed in "Real Life"

Wreath #1 ⎰ Third-person idyll ("Two girls")
⎱ (Allegorical autumn-couplet and its sequelae)
Idyll recalled ("Two girls")

Part II, stationed in the "Afterlife"

Second-person address ("Dear shadows"), aphorisms and sage-truths

Wreath #2 ⎰ Second-person pleading ("Arise and bid me strike")
⎱ First-person plural self-inculpation ("We the great gazebo built")
Second-person pleading ("Bid me strike")

This structure graphs the superposition of afterthought on life, as the second wreath "takes revenge," on the plane of imagination, on all the mistakes of the first wreath of lived history. But before the second wreath can be made, Yeats must enunciate, through aphorisms, the moral conclusions of the poem, judging himself and the sisters. (The aphorisms come in the middle, between the two "wreaths," because closing the poem with them would make too tame an ending, representing Yeats's resignation to Fate and time's enmity.) Together, Yeats recognizes, he and they created the uninhabitable "gazebo" or "folly" of Anglo-Irish culture in an Ireland that was bound to expel their gazebo-architecture in favor of its own Catholic and (in Yeats's view) materialistic constructions. Both he and the Gore-Booths (he now acknowledges) were guilty of entering into the fight against the "common" wrongs or rights of their day—they in violence, conspiracy, and vague Utopian schemes, he in political writing and social action, especially in his youth.[13] He and they have been undone alike by time: if he did not join them in life, then now, when the sisters are "shadows" (and when, by addressing them, he has relocated himself into their Hades-space), he will conspire with them in his own self-consummation as all three revenge themselves on destructive time, exculpating themselves before the sages by the animating force of their apocalyptic imagination.

Elegy's "repairing" of actual history is a perennial impulse ("let our frail thoughts dally with false surmise"). Yeats would not admit—at least not in a poem in "square" four-beat quatrains—to "frail" thoughts, nor would he characterize his fantasy of afterlife militant cooperation with the sisters as a "false surmise" (though it is that). We might see the second part of the poem more sympathetically if we think of it as Yeats's overdue and late-felt act of apology, and as an enactment in fantasy of that visit to the sisters which he never, in life, found himself able to undertake. The moral center of the poem is the first-person "we" and "us" by which Yeats, late in the poem, admits his part in collective guilt: "We the great gazebo built, / They [the sages] convicted us of guilt."[14] Only in Hades, in the realm of the sages, he acknowledges, does everyone "know" the moral aphorisms that he recited in the center of the poem; he therefore places the aphorisms within the afterlife of part II rather than in the historical years of part I. That reflective realization of life's "folly" enables his eventual sympathy for the sisters and his deference to them as those who are already inhabitants of the afterlife-realm of wisdom.

The versatility of the tetrameter line, and the flexibility of the *In Memoriam* quatrain, are manifest here as the poem advances from its initial iambic harmony ("The light of evening") to trochaic anger ("But a raving autumn"); from anger ("withered, old") to sympathy ("Dear shadows"); from sympathy to instruction ("The innocent and the beautiful"); and from instruction to a martial energy ("Arise and bid me"). This versatility of form arises in part from Yeats's management of sound and rhythm, as in the alliterating trochees of the last three lines, which pick up the harsh sound effects in "*b*" and in the hard "*c*" and "*g*" that earlier denigrated the sisters, but now characterize the poet as well:

> We the **great ga**zebo **built,**
> They **convicted** us of **guilt;**
> **Bid** me strike a match and **blow.**

A Yeatsian inventiveness can also be felt in the poet's handling of the *In Memoriam* quatrain, which imposes on the reader a very long (11-beat) wait between the occurrence of the first rhyme-sound (beat 4) and its counterpart-sound (beat 16). The distribution of beats with respect to the refinding of the opening rhyme could be represented graphically as follows:

```
 1        2       3   4
The light of evening, Lissadell,
      5      6   7     8          9     10   11    12  13   14  15     16
Great windows open to the south, Two girls in silk kimonos, both Beautiful, one a gazelle.
```

The long suspension of the rhyme-arc gathers into our mind, as a single segment, everything that happens between -**dell** and -**zelle;** the unobtrusive slant-rhyme *south-both* scarcely makes itself felt during the suspension. We expect, given the *abba* rhyme scheme, to be brought to some resolution with the completion of each new "outer" rhyme. We are consequently unsettled when we are asked to consider as a "quatrain" a group of words, such as the one below, that both begins and ends in the middle of a sentence:

An image of such poli**tics.**
Many a time I think to seek One or the other out and speak Of that old Georgian mansion, **mix**[.]

We see that *all* the stanzas of this poem, except the first, violate the usual Yeatsian desideratum of matching sentence to rhyme-unit. The last stanza, although Yeats makes it possible to read it as syntactically complete, actually begins in the middle of a sentence:

Run till all the sages **know.**
We the great gazebo built, They convicted us of guilt; Bid me strike a match and **blow.**

Yeats thus redefines the *In Memoriam* quatrain, and its tetrameter line, as something continuous and agitated rather than (as it is in Tennyson) stanzaic and reflective, something disturbing rather than consoling. The quatrain is so intensely at cross-purposes with the sentence throughout most of this sequence, and the lines are so frequently enjambed rather than end-stopped, that each part becomes a current of wreath-continuity rather than a composition of perceived recurrent line-length and felt quatrain-form.

A poet, as the Gore-Booth elegy suggests, can silently cooperate with his chosen meter, play ostentatiously with it, or even contend against it. To exemplify the last course, I will discuss two tetrameter poems in which Yeats opposes himself to the natural pulse and propulsion of the tetrameter, so visible in "To a Wealthy Man" or "In Memory of Eva Gore-Booth." Yeats placed these two short war-poems side by side as near-twins, enclosing them (as parts V and VI) in the sequence "Meditations in Time of Civil War." The first, the three-stanza poem "The Road at My Door," is melancholy; the second, the four-stanza "The Stare's Nest by My Window," is utopian. Both poems are composed in tetrameter because it is *the* martial march-measure, and these are war-poems. But, oddly, both poems are made of cinquains. (The cinquain is a short five-line stanza with a rhyme-scheme extended from the quatrain's *abab;* here, it displays an "extra" line inserted between lines 2 and 5: *abaab.*) In a stanza of such limited length, the tetrameter never has a chance to get its full swing under way: even "The Song of Wandering Aengus" has stanzas of eight lines, allowing for a narrative energy in each.

"Meditations in Time of Civil War," composed in 1923, reflects on the internecine conflict that had broken out in Ireland after one group among the Republicans, who would not accept partition, objected to the signing of the 1921 Anglo-Irish treaty establishing the British-approved Free State. (The civil war had been preceded by the guerilla warfare between the British Black and Tans and the IRA, memorialized, as we saw in Chapter III, in "Nineteen Hundred and Nineteen.") In "The Road at My Door" (423–424), Yeats, in his ancient stone tower in Gort, is successively visited in neighborly fashion, during a cessation of hostilities, by military representatives from each side of the war. Instead of asserting a political position of his own, the poet envies both sets of men because they are men of action, while he, as a writer, is isolated not only from them (they represent society in war-costume) but also from the "natural" biological life of the nearby moor-hen and her young, on whom he bends his gaze before he sadly turns away. As he climbs the winding stair to his writing-chamber high under the roof of the tower, he might as well, he feels, be ascending to another sphere, so immediately estranged is he from the actual outer world (both social and biological). I reproduce part V not as it appears on the page (in three successive stanzas) but so as to reflect its even-handed internal political structure, and to show its dissolution into estrangement:

V

The Road at My Door

| | |
|---|---|
| An affable Irregular, | A brown lieutenant and his men, |
| A heavily-built Falstaffian man, | Half dressed in national uniform, |
| Comes cracking jokes of civil war | Stand at my door, and I complain |
| As though to die by gunshot were | Of the foul weather, hail and rain, |
| The finest play under the sun. | A pear-tree broken by the storm. |
| | |
| I count those feathered balls of soot | |
| The moor-hen guides upon the stream, | |
| To silence the envy in my thought; | |
| | And turn towards my chamber, caught |
| | In the cold snows of a dream. |

This is a poem about silence concealed under small talk: killing remains the unmentioned fact. Hideous incidents have happened in Yeats's neighborhood, incidents which may well have been brought about by these Irregulars of De Valera's IRA—or, equally probably, by the Free State lieutenant and his men. We recall that Yeats had described an earlier such horror in "Nineteen Hundred and Nineteen":

> Now days are dragon-ridden, the nightmare
> Rides upon sleep: a drunken soldiery
> Can leave the mother, murdered at her door,
> To crawl in her own blood, and go scot-free.

Nobody, however, can bring up such atrocities during a personal neighborhood encounter. The IRA Irregular makes jokes; the poet complains of the weather to the Free State lieutenant. Such a conspiracy of silence is intolerable to the man of words; and yet the ascent to a solitary chamber in order to transform event into symbol isolates one from life—not only the current social life of brutal wars coexisting with superficial threshold pleasantries but also the natural organic life of sexuality, breeding, and mothering implied by the moor-hen and her young.

The structure of the poem is self-evident: one stanza for the Irregulars, one stanza for the Free Staters, one (divided) stanza for the poet looking left at the moor-hens and right at his tower. Yeats awards a whole stanza to himself, as though he constituted a third political party rivaling the Irregulars and the Free Staters—as, in one sense, he does. The main feature of the stanza in which Yeats couches both this poem and its companion is the long wait for the fifth-line *b* rhyme to match the second end-word. The wait is, of course, no longer in fact than the wait for the second rhyme-word in the *abba* stanza of "In Memory of Eva Gore-Booth," yet here it *seems* longer because we so strongly expect the rhyme-sequence *"soot/stream/thought/—?"* to engender immediately a rhyme to match *stream*. But instead it engenders *caught*, putting us off our stride. The forward march of the tetrameter is impeded not only by the stop after each five lines, as Yeats distinctly separates the vignettes of opposing soldiers, but also by the delaying "extra" lines ending in "were" and "rain" and "caught." And at the end Yeats actually expunges the four-beat "martial" line in which the poem has been composed. As he retreats to his chamber, "caught" in the "cold snows" of his dream, that dream creates its own anomalous rhythm, the trimeter with which the poem closes: "In the **cold snows** of a **dream**." The "defeat" of the martial four-beat march-rhythm as it fades away into trimeter suggests the fundamental defeat of war by the poet's act of solitary imagination. Yet by keeping the bloody aspects of war out of sight as he converses with the soldiers, Yeats has suffered the shame of the non-participant bystander as well as the shame of a poet uttering "polite meaningless words" to the soldiers at his door.

Perhaps for this reason, the near-twin to "The Road at My Door"— the immediately following part VI of "Meditations," "The Stare's Nest by

My Window" (424–425)—emphasizes war's destructiveness, both physical and spiritual. Like "The Road at My Door," "The Stare's Nest" uses the cinquain-stanza's "extra" line to retard forward motion. The effect achieved, however, is altogether different here because the poet, in this penultimate poem of "Meditations in Time of Civil War," turns the last line of the cinquain-stanza into a refrain. "The Stare's Nest by My Window" is not so much a poem in cinquains as it is a poem in quatrains with a choral refrain. The first stanza, in its tranquil depiction of the natural order of things, contrasts strongly with the subsequent three, which rehearse the terrors of civil war—general, specific, and psychological. I reproduce the poem below according to its internal structure, in which a pleading refrain of choral effect follows the poet's individual quatrains:

VI

The Stare's Nest by My Window

The bees build in the crevices
Of loosening masonry, and there
The mother birds bring grubs and flies.
My wall is loosening;

          honey-bees,
Come build in the empty house of the stare.

We are closed in, and the key is turned
On our uncertainty; somewhere
A man is killed, or a house burned,
Yet no clear fact to be discerned:

Come build in the empty house of the stare.

A barricade of stone or of wood;
Some fourteen days of civil war;
Last night they trundled down the road
That dead young soldier in his blood:

Come build in the empty house of the stare.

We had fed the heart on fantasies,
The heart's grown brutal from the fare;
More substance in our enmities
Than in our love;

          O honey-bees,
Come build in the empty house of the stare.

Such a layout (graphically displayed above for clarity, but certainly implicit in the poem as printed) represents—after a first stanza of normalcy—repeated reports of war assaulting the poetic imagination as it endeavors to restore the life of benevolent nature. The poet's imagination—always in immediate sensory connection to its natural surroundings—remarks indolently, as the poem begins, on the eventual victory of nature over culture; the masonry wall is loosening, the bees are finding its crevices suitable for storing honey, and the birds take advantage of the crevices to make nests for their expected young. Later, when the mother starling's nest is empty, its crevice will invite inhabitation by further bees producing honey. The poet's first invitation to the honey-bees follows "naturally" from his perceiving their presence in the openings of the wall. But his subsequent pleas are uttered—almost as a prayer—against the overwhelming and reiterated evidence of violence. Yeats suggests that he knows of no poetic way to counter the political situation in its own terms; he cannot change the political scene by casting his own opinion on one military side or another. The only possible poetic reply is one pitched on a different plane altogether.[15]

The rational, historical mind is here given all the "powerful" tetrameter lines. Nothing could be more grimly memorable than the martial advance of iambs in the bloody narrative of the third quatrain; nothing could be more crisply put than the sinister aphorisms of the fourth.[16] Against all this accurate strict tetrameter reporting, the heart can utter only its unadvancing and immobile choral sentence, "Come build in the empty house of the stare." But that refrain sounds out a rising dance-lilt in its iambs and anapests; and the faint buoyancy of its exhortation, opposing the bitter news in the three war-quatrains, keeps being generated almost in spite of the evidence. The refrain appears first at its most enlivened, containing (counting its half-line lead-in) three trisyllabic feet:

˘ ´ ˘ ´ ˘ ˘ ´ ˘ ´ ˘ ´ ˘ ˘ ´ ˘ ´ ˘ ˘ ´

My wall is loosening; honey-bees, / Come build in the empty house of the stare.

In the refrain's reappearances in stanzas 2 and 3, the heartening trisyllabic feet have been reduced to two; but when the refrain closes the poem it has regained, with its invoked honey-bees, its original three anapests. This is a sign of hope, flickering within the poetic mind, which can do no more than reiterate—almost blankly, in yearning words—the possibility of new life, in a rhythm antithetical to martial grimness. Like the "defective" trimeter line that closes "The Road at My Door," the stubborn trisyllabic feet of the brief refrain in "The Stare's Nest" argue for the eventual defeat of the sternness of the strict march-rhythms in lines 1–4 of each stanza.

In "The Stare's Nest" Yeats makes the refrain *necessary* to the rhyme-completion of each stanza (as he had in "September 1913"), so that its hope cannot be viewed as a sentimental addition unrelated to "reality." If the poet does not include the mental presence of embodied longing, the structure of "reality" (however victorious its warlike aspects may appear) is not complete. The refrain—although weak in its single-line smallness against every four strong lines—plays an indispensable part in the completion of each stanza; and it has, in its repetition of "stare," not only the last word but also the concluding long-vowel rhyme, winding up the charm. The refrain is a pleading line, unable to assert that its plea will ever be answered. But the persistence of natural forces in the first stanza suggests that the honeybee-refrain is not without valid hope; its trisyllabic accents, reconceiving what a four-beat line might sound like in a more hopeful moment, mitigate the otherwise despairing wartime brutality of the poem's tetrameters.

## Last Tetrameter Poems

Yeats, in his last years, chose the tetrameter line for both "Lapis Lazuli" (1936) and "The Man and the Echo" (1938). In its form of restless advance, tetrameter is suitable for "Lapis Lazuli" (565–567), with its panoramic view of one culture after another rising up and being destroyed. Like many of Yeats's late poems, "Lapis Lazuli" tests the amount of the grotesque admissible in a "serious" poem, in order to set off more strongly the detached, meditative gaiety it recommends at the end. Among its explorations of the grotesque, it ventriloquizes the childish diction of "hysterical women" who say

> They are sick of the palette and fiddle-bow . . .
> For everybody knows or else should know
> That if nothing drastic is done[17]
> Aeroplane and Zeppelin will come out,
> Pitch like King Billy bomb-balls in
> Until the town lie beaten flat.

It reduces the soliloquies of Shakespeare's most complex characters to rambling and raging:

> Though Hamlet rambles and Lear rages,
> And all the drop-scenes drop at once
> Upon a hundred thousand stages
> [Tragedy] cannot grow by an inch or an ounce.

It mimics the mass migrations of culture in an absurdly packed line, with eight nouns (four used adjectivally, four as an invariable repeated animal "back") in nine syllables:

> On their own feet they came, or on shipboard,
> Camel-back, horse-back, ass-back, mule-back.

"Lapis Lazuli" takes a long view of massacre, and airily overlooks the fate of those "put to the sword," who have fallen together with their fallen "things" and are certainly not "gay":

> Old civilizations put to the sword. . . .
> All things fall and are built again,
> And those that build them again are gay.

The poem matches the hysteria of the frightened women by its own hysteria of alliance with the new victors.

It is one of the chief strengths of "Lapis Lazuli," given its frequent oscillation from the grotesque to the serious, that it so ingeniously paces its tetrameters. Amid the "hardness" of speeded-up, far-focus representation of the rise and fall of cultures, Yeats inserts delays, emotional moments of lament and close-focus commentary. Sometimes these bring in the softening influence of trisyllabic feet, changing march-step to dance:

> No handiwork of Callimachus,
> Who handled marble as if it were bronze,
> Made draperies that seemed to rise
> When sea-wind swept the corner, stands;
> His long lamp-chimney shaped like the stem
> Of a slender palm, stood but a day.

At other times (as we shall see in a moment), Yeats slows down his tetrameters by means of middle- and end-punctuation. Except in its variety of pacing, "Lapis Lazuli" does not offer technical novelty within Yeats's use of the tetrameter; rather, it does again what Yeats has done before, as its powerful enjambed quatrains sweep through civilizations from ancient Greece to modern Dublin, with nothing stopping their streaming through the "tragic scene."

The only thing that can arrest that relentless march through eras is mental withdrawal into the suspended time of meditation, exemplified first by Yeats's own careful visual reconstruction of his tall carved piece of lapis lazuli. He impedes the tetrameter-advance by the short descriptions of the figures carved on the stone; here, the compositional unit of the poem, the quatrain, is "reduced" (by a series of commas, a semicolon, and a period) to end-punctuated two-line syntactic units. Each of these is allotted to a different inhabitant or inhabitants of the carving, carefully stationed: two Chinamen; above them, a long-legged bird; behind them, a serving man.

> Two Chinamen, behind them a third,
> Are carved in lapis lazuli,
> Over them flies a long-legged bird,
> A symbol of longevity;
> The third, doubtless a serving-man,
> Carries a musical instrument.

The suspension of time, as Yeats dwells on the lapis-lazuli scene, is completed by his Keatsian imagining of the moment when the three "Chinamen" depicted on the stone bas-relief will have reached the (equally carefully stationed) "little half-way house" they climb toward. There, adopting the remote perspective on current events that the poet himself was unable to summon up earlier in his irritation at the "hysterical women," the Chinese sages will compose themselves for meditation, far above the wrack of history. The tetrameters are now slowed to a walk by further punctuation: line, period; line, semicolon; line, period; two lines, period. The only vivacity is contributed by the starting up of a trisyllabic foot after the Chinaman's request for music; a comparable "glittering" foot ornaments each of the last three lines, insisting metrically on the speculative light in the eyes of the staring ancients, who are immune to being moved to tragic feeling even by a tragic spectacle:

> On all the tragic scene they stare.
> One asks for mournful melodies;
> Accomplished fingers begin to play.

Their eyes mid many wrinkles, their eyes,
Their ancient, glittering eyes, are gay.

In contrast to the "coldness" and chilly gaiety of the telescopic view adopted by "Lapis Lazuli" and its Chinese ancients, Yeats's last tetrameter poem, "The Man and the Echo" (632–633), written in 1938,[18] ends in a close-focus pang, with the cry of a wounded rabbit that "distracts" the poet from his dark examination of conscience:

But hush, for I have lost the theme,
Its joy or night seem but a dream;
Up there some hawk or owl has struck
Dropping out of sky or rock,
A stricken rabbit is crying out,
And its cry distracts my thought.

By giving this six-line ending the last word, Yeats balances present animal agony against his earlier reflectiveness, and demonstrates that a single cry—even if only one of animal pain—is sufficient to efface, or at least distract, his meditation. (He is arguing, here, against the impassiveness of the ancient "Chinamen" of "Lapis Lazuli.") On the other hand, the previous forty lines of the poem have been devoted to "the spiritual intellect's great work," suggesting that this is a concern of substantial importance, if not equal in immediacy to fatal pain. As in "Lapis Lazuli," we see a slowing down of the tetrameter in the six-line close above, when the natural propulsiveness of the line is tamed into distinct units: first, a couplet to hush the preoccupations of the forty previous lines; second, a couplet devoted to the unseen predatory hawk; third, a single line for the stricken rabbit; and finally, a single line showing the humane (if temporary) victory of shocked sympathy over detached reflection.

How is "The Man and the Echo" different from the tetrameter poems we have so far seen? Like others, it has a prelude (five lines) and a coda (six lines); and like others, it has an interest not only in the tetrameter's ability to "hurry ahead," but also in its potential for distinct and striking epigrammatic couplets. Yeats distinguishes "The Man and the Echo" from his earlier tetrameter poems by placing it in the centuries-old genre of the echo-poem. The distinct units of the poem, as couplets that have less "space" within them than quatrains do, lend themselves to being sharply "bitten off"—but, like all forms, they can be "contradicted" by the poet's using them against their natural grain. It is the epigrammatic force of this form that Yeats calls on for the successive couplet-questions of his self-interrogation.

Yeats begins by explaining that he has come to a hidden "pit" of "broken stone" to "shout a secret to the stone." The "secret" is that he now feels, at the end of his life, that everything he has done has been evil (an admission he could hardly make in public, but which is so obsessive now that he must "shout" it out to relieve its crushing pressure):

> In a cleft that's christened Alt
> Under broken stone I halt
> At the bottom of a pit
> That broad noon has never lit,
> And shout a secret to the stone.

He delays revealing the secret until after he poses the questions that will evilly turn into the asserted substance of his "secret":

> Did that play of mine send out
> Certain men the English shot?
> Did words of mine put too great strain
> On that woman's reeling brain?
> Could my spoken words have checked
> That whereby a house lay wrecked?

In spite of Paul Muldoon's ventriloquially witty answer from Auden ("Certainly not") to the first of these questions,[19] they still strike a reader, in their hammering sequence, as a classic formulation of self-reproach in the watches of insomniac nights. Yeats's questions here, we notice, all concern words: the words of a political play, words to an unstable woman, words unuttered in a crisis. That resemblance among his acts allows the poet the summary of his "secret": "And all seems evil."

But later in the poem, when the poet's couplet-questioning resumes, taking the same rhetorical form (one question immediately following another), the content of the questions has shifted entirely away from words. The first (unanswerable) question asks whether the final judgment on one's life will be positive; the second (a purely rhetorical question) turns away from speculation on the afterlife to our confinement in this life:

> O Rocky Voice,
> Shall we in that great night rejoice?
> What do we know but that we face
> One another in this place?

The second of these questions is the fulcrum on which the poem turns from thought to pain, from self-examination to sympathy with other beings.

Between these two passages of atomistic couplet-questions, Yeats works against the tendency of the couplet-form to segregate itself syntactically into distinct small units. As he had done in writing "In Memory of Alfred Pollexfen," he "forces" the couplets here to become continuous as he reflects on "the spiritual intellect's great work," admitting that the flow of life (symbolized in the couplet-flow) has allowed him to evade self-judgment, which will be the posthumous work of the soul in the afterlife. That spiritual work has prematurely arrived to afflict him now (with its harassing couplet-questions) only because he is "old and ill," lacking the narcotics of "wine or love." Here are the couplets that Yeats articulates into a single continuous twelve-line sentence:

> While man can still his body keep
> Wine or love drug him to sleep,
> Waking he thanks the Lord that he
> Has body and its stupidity,
> But body gone he sleeps no more,
> And till his intellect grows sure
> That all's arranged in one clear view,
> Pursues the thoughts that I pursue,
> Then stands in judgment on his soul,
> And, all work done, dismisses all
> Out of intellect and sight
> And sinks at last into the night.

It seems as though Yeats cast "The Man and the Echo" into couplets to make the fundamental unit of the poem a restless, short, tight one, the interrogative or speculative couplet, matching the reiterated self-reproach that is the emotional heart of the poem. The theatrical setting below Knocknarea in the "cleft that's christened Alt" (the deep and wide walkable fissure between two steeply rising rock walls) emphasizes the poet's solitude. Nothing from society can touch him here: he is "At the bottom of a pit / That broad noon has never lit." It is only here that he can find a place where his peculiar action—to "shout a secret"—will not be overheard. As he "shouts" his shaming conclusion, that "all seems evil until I / Sleepless would lie down and die," the Rock Wall, to his astonishment, echoes evilly back: "Lie down and die." This frightening development (occurring late, after eighteen lines) breaks the tetrameter line into two fragments, and brings the poem into the genre of the echo-poem, in which the poet always hears his own words called back to him. In the wittiest of such poems, "Heaven," George Herbert makes the celestial echo punningly sound out his own phonemes while changing their semantic content:

> Oh who will show me those delights on high?
> *Echo:* I.
> Thou echo, thou art mortal, all men know.
> *Echo:* No.

Herbert's echo speaks nine times, each time more reassuringly. But Yeats's echo is neither so inventive nor so kind; it repeats the man's darkest words without changing them, forcing him to hear—by external repetition—what he has himself been saying. As soon as someone *else* (the echo) says back to him "Lie down and die," he immediately repudiates the idea: "That were to shirk / The spiritual intellect's great work." He succeeds in reestablishing his self-respect by pursuing the idea that he still has time to accomplish that necessary work: "Nor can there be work so great / As that which cleans man's dirty slate." But after that work is done? Once again, the man's thought turns dark, as he acknowledges that at last he will sink "into the night." And once again, the menacing half-line echo breaks into the tetrameter with its grim seal of sagacity—"Into the night."

> *Man*
>
> And, all work done, dismisses all
> Out of intellect and sight
> And sinks at last into the night.
>
> *Echo*
>
> Into the night.

*Man*

> O Rocky Voice,
> Shall we in that great night rejoice?
> What do we know but that we face
> One another in this place?

The fact that the length of the echo's second utterance (four syllables: "Into the night") matches exactly that of its previous utterance ("Lie down and die") tells us that the echo is capable of only half-line utterances—rather little, against the scores of lines uttered by the man. Yet the poet flinches, again, from the repetition by another voice of his fearful "into the night." It is as though he has found himself in the precinct of an alien chthonic voice (not the still, small voice of conscience that posed the earlier self-interrogatory questions, but the distinct voice of death). Among the man's "shouted" words, the cliff echoes only those that are doom-laden, as though it can choose the words it wants to ratify. The poet's affrighted consciousness of the voice, after it speaks a second time, causes him to personify it, give it a name, make it a conscious being like himself. He calls it by name: "O Rocky Voice,"[20] and—in a departure from the rest of the poem—now puts questions to this exteriorized version of his voice rather than directly to his insomniac self, as he had earlier done. The self-identification is made explicit in the back-and-forth repetition of a mutually owned phrase: "into the night" (the man), "Into the night" (the echo), followed by "in that great night" (the man).

Like the earlier questions about words, the two later ones are couplet-questions (the first truncated by having to accommodate the "Into the night" of the echo). But unlike the earlier questions in the first person singular ("that play *of mine,* words *of mine, my* spoken words"), these questions are phrased in the collective "we," and represent the turning of the man's mind to others and his collective relation to them: "Shall *we* . . . rejoice?" "What do *we* know but that *we* face / *One another* in this place?" "This place" does not refer to the cleft where the man has gone to shout his secret, but rather to the social world which he shares with others. Yet, physically speaking, the man is still "imprisoned" in the depth of private shame and solitary shouts; he can see no other being in that "pit." The only sense unimprisoned by the deep cleft is the sense of hearing; and to hear the outside world, the man must quiet both his voice and that of the echo: "But hush, for I have lost the theme." The cry the man hears comes from "up there," the high ground on either side of the fissure, and although its animal source can in fact only be guessed at, Yeats's imagination leaps to solicitude, creating by conjunction a verbal echo: the hawk that has struck, the rabbit that is stricken. By rhyming "out" and "thought" in his last couplet, Yeats admits to the irreparable separation between external concern and interior meditation: they cannot coexist, but must yield alternately, one to the other, in the human mind, as the one "distracts" the other. His meditation cut short, the poet must return "up there" and live out his troubled life facing others.

"The Man and the Echo" distinguishes itself by its predominance of trochees: almost half the lines begin with a stressed syllable. Yet the trochaic rhythm disappears in the passage of "flow" describing "the spiritual intellect's great work" (lines 25–36), where only line 35 ("Out of intellect and sight") begins trochaically. The agitated spiritual questions bring initial trochees again ("**What** do we know but that we face / **One** another in this place"), as does the hawk "**Drop**ping out of sky or rock." "The Man and the Echo," by its insistent trochaic couplet-questioning, achieves a contour unlike those of Yeats's other tetrameter poems, and illustrates the poet's lifelong capacity to evoke variations on prosodic forms. By his large and small adjustments of rhythm and stanza form, Yeats reveals to us the many possibilities harbored within the four-beat line. Each of his inventions using this line widens the horizon of its aptness, while exploring its capacity for expansion, propulsiveness, and (in couplets) epigrammatic terseness.

## IX

## ᐁ THE MEDIUM OF INSTRUCTION:
## DOCTRINE IN BLANK VERSE

When we think of Yeats's poetry, it is, understandably enough, rhymed poems that come to mind. Yeats used most of the conventional forms of English rhyme, and brilliantly revived such stanzas as the trimeter *abab* quatrain and *ottava rima*. But Yeats also wrote unrhymed poems, most of them in blank verse,[1] unrhymed iambic pentameter. What fundamental difference existed for him between rhymed verse and blank verse that led him to cast some materials into that unrhymed form? It is odd that there is relatively little blank verse in Yeats's lyric poetry (by contrast to his narrative and dramatic poetry),[2] considering the prestige that lyric blank verse had acquired from its use in Wordsworth (rumination), Coleridge ("conversation poems"), and so on, down to Tennyson's and Browning's dramatic monologues. Blank verse is one of the supreme English forms in drama and narrative (by Shakespeare and Milton); and perhaps that very fact kept Yeats the Irish nationalist from resorting to unrhymed pentameter with any frequency in his youth.[3] He avoided it then as he avoided the Shakespearean sonnet.

What sort of poetic content required, in Yeats's mind, "lyric" blank verse? The short answer to the question is that Yeats thought blank verse a good medium for two sorts of expository lyric occasions: dialogue on the one hand, and doctrine on the other. In the long run, doctrine supplanted dialogue.

Dialogue is a genre that exists halfway between the solo voice of lyric and the choral (or social) voice of drama. The content of lyric dialogue, if it is to embody the poet's quarrel with himself, must be confrontational, and Yeats would ultimately realize that fact. But his earliest use of blank-verse dialogue does not aim at conflict: he simply adopted blank verse as the conventional medium for middle-level speech of any sort, and his first blank-verse dialogues are sites of mutual reinforcement rather than sites of debate.[4] The 1889 "Ephemera" (79–81; written, according to *NC*, in 1884 when Yeats was nineteen) is spoken by two lovers who engage in no conflict but instead join in agreement that their love is waning. The man suggests at the end that mourning that fact is not necessary, "for other loves await us" in future incarnations. In this instance, Yeats does not trust conversational dialogue to bear the whole emotional burden of the poem: although "Ephemera" opens and closes with dialogue, a narrator (initially heard from in lines 3 and 10) takes over the poem in lines 13–20, as if, in order to interpret the lovers' speeches, we need to be helped by a verbally visualized setting aided by editorial metaphors. In a foretaste of "The Wild Swans at Coole," the poem situates its lovers at a lake: "Pensive they paced along the faded leaves." Between portions of their dialogue, the narrator inserts stage directions:

> The woods were round them, and the yellow leaves
> Fell like faint meteors in the gloom, and once
> A rabbit old and lame limped down the path;
> Autumn was over him; and now they stood
> On the lone border of the lake once more:
> Turning, he saw that she had thrust dead leaves
> Gathered in silence, dewy as her eyes,
> In bosom and hair.

The limping hare is lifted from "The Eve of St. Agnes," while the melancholy female figure with dewy dead leaves in her bosom and hair seems borrowed from the Pre-Raphaelites. The blank verse, with its mournful Tennysonian cadence, lies as far as possible from the energetic blank verse of the English stage. The narrator's additive syntax links together its observations with languid "and's" that set everything on the same visual plane. The woods are round them, *and* the leaves fall, *and* a rabbit limps by, *and* now the lovers stand again at the lake. Yeats is not constructing his blank verse in this fashion out of inadvertence: he is giving it a Pre-Raphaelite flatness of perspective, so that the figures—leaves, rabbit, the lake, the lovers—become two-dimensional, rather than realistic in volume. And the lovers' dialogue—although it is the cause of Yeats's casting the poem into blank verse—seems less interesting to the poet than the scenic descriptions of the narrator. There is mere poetic filler in lines such as "How far away the stars seem, and how far / Is our first kiss, and ah, how old my heart!" But "the yellow leaves / Fell like faint meteors in the gloom," whatever its debt to Tennyson, springs from a poetic imagination.

We find a second blank-verse dialogue between lovers, a lengthy one, in the 1887 playlet "Anashuya and Vijaya" (70–75), a poem probably inspired by dialogues in the Bhagavad Gita, since the lovers are situated in "a little Indian temple of the Golden Age." Anashuya for a moment doubts her lover's fidelity, but she is reassured when Vijaya assures her that he no longer loves his former beloved, Amrita. No further conflict appears, and nothing characterizes the personages of this little dialogue but their name and gender. Perhaps because Yeats recognized the feebleness of the lovers' blank-verse conversation, he interrupts it three times with interposed short lyrics, as if the lovers' deeper feelings required a singing meter more intense or exalted than workaday blank verse. And the blank verse itself scarcely knows its own mind. At one extreme it is loftily Miltonic, as when Anashuya remarks that the "sacred old flamingoes" now appear and

> seek their wonted perches
> Within the temple, devious walking, made
> To wander by their melancholy minds.

"Devious walking," with the adjectival form of the modifier acting as an adverb, is pure Milton. On the other hand, when, six lines later, Anashuya tells Vijaya to ward off the flamingo that wants to eat her rice, the blank verse, in search of "vivacity," descends to triviality:

> Ah! There he snaps my rice. I told you so.
> Now cuff him off. He's off! A kiss for you,
> Because you saved my rice.

Blank verse of this degree of inanity demonstrates that although the young Yeats wants to find a suitable vehicle for a descriptive and conversational middle style, he cannot yet manage it.

Blank-verse dialogue that articulates some real drama between two speakers at last appears in the 1892 "Fergus and the Druid" (102–104). Although Fergus the poet-king has laid aside his crown in favor of his stepson Conchubar, he complains to the "thin grey" Druid that he still feels himself to be "A king and proud!" adding, "and that is my despair." Fergus has so identified his personal identity with his former role as ruler that he can no longer imagine an independent selfhood. Yeats does not attempt to make the conversation between Fergus and the Druid appear "realistic," as in the earlier Indian playlet. Instead, the Druid expresses himself in stately ritual speech, and says the same thing three times (the third time in abbreviated form): "What would you, king of the proud Red Branch Kings?" Fergus re-plies that he wishes to "be no more a king," and also that he wishes to "learn the dreaming wisdom" of the Druid (he is undeterred by the Druid's display of his weak grey body, useless for love or battle). The Druid, com-plying, gives Fergus a small slate-colored bag of dreams, which turns out to both "solve" and "multiply" Fergus's original melancholy. From the bag of dreams, Fergus learns that over the centuries he has had many identities—inanimate, animate, human; this revelation multiplies his original sorrow into "great webs of sorrow," because he has learned that no identity perma-nently fits the self. Yeats's blank verse picks up rhythmic vitality as Fergus, in his stirring closing speech, forsakes the dreamy paratactic "and's" of his sequential narration in favor of a scene-by-scene montage of all his different past lives:

> I have been many things—
> A green drop in the surge, a gleam of light
> Upon a sword, a fir-tree on a hill,
> An old slave grinding at a heavy quern,
> A king sitting upon a chair of gold.

The quickening of the pace by means of a rapid montage suggests that Yeats has begun to understand how to create urgency in blank verse. He learns as well how to use different speech-acts to enliven his unrhymed lines. At the close of the poem, Fergus, having viewed the sequence of his past lives, and feeling their cumulative emotional weight, perceives, with a sigh, that the "dreaming wisdom" of the slate-colored bag of dreams blurs identities into extinction:

> And all these things were wonderful and great;
> But now I have grown nothing, knowing all.

A sudden change of speech-act, in the closing exclamatory burst by Fergus, vivifies the blank verse:

> Ah! Druid, Druid, how great webs of sorrow
> Lay hidden in the small slate-coloured thing!

Portioned out among the diverse visions of his past identities, Fergus feels a greater sorrow than he did in his original confined identity as king. This terse modulated blank verse has no padding; it leads to an unexpected climax, and the ritual speech of the Druid forms a rhetorical counter to Fergus's conversational exposition. Although Yeats's later blank-verse dialogue poems—"Ego Dominus Tuus" and "The Phases of the Moon"—continue the pursuit of wisdom, they do so not under the Celtic sign of "Druidic" myth but under occult directives. Still, they originate from the same impulse as this dialogue between Fergus and the Druid: the desire to find a way to become one of the "most wise of living souls" and impart to others instruction concerning that path.

The last vestiges of the Yeats of dreamy additive blank verse appear in the meditative unrhymed sonnet of 1902, "In the Seven Woods" (198), which serves as proem to the volume by that name. Its additive nature is at first conspicuous: we find six "and's" in the octave (though only one in the sestet). Here blank verse serves Yeats not as a conversational mode but as a descriptive medium—at least the sonnet begins in description, and seems to be enlisting the natural beauty of Coole as a recourse against political bitterness. However, the poem will not end there (see my fuller discussion of this sonnet in Chapter VI). To forecast its apocalyptic end, Yeats manages to impose on the octave's paratactic structure of "and's" an anger that such a ruminative syntax would normally preclude. Although the blank verse of "Fergus and the Druid" had tended toward end-stopped lines, "In the Seven Woods" gains momentum for its octave by relentlessly enjambing every single line, so that the reader must surge on from tranquil Coole of the seven woods to the English vandalizing of Tara to the scandalous celebrations, in Dublin itself, of the coronation of Edward VII:

> I have heard the pigeons of the Seven Woods
> Make their faint thunder, and the garden bees
> Hum in the lime-tree flowers; and put away
> The unavailing outcries and the old bitterness
> That empty the heart. I have forgot awhile
> Tara uprooted, and new commonness
> Upon the throne and crying about the streets
> And hanging its paper flowers from post to post[.]

The blank-verse octave becomes dramatic by the contrast between the pastoral pigeons and bees of the Seven Woods and the poet's political bitterness, especially since the sardonic negative phrases of the octave claim twice as much space as the initiating calm of the Coole murmurs.

In addition to giving his blank verse momentum by enjambment and a drama of contraries, Yeats has begun to insert into this supposedly un-rhymed form, in order to bind his lines together, something resembling rhyme. Here, *bitterness* "rhymes" with *commonness; away* calls out to *awhile;* the lime-tree *flowers* are echoed by the slavish paper *flowers* of monarchic celebration; and the poet's own unavailing out*cries* are replaced by the vulgar *crying* in the streets. Also, Yeats takes care that when reversed feet appear, they do so not randomly, but only where they are warranted, sometimes to emphasize main verbs (*"Make"* and *"Hum"*), sometimes to express outrage (*"Tara* uprooted"). "In the Seven Woods" seeks to make its blank verse so ornately self-sustaining—by internal "rhymes," by syntactic parallelism—that it could be almost as easily recalled to memory as a rhymed form. This aim—a different one from Yeats's resort to blank verse as a conventional index of middle-style conversation—remains a powerful one for the poet (as we will see later in "The Second Coming" and in "Ribh at the Tomb of Baile and Aillinn").

The next blank-verse dialogue, the 1915 poem "The People" (351–353),[5] is the first in which Yeats imitates "real-life" conversation in non-rhymed lines, "reporting" an exchange nine years earlier between himself and Maud Gonne.[6] Of the thirty-seven lines of "The People," all but five render conversation. Unlike "Anashuya and Vijaya" (that earlier conversation between lovers), "The People" does not flee away from blank verse into interspersed songs, but creates a block of blank verse that moves easily between exposition and lyric emotion. When Yeats complains (accurately) about what he has suffered from "the daily spite of this unmannerly town," Maud replies, equally accurately, that she has undergone the same attacks, "'Yet never have I now nor at any time, / Complained of the people.'" The poet, seeking to account for their sharply different responses to the same hostile local audience, explains to Maud, in the most expository passage of the poem, that while her life is one of action, he must, as an artist, live in reflection, analytic observation, and compelled expression:

> 'You, that have not lived in thought but deed,
> Can have the purity of a natural force,
> But I, whose virtues are the definitions
> Of the analytic mind, can neither close
> The eye of the mind nor keep my tongue from speech.'

This vigorous and intellectual sentence is typical of the sinewy blank verse of Yeats's maturity. He is unafraid of inserting analytical remarks into conversational exchange, and unafraid as well of the complex syntax of thought. Dissatisfied with contemporary Ireland, he imagines how much easier his life would have been had he been living during the Renaissance in Ferrara or Urbino, in the company of nobles and writers, talking through the night like the group described by Castiglione in *The Courtier:* "'I might have lived . . . / In the green shadow of Ferrara wall; / Or climbed . . . / the steep street of Urbino . . .'":

> 'I might have had no friend that could not mix
> Courtesy and passion into one like those
> That saw the wicks grow yellow in the dawn;
> I might have used the one substantial right
> My trade allows: chosen my company,
> And chosen what scenery had pleased me best.'

Yeats's counterfactual sixteen-line sentence, with its descriptions of the intimate geography and the intimate company possible in a different life, implies by contrast the poet's real life in Ireland, circumscribed by a quarrelsome town and exhausted by controversy. Somewhere behind the ornate parallel clauses ("'I might have . . .'") of such blank-verse self-scrutiny lie the soliloquies of Shakespeare.

Steadily writing plays for the Abbey Theatre, Yeats worked at making speech dramatic, and the vigorous blank verse of "The People" bears witness not only to his tightening up of syntax into concise hypotactic forms but also to his increasing capacity for enunciating true counter-positions. Such intellectual debate animates another dialogue-poem of 1915, "Ego Dominus Tuus" (367–371), spoken by two interlocutors named only by the Latin deictic pronouns *Hic* ("this one") and *Ille* ("that one"). "Ego Dominus Tuus" stems from Yeats's work on *A Vision;* Jeffares[7] cites Yeats's letter to his father claiming that the poem "has given me a new framework and new patterns." These "new patterns" were the antinomies so basic to Yeats's later thought and writing: Will and Mask, the antithetical and the primary, the subjective and the objective, the waxing gyre and the waning gyre.

"Ego Dominus Tuus" is significant in Yeats's development because it inaugurates his fusing, in his blank verse, dialogue with doctrine. *Hic* is the nineties poet of sorrowful introspection and emotional expression that Yeats used to be, while *Ille* is Yeats the modernist, discovering a new firmness in calling upon an anti-self, an image that is his own opposite, one that will round out what he knows of self and world:

> *Ille.*           By the help of an image
> I call to my own opposite, summon all
> That I have handled least, least looked upon.
> *Hic.*    And I would find myself and not an image.

In the debate, the sensitive *Hic* has the first word, but the objectifying *Ille* the last. The two speakers differ not only in the value they set on introspection but also in the attitude they think art may embody. To the Yeatsian modernist *Ille,* all literature is tragic because life is. *Hic,* finding this a hard doctrine, objects wistfully,

> Yet surely there are men who have made their art
> Out of no tragic war, lovers of life,
> Impulsive men that look for happiness
> And sing when they have found it.

The debaters have opposite notions, too, on how style is to be attained. *Hic* speaks up for tradition and technique: "A style is found by sedentary toil / And by the imitation of great masters," while *Ille,* in the most categorical of his statements, swears by poetry's emotional motive as the path to style, declaring that "Those men that in their writings are most wise / Own nothing but their blind, stupefied hearts." This is a debate that is real, not confected: it is a debate Yeats had conducted within himself for decades. He had himself, by sedentary toil, found a style; but in his maturity, with his style well-practiced, he urged passion as indispensable to poetry, and found in the blindness of the "stupefied heart" a wisdom unknown to stylistic "toil."

In "Ego Dominus Tuus," Yeats has chosen blank verse as a neutral conversational ground on which to base a doctrinal confrontation between two artists of conflicting views. Of course *Ille,* the modernist with the stupefied heart, is given the best lines, and I take one of his manifestos as an example of the kind of blank verse which the mature Yeats can now devise for exposition. *Hic* has just proposed, as we recall, that there can be poets that look for happiness and "sing when they have found it," to which *Ille* responds with a magnificent contempt for rhetoricians and sentimentalists alike, voiced in a blank verse that has become irreproachable:

> *Ille.*               No, not sing,
> For those that love the world serve it in action,
> Grow rich, popular and full of influence,

And should they paint or write, still it is action:
The struggle of the fly in marmalade.
The rhetorician would deceive his neighbours,
The sentimentalist himself; while art
Is but a vision of reality.
What portion in the world can the artist have
Who has awakened from the common dream
But dissipation and despair?

Yeats here dramatically disposes his blank verse in powerful organizing an-
titheses: *sing* versus *action; rhetorician* versus *sentimentalist;* both *rhetorician*
and *sentimentalist* against *artist;* deceiving one's *neighbours* versus deceiving
*oneself;* the *common dream* versus *a vision.* And he refines analytical categories
into subcategories, compelling us to distinguish—among ways of being
worldly—growing *rich,* growing *popular,* and growing *full of influence;* or
making us see, by their relative placement, how *dissipation* leads to *despair.*
The meter is managed equally ably: the commercial swing of "Grow rich,
popular and full of influence" derives from the extra syllable of "popular"
as well as from the jocose reversed second foot that gives stress to both
"rich" and "popular." This sort of false social energy is drastically under-
mined by the dismissive irony of Yeats's regularly-metered line "The strug-
gle of the fly in marmalade" (an unequaled image of the feeble activist
writer drowning in his propagandistic medium). Yeats has mastered, as this
line demonstrates, the Shakespearean ability to construct an entire blank-
verse line out of a few (here three, sometimes only two) emphasized words,
with the other unimportant words dropping to invisibility "below" the line:

| struggle | fly | marmalade. |
|---|---|---|
| (The) | (of the) | (in) |

Another such line—"Is but a vision of reality," with its two powerful
nouns—is the brief but crowning line of this stern blank-verse passage, the
one that makes the greatest claim. A poet who makes writing a form of ac-
tion directed toward serving the world, says Yeats, is either writing with one
eye on public reaction (the rhetorician aiming to deceive his neighbors) or
with an eye to making himself look agreeable (the sentimentalist deceiving
himself). The way of the artist, by contrast, is to look neither at his audi-
ence nor at himself, but at reality. Art is "but"—a great deprecatory "but"—

a vision of reality. Although reality is its object, art cannot be a literal transcription of what is outside us, because each of us sees reality through the scrims of temperament, particular knowledge, and individual feeling. What we see is in one sense reality and in another sense a "vision"—a symbolic construct on an imagined plane—of reality. The true artist, who has not covertly trained his eye on his neighbors' image of him or his own image of himself, has a better chance of approaching reality through his "vision" than the rhetorician or the sentimentalist. It is hard to realize that the line "Is but a vision of reality" has ten syllables—it has such a careless, "throwaway" sound after the magniloquent "The rhetorician would deceive his neighbours." The understatement of the line guarantees both its purity of assertion and its subversive impact. By bringing into conjunction two words—"vision" and "reality"—that normally form an antithesis, Yeats makes them mirror each other.

In the closing words of this doctrine of authenticity, Yeats is remembering the "tragic generation," the poets of the nineties who woke from the "common dream" and, having nothing but introspection to fall back on, yielded to "dissipation and despair." His friends' collapses into alcoholism and mental illness were only too familiar to Yeats. By putting the line about dissipation interrogatively, not scornfully as he had the lines about rhetoricians and sentimentalists, Yeats manages here a nuanced succession of speech-acts in his blank verse: the tone suddenly darkens into a suicidal alliteration in "dissipation and despair." Yeats's rhythmic variety and syntactic command—coupled with the imagination that conjures up the fly in marmalade—enable him here, without the ornament of rhyme, to make ringing poetry out of a blank verse stamped with the image of his syntactically complex style.

"The Phases of the Moon" (372–377)—also cast into blank verse because it expounds doctrine—is less vivid than "Ego Dominus Tuus" simply because there is no debate: Owen Aherne is merely a companion and interlocutor to Michael Robartes, the expounder of the moon's phases:

> *Aherne.* Sing me the changes of the moon once more;
>   True song, though speech: 'mine author sung it me.'
> *Robartes.* Twenty and eight the phases of the moon . . .

After the 25-line recitation of the moon-phases, Aherne merely replies, "Sing out the song; sing to the end, and sing / The strange reward of all that discipline," whereupon Robartes continues his instruction of Aherne through the end of the poem. The task Yeats set himself in this poem was to present in verse, without becoming either unintelligible or predictable, his periodic table of human psychological elements arrayed under the phases of the moon. This piece of doctrinal exposition has probably never been anyone's favorite work. But Yeats's blank verse here, in its best moments, can exhibit the epigrammatic compression and acid scorn that we have seen in "Ego Dominus Tuus," not least when it claims that those who fear and flee the imagination's dream create in themselves a deformity of soul. The socially approved "best" citizens of both sexes, needless to say, have the most deformed souls:

> *Robartes.* Reformer, merchant, statesman, learned man,
>     Dutiful husband, honest wife by turn,
>     Cradle upon cradle, and all in flight and all
>     Deformed because there is no deformity
>     But saves us from a dream.

Yeats was sometimes annoyed at his own turn to versified dogma, complaining about one unpublished prose narrative concerning Robartes and Aherne (which was to become *Michael Robartes and his Friends*) that "I must amend and find a place for [it] some day because I was fool enough to write half a dozen poems that are unintelligible without it."[8] But in spite of such slighting words, Yeats's own "system," expounded in *A Vision,* enthralled him for some years, and he strove to analogize it to better-known dogmatic systems, chiefly the Christian one, so that it might become intelligible to others. As he said in his collective note (in the 1933 *Collected Poems*) to "The Phases of the Moon," "The Double Vision of Michael Robartes," and "Michael Robartes and the Dancer," the figures of Michael Robartes and Owen Aherne "take their place in a phantasmagoria in which I endeavour to explain my philosophy of life and death. To some extent I wrote these poems as a text for exposition" (821).

In his single best-known blank-verse poem, the 1919 "The Second Coming" (401–402), Yeats queries whether his "system"—which embodies the old millennial myth of a third era to succeed the classical and Christian ones—predicts the Second Coming of Christ. (Of course, it is not the *parousia,* Christ's return, that the apocalyptic imagery foretells; it is the arrival of a monster, half-beast, half-man, bent on inhabiting a cradle at Bethlehem.) It is because "The Second Coming" is a doctrinal poem that Yeats casts it into blank verse (I have treated it at more length in the chapter on

Yeats's sonnets; here, I am considering its line rather than its architectonics). Yeats is no longer using blank verse to simulate dialogue: here there are no *Hic* and *Ille*, no Aherne and Robartes, not even a Yeats and a Maud. Instead, Yeats creates a single speaker, who at first struggles with his present sense of the world and then conveys to us his unexpected revelation. Yet this single speaker is interiorly divided, engaging in a dialogue of the mind with itself (to use Matthew Arnold's term). Yeats's speaker discovers as he muses that he can adopt either the objectivity of the prophet (which enables his first octave) or the subjectivity of the sufferer, but not both at once; and, abandoning his initial stance as a prophetic observer, he finishes his poem in ambivalent subjectivity. In the opening octave we hear only apodictic impersonal statements that are epigrammatic in form; but then a white space, denoting a change in focus, appears after line 8, stopping the poem in its tracks. Two unsure "surely's" move the poem into a subjective first-person mode, away from its earlier prophetic stance. The indignant desert birds stand for the human indignation before change that succeeds the initial inhuman, omniscient assertions by the Yeatsian speaker.

What can we say about the perfected blank verse of "The Second Coming"? Like almost all blank verse, it exhibits both end-stopped and enjambed lines. In Yeats's other blank-verse poems these kinds are frequently intermixed, but in "The Second Coming" the poet tends to separate a passage with end-stopped lines from an enjambed passage, so that each may have its own effect. Yeats's blank verse is especially formal at the omniscient "objective" opening of the poem; the prophetic voice pronounces the last three of its initial four lines in stern end-stopped clauses, as though each line or half-line contained a formula for the end of the world:

> Turning and turning in the widening gyre
> The falcon cannot hear the falconer;
> Things fall apart; the centre cannot hold;
> Mere anarchy is loosed upon the world[.]

In place of rhyme, these lines substitute an internal coherence intensified not only by repetition ("Turning . . . turning; falcon . . . falconer; cannot . . . cannot") but also by end half-rhyme ("gyre . . . falconer; hold . . . world), internal rhyme ("hear . . . mere"), and irrational graphic binding (**fal**-con . . . **fal**-coner . . . **fall**"). We read the next two couplets of the poem semantically as four grim free-standing statements, as confident as the end-stopped pronouncements of the first four lines:

> **The blood-dimmed tide is loosed;**
>     (and everywhere)
> **The ceremony of innocence is drowned;**
> **The best lack all conviction;**
>     (while)
> **The worst are full of passionate intensity.**

The "trick" of the blank verse here, as we saw earlier in "Ego Dominus Tuus," is to charge every word in the "free-standing" statements with such significance that "insignificant" words such as "and everywhere" and "while" melt almost into invisibility, leaving the four free-standing statements solidly frontal. The copulative verbs are also relatively invisible, in that they could (without sacrificing meaning) be replaced by adjectives: the loosed tide, the drowned ceremony, the passionately intense worst.

But when the prophet's boldly assertive stance is replaced by the first-person visual confrontation with the suddenly manifest Sphinx-like creature, no such free-standing abstract assertions about the best and the worst can be uttered. Telling is replaced by showing; the mental image cannot be explained, it can only be exhibited. We are made to see the image by the rising momentum of a single descriptive sentence, interrupted only by commas:

> Somewhere in sands of the desert
> A shape with lion body and the head of a man,
> A gaze blank and pitiless as the sun,
> Is moving its slow thighs, while all about it
> Reel shadows of the indignant desert birds.

The chief stylistic "trick" of this passage is to anatomize the beast in disjunctive parts—lion-body, male head, a blank gaze, slow thighs—so as to reproduce within the reader the speaker's unfamiliar and slowly accretive experience of the "shape." (Yeats adopts this indefinite noun from Milton, who uses it for the indescribable allegorical figure of Death in *Paradise Lost*.) The "shape" is twinned with "somewhere"—an equally indescribable location. "In sands . . . A shape . . . A gaze": these phrases single out parts that do not add up to a *gestalt;* the disturbed birds too appear obliquely and uncategorizably, as "shadows." Yet there do exist here some undeniable specificities: sands, lion, man, thighs, birds. Like an image in a dream, the thing seen in the vision is both entirely clear and entirely indefinable. The blank verse line is used here in two full-length extensions, twinned by anaphora ("A shape . . . / A gaze"), to denote the vision, and yet within each of these two lines the nouns brought into conjunction are discordant: in the first, *shape, lion, body, head, man;* in the second, *gaze* and *sun.* The blank verse about the blank gaze rolls on without hindrance through its ten syllables, but its bizarre content belies its apparent coherence. As he did earlier, in "Leda and the Swan," Yeats pushes the pentameter line here from statement to a final question, one that has become as famous as the one that closes "Leda." As Seamus Heaney has remarked, the assertiveness of the verse of "The Second Coming" says "Yes" to the question of "Do I know?", while the query at the end suggests that that knowledge is at best partial. A final question is not a common occurrence in the blank-verse lyric tradition.

"The Second Coming" marks, with respect to technique, the end of the story of Yeats and blank verse, whether as a vehicle for conversational dialogue, as a sterner vehicle for doctrine, or both (as in "Ego Dominus Tuus"). After writing "The Second Coming," Yeats really had nothing more to learn about making supple, symbolic, economical, and memorable blank verse—a form that had now outgrown, in his work, its Tennysonian origins and its paratactic clauses.[9] But I do want to mention, in closing, two later blank-verse lyrics: "Ribh at the Tomb of Baile and Aillinn" and "In Tara's Halls." The first of these (the opening poem of Yeats's 1934 sequence called "Supernatural Songs") is discussed at greater length in Chapter XII. Here, it is enough to say that it is cast in blank verse because it is the doctrinal prologue to the eleven following poems of "Supernatural Songs"; none of the others is composed in blank verse. In his prologue, the monk Ribh explains to curious passersby that the light by which he reads his book in the dark is generated by the recurrent embrace in the afterlife of the mythical lovers Baile and Aillinn. After Ribh's two-line prelude, the sentences of instruction—in a familiar Yeatsian pattern—gradually lengthen to three, four, seven, and eight lines respectively, with the two longest sentences reserved for doctrine and for visionary recapitulation. Yeats's blank verse fits sentence-length to drama, symbolizing by the longest sentence the recapitulatory nature (with respect to the earlier sentences) of the literary tale that Ribh retells.

I said earlier that Yeats's aesthetic aim in creating his distinctive form of blank verse is to make it so intricately self-referential (lexically and syntactically) that we remember it as if it were rhymed. We can see this practice at work in "Ribh at the Tomb of Baile and Aillinn" (quoted in full in Chapter XII), as the monk Ribh relates to unnamed auditors his vision of "the inter-

course of angels," in fact the dead lovers Baile and Aillinn, who by their em-
brace generate a miraculous light enabling Ribh to read his book in the
dark. In the first *sixteen* lines of "Ribh at the Tomb of Baile and Aillinn"
there are only five internally repeated words *(speak, heard, join [is joined],
touching, whole),* but in the *ten*-line reprise occupying the last third of the
poem (lines 17–27) so many additional words are repeated or paralleled
from the first two-thirds that the poem becomes, by such increased back-
stitching, an overlay of self on self:

| Lines 1–16 (Tale) | Lines 17–27 (Reprise) |
| --- | --- |
| in the pitch-dark night | in the pitch-dark atmosphere |
| with open book | my holy book |
| my tale | their tale |
| this head . . . this voice | these eyes |
| heard | heard |
| speak | speak |
| leaf | the leaves |
| the apple and the yew | the apple and the yew |
| their bones | bone |
| such a death | their death |
| pure substance | purified |
| join | is joined |
| no touching | nor touching |
| here | here . . . here |
| whole | whole |
| a light | that light . . . that light |
| the anniversary | the anniversary |

Yeats superimposes, in the fashion of a palimpsest, three things: the original
mythical narrative of the doomed love of Baile and Aillinn; Ribh's doctrine
of the light given off by "the intercourse of angels"; and the present light-
generating embrace of the translated lovers. This "matched" overlaying,
"guaranteeing" the trustworthiness of Ribh's tale, creates such a number of
semantic "rhymes" that we may for a moment be unaware that we are read-
ing blank verse.

By casting "Ribh at the Tomb of Baile and Aillinn" into blank verse,
Yeats removes the matter of the poem from the realm of legend and super-
stition (where we might place it in reading Yeats's earlier lyrical tetrameter
version of the lovers in "Baile and Aillinn"), and brings it into the realm of
discursive seriousness. We are of course to take its structure imaginatively:
it serves as an example of the miraculous symbolic mutual "fit" of the plane

of archaic myth, the plane of literary tale, the plane of doctrinal formulation, and the plane of incandescent recursive recapitulation of myth within the virtual space of the meditating mind.

The last of the blank-verse poems, "In Tara's Halls" (609), was written in 1938, a year before Yeats's death. An argument against dependency, spoken by an anonymous narrator, it too is a doctrinal parable even though it masquerades as a narrative: it exists to assert the power of the resolved will. The narrator says that a certain man (Yeats's draft calls him "A certain King") fears, now that his hundredth year has ended, that he is about to enter the stage of dependency, and, finding the thought intolerable, he wills himself to die. He announces to all that his independence has been so fierce that he has never asked for love from the women he has known; nor will he now, in old age, ask return of love from God, either:

> 'God I have loved, but should I ask return
> Of God or woman, the time were come to die.'

After quoting this speech of the resolved centenarian, the narrator continues in his own voice and shows us the man a year later. Describing the man's last days, he ascribes to him six ceremonious verbs, of which three occur in the last line of the poem. I italicize the verbs:

> He *bade,* his hundred and first year at end,
> Diggers and carpenters make grave and coffin;
> *Saw* that the grave was deep, the coffin sound,
> *Summoned* the generations of his house,
> *Lay* in the coffin, *stopped* his breath and *died.*

Here, by contrast with the gradually expanding sentences of Ribh, the clauses shrink in length: two lines for the first verb ("bade"); one line each for the next two ("saw" and "summoned"); and finally one single line for the last three verbs ("lay," "stopped," and "died"). Yeats has his centenarian and his narrator both speak in blank verse because he wishes to present this terminal exertion of will less as anecdote than as moral doctrine. We know nothing of the narrator of the poem (whom we can think of as Yeats) except that he praises a nameless man ("A man I praise that once in Tara's halls"), and that this man is identified, by the phrase "in Tara's halls," with archaic epic strength. The story is a nationalist exemplum recounted for our admiration and imitation; its "miracle" of mind over matter, a self-willed extinction, resembles the miraculous insensibilities of the Hindu monks in "Meru." This stoic old man of stern executive will is the immobile opposite of the volatile old men of Yeats's rhymed poems, who (except in the sonnet "Meru") are granted creative "frenzy," or go mad because of the tragedies they have seen where there is "no finish worthy of the start" ("Why should not Old Men be Mad?").

The late rhyming poems of this sort, consecrated to the frustrations of life as it approaches death, remain on the human plane. Those of Yeats's blank-verse poems that represent ordinary conversation between, say, the poet and Maud Gonne also take place on the human level. Those that contain occult dialogue, such as "The Phases of the Moon," oscillate between the human plane and some other realm—the plane of Phase 14, or a plane of ideal song. But the poems in blank verse that either expound Yeatsian doctrine, exhibit visionary palimpsests, or offer stoic moral fables are constructed to exist entirely on a hypothetical abstract plane, often geometrical, always exalted. To the end of his life, Yeats observed the division between experiential suffering that required the consolation of rhyme, and the sort of dialogue or philosophical instruction that demanded the dry dignity of blank verse.

## ᔕ— THE RENAISSANCE AURA:
## *OTTAVA RIMA* POEMS

The stanza known as *ottava rima* (for its eight lines) was one of Yeats's favorite forms.[1] Because it rhymes *ababbcc*, it "naturally" falls into two parts, a six-line portion and a closing couplet. The reader of Yeats's *Collected Poems* first encounters *ottava rima* in "Sailing to Byzantium," the opening poem of *The Tower*. Though "Sailing to Byzantium" is neither the earliest-composed poem in *The Tower* nor the title poem (which Yeats placed second), it was given pride of place not only for its thematic relevance in this volume treating old age, but also because it announces, opulently, the appearance of a new metrical form for Yeats—one that he would continue to explore for the rest of his life, not only in single poems but also in some of his most famous sequences. We see, among the *ottava rima* poems in *The Tower*, not only "Sailing to Byzantium" and "Among School Children" but also two parts of "Meditations in Civil War" ("Ancestral Houses" and "My Descendants"), as well as the first part of "Nineteen Hundred and Nineteen" ("Many ingenious lovely things are gone"). In *The Winding Stair*, there are several more instances of *ottava rima*: the one-stanza poem "The Choice" (originally the penultimate stanza of "Coole Park and Ballylee, 1931"); the two Coole Park poems of 1929 and 1931; parts II ("A tree there is") and III ("Get all the gold and silver") of "Vacillation"; and part VIII ("Her Vision in the Wood") of "A Woman Young and Old." Subsequently, "Parnell's Funeral" (part I, "Under the Great Comedian's Tomb"),[2] "The Gyres," "The Municipal Gallery Revisited," "The Circus Animals' Desertion," and "The Statues" arrive to fill out the list.

What is this form that meant so much to Yeats? As its name implies, it is an Italian stanza, first brought into English by Edward Fairfax's translation of Tasso's *Gerusalemme Liberata* (1600). Although Byron (drawing on Ariosto) adopted it to comic effect in *Don Juan,* Yeats was attracted to it chiefly by reading Shelley ("The Witch of Atlas," "The Zucca," the Homeric "Hymn to Mercury"). Shelley's *ottava rima* relies on diffuse atmospherics, while Yeats (as usual in his later life) was bent on a precise and forthright speech. As Seamus Heaney describes it, the stanza is a "strong-arched room . . . which serves as a redoubt for the resurgent spirit. . . . The unshakably affirmative music of this *ottava rima* stanza is the formal correlative of the poet's indomitable spirit."[3] It is Yeats who established *ottava rima* as a viable modern form, fit for everything serious—valediction, ode, historical meditation, fantasy. But what atmosphere did Yeats wish to confer on a poem when he decided on *ottava rima* for its form?

Yeats's 1907 six-week trip to Italy with Augusta and Robert Gregory gave him the confidence to think of the Italian Renaissance as a potential cultural model for Ireland. By invoking the success of Italian patronage in fostering art, he could evade invoking as a model Renaissance England (an act impossible for him as an Irish nationalist). *Ottava rima,* given its origins, was adopted by Yeats as a shortcut to mean, ideologically speaking, "courtliness," "stateliness," "aristocratic personhood," "a patronage culture," and "the Renaissance"; and these values are often explicitly evoked in his *ottava rima* poems (as in "Ancestral Houses"). But the stanza had another value for Yeats, a structural one: its expansive sixain and conclusive couplet enabled a geometrically exact "placing" of internal elements (as we saw in "Sailing to Byzantium" in Chapter II).

The eight-line *ottava rima* stanza is formally linked, by its pentameter width, to other substantial blocks of rhymed pentameter. Its closest relative is the octave of the courtly Italian sonnet *(abbaabba),* its next-closest the seven-line "aristocratic" rhyme royal *(ababbcc)* reserved by Yeats exclusively for Maud Gonne ("A Bronze Head") and the group of beloved "noble" women with whom he numbered her ("Hound Voice"); see Chapter XIII, "Rare Forms." Among the lyrics of the Western tradition, poems in pentameter lines are the weighty ones, useful for sublime or philosophical topics. Although lyrics in *unrhymed* pentameter (blank verse) are, as we have seen, imitative of both ordinary speech and exposition, *rhymed* pentameter poems are imitations not of speech but of lofty song. Their rhymes bring them into the tradition of song, but their pentameter breadth prevents their being considered "songs" in the idiomatic sense of folk or art songs. Instead, pentameter rhyming poems are closer to sacred song: ode, choral commentary, public hymn. (A student of mine, Nathan Rose, once said of Yeats's *ottava rima* that it is Yeats's "senatorial" form.)

The expected way to fill up the asymmetrical 6 + 2 formal shell of the *ottava rima* would be to offer a sustained six-line description or speculation followed by an epigrammatic couplet. And indeed Yeats sometimes filled out the shell in just that way:

> An aged man is but a paltry thing,
> A tattered coat upon a stick, unless
> Soul clap its hands and sing, and louder sing
> For every tatter in its mortal dress,
> Nor is there singing school but studying
> Monuments of its own magnificence;
> And therefore I have sailed the seas and come
> To the holy city of Byzantium.

After the six third-person lines about the generalized "aged man" and his needs, there arrives a first-person conclusive couplet, fortified by its resonant and unusual rhyme ("come/Byzantium"), itself made salient by being repeated in reverse order at the end of the poem, when the golden bird will sing "To lords and ladies of Byzantium / Of what is past, or passing, or to come." In "Sailing to Byzantium" these grand echoing couplets mark, respectively, the halfway point of the poem and its close, showing us how useful as a punctuation-point the sonorous couplet of the *ottava rima* stanza can be.

To Yeats, the *ottava rima* stanza often seemed not so much a stanza as a station, a place, a location. He had begun (in his 1919 elegy "In Memory of Major Robert Gregory") the practice, which became common in and after *The Tower* (1928), of prefacing the separate stanzas of certain poems with Roman numerals. This formal numbering bestows on each stanza the importance we normally ascribe to a member of a sequence. "Sailing to Byzantium," for example, is transformed by its four Roman numerals into a solid four-poem sequence, with each part representing a significant step into a different spatial "environment"; I call these environments "stations," since the speaker is stationed within them. As we saw in Chapter II, the stations in this poem might be named as places: I: The Country of the Young; II: Byzantium; III: Hagia Sophia; IV: The Emperor's Palace. The stately self-conscious amplitude of Yeats's numbered *ottava rima* stanzas reinforces our impression of the function of the Roman numerals—that they are there to make the poem a deliberated "sequence" which steps, with each numeral, to a different mental location, rather than a spontaneous "lyric."

When Roman numerals are absent, another way of sharpening the focus of an individual *ottava rima* stanza is a marked internal change in the register of its diction, as in the single-stanza poem "The Choice" (495). The first four lines are framed in three classic forms of Christian diction: the diction of moral choice ("No man can serve two masters"); the diction of personal salvation ("In my father's house there are many mansions"); and the diction of damnation ("They shall be cast into outer darkness amid weeping and gnashing of teeth"):

> The intellect of man is forced to choose
> Perfection of the life, or of the work,
> And if it take the second must refuse
> A heavenly mansion, raging in the dark.

To choose perfection of the life is the way of the saint. To choose perfection of the work is the way of the artist—and for this choice, according to the Christian view (as Yeats interprets it), the artist is damned. All this has been put very concisely in this first half of the *ottava rima* stanza, a splendid and uncompromising quatrain pitched at a religious height. But the two lines that follow jeer, in their commonness ("what's the news?") and materiality ("toil" that leaves a "mark"), at the aloof sublimity of the first quatrain with its Judeo-Christian myths of heavenly mansions and demonic darkness. No matter which choice is made, says the newly derisive speaker, at the end of life one is old and worn out:

> When all that story's finished, what's the news?
> In luck or out the toil has left its mark[.]

How can such a poem end? Which side will win—the sublime or the sardonic? And what diction can the final couplet use, after the declaration that religion is bankrupt and that the end-result of perfection of the work—work now denigrated to "toil"—is simply a scarring of the self?

The remarkable closing couplet of this example of *ottava rima* consists, basically, of four finely chosen nouns: the alliterating "perplexity" and "purse," and the antithetical "vanity" and "remorse":

> That old perplexity an empty purse,
> Or the day's vanity, the night's remorse.

This couplet serves to explain the mark left by the life's toil. Each of the lines is an epigram: the first considers the original intellectual problem ("that old perplexity") of choice between two vocations, while the second judges the poet's conduct. In the first line, the old perplexity—whether to choose sainthood or an artistic vocation—turns out to be "an empty purse," profitless and unrewarding, because one is chosen by, rather than chooses, a destiny.[4] In the second line, the work one was so vain about in the daytime becomes, in the watches of the night, matter for remorse (as in "The Man and the Echo"). The double epigram in the couplet can in this way be regulated into sense, but I am more interested here in its aesthetic effect. The two nouns of the first line—*perplexity, purse*—reinscribe the contest between the lofty and the vulgar dictions of the first six lines; but the two nouns of the second line—*vanity, remorse*—belong to a single register of diction, that of moralized personal emotion. Although they clash in content, they do not clash in plane: they are located on the same plane (the psychological plane where one evaluates one's conduct), whereas *perplexity* and *purse* come from two different planes entirely (the moral and the material).

To summarize: lines 1–4 are composed on the religious plane of diction, and are jeered at by lines 5–6, which are composed on a vulgar plane. Line 7 resumes this conflict between the lofty and the vulgar in epigrammatic fashion; but in line 8 Yeats finds a way to resublimate the artist's life, not lifting it to the heaven of reward, nor letting it rest in the gutter with the castaway "empty purse," but rather judging the creation of art by referring it to the intellect's scale of ethics, registering its original exaltation in vanity and its subsequent self-critique in remorse. Every line of the *ottava rima* counts, but the last counts most.

In reading Yeats's poems in *ottava rima,* we need to be aware of the attention he paid to the pacing of what is normally (in its serious, non-Byronic form) a very steadily-stepping stanza. The sharpest change in pace in all of Yeats's *ottava rima* poems occurs in part I of "Nineteen Hundred and Nineteen" (428–430), where at first, as we saw in Chapter III, the formal elegiac beginning ("Many ingenious lovely things are gone") confers an oratorical stateliness that continues even through the mention of the guardsmen's "drowsy chargers." Suddenly, as the fourth stanza opens and "the Troubles" enter the poem, the pacing changes. The collapse of liberal faith in progress generates a fierce set of enjambments followed by a "spillover" of the six-line body of the stanza into the seventh line, and finally a violent drop into an abyss at the end:

> Now days are dragon-ridden, the nightmare
> Rides upon sleep: a drunken soldiery
> Can leave the mother, murdered at her door,
> To crawl in her own blood, and go scot-free;

> The night can sweat with terror as before
> We pieced our thoughts into philosophy,
> And planned to bring the world under a rule,
> Who are but weasels fighting in a hole.

The fantasy material here—dragon and nightmare—bursts in upon the poem in a demotic incursion of the sort we saw in lines 5–7 of "The Choice." Words of a raw reality thrust themselves forward: *drunken, murdered, crawl, scot-free, sweat, fight, weasels, hole*. These words jostle for place, swarming around the scornfully discounted "lofty" words of the stanza—*thought, plan, rule, philosophy*. With each new verbal or participial theater of action of the stanza, there arrives a new agent—*days, dragon, nightmare, soldiery, mother, night, we, weasels*—making the clauses scramble helter-skelter, one after the other. The headlong pace is crucial: fighting weasels cannot be asked to inhabit the ceremoniously paced lines of normal *ottava rima*.

Our sense of Yeats's *ottava rima* stanza is affected not only by its pacing, but also by its varieties of inner structure. In one sort of experiment with *ottava rima*, Yeats deliberately violates the normative thought-division into 6 and 2, and plays up instead the two-quatrain possibilities of the eight-line stanza. We can see in the three-stanza "My Descendants" (422–423)—part IV of "Meditations in Time of Civil War"—how Yeats makes the two-quatrain division of his stanza act symbolically in the first two stanzas of the poem. In the first stanza we find, initially, a proud quatrain of flourishing:

> Having inherited a vigorous mind
> From my old fathers, I must nourish dreams
> And leave a woman and a man behind
> As vigorous of mind . . .

But these purposeful lines quickly sponsor a pang, an "and yet" which creates four antithetical lines of decline:

> and yet it seems
> Life scarce can cast a fragrance on the wind,
> Scarce spread a glory to the morning beams,
> But the torn petals strew the garden plot;
> And there's but common greenness after that.

The second stanza of "My Descendants" is also divided into two quatrains, distinguished from each other by their respective speech-acts. The first quatrain, a question, fears the decline of progeny:

> And what if my descendants lose the flower
> Through natural declension of the soul,
> Through too much business with the passing hour,
> Through too much play, or marriage with a fool?

The second quatrain, an annihilating prayer, prophesies a decay of masonry paralleling the decay of family:

> May this laborious stair and this stark tower
> Become a roofless ruin that the owl
> May build in the cracked masonry and cry
> Her desolation to the desolate sky.

These angular four-line slants of the first two stanzas of "My Descendants"—a slant of upward flourish followed by an equal and opposite slant of decline, then a downward dynastic slippage paralleled by an equal downward architectural slippage—are sharply contradicted in stanza 3. Stanzas 1 and 2 have suggested angular comic and tragic views of life, which must exhibit either a flourishing or a decline. But Yeats no longer trusts either of those models, and he counters their sharp slants by the geometric counter-figure of the circle.

Unlike its two predecessors, the "circular" stanza 3 is not composed of equal quatrain-slants of directed motion up or down; in fact, it opens with a two-line repudiation of such slants as distasteful to the First Mover of the universe, who prefers circles to such an extent that he has installed them everywhere, down to the instincts of birds:

> The Primum Mobile that fashioned us
> Has made the very owls in circles move.

(I must add that the horizontal circle in which the owls move has been foreshadowed in the vertical echo-circuit in stanza 2, by which the owl in the ruin cries "her *desolation* to the *desolate* sky" [italics mine].) This closing third stanza "proves" its assertion of the superior value of circular form by shaping itself into the figure of speech which represents a circle, the *abba* figure of chiasmus, which bites its own tail. Here, the chiasmus consists of the four words *love: friendship :: friendship: love,* which make up an "inner quatrain" (lines 3–6) within the *ottava rima* of stanza 3, constructing a circlet enclosing (the unnamed) Augusta Gregory and George Yeats within a wreath of love and friendship:

> And I, that count myself most prosperous,
> Seeing that **love** and **friendship** are enough,
> For an old neighbour's **friendship** chose the house
> And decked and altered it for a girl's **love**[.]

This stanza of circles closes with a two-line couplet dismissing linear models of "flourish and decline." But it still hopes to defeat the turbulence of the Primum Mobile's gyres by an image of material endurance. The stones of his ruined tower, Yeats prophesies, will remain stable even if generations enter and exit:

> And [I] know whatever flourish and decline
> These stones remain their monument and mine.

Thus the complete thought-structure of the last stanza of "My Descendants" is an unusual 2-4-2 one—couplet, quatrain, couplet—and, by enclosing in the quatrain a "circlet" of its own, this final stanza contradicts the rigid 4-4 slants of flourish or decline of the preceding two stanzas of the poem.

"My Descendants" could not have seemed aesthetically credible to Yeats (I would argue) unless its *thematic* notions found a mimetic reflection in the structure of the stanzas narrating them. The five models of history to which Yeats has recourse—first a comic model of rise, then a tragic model of fall; then a catastrophic model of repeated falls; and finally a comic "circular" model of eternal return combined with a "horizontal" static model of endurance—are not in themselves new. What *is* new is that they are made convincing in stanzas that act out the slants in formally equal quatrains and in a final stanza centered on a circular chiasmus. It is always worthwhile to search beneath Yeats's fixed rhyme schemes to observe the structural arrangements within his stanzas. The double decline of stanza 2, for instance, reveals that Yeats has not really been convinced of anything but catastrophe before he is reassured by the Primum Mobile's preference for circles. And the last stanza, which so obviously participates, by its inner chiasmus, in the circular determinism of the Primum Mobile, tells us that even what once seemed inalterable and universal historical decay (the slants) can be interpreted in a wider way, can be seen as part of normal recurrences and (with the stones) as an enduring state.

Yeats's single most sustained use of agitation within his *ottava rima* occurs, not surprisingly, in "The Statues" (610–611), his last work in the form. The large cultural sweep of this poem—from Pythagoras to Pearse—duplicates the tumultuous role, throughout history, of the invention, embodiment, and migration of art. Austere Pythagorean geometries of form, though a necessary condition for the existence of art, are not in themselves sufficient. Only an overlay of "casual flesh," met by a responsive kiss, gives statues character. Conceptual power is nothing without embodiment in a medium. It was, after all, the Phidian statues (storing within themselves powerful cultural energy) that allowed the outnumbered Greeks to defeat the swarming Persians at Salamis. And power within a single culture is not enough to maintain art; art's inherent force spreads to colonize other cultures, just as Alexander colonized the known world. However, as art spreads from colonizer to colonized, from Greece to India, the colonized take silent possession by gradually transforming the art of the colonizer into something of their own. Who now, except a connoisseur, would recognize in Ghandaran Buddhas their Hellenic prototypes? In those statues of Buddha, the Hellenic has been made Asiatic. Finally there arrives, inevitably (according to Yeats's Spenglerian narrative), the decadence of any cultural form, no matter how great its earlier power. Representation loses real-life reference, and "mirror on mirror mirrored is all the show." Greco-European meaning is lost in the meditative emptiness of Buddha.

In Yeats's mapping in "The Statues," the spirit of sculptural passion has moved from Egypt to Greece to India, and this spirit, says the poet, will now begin its work anew, this time in Ireland, where Pearse's revolutionary passion enables the geometries of the past to arise again:

> When Pearse summoned Cuchulain to his side,
> What stalked through the Post Office? What intellect,
> What calculation, number, measurement, replied?

These two climactic questions begin the final stanza of "The Statues"; in this respect the last stanza resembles the first, which began with a first-line question: "Pythagoras planned it. Why did the people stare?" In a reversal of the normal six-plus-two proportion of the *ottava rima* stanzas, these first and fourth stanzas of "The Statues" are "up-ended," having their "little part" at the opening and their "long part" at the end. In fact, looking back over "The Statues," we discover that *all* the stanzas of the poem are similarly asymmetrical in the irregular way in which they articulate their sentences. Although the two middle stanzas of the poem obey the "rule" of giving the couplet its own syntactic unit (here, a sentence), the management of the sentences preceding the "regular" couplet is so erratic that even the "obedient" closing couplets are insufficient to calm the turbulence that precedes them. For instance, in stanza 3, it is quite some time before the opening noun, "One image," which "crossed" and "sat" and "grew," is identified as "a fat / Dreamer of the Middle Ages":

> One image crossed the many-headed, sat
> Under the tropic shade, grew round and slow,
> No Hamlet thin from eating flies, a fat
> Dreamer of the Middle Ages.

And even when we find the vague medieval analogy to that "one image," we do not know where or in what shape the "one image" landed after it had crossed the "many-headed" foam of the sea. Only when we arrive at the penultimate word of the entire stanza—"Buddha"—are we permitted to know what appearance the Greek image assumed in India after its long journey. Such a stanza negates, in every way, the serenity and graciousness of the normative *ottava rima* stanza.

The torsion that Yeats inflicts on his *ottava rima* is of course only one of the many forms of agitation pressed into service for "The Statues." Other "disturbances" in the poem include a plethora of culturally heterogeneous proper names (from Phidias to Hamlet, from Grimalkin to Buddha and Cuchulain); the presence of sudden questions and an exclamation ("No!"); the noticeable number of extremely active verbs *(stalk, throw, wreck, climb)*; the varied *dramatis personae* (from Phidias to Cuchulain). These are all unreposeful assemblages. The frequent enjambment, too, destroys the steady rhythm characteristic of "normal" *ottava rima*. Even the rhymes of "The Statues," except for those in the couplets, avoid conclusiveness, as Yeats rhymes *stare* and *character* and *were; men, down,* and *upon; slow* and *knew*. It is not until his concluding stanza that Yeats creates only "perfect" rhymes *(side, replied, tide; intellect, sect, wrecked; trace, face)*. By making agitation— rather than repose or steadiness—the characteristic mark of the *ottava rima* of "The Statues," Yeats turns the form on its head, letting its earlier connotation of the "aristocratic" stability of art be troubled by the historical migrations, transformations, and revolutionary upheavals in which art participates.

The value of *ottava rima* to Yeats can be seen differently in the three-part sequence "The Circus Animals' Desertion" (629–630), the last-placed of the *ottava rima* poems in the *Collected Poems* (though not the last written, which was "The Statues").[5] "The Circus Animals' Desertion" is anomalous among the *ottava rima* poems with numbered parts because it bestows its middle Roman numeral, II, not on a single stanza but on a group of three stanzas (2–4). The sequence consists, then, of a one-stanza prelude, a three-stanza body, and a one-stanza coda. Given the close verbal connections among all five stanzas, how are we to understand the need for numbering at all? And then how are we to explain the asymmetrical tripartite division of the poem? What is Yeats finding to do with the *ottava rima* here that could not be accomplished either by omitting numbering altogether or by giving a single numeral to each stanza, as was his usual practice?

The part I prelude of "The Circus Animals' Desertion" is one of Yeats's "topsy-turvy" stanzas, in which the first two lines form one unit and the last six another, thus exhibiting his characteristic unsettling old-age counterpoint between prosody and period. The striking confession in the first two lines exposes the "writer's block" (as we would now call it) from which the poet suffers, and which "causes" the rest of the poem:[6]

> I sought a theme and sought for it in vain,
> I sought it daily for six weeks or so.

The three "sought's", and the precision of "daily," move us to count to see just how miserable the writer has become. Day 1, no theme; day 2, no theme; day 3, day 4, day 5 . . . to day 10, 20, 30, 40 . . . on to day 42 ("or so"). The disconsolate first stanza suggests that the poet, because he has become old and broken, must cease to hope for future performances of his art. He has, alas, been abandoned by its compositional elements, his images, referred to ironically as his "circus animals":

> I
> I sought a theme and sought for it in vain,
> I sought it daily for six weeks or so.
> Maybe at last, being but a broken man,
> I must be satisfied with my heart, although

> Winter and summer till old age began
> My circus animals were all on show,
> Those stilted boys, that burnished chariot,
> Lion and woman and the Lord knows what.

According to the metaphor that closes this stanza, a new theme, generating fresh images, would provide a next act for the year-round circus of which Yeats has been ringmaster. It is (and is meant to be) rather chilling that Yeats numbers among his circus *animals* "stilted boys" and "woman" as well as the more conventional lion and chariot. (As we shall see, a different symbol for poetic images will eventually displace that of the coerced performances of the animals.) The artificiality of art (in Yeats's bitter metaphor) turns one's companions, even one's beloved, into live-animal acts directed by oneself. But the ringmaster has awakened to find his tent forsaken; his circus animals, on whose loyalty he has depended, have deserted him, permanently. (The poet does not, at this point, accept any responsibility for his depressed and uncreative state; it is the animals alone who have caused it by their "desertion" of their post and their master.)

The next three stanzas, grouped under the Roman numeral II, begin with an even more "upside-down" stanza, opening with a helpless single-line question that responds to the two-line frustration of "I sought a theme, and sought . . . I sought"—"What can I but enumerate old themes?" If the poet cannot find a new theme, he can perhaps prime the pump by reminding himself of old themes that had succeeded in the past. I quote for the moment, of the three-stanza part II, only the two initial stanzas, truth and counter-truth:

> II
> What can I but enumerate old themes?
> First that sea-rider Oisin led by the nose
> Through three enchanted islands, allegorical dreams,
> Vain gaiety, vain battle, vain repose,
> Themes of the embittered heart, or so it seems,
> That might adorn old songs or courtly shows;
> But what cared I that set him on to ride,
> I, starved for the bosom of his faery bride?
>
> And then a counter-truth filled out its play,
> *The Countess Cathleen* was the name I gave it;
> She, pity-crazed, had given her soul away,

But masterful Heaven had intervened to save it.
I thought my dear must her own soul destroy,
So did fanaticism and hate enslave it,
And this brought forth a dream and soon enough
This dream itself had all my thought and love.

In the enumeration occupying part II, the old works are allotted a stanza apiece: one for *The Wanderings of Oisin*, one for *The Countess Cathleen*, and one (yet to come) for *On Baile's Strand*. These stanzas follow a predetermined template—each must include a mention (not necessarily by name) of four things: the work; its hero or heroine (Oisin, the Countess, Cuchulain); the "heart-mysteries" that were its source; and the writer's ultimate preference (or so it seems) for the generated art-work over the life-events from which it arose. As Yeats attempts to sort out his past accomplishments and attitudes, these three stanzas, in order to create a texture of fruitless introspection, juggle the words *theme, dream,* and *heart* in deliberately entangled ways.[7] The "allegorical *dreams*" of *Oisin*, asserted to be "*themes* of the embittered *heart*," are followed in antithetical fashion by the "count-er truth" of *The Count-ess Cathleen*. The appearance of the word "counter-*truth*" suggests that the poet now perceives, retrospectively, that the events of *The Wanderings of Oisin* (although lately scorned as "*dreams*, / Vain gaiety, vain battle, vain repose") were in fact also a *truth*, though one different from the Countess's counter-*truth*.[8] In the composition of *The Countess Cathleen*, the poet's *thought* (of Maud Gonne's possibly disastrous future) brought forth a *dream* (the idea for the play); and with that birth, the original *thought* about the beloved and the poet's love for her ("my dear") are translated into concern about the fictional Countess: "this *dream* itself had all my *thought* and *love*."

The rather relaxed single-sentence account of *Oisin*, which occupies seven lines of its stanza, "tucks in" its antecedent heart-mysteries, but then returns to their literary equivalent, the "faery bride." The more vexed account of *Cathleen* (four lines on Cathleen, two lines on Maud Gonne, and two lines on literary dreaming) never returns to the literary artifact, the named play, but stops on the dream generating the drama; yet it too occupies its whole stanza with the encompassing narrative that had begun with "First that sea-rider Oisin," and that continues here with "And then." The third stanza about a work of the poet—this time, *On Baile's Strand*—seems to want to continue the narrative: "And when the Fool and Blind Man," etc. Yet it does not entirely resemble its two predecessors. After its first four

lines, this stanza departs sharply from the previous genre of narrative to of-
fer, in two lines, a sterner pattern and a harder aesthetic abstraction:

> And when the Fool and Blind Man stole the bread
> Cuchulain fought the ungovernable sea;
> Heart-mysteries there, and yet when all is said
> It was the dream itself enchanted me:
> Character isolated by a deed
> To engross the present and dominate memory.
> Players and painted stage took all my love,
> And not those things that they were emblems of.

This narrative, unlike those before it, forcibly compresses the description of
the actual Yeatsian artifact into two lines, sub-plot and plot:

> And when the Fool and Blind Man stole the bread
> Cuchulain fought the ungovernable sea.

An equal terseness governs the expected conflict of heart and dream, as the
poet admits, in the next two lines, that he remained as "enchanted" by
dream as Oisin was in his "enchanted" islands.

The *ottava rima* of this stanza has become—we recognize the fact as we
read—peculiarly staccato, with a stop (semicolon or period) after every two
lines. The stanza displays a series of four short punctuated two-line utter-
ances, each springing from a different vantage point—first a summary of a
play plot, then meditative introspection, then literary theory, then recapitu-
lation of the artist's exchange of life for art. The increasingly epigrammatic
style of Yeats's stanza reaches its apogee in the unexpected allusion to Aris-
totle's theory of drama: Yeats claims that his play, like those described in the
*Poetics*, presents character (larger than life, as in the case of Cuchulain) iso-
lated by a deed (in the classical past, one of hubris, but in Cuchulain's case,
his killing of his son). And Yeats's play is so powerful that, like the Greek
dramas on which Aristotle based his analysis, it not only "engrosses" (ab-
sorbs the attention of, inscribes itself upon) the era when it is first being
played, but for generations to come will "dominate memory." To alert us to
the classical character of this theoretical description of drama, Yeats writes
his claim in a Latinate diction easily translated back into its classical origins
("present," "dominate," and "memory" are all derived from Latin, although
"engross" is from the French).

This couplet of compositorial poetics ("character," etc.) and literary reception ("to engross and dominate") could not possibly have been part of either of the two previous narrative stanzas. Literary theory of the Aristotelian sort implies a distance from the writing moment, and it espouses judgment of *aesthetic* success or failure (rather than solely judgments of "mystery" or "truth"). These two lines of literary evaluation, of successful "engrossing" and "dominating," are for Yeats conclusive. We are, I think, expected to ascribe, retrospectively, the Aristotelian phrases used of *On Baile's Strand* to each of the other works in Yeats's three-stanza overview: *character* (Oisin) *isolated* (from other Fenians) *by a deed* (his flight to the faery otherworld); *character* (Cathleen) *isolated* (from Catholicism) *by a deed* (selling her soul to the Devil for bread for the poor). The hard "masculine" abstractions of the Aristotelian passage do not resemble the narrative and emotional diction earlier employed by Yeats in describing his past compositions. It is as though the poet has realized, as he comes to the end of his part II retrospection, that his past writings, although they indeed represent authorial "heart-mysteries" and imagined "dreams," now also exhibit the objective existence, authority, power, and longevity of successful works of art.

If we look back, now, to the three *ottava rima* stanzas grouped under the Roman numeral II, we can see that each has a well-defined closing couplet (as the first, the prelude-stanza I, did not), but that the structure of the preceding six lines is different in each case. Though the three stanzas are intimately linked by retrospection, repeated words, and an invariable use of a well-formed couplet at the end, they grow in density of language and syntax as they progress, until they arrive at the two "classical" lines in which pregnant words follow each other with almost no gaps: *character, isolated, deed, engross, present, dominate, memory.* No poem of Yeats better shows the cumulative possibilities of the *ottava rima* stanza: the form is self-contained enough to make a strong freestanding unit, but short enough so that an allusion to a previous stanza, by word or reference, is instantly grasped by the reader and added to the ongoing effect of the whole. It entertains narrative, but it also entertains philosophical reflection. Changes in the register of diction are usually marked by audible rhythmic changes in the stanza (as in the staccato syntax of the fourth stanza here). *Ottava rima*'s pentameter has the breadth for sustained exposition, but the couplet is always bringing epigrammatic possibilities into view.

What does Yeats's part III coda add to the fruitless theme-searching of the prelude-stanza and the enumeration of past themes in the body of the poem?[9] When the coda of "The Circus Animals' Desertion" opens, Yeats remains in his original predicament; but now, instead of blaming his silence on the desertion of his circus animals, he begins to scrutinize his own past writing-processes, just reviewed in part II. In doing so, he has to redefine the heart, previously only a repository of "mysteries." The most forceful imaginative move of the coda is the conceiving of the heart as a rag-and-bone shop with a "raving slut" at the till, and the poet as inhabitant of this location. The grimly startling image of the shop replaces, and thereby "corrects," the initial prelude-image of the ringmaster and his circus animals. Borrowing the word "masterful" from his earlier part II line "But masterful Heaven had intervened to save it," Yeats's coda sets the past images generated by the poet's past themes on a par with Heaven: they were "masterful images" that grew in "pure mind":

III

Those masterful images because complete
Grew in pure mind, but out of what began?
A mound of refuse or the sweepings of a street,
Old kettles, old bottles, and a broken can,
Old iron, old bones, old rags, that raving slut
Who keeps the till. Now that my ladder's gone,
I must lie down where all the ladders start,
In the foul rag-and-bone shop of the heart.

After the marmoreal Aristotelian abstractions centering the Cuchulain stanza, we are jostled by the cascade of concrete nouns answering the poet's opening question concerning his literary images, "Out of what began?" Only the unnerving appearance of the raving till-keeper can bring to an end the poet's shocked pell-mell inventory of the shop's contents. The masterfulness of his previous images, the poet tells us, arose from their having climbed up the Platonic ladder to the zoo of Pure Forms: to *pure mind*. Such images appear, to the reader of literature, to be "alive," able to "put on a show." But, as we now learn, the origins of Yeats's "circus animals" are almost entirely inorganic: they have been constructed chiefly from foul detritus, garbage and metal and rags, with only a whisper of an organic component in "old bones." The Muse is suddenly seen as one of the "raving" Furies, available, as a slut, to all who will pay, mercilessly exacting her price. That "stilted boy"—Oisin or, grown old, Malachi Stilt-Jack (of "High-Talk," recently composed)—must descend from his stilts and his ladder and lie down within the precincts of the unlovely rag-and-bone shop.

"The Circus Animals' Desertion" comes to rest on the most important of its repeated words, *heart*—its "mysteries" now grossly demystified. Yet the recycling-center of the heart, for all its squalor, is a far more humane image of art than the ringmaster's show; and though the ringmaster seemed to put on his circus at no cost to himself, the truer picture at the close says that the artist must pay that "raving slut / Who keeps the till," his exacting Muse, in some unspecified currency for everything he removes from the shop as raw material for his art-work. The crisp vignette of the shop at the end, matching the equally crisp vignette of the year-round circus at the beginning, suggests the summary function of both prelude and coda, by contrast to the more retrospective and reflective function of the three middle stanzas. One can experience the "The Circus Animals' Desertion" as something resembling an armillary sphere, with two crossed outer bands (one saying "Circus," the other saying "Shop") that enclose three crossed inner bands of a different metal, labeled "Oisin," "Cathleen," and "Cuchulain," with all the parts revolving by means of gears of subtly different sorts.

It is, we see, the poet's earlier conception of his images as things that must "grow" organically in "pure mind" that has been preventing him, day after day after day, from finding a theme. He has only to decide to *excavate* the "heart-mysteries" to find themes thrust on him a hundredfold: old iron, old kettles, old rags, old bones. The old iron was once a sword, the old kettle a divine cauldron, the old rags his coat covered with embroideries, the old bones those of the Fenian heroes. In old age, he has become capable of seeing the sword, the coat, the heroes in their raw unsublimated form, as obsessions of his heart. Themes, in fact, lie all about him, a whole shopful of them; and he is at home among them as consort to his promiscuous Fury-Muse. At this point of abundance, as the poet finds a plethora of new themes, the Yeatsian *ottava rima* regains its composure. There is something almost regal in the poet's final self-disposition in the closing couplet, as his "aristocratic" ringmaster's-throne, so "suitable" formerly in its artifice and superiority, is displaced by a lowly bed:

> I must lie down where all the ladders start,
> In the foul rag-and-bone shop of the heart.

The popularity of "The Circus Animals' Desertion"—generated by the pathos of its deluded opening search, its "brokenness," its autobiographical reminiscence, and its immediately comprehensible images—should not lead us to overlook the intellectuality of its 1-3-1 patterning of "stations," the inner elaborations of its central words, and its beautifully symmetrical vignettes of prelude and coda. By making the last station of his "lofty" and "courtly" Renaissance stanza a demystifying encounter with the hitherto occluded rag-and-bone shop of the heart, Yeats asserts formally that under the most highly wrought art-surface (such as those reviewed in part II of the poem), there abound not unsearchable "heart-mysteries" but the unruly and unprepossessing libidinal emotions from which all art-works originate.

Although there is a masterful quality to all of Yeats's *ottava rima* poems, the great "philosophical" poem, "Among School Children," stands supreme among them. Because it concerns the depression of old age and the heart-break of human attachment, we might ask why it should be cast into the *ottava rima* that bears such strong overtones of art, cultural achievement, and past civilization. It is not until the last couplet of "Among School Children" that Yeats's choice of *ottava rima* becomes truly explicable. Until that point, the themes of the poem might have been expressed in any one of Yeats's "spacious" eight-line forms—that of "In Memory of Major Robert Gregory," perhaps, or of "Byzantium." Having a sense of what the *ottava rima* form means to Yeats helps us to interpret such a poem as "Among School Children." Does it, as its stanza form promises, express a philosophy of art, and if so, how and where?

"Among School Children" is set up, from the beginning, to establish a stark opposition between youth and age. Its first half—four "stations"—is narrative. The "sixty-year-old smiling public man," W. B. Yeats the senator, finds himself, as an official visitor, walking through a "progressive" Montessori school, with the *ottava rima* courteously keeping pace:

> I walk through the long schoolroom questioning;
> A kind old nun in a white hood replies[.]

We then hear, in indirect discourse, the voice of the nun as she explains, with artless pride, the successful socialization of her pupils:

> The children learn to cipher and to sing,
> To study reading books and history,
> To cut and sew, be neat in everything
> In the best modern way . . .

But her sing-song lines are sharply interrupted:

> —the children's eyes
> In momentary wonder stare upon
> A sixty-year-old smiling public man.

The element that has upset the serene *ottava rima* walk of elderly visitor and elderly nun, even as it was extending itself into its seventh line, is the poet's meeting of the gaze that the young school children bend on their unknown visitor. The poem's central confrontation of age and youth has begun.

Bored with his official duties, Yeats—as we would expect in a poem-sequence of numbered "stations"—moves in the second stanza into a different period of his life, dreaming back in memory to a day when the youthful Maud Gonne had confided to him an event from her school days that "changed some childish day to tragedy." As Maud opened her past to him, his sympathy with her made him feel that she and he had blended into a single Platonic sphere—or rather into Ledaean twinship ("into the yolk and white of the one shell"). In the third station, Yeats's mind moves back into the schoolroom, speculating idly (recalling the story of the Ugly Duckling who was not yet recognized as a swan) whether his Ledaean Maud Gonne might have resembled in her youth one of the children before him, and his imagination, while he stands in the schoolroom, diverges again—not to a memory this time, nor to the sight of an actual child in the classroom, but to a visionary plane: "She stands before me as a living child." Opening on the very same plane of mental vision, the fourth station conjures up the present emaciated image of Maud in old age, which stands in horrible symmetry with her appearance, a line earlier, as a "living child." Maud Gonne as Child becomes opposed, as in a diptych, to Maud Gonne as Crone (her face "Hollow of cheek as though it drank the wind"). At the close of the fourth "station," the poet creates another mental diptych of youth and age paralleling the one of Maud Gonne from which he has flinched: now the diptych consists of himself when young ("I . . . had pretty plumage once") and himself as "a comfortable kind of old scarecrow."

After completing his first four stations, the poet never returns to the narrative of his visit to the schoolroom. He uses his visit "among school children," and the cruel double diptychs of Youth and Age, as a springboard to the philosophical reflection that occupies the second half of the poem. In the fifth station, in a thought-experiment, Yeats creates another diptych: the baby on the mother's lap versus the same son at the poet's own age, "with sixty or more winters on its head." (Yeats wrote "Among School Children" on the day after his sixty-first birthday.) Would the mother, if she could see what her son would be at sixty, think it worthwhile to have borne him? The sexual "honey of generation" has betrayed the child into existence, deprived it of its Platonic pre-existence, given it only two alternatives in life: to sleep a drugged sleep unconscious of its celestial past or, when it remembers its former Platonic happiness, to "shriek [and] struggle to escape" its earthly condition. The hypothetical situation of the mother's repudiatory evaluation of her sixty-year-old child ends in a rhetorical question; the *ottava rima* couplet hangs in suspense.

In the sixth station, the Platonic pre-existence of the child calls up in Yeats the briefest of all histories of ideas, by its brevity made ironic: first there was Plato, then Aristotle, then Pythagoras. Plato was the idealist, "solider" Aristotle the pragmatist, Pythagoras the aesthetician who (by determining the ratio of strings for making music) brought into material existence "what a star sang and careless Muses heard." This enumeration of philosophers—resembling the ornamental depictions of them in illuminations or on frescoes—is deployed like a fan: two lines for Plato, two for Aristotle, but three (for pride of aesthetic invention) to Pythagoras. At this point, a single line sends the whole assemblage crashing, as the philosophers are deflated into "old clothes upon old sticks to scare a bird." Before our eyes, the togas of the philosophers turn into the rags of scarecrows—and this one final line outweighs all the ceremony of arduous philosophical succession that has preceded it. We once again see a diptych, but this one has a triple frame on each side: the three classically clad philosophers on the left are diminished into three scarecrows in old clothes on the right. Once again, the "couplet" is not whole: whereas in the previous stanzas it had always been deprived of freestanding status by being enjambed into what preceded it, here it is diminished by syntax into a single line. With the dismissal of philosophy, the ultimate aim of schooling—cultural knowledge—is dismissed as well.

Having denigrated the philosophers as part of our cultural detritus, Yeats speculates in the seventh station not on school-knowledge, but on the human relations that he has been seeing and remembering in the classroom: first the old nun and her life of worship (represented by the "white hood" of her religious habit); then himself and Maud Gonne as lovers; then the hypothetical mother and her child. Seeking what these relations have in common, he realizes it is the tendency to idealization: the nun, in her piety, worships her imagined God through the bronze or marble images she sees in her candlelit chapel; the mother, in her affection, worships the image of what her newborn child might become. (And the lover: what does he worship in his passion? his idealized image of the beloved.) However different the maternal image of the child and the marmoreal images worshipped by nuns may be, they have, the poet realizes, one thing in common: they both, in time, break the hearts of those adoring them. It is only in the next line, as the poem rises to become an encompassing ode of sublime address, that the poet mentions (with a single word, "passion") his own heartbreak. But he gives that passion pride of place, mentioning it as the first of the emotions generating those worshipped "Presences":

> O Presences
> That passion, piety, or affection knows,
> And that all heavenly glory symbolize—
> O self-born mockers of man's enterprise;

And with that startling semicolon the seventh station ends. Each preceding station had come to a full stop at its end, with a period or a question mark. No matter how interiorly stressed the previous stanzas had been, unable ever to achieve a freestanding reposeful couplet, they at least ended where an *ottava rima* stanza is supposed to end—at the completion of its eight lines. This seventh station, in which the poet realizes that worship itself is necessarily a fallible sentiment, that self-created idols always have feet of clay, breaks off in the middle of a sentence, wholly unable to continue on the capitalized plane of the odal sublime ("O Presences"). He repudiates that plane in a heartbroken lowercase echo, "O self-born mockers." The presences are not Divinities to be addressed in vertical aspiration; they are self-born and deceiving solaces, created by our longing for perfection in the things we love.

It takes only a brief survey of the conduct of the *ottava rima* in the seven stations to perceive how unsettled it is, how each stanza is written from a different vantage point, how enjambment and a troubled syntax both work against the 6-2 pattern that "should" prevail in each stanza—and above all to register how all the unease culminates in the rupture at the end of the seventh, "philosophical" station. We come to realize that the poem—in spite of its *ottava rima*—has *not* been reflecting on works of art, "ingenious lovely things"; it has concerned itself, rather, with passion, piety, and affection, those primary emotions of engagement with another—a beloved, God, or a child. And though such idealizing "worship" may symbolize all that we desire, all celestial glory, it always and everywhere ends in heartbreak, mocking the human "enterprise"—whether of love, of religion, or of motherhood—that engendered it.

Yeats knows that in the religious life of mortification, body is bruised to pleasure soul; that in the philosophical life, the reward of midnight oil is a blear-eyed wisdom; that only by the advent of a lover's despair is beauty forced into being. What, he wonders—as the eighth station sets out to find some vision of life that does not end in heartbreak—would a realm be like where soul and body could equally take pleasure, where wisdom did not destroy the bright gaze of youth, where beauty could grow from love, not from love's despair? In its first quatrain, the eighth station moves to a place of prelapsarian fantasy, where Adam's curse has been repealed, and where labor is no longer effortful, but spontaneous and beautiful:

> Labour is blossoming or dancing where
> The body is not bruised to pleasure soul,
> Nor beauty born out of its own despair,
> Nor blear-eyed wisdom out of midnight oil.

But who might be those who could labor in such Edenic ways? The available beings, existing implicitly in their present participles above, are a blossomer and a dancer. These agents become reified in the last four lines of the poem, as the station moves from its speculative plane to earthly being. By situating earthly life in the same numbered "station" as its Edenic fantasy, the poet suggests that the two *can* converge on the human plane, that in fact they occupy, rightly perceived, the same "place."

The eighth station concludes with two 2-line questions, of which the first examines what it would be to be a blossomer:

> O chestnut-tree, great-rooted blossomer,
> Are you the leaf, the blossom or the bole?

There is much to be said for the venerable chestnut tree as a non-tragic metaphor for earthly existence. It blossoms effortlessly every spring, even in its rooted old age. And when we behold the organic tree, we never question the visual unity composed by its inextricably connected leaf, blossom, and bole. The question is of course a rhetorical one: Yeats does not mean to ask, seriously, whether the tree is the one or the other or the third of its components; he means to imagine a joyous unity of being. This image nonetheless turns out to be unsatisfactory, as we shall see.

If Yeats has found an image of spontaneous and effortless labor, and has named the essence of the tree as generative by bestowing on it the noun "blossomer," and if that beautiful labor can continue even into old age, why cannot the poem end here? The Edenic tree is in old age the same blossomer that it was in its beginning; its mother would not have to repudiate it, its lover would not have to see it grow hideous in age. But something is wrong, for Yeats, with the chestnut tree as a positive way to regard age, as we conclude when we see him replace it with a different image. It is not until we come upon, in the very last lines of the poem, the poet's true solution to the dilemma of his shocking earlier diptychs of youth and age, that we recognize the deficiencies of the chestnut tree as an image for successful human "enterprise." The chestnut tree has no free will; its capacity for sexual generation into old age is not ours; its beauty in late blossoming is not ours; its immobile species-nature is not ours. The specters of scarecrow and crone cannot be "rehabilitated" by the unity of being of the chestnut tree; they can be "corrected" only by some image of *human* existence that does not participate in the diptychs of idealization and heartbreak, but that is nevertheless a true representation of personal life, life as it moves its location and changes its selfhood over time (as the chestnut tree does not).

We can best understand the closing couplet—and therefore the whole poem—by recalling one of its original drafts. The closing couplet as we have it is:

> O body swayed to music, O brightening glance,
> How can we know the dancer from the dance?

The final couplet begins with the odal "O" of the poem's preceding stanza, but the "O" is here allowed to persist without a mocking echo; thus it "cures" both the celestially exalted and the disheartened tragic "O's" of the preceding stanza, "O Presences . . . / O self-born mockers." The joyous and celebratory closing couplet offers, we feel, an odal counterspell to the poem's despair; but how do its elements work to "cure" the hideous collapse, previously beheld, from promising child to repellent scarecrow? Yeats's earlier binary model of youth versus age resembles the view espoused by the resentful old man at the opening of "Sailing to Byzantium," who, in his summation of the sexual creatures' song, refers to it as commending "Whatever is begotten, born, and dies." He has omitted the whole middle of life that extends between birth and death, just as Yeats's cruel diptychs have done. There is no life-span depicted between beautiful "living child" and catastrophic "present image," between the "shape" on a mother's lap and "that shape / With sixty or more winters on its head." The "false" diptych-model needs to be "stretched out": the long, ongoing course of life that connects beginning and end must be allowed its part in any adequate image of life, one that could close "Among School Children."

At first, Yeats had thought that the way to be fair to "stretched-out" life was to concede that there was something to be said for the middle of it—it had rejoiced in sexual love. The sole episode between childhood and age allowed into "Among School Children" so far was the precious moment of "youthful sympathy" in which the lovers' "two natures blent / Into a sphere." Salvaging that memory of erotic blending, the poet abstracts it, in a draft, into two symbols—the first, the spring-blossoming of a hawthorn tree; the second, the immemorial sexual image of a dancing couple moving in perfect synchrony and gazing into each other's eyes:

> O hawthorn tree, in all that gaudy gear
> Are you it all, or did you make it all
> O dancing couple, glance that mirrors glance,
> How can we know the dancer from the dance?[10]

But (as Yeats realizes) to isolate the sexual moment for commendation does nothing to salvage the rest of life, nor does it take into account the brevity of the span of sexuality for many human beings. Yeats himself is, at sixty, far distant in time from the sexual ecstasy and mirroring of gaze represented by the image of the dancing couple. What image, then, will be a "befitting emblem" for his own life-course as he now sees it? With courage and accuracy, Yeats erases from the draft the sexually "gaudy" (from *gaudium,* joy) hawthorn tree ("Let's have one other gaudy night," says Antony to Cleopatra) and—in his most radical revision—halves the image of the dancing couple. He chooses to make his dancer solitary, ungendered, unmirrored by a responsive human look. "O body, O glance," he exclaims (again rising to the odal plane), and then asks what might be said about the actions of that single human body and that solitary glance. The body must obey the music that sways it, yes: the dance must be performed to the given, not chosen, music of time and Fate. But the music leaves open an infinite number of expressive possibilities for self-choreography, and the body's "brightening glance" is perpetually conceiving new steps.[11] The progressive verb "brighten" (like other progressive—or regressive—verbs such as "redden" or "wane") never ceases to act; the glance is always "brightening" into future dance-conceptions (just as Aengus's beloved disappeared into the ever-"brightening" air of dawn). Yeats has been able to find, in the dance, an image for the continuum of life occupying the extended space between birth and death; he no longer emphasizes the cruel and distorting end-point, nor (as in the chestnut tree) an instinctual unity of being, but rather the necessary evolution of our consciousness throughout our lifetime. We can imagine new potentials for our existence, as the chestnut tree cannot. The life-shape that we generate is in part determined (by the music) but in part free (as we invent our steps to the music). And we must create that life-shape by ourselves—no partner can do it for us.

If our identity is not determined by our fated end as old scarecrows, then we can define identity as a continuum in time, constantly being altered as our lives unfold. Who are we? We are the dance we go on creating from birth to death. Conceiving ourselves as a body responding with steps invented by our constantly brightening eye, we gain a far more generous (and far more accurate) sense of existence and identity than that provided by the inflexible opposed diptychs of youth and age that drove the poem to despair. Like the question to the chestnut tree, "Are you the leaf, the blossom or the bole?" the question closing the poem—"How can we know the dancer from the dance?"—has the same obvious answer: we cannot know (that is to say, distinguish) the dancer from the dance, identity from its deployment in time. The question implies wonder and joy, rather than an unanswerable enigma. Yeats has found something to say for life: it is a solitary but nonetheless endlessly satisfying set of creative inventions. By locating joy and identity in the "enterprise" of our devising an individual dance, Yeats can acknowledge the truth of universal heartbreak without letting it entirely destroy the energy, delight, inventiveness, and continuity of being.

What does Yeats's choice of *ottava rima* contribute to our sense of "Among School Children"? I have promised that we will find a poetics within the poem, that the aristocratic and aesthetic connotations of Yeats's chosen stanza will "prove out" by the end. It is not enough to say that the poem ends by invoking an art form, that of the dance. It does that, of course, and it does specify that the dance is self-choreographed by the continuously inventive eye of the dancer. In emphasizing the function of the glance, as well as that of the body, in the creation of the dance, Yeats is perhaps remembering Blake's divine Creator in "The Tyger" who needs eye as well as hand to forge the tiger:

> What immortal hand or eye
> Could frame thy fearful symmetry?

Blake again emphasizes the dual nature, both physical ("shoulder") and intellectual ("art"), of creativity:

> And what shoulder, & what art,
> Could twist the sinews of thy heart?

And finally, the courage needed for original creation is made salient by Blake's final change of verb from "could" to "dare":

> What immortal hand or eye
> Dare frame thy fearful symmetry?

Blake's insistence on bodily agency (hand, shoulder), on intellectual creativity (eye, art), and, in the close, on aesthetic daring, stands behind Yeats's comparable emphasis on the contribution to identity of both sensuous body *and* intellectual glance, and on the courage to become the dance you invent.

Although we have been given (fittingly for an *ottava rima* poem) an art form—the dance—as a "solution," Yeats has, in an act of spectacular generosity, made his closing art form available to all. We are not seeing a specific "trained" dancer (such as one of Loie Fuller's "Chinese" dancers); nor are we offered artworks such as the mosaics or golden bird of Byzantium, which must be made by skilled artificers. The poet is not praising here the arts that need training, that produce an art-product: the "golden grasshoppers and bees" of the *ottava rima* of "Nineteen Hundred and Nineteen," the architect-designed "ancestral houses" of the opening of "Meditations in Time of Civil War," or the set of accomplished paintings in "The Municipal Gallery Revisited." He does not set before us for emulation a set of literary dramas as in "The Circus Animals' Desertion," nor a set of world-famous sculptures as in "The Statues." Nor does he suggest that life can be enhanced by aristocratic patronage from a "laurelled head" in an "ancestral" house, as in the two *ottava rima* Coole Park poems, praising Lady Gregory, of 1929 and 1931. No: "Among School Children" offers as its example of an art-work the self-choreographed articulation of a life over time—an enterprise that every conscious creature must in some way undertake. By making personal soul-making equal in "aristocracy" and "aesthetic significance" to all the other art-practices he has called into being within his *ottava rima* pieces, Yeats has written a philosophical poem for everyone. He has stepped outside his own life, and that of other creative artists who produce the sort of visible artifacts to which the Yeatsian *ottava rima* has paid homage. He has stepped into the life of Everyman, and the poem is the greater for it. And he has rewritten the conclusion of the other great philosophical poem of youth and age, Wordsworth's "Ode on the Intimations of Immortality." There, early joy has been lost, but Wordsworth affirms that greater capacities—human sympathy in the soul, and the ability, by metaphor-making, to read nature as analogous to human life—have replaced it. Yeats too believes that there have been profound losses over time, but that the joy of self-invention, of self-formation, is as alive at sixty as it ever was.

There is another contribution of the *ottava rima* to "Among School Children"—this time a purely formal one. The despair of the poet—visible in the opening diptychs of Maud and himself that are awakened by the schoolroom, and perpetuated in the latter, "philosophical" half of the poem in the abstract diptychs of mother and child, philosophers and scarecrows, and worship and heartbreak—has not been alleviated by the Edenic fantasy of a consequence-free "labour" of spiritual delight, beauty, and wisdom, nor has it been removed even by the "organic" fantasy of the ever-blossoming chestnut tree. It is only in the last two lines of the poem, with the invention of the solitary dancer, that "Among School Children" finds true resolution. These two lines constitute the only true freestanding closing couplet in the whole poem. After the agitated or enjambed couplets preceding it, the final couplet at last radiates the confirmed "natural" beauty of the *ottava rima* form.

And there is yet another effect of Yeats's choice of *ottava rima*. The poem's continued display of life's losses—until the last couplet—suggests that life is radically imperfect, that no kind of perfection can be found on this earth. "I read, and sigh, and wish I were a tree," writes George Herbert in depression, for at least as a tree he would be of some service, he could bear fruit or house a bird. Like Herbert's, Yeats's wishing he were a tree offers no real image of a perfection attainable in *human* life. But with the miraculous "solution" of the individually created identity-dance, the poem brings a form of perfection at last into view—and because the solution occurs at line 64, we realize that "Among School Children" has suddenly snapped—at its closing question mark—into a perfect square, 8 stanzas of 8 lines each, a "magical" symbol of perfection (of the sort we have already seen in the 4 × 4 perfect square of "An Irish Airman"). The poem has replicated, in its own changes of genre and address, in its multiple variations in stanza-proportions and metaphor, the actual inventive choreography of the spontaneous-but-responsive dance, exemplifying its own fidelity to what it has discovered. But it remains nonetheless true that no poem can obliterate or disavow the reflections in which it has engaged en route to its arrival at a "solution." Yeats's discovery of the great importance of the creative continuity of life—the exhilarating articulated and extended dance—cannot erase what he has seen of the shriek of infancy and the tragedy of idealizing attachment. It is part of the seriousness of the poem that it does not subside in the fantasy of a suffering-free existence as chestnut tree.

Reading over this poem and others, we recognize that a new form—which we can now name the Yeatsian *ottava rima*—has been added to the repertoire of poetry. It comes trailing clouds of glory from its Renaissance associations, but it is brought forcibly into modernity by Yeats's modifications of its traditional architectonics, its diction, and its "flow." By numbering individual stanzas in some poems, creating distinct "stations," Yeats contributes substantial weight and presence to the form; by allowing in his *ottava rima* poems a maximal psychological complexity, he has removed the genre from a chiefly descriptive or speculative function, and made it sympathetic to intellectual and emotional autobiography. As we grow more and more familiar with the *Collected Poems,* assembling, as we reread, formally similar poems into "family" groups, we come to Yeats's *ottava rima* pages with alerted expectation and richer satisfactions than when we first encountered them. The sixteen *ottava rima* poems, taken together, make up the most accomplished chapter in the history of Yeats's styles.

# APPENDIX: Yeats's *Ottava Rima* Poems

"Sailing to Byzantium"

"Among School Children"

from "Meditations in Time of Civil War":
      I: "Ancestral Houses"
      IV: "My Descendants"

from "Nineteen Hundred and Nineteen":
      I: "Many ingenious lovely things are gone"

"The Choice"

"Coole Park, 1929"

"Coole Park and Ballylee, 1931"

from "Vacillation":
      II: "A tree there is that from its topmost bough"
      III: "Get all the gold and silver that you can"

from "A Woman Young and Old":
      VIII: "Her Vision in the Wood"

from "Parnell's Funeral":
      I: "Under the Great Comedian's tomb the crowd"

"The Gyres"

"The Municipal Gallery Revisited"

"The Circus Animals' Desertion"

"The Statues"

## XI

## ↷ THE SPACIOUS LYRIC:
## LONG STANZAS, IRREGULAR LINES

In the spectrum of Yeats's lyric poetry, the space between his short, sometimes terse, pieces and his extended sequences is filled by what I think of as his "spacious" lyrics. These are the leisurely, meditative single lyrics in which a great deal of matter is compressed. The poet does not have in single poems, as he does in the sequences, the option of approaching a complex theme through separate aspects which motivate different verse forms. The spacious lyrics keep to a single stanza form, and they must offer, in spite of their often heterogeneous contents, at least an appearance of coherence and continuity. The rubric "spacious lyric" includes several of the *ottava rima* poems, such as "Among School Children," but since I have discussed the *ottava rima* lyrics earlier as a separate class, they do not appear here. I'll consider first some of the poems written in octave-stanzas *other* than *ottava rima:* this group includes "In Memory of Major Robert Gregory" (1918), "A Prayer for My Daughter" (1919), and "A Dialogue of Self and Soul" (1927). Although the great poem "Byzantium" (1930) belongs to this group, it has been treated in Chapter II on Yeats's paired poems; nonetheless, we should not forget that it is the "spacious lyric" *par excellence.* I have already taken up in Chapter III the poems in Yeats's ten-line stanza originating in "All Souls' Night" and returning in "Nineteen Hundred and Nineteen" (parts II and III) and "Meditations in Time of Civil War" (part II), so I will not return to them here; but we should keep in mind the way Yeats handled that long "labyrinthine" stanza with virtuosic self-possession in those spacious lyrics.

It is in composing "In Memory of Major Robert Gregory" (323–328) that Yeats first uses the "spacious" octave-stanza that he adopted from the elegy "On the Death of Mr. William Hervey" (the discoverer of the circulation of the blood) by Abraham Cowley (1618–1667).[1] Cowley's stanza (rhyming *aabbdccd*) is an interesting one which, while interspersing shorter lines among longer ones, regulates the moments when such briefer lines occur. Its effect, therefore, is not one of *canzone*-like "spontaneity" with the irregular insertion of lines of different lengths, as in "Lycidas," but rather one of inviolable but paradoxically "irregular" rules. Here is a single stanza, the last of nineteen, from Cowley's poem on the death of his friend. Like many other poets, Cowley indents his shorter lines, with pentameter lines flush left and the tetrameters (in lines 4, 6, and 7) indented:

> And if the glorious *Saints* cease not to know
> Their wretched Friends who *fight* with *Life* below;
> Thy Flame to *Me* does still the same abide,
>     Onely more pure and rarifi'd.
> There whilst immortal Hymns thou dost reherse
>     Thou dost with holy pity see
>     Our dull and earthly *Poesie,*
> Where *Grief* and *Mis'ery* can be join'd with *Verse.*

This is the stanza form Yeats adopted. Although Cowley allowed trimeters to be substituted for tetrameters in all three tetrameter positions,[2] Yeats keeps strictly to pentameters and tetrameters, in effect making his poems that use this form more regular than Cowley's.[3] However, Yeats "concealed," by suppressing indentation, the irregularity of line-length that the printing of Cowley's poem makes so explicit. It is by no means apparent to the eye, in the block-like look of the following stanza from "In Memory of Major Robert Gregory," that some lines are metrically shorter than others. At first glance, it could almost appear to be a passage of pentameter:

> For all things the delighted mind now sees
> Were loved by him; the old storm-broken trees
> That cast their shadows upon road or bridge;
> The tower set on the stream's edge:
> The ford where drinking cattle make a stir
> Nightly, and startled by that sound
> The water-hen must change her ground;
> He might have been your heartiest welcomer.

If Yeats had followed Cowley's mode of indentation, thereby calling attention to his own stanza's different line-lengths, his elegy would appear "old-fashioned," "metaphysical," and "formal" rather than "modern," "literal," and "casual":

> For all things the delighted eye now sees
> Were loved by him; the old storm-broken trees

That cast their shadows upon road or bridge;
The tower set on the stream's edge;
The ford where drinking cattle make a stir
Nightly, and startled by that sound
The water-hen must change her ground;
He might have been your heartiest welcomer.

Borrowing from Cowley (in a hidden, flush-margined way) turned out to be a fruitful exercise for Yeats.[4] The non-*ottava rima* octave-stanza, dividing itself by its meter into two asymmetrical parts, spurred him into a distinct exploration of prosodic means that were less measured, less stately, more agitated than those of the ceremonious *ottava rima*.

Yeats invented three forms of the non-*ottava rima* octave-stanza. The first follows Cowley's pattern; the second (in "Byzantium") changes some line-lengths but keeps the rhyme-scheme; the third (in "A Dialogue of Self and Soul") keeps the line-lengths but changes the rhyme-scheme, as follows:

**A. Cowley's model (excluding Cowley's occasional substituted trimeters):**

| Title | Rhyme-scheme | Line-lengths |
|---|---|---|
| "In Memory of Mr. William Hervey" | *aabbcddc* | 5-5-5-4-5-4-4-5 |

**B. Yeats's three forms of non-ottava rima octave stanzas:**

**1.** Direct imitations of Cowley, in both line-lengths and rhyme-scheme:

| | | |
|---|---|---|
| "In Memory of Major Robert Gregory" | *aabbcddc* | 5-5-5-4-5-4-4-5 |
| "A Prayer for My Daughter" | | |
| "The Tower" (II) | | |
| "Colonus' Praise" | | |

**2.** Imitation keeping Cowley's rhyme-scheme but changing his line-lengths:

| | | |
|---|---|---|
| "Byzantium" | *aabbcddc* | 5-5-4-5-5-3-3-5 |

**3.** Imitation changing Cowley's rhyme-scheme but keeping his line-lengths:

| | | |
|---|---|---|
| "A Dialogue of Self and Soul" | *abbacddc* | 5-5-5-4-5-4-4-5 |

The Cowley-Yeats first type of stanza (appearing in "In Memory of Major Robert Gregory," "A Prayer for My Daughter," and "The Tower," II) falls into three rhyme-units:

a rhyming pentameter couplet (*aa; 5-5*);

a rhyming non-isometric couplet, pentameter followed by tetrameter (*bb; 5-4*); and

a quatrain in embraced rhyme in which two pentameters enclose two tetrameters (*deed; 5-4-4-5*).

The "feel" of such a stanza is unusual. We are initially reassured by the solid presence of the introductory rhyming pentameter couplet; but then we feel unsettled when in the next couplet the two lines, although they rhyme, are of unequal length. The third unit, to our surprise, is not a third rhyming couplet (whether symmetric or asymmetric), but rather two lines of different length that do *not* rhyme. We are therefore perplexed again, waiting to find the rhyme that will match that of line 5—but we do not arrive at it until line 8. Rhythmic unease is generated in both ear and mind (an unease that would have been considerably mitigated had Yeats indented his shorter lines to alert his reader to the evolving shape of the stanza).

In this stanza Yeats, unlike Cowley, feels no obligation to make syntax match rhyme-units, confusing the ear still further. We are accustomed to ordinary *abba* quatrains, and also to closed pentameter couplets (Pope) and run-on pentameter couplets (Keats); but we are not used to pentameter couplets and irregular quatrains of the sort that Yeats produces in "The Tower":

> Good fellows shuffled cards in an old bawn;
> And when that ancient ruffian's turn was on
> He so bewitched the cards under his thumb
> That all but that one card became
> A pack of hounds and not a pack of cards
> And that he changed into a hare.
> Hanrahan rose in frenzy there
> And followed up those baying creatures towards—

Unlike someone listening to stable *ottava rima,* someone hearing such a stanza read aloud would be hard put to perceive, let alone remember, its line-lengths and rhyme-scheme (the latter made even less evident by the slant rhymes "thumb"/"became" and "cards"/"towards"). In the later work of Yeats, as here in "The Tower," apparent lexical and syntactic informality obscures a strict formality of stanza-construction.

Toward the end of the famous elegy for Robert Gregory, however, the formality of stanza form is not concealed, and can even become intrusively evident. There is, it seems to me, something brittle about the reiteration, in three successive stanzas, of the phrase "Soldier, scholar, horseman, he," an ostentatiously ritualized repeated praise that departs, with intent, from the original rhetorical premise of the poem—that the poet will mention to his new bride, stanza by stanza, the friends he would have invited to meet her.

By the repetition, in three successive Gregory-stanzas, of the three epithets for Gregory, the poet distinguishes, it is true, the "stalled" vignettes describing his elegiac subject from the preceding single-stanza sketches of dead friends. And by showing himself temporarily unable to proceed beyond the reiteration of the triple epithets, Yeats perhaps thinks to demonstrate how he could not continue his enumeration of dead friends once he had arrived at Gregory's too-recent, too-premature, and too-violent wartime death. Yet even if Yeats's epithet-repetition is an aesthetically mistaken gesture, no one can fail to see that it is in the Gregory elegy that Yeats first successfully undertakes the sort of sweeping and (putatively) random reminiscence that will pervade "The Tower" (II), "All Soul's Night," and "The Municipal Gallery Revisited." In these poems he establishes a powerful new genre of Yeatsian lyric: a "realistic" autobiographical meditation that expresses both ordinariness and dignity. "Robert Gregory" offers glimpses into the ordinary life and acquaintance of a contemporary man who settles in his new house with his wife and will soon climb up the winding stair to bed. Some of the mentioned friends are artists and writers, some not; one is a relative. The speaker is a man who has been to horse races, who mentions Clare and Galway and Mayo, who notices how water-hens are startled and move away when disturbed by cattle who have come down to drink, who is conversant with astrology, who has read Philip Sidney. These glimpses, successively proffered, have the heterogeneity of snapshots.

And indeed "In Memory of Major Robert Gregory" is, as I have written elsewhere, a heterogeneous poem that shifts genres as it goes.⁵ The casualness of its beginning is peculiarly deceptive. It is only in the closing lines that we learn that the poet had wanted to write an epithalamion (no doubt with Spenser's in mind) for his bride, but felt he lacked inspiration. He decided that until imagination inspired him to "a fitter welcome" for her, he would fill in the lack with some mention of the (now dead) friends he wishes he could have invited to a wedding supper, adding about each "some appropriate commentary." These deliberate words sum up a style entirely other than the warmly joyful one suitable to an epithalamion; for the friends, Yeats proposes a middle style, elegiac, distanced from immediate mourning. Stanzas II, IV, and V present vignettes—of a sort we meet again in "The Tower" (II) and "All Soul's Night"—of Lionel Johnson, John Synge, and George Pollexfen. These three stanzas are "matched" by three parallel stanzas—those containing "Soldier, scholar, horseman, he"—describing Gregory. (The sedulous equality, three to three, testifies to Yeats's drive toward architectonic formality within apparent spontaneity of recollection.)

The elegiac tolling of the three "Gregory" words—"soldier, scholar, horse-man"[6]—distinguishes these vignettes from the earlier single ones of friends. The friends are all "characters"—Lionel Johnson in his social isolation, his desire for sanctity, his apocalyptic fantasies; John Synge by his almost post-humous life and by his unusual choice of "a most desolate stony place" (the Aran Islands) as his fated terrain; and George Pollexfen as an example of an athletic youth turned "sluggish and contemplative" in middle age. Greg-ory, by contrast, is less a "character" than an idealized form. He is the dreamed-of "great painter," the aesthetic counselor, the person who lives so vividly that he exhausts life in a brief time. (The stanza inserted at Margaret Gregory's request, on Gregory as a horseman, is, however, laden with spe-cificity of time and place—Galway, Castle Taylor, Roxborough, Esserkelly, Mooneen—and therefore breaks Yeats's original convention of the general-ized three archetypal nouns.)

The Yeatsian separation of the quotidian detail attached to dead friends from the iconic idealization accorded to Gregory, natural in a poem that turns from distanced reminiscence to immediate elegy, suggests that Yeats is developing a repertoire of different modes of recollection. Here, each memory of a dead friend is placed in a separate stanza-frame of its own. The comparable vignettes of friends in "All Soul's Night" are still formally separate, but because each one spreads out over two long (ten-line) stanzas, they seem more desultory and *ad hoc* than the compact single-stanza vi-gnettes of "In Memory of Major Robert Gregory." In "The Tower" (II) and "The Municipal Gallery Revisited," Yeats renders the passage from vignette to vignette far more fluidly, each one (in "The Municipal Gallery") called up by a different painting catching the poet's eye. Some of the paintings deserve only glancing attention ("A revolutionary soldier kneeling to be blessed"), some arrest the poet for several lines (the woman met fifty years ago), and one elicits an entire stanza (Augusta Gregory).

In the concluding stanza of "Robert Gregory," Yeats announces that the elegy for Gregory has superseded not only the epithalamion he was unable to rise to, but also his proposed listing, for his wife, of the friends from each stage of his life whom he wishes he could have invited to meet her:

> I had thought, seeing how bitter is that wind
> That shakes the shutter, to have brought to mind
> All those that manhood tried, or childhood loved
> Or boyish intellect approved
> With some appropriate commentary on each;

> Until imagination brought
> A fitter welcome; but a thought
> Of that late death took all my heart for speech.

We can see in this eloquent close the potential for expressiveness in Yeats's irregular non-*ottava rima* stanza derived from Cowley. The lapse into modesty about adolescent admiration—"Or boyish intellect approved"—suits the lapse in energy denoted by the four-beat line after three five-beat ones; the middle-aged breadth of "With some appropriate commentary on each" justifies the resumption of the pentameter; the swift hope of the enjambed lines "until imagination brought / A fitter welcome" is stopped short by an "unnatural" semicolon breaking the latter line in two, as the thought of Gregory's death breaks in. And our long wait (from line 5 to line 8) while the word "each" seeks its rhyme is rewarded when the (slight) complacency of the polysyllabic "appropriate commentary" is deflated by the blank mimetic monosyllables of "but a thought / Of that late death took all my heart for speech." The final apologetic pentameter rebukes, with its stifled words of present grief, the deliberate plan of "appropriate" elegiac rhetoric for the not-recently-dead friends. As we follow a Yeatsian stanza through its unfolding, we often come to admire the way in which unusual or irregular stanza-rhythms and thought-rhythms seem effortlessly to agree.

Yeats found new uses for the "Gregory" stanza a year later in "A Prayer for My Daughter" (403). Is he repeating himself? Yes, in the sense that he returns here to certain discoveries made in the course of writing the earlier poem, using the form of his earlier vignettes in the brief sketches of "A Prayer"—those of Helen and Venus as mythical archetypes of erotic disaster, and that of (the unnamed) Maud Gonne as the contemporary representative of the disaster of political rhetoric and party-line "opinions." ("Opinions" is a word which Yeats invariably uses scornfully in the sense of views borrowed from fashion, politicians, propagandists, newspaper pieces, and so forth; "opinions" are never, in Yeats, personally discovered insights.) On the other hand, the vignettes of "A Prayer" include debased language that would have been foreign to the stately portraits of "Robert Gregory," and there are new stanza-effects that I will return to after a brief sketch of the matter, overt and covert, of the poet's prayer for his daughter.

"A Prayer for My Daughter" has been misread by critics who have found it misogynistic. It belongs to the genre of christening poems, and Yeats could hardly have suitably christened a daughter in a poem expressing dislike for women as a group, or even singly. Some critics have decried Yeats's aims for his daughter in envisaging her future solely in terms of marriage. (In the event, of course, Anne Yeats did not marry or have children, and this irony satisfies antagonistic readers.) But in the economics of Yeats's day, it was not reasonable for a father lacking family wealth to think that his daughter could in the future live on her own means, and most middle-class women had no expectation of a paid career. For Anne to flourish, her father thinks, she will need someone to make a suitable home for her and enable her to attain her potential for happiness. The peace and love and joy that Yeats hopes for his daughter would be among the blessings that any parent would wish to be able to guarantee for a child; and those blessings, Yeats thought, could be secured for his daughter (in Ireland's foreseeable historical circumstances) only within marriage.

To my mind, "A Prayer for My Daughter" is Yeats's hidden poem about his mother.[7] Hers is the mistaken life that principally shadows and motivates the poem: her unfortunate marriage (to a barrister who refused to practice law); her precarious status as the wife of a painter; her nomadic changes of address as the family shifted about in rented premises in England and Ireland (Susan Yeats never had a house to call her own); her depression and lack of personal self-determination; her silent quarrel with her husband that led her to return often to her parents' house in Sligo—once for as long as two years. Of whom must Yeats have been thinking when he hoped, for his daughter, that *she* might live "like some green laurel / Rooted in one dear perpetual place"? Of whom was he thinking when he observed that, to know happiness, a woman's soul needed to be "*self*-delighting / *Self*-appeasing, *self*-affrighting," confident that its will is Heaven's will? Of whom was he thinking when he prayed, with the last breath of the poem, that his daughter's bridegroom would bring her to "a house / Where all's accustomed, ceremonious"? I hear those lines with (in Yeats's mind) a contrastive under-echo: "And may *her* bridegroom [unlike my mother's husband] bring *her* to a house / Where all's accustomed, ceremonious." The sight of his mother—sinking into melancholy and illness as she tried to bring up children in temporary rooms, in a poverty sometimes lacking even such necessities as tea and candles, with a husband who had been no munificent bridegroom but a feckless and wayward artist—might well have led Yeats to think that a happy, non-quarrelsome, decorous, and abundantly provided house was the least a woman needed to achieve happiness. Yeats had himself seen the unhappy consequence of his father's incapacity to provide for the family: not only Susan Yeats's distress, but also the lack of dowries for his two sisters (who remained unmarried and had to be supported in part by their brother).

Although it is true that in "A Prayer" Maud Gonne is the chief overt exemplum of a woman making a wrong marital choice, her disastrous dissolved marriage to John MacBride was public and could be commented on, as Yeats's mother's marriage could not. Both of the women Yeats cared most about—his mother and Maud Gonne—had the "wrong" sort of life; and it is no surprise that in thinking about why their lives went wrong, the poet saw as at least partial causes the mistaken marital choices of both. As he ponders his daughter's future, Yeats cannot bear the thought that her life might evolve as tragically as theirs. Had he not had the examples of his mother and Maud Gonne in mind, his prayer for his daughter might have been different; but his wishes sprang out of pained love for his mother and Gonne, and his frustration at their sexual choices and consequent unhappiness. The poem exhibits not misogyny toward Maud, "the loveliest woman born," but sympathy and anger at the fate that befell her because she chose wrongly.

However, it is not solely the economics of gender that determines Yeats's closing wishes for Anne in "A Prayer for My Daughter." The earlier drafts of the ending reveal the great difficulty Yeats had in concluding the poem. At first, he thought to end it by picturing Anne, at twenty-five, returning to Coole and thinking of her dead father as she walked the paths there. (The following lines—which, for ease of reading, I have regularized slightly from the published drafts—follow the stanza beginning "An intellectual hatred is the worst"):

> Daughter if you be happy & yet grown—
> Say when you are five & twenty—walk alone
> Through Coole Domain & visit for my sake
> The stony edges of the lake,
> Where every year I have counted swans, & cry
> That all is well till all that's there
> Spring sounding on to the still air
> And all is sound between the lake and sky . . .
>
> No common man will mock the cry
> Nor think that being dead I cannot hear.

There follows an apparent alternative to these tentative closing lines imagining Anne at Coole after her father's death. Here Yeats returns as a spirit, recalling, equally regressively, his days at Coole with Lady Gregory:

> For it is certain that I shall appear
> Standing to think where I have often stood
> By the lake's edge, in that blue wood
> Where the path climbs between a rock & root
> Or else, where twenty years or so
> My friend & I paced to and fro
> Hurrying thought driven on a vaporous foot[.][8]

The stanzas uniting his dead self and an adult Anne are dated April 1919, and variants of them continue in subsequent handwritten drafts. It is not until the later typescript of June 1919 that the stanza of the bridegroom—which replaces these stanzas and brings the poem to an end—makes its appearance. In rethinking the poem, Yeats must have seen the incestuous implications of asking an unmarried twenty-five-year-old daughter to return to Coole and think of her father. By choosing a different ending, in which he performs the traditional role of the father in "giving away" his daughter to the bridegroom, Yeats releases his daughter into a new family unit, where she is a wife (and potential mother, a role implied in the image of the cornucopia). He had thought of these possible roles earlier as he drafted the poem. The stanza now beginning "May she become a flourishing hidden tree" had originally begun (again, I regularize):

> Grant her an even temper & good health
> A husband, children & a little wealth
> Yet not enough for joy to have no part
> In the self-delighting heart.[9]

These lines, though cut in revision, provided the seed for the concluding marriage-stanza. In giving up the sentimental hope that an unmarried Anne would return to Coole and think of her dead father, in allowing her to delight another man's eyes, Yeats repeats his generous gesture at the end of "The Wild Swans at Coole" in which he relinquishes the swans to others, leaving himself as their merely transient possessor.

I return now to form, to ask how Yeats, in "A Prayer for My Daughter,"
improves on his earlier use of the irregular octave-stanza. But first I must
mention one significant formal difference between the first printing of the
poem in *Poetry* and *The Irish Statesman* in November 1919 and its subsequent
appearance in the 1920 *Michael Robartes and the Dancer:* in book form the
poem has lost the Roman numerals prefacing its stanzas, which had per-
sisted into the June 1919 typescript submitted for publication to *Poetry*.
There is no absolute consistency in Yeats's practice of prefacing the stanzas
of some individual poems with Roman numerals: the vignettes in the Greg-
ory elegy have them, for instance, while the two-stanza vignettes in "All
Soul's Night" do not. Still, it is evident that the presence of a large and im-
posing Roman numeral before each stanza interrupts, slows down, and
tends to shift the locus of a poem; and in finally choosing to print "A Prayer
for my Daughter" without such interpositions, Yeats gives the poem a single
local "station" as, on the battlements of his tower, he progresses through
his prayer.

"A Prayer for My Daughter," though written in the same stanza form as
"In Memory of Major Robert Gregory," uses the stanza with considerably
more freedom. There are two opposite effects natural to this stanza: the
first is the "rational" one of the initial pentameter couplet, which can set a
scene or propose a thesis; the second is the "lyric" effect created by the in-
ternal tetrameter rhyming couplet (lines 6–7) of the closing embraced-
rhyme quatrain. The internal couplet often introduces a note of simplicity,
sometimes ironized, sometimes not. The Gregory elegy makes ample use
of the expository possibility of the first, pentameter, effect, as these down-
to-earth examples suggest:

> Now that we're almost settled in our house
> I'll name the friends that cannot sup with us[.]
>
> Always we'd have the new friend meet the old
> And we are hurt if either friend seem cold[.][10]

In addition to using an initial pentameter couplet-statement, Yeats also ex-
ploits, in the Gregory elegy, the "lyric" possibilities of the internal four-beat
couplet. He foregrounds that couplet, of course, in the three stanzas that
repeat "Soldier, scholar, horseman, he" (IX, X, and XI), but that ritualized
insistence tends (to my mind) to appear mechanical in its reappearances. If

we look at the other stanzas, the first internal couplet gathers up the contemplated guests:

> Discoverers of forgotten truth
> Or mere companions of my youth . . .

The sixth stanza sets forth epithets:

> But not that my dear friend's dear son,
> Our Sidney and our perfect man . . .

But in the remaining stanzas the expressive potential of the internal rhymed couplet is not made salient.

When we come to "A Prayer for My Daughter," we find that the initial pentameter couplets recall, in their expository function, those in the Gregory elegy. But the internal tetrameter couplets now draw more of Yeats's attention, as he becomes conscious of the aesthetic energy they can be called upon to provide. We see him emphasizing the strong emotional rhythm, whether sinister or sardonic, of the short-breathed couplet (by contrast to the more intellectual effect of the initial pentameter couplet):

> That the future years had come,
> Dancing to a frenzied drum . . .

> It's certain that fine women eat
> A crazy salad with their meat . . .

> She can, though every face should scowl
> And every windy quarter howl . . .

In "The Tower," part II, Yeats continues to confer striking effects on the internal couplet. Sometimes the tone is brisk or racy:

> Ran, and with the garden shears
> Clipped an insolent farmer's ears . . .

Or the couplet may emphasize a unity mentioned in the poem:

> O may the moon and sunlight seem
> One inextricable beam . . .

Or it may group consequences together:

> And had but broken knees for hire
> And horrible splendor of desire . . .

In "Colonus' Praise," the rhythmic dance-potential of the four-beat line is recalled in the internal couplet:

> Immortal ladies tread the ground
> Dizzy with harmonious sound[.]

And still later, in "A Dialogue of Self and Soul," Yeats uses the internal tetrameter couplet for the Soul's dismissive summary of the intellect's adventures:

> And intellect its wandering
> To this and that and t'other thing . . .

Another couplet marks the Soul's theological complacency:

> That is to say, ascends to Heaven;
> Only the dead can be forgiven . . .

In the same poem, an ecstatic trochaic Blakean couplet expresses the joy of the self that has cast out remorse:

> We must laugh and we must sing,
> We are blest by everything . . .

Yeats has become, it is clear, keenly aware of the potential—expository or lilting—of the distinct parts of his Cowley stanza. When he takes up a stanza form over and over, he is always attempting to explore and exploit more fully its expressive limits.

Because the Cowley stanza had been so successful in the Gregory elegy and in "Prayer for My Daughter," we are at first surprised that when Yeats came to write "Byzantium" in the same rhyme-scheme, he adopted a different rhythm. He must have known instinctively that he could not allow into his turbulent death-poem the one-two, one-two dance potential of mocking or ecstatic four-beat couplets. He therefore reduces the measure of the internal couplet from the left-right symmetry of four beats ("That is to say, as-cends to Heaven") to the asymmetrical measure of three beats, with an im-plied pause for reflection (like a musical rest) after each line:

> All that man is, [*rest*]
> All mere complexities; [*rest*]
>
> Dying into a dance, [*rest*]
> An agony of trance; [*rest*]
>
> Those images that yet [*rest*]
> Fresh images beget [*rest*]

To sum up, the measure that Yeats chose in the non-*ottava rima* eight-line stanza—one that rocks back and forth between pentameters and te-trameters (or, in "Byzantium," among pentameters, tetrameters, and trim-eters)—was a more disturbing measure than the historically stabilized pace of the pentameter *ottava rima*. Although the rhyme-schemes of his alter-nate eight-line stanzas—couplet, couplet, embraced quatrain (*aabbcddc*), or two embraced quatrains (*abbacddc*, as in "A Dialogue of Self and Soul")—suggest a potential division into quatrain sense-units, Yeats usually divides up the stanza syntactically into anything but quatrains. In "A Prayer for My Daughter," for instance, only one stanza—the second—is divided syntacti-cally into two quatrains. The rest vary wildly, from a single unbroken eight-line sense-unit in stanza 3 ("May she be granted beauty") to an asymmetri-cal set of units like those found in stanza 5 ("In courtesy I'd have her chiefly learned"): 1; 2; 5. In the prayer for his daughter Yeats repeats his pattern of syntactic units only once, when stanza 9 (5; 3) repeats stanza 7 (5; 3). Yet be-cause stanza 9 is a single sentence, while stanza 7 is split into two sentences, the actual effects of the similar syntactic division differ from stanza to stanza.

By the time he writes "A Prayer for My Daughter," Yeats is allowing himself great freedom to range the lexicon (from "heart-revealing inti-macy" to "a bandy-leggèd smith"). Part of the appeal of the poem lies in this freedom: a man of fifty-five is not about to tailor his language to the diction of the conventional christening-poem. Since every poem reveals the mind of its author as well, we may ask ourselves what we can say about the mind of the man who composes these spacious poems, with their eight-line stanzas that enable him to write on several planes at once. In "A Prayer" the first plane is that of external factual narrative in which the outside *wind* disturbs (on another plane) the *mind* of the man who has recently become a father. *Mind* and *wind* are rhymed twice more in the poem, in stanzas 7 and 8, reinforcing both the actual disjunction and the symbolic nearness of the two planes, physical and mental. A third plane to which Yeats moves is that of desacralized myth (Helen, Venus); the fourth is that of symbolic Nature (the storm, the linnet, the laurel tree); the fifth that of contemporary distressed women (Maud, the poet's hidden mother); the sixth, a meditative plane ("Hearts are not had as a gift"); the seventh, psychological ("To be choked with hate / May well be of all evil chances chief"); the eighth, overtly allegorical (the horn of Plenty as Ceremony, the "spreading laurel tree" as Custom). And one could probably add others. This imaginative freedom of motion through planes—as Yeats moves his hands up and down, one might say, from one keyboard to the next and back again—is matched by the freedom of syntactic division, as each stanza unfolds differently from its fellows.

I mention these technicalities of construction to explain what causes the impression, when we read the Yeats of the spacious poems of octave-stanzas, that we are encountering a free-associating discourse that paradoxically exhibits total formal control. As each of these poems unrolls, we take in (if only subliminally) its formal patterns: the recurrence of rhymes and line-lengths, of stanzaic shape, of incremental repetition of words and themes. The apparent spontaneity with which these masterful effects are deployed conveys a powerful sense of a mind that has arrived at personal, intellectual, and emotional freedom. Such long poems as the elegy for Gregory and the father's prayer are the bridge to the even more ambitious Yeatsian sequences (seen in Chapters III and XII) that can no longer contain themselves within one prosodic order or genre, but rather need to multiply themselves internally into a group of non-isometric poems.

When composing, in 1927 or 1928, "A Dialogue of Self and Soul" (477–479), Yeats used a variant of the stanza appearing in "In Memory of Major Robert Gregory," "A Prayer for My Daughter," and "The Tower," part II. In "A Dialogue," although the irregular *line-lengths* remain the same (5-5-5-4-5-4-4-5) as in his regularized version of the Cowley stanza, Yeats alters the *rhyme-scheme,* making both quatrains embraced ones *(abbacddc).* Yeats's master-stroke in "A Dialogue" is to insist, in part I, on retaining a *single* stanza form as the shape common to *both* Soul and Self (in spite of their drastic thematic opposition). Self and Soul (says the single shared stanza form) inhabit the same body in life; they are coerced by their cohabitation into the same external, material, stanzaic outline. The formal thesis of this poem says that we are unable to imagine, in this life, Soul dwelling in one shape and Self in another. As long as Soul and Self remain embodied, they must share a single habitation, a single "shape," a single stanza form.

Nonetheless, Yeats must somehow differentiate, in part I, Soul from Self, Self from Soul. He does this thematically, as the Soul recommends that the Self not only repudiate eros and thanatos, Love and War (the old Homeric themes), but also repudiate thought, imagination, and memory. These are to be replaced by spiritual ascent, oblivion of the senses, a merging into the darkness of non-identity, a petition for forgiveness of "the crime of death and birth" (that is, embodiedness itself), and, ultimately, the silencing of the tongue. The Self, by contrast, dwells on its sole valued possession, a single 500-year-old emblem of triple aspect: a Japanese sword ("Sato's ancient blade"), its wooden scabbard, and a piece of embroidered cloth wound around it. These stand not only for sexual union—blade in scabbard—but also for Yeats's persistent Homeric pair: war and (in the embroidery that was a soldier's guerdon) love:

> all these I set
> For emblems of the day against the tower
> Emblematic of the night.

The Self, transformed metaphorically into a soldier by its possession of the master-forged sword,[11] claims "as by a soldier's right / A charter to commit the crime [of death and birth] once more."

Daringly, Yeats in part I gives the Soul not only the first word but the last, seeming to award the victory to the nihilism and silence of death. But he then appends part II—four stanzas spoken (still in the same stanza form) by the Self alone, dialogue having vanished with the banishing of the Soul. By the end of the poem, Self has acquired six stanzas to the Soul's three, gaining in part II a last word both long and resonant. The literal disappearance of Soul leaves Self in sole possession of the stanza form, that symbol of embodied being.

The drafts of the "Dialogue," quoted below from the Cornell manuscripts of *The Winding Stair,* are exceptionally full and interesting.[12] The first draft is a bare skeleton (slightly regularized here, as are subsequent citations of the drafts, for better intelligibility). Already the poem is a dialogue ("He" versus "Me"); already its terms (God versus love and war) are set; and already Self's emblems (court-dress and sword) are pictured; but this draft insists on a divided personhood, a first-person versus a third-person self, by labeling only one voice (the one that will become Self) "Me" (while the other, who will become Soul, is "He"). As I reproduce Yeats's disordered spacing of the words on the first manuscript page, I underline the words representing the speakers in order to make Yeats's draft-organization clear as he sketches his Arabic-numeraled stanzas:

<u>He</u>

1

Stair

Stands

<u>Me</u>

2

I know emblems
    & set up
    Show court dress.

3 <u>He</u>

What use to you now
    love & war

    4—<u>Me</u>

I pray to god [?to] send me back to the world

    5 <u>He</u>

What seek you there
Are you not tired of men & of strife

    <u>Me</u>

Never enough of women

    <u>He</u>

That which you have sought in [?them]
    he offers

    <u>Me</u>

[?No] only the sword gives truth—
            (WS, 23)

The comprehensiveness of the conflict between the secular and the sacred, women and God, is clear even in this naked outline: "That which you have sought in [?them] he [God] offers."

The next draft (*WS*, 24) shows Yeats choosing a pentameter measure for his opening line ("The time approaches for the winding stair"), and perhaps for subsequent lines ("The cold starlight, & the breathless air"). By the third draft (*WS*, 27), sure of his pentameter, he is oscillating (for his shorter lines) between tetrameter and trimeter, and has not decided whether lines 3 and 4 should both be pentameters (as in III below) or whether line 4 should be a tetrameter (as in I below). In spite of this indecision about line-length, the poet has settled, by stanza III, on his final rhyme-scheme: two embraced quatrains. The first speaker (formerly "He") has become "The Soul," and the second speaker (on the way to his ultimate name, "Self") is now named not "Me" but "Myself":

The Soul

I

I summon to the winding ancient stair;
Set all your mind upon the steep ascent
Upon the broken crumbling battlement
Upon the breathless starlight air
But set it most upon
The quarter where all thought is done,
The pole star & the silence at the pole.

II

Myself

III

The consecrated sword upon my knees
Is Sato's ancient sword, still as it was,
Still razor sharp & still a looking glass
Unspotted by the slattern centuries
The silk embroidered wrapping was a part
Of some court lady's dress—I vow
The pretty blossoms of the bough
Picture the red & purple of her heart.

The temptation toward having a three-beat line somewhere in the second quatrain (as in stanza I above) persists even into the published poem, where the second quatrain of the penultimate stanza contains a trimeter in the line "The folly that man does":

> Or into that most fecund ditch of all,
> The folly that man does
> Or must suffer, if he woos
> A proud woman not kindred of his soul.[13]

By the third extant draft of "A Dialogue," Yeats has achieved his new stanza, with embraced rhyme in both quatrains. He has also taken the crucial decision (in the same draft) to have "The Soul" and "Myself" speak in identical stanza form. He has changed his earlier prefacing Arabic numbers to Roman numerals, and the "He" and "Me" of the first draft have mutated into "The Soul" and "Myself." (Later—in the draft entitled "Silk, Sword, & Tower" and in the published poem—they will move closer to each other by being named "My Soul" and "My Self" [*WS*, 45]. The title of the published poem—"A Dialogue of Self and Soul"—by omitting the personal pronoun, universalizes the reference of the two nouns.)

Having compelled himself to give Self and Soul identical stanzaic form, it is now only through idiom that Yeats can differentiate the two debaters. Into the Soul's mouth, Yeats puts language which is religious, authoritative, astrological, astronomical, occult, cruelly dismissive, paradoxical, and trans- or super-categorical (as the Soul announces the obliteration of the usual distinction between fact and value):

> The intellect no longer knows
> How to [?divine] the knower from the known
> And knowing everything knows nought
> Of the "is" & of the "ought."
> (*WS*, 35)

Against the idiolect of the Soul, what idiom must the Self produce? First, the Self repeats the very words used by the Soul, in order to contest the Soul's right to "own" the concepts behind the words. The words of the Self concerning the sword, and some subsequent draft-words about its embroidery, argue for a secular sanctity as good as that offered by God's obliterative darkness: "the *consecrated* sword upon my knees / Is Sato's ancient sword" (*WS*, 27); "And not less *sacred* than the blade the bit / Of some court lady's dress" (*WS*, 29; italics mine). If the Soul summons to an "*ancient* stair," the Self will retort that it too has archaic warrant—"Sato's an-

*cient* blade" (italics mine). If the Soul concedes that its theocratic battlement is "broken" and "crumbling," the Self likewise concedes that one of its aesthetic talismans is "tattered" and "faded." These overlappings in diction symbolize the fact that the argument is taking place within a single man, who values the sacred and the ancient whether he is speaking as Self or as Soul.

Yet "Myself" (as the drafts continue) is also at pains to differentiate himself from "The Soul." While conceding the effect on the embroidery of time's ravages, he asserts that the lady's token can still protect and adorn; and he adds that his other talisman, the sword, has escaped such disfiguration and has lost nothing to time, since it is "still razor-keen, still like a looking glass / Unspotted by the centuries" (*WS*, 27). Although the Soul wishes to abolish time (to "deliver from the crime of death and birth"), the Self loves history and wishes to remain in continuity with the past, finding it important to name the maker of the sword: "Montashigi, third of his family, fashioned it." If the Soul seeks night, the Self seeks day, with its doomed but classical occupations, love and war.

So far, in this dialogue, the Soul, who speaks first, has set the terms of debate, and the Self has merely defied them with its own version of sacredness, its own noble emblems. In part II, however, when the Self, no longer confined by the Soul's leading voice, can invent its own terms, it resorts to extremes of diction that we would never have expected from the courtly devotee of those high abstractions, "love" and "war," and their aristocratic symbols, embroidery and sword. The Soul's challenge has forced the Self to confront directly the bestial and blind things that actually go on in war and in love, and the Self must assert his response to these not in his courtly language of part I but in a newly sordid first person: "I am content to live it all again":

> I am content to live it all again
> And yet again, if it be life to pitch
> Into the frog-spawn of a blind man's ditch,
> A blind man battering blind men;
> Or into that most fecund ditch of all,
> The folly that man does
> Or must suffer, if he woos
> A proud woman not kindred of his soul.

The sexual frog-spawn and the biblical blind battering ("Shall they not both fall into the ditch?") are the utmost reduction of love and war, abased even beyond the abstract "lust" and "rage" found in "The Spur" (1936) or "the fury [rage] and the mire [lust] of human veins" found in "Byzantium." The Self's idiom in part II, though stimulated by the Soul's commands, reveals for the first time that there is a conflict of Self with Self, a conflict provoked by the Self's social experience. The Self lives within the archetypal world of sword and embroidery, yes, but it lives equally within part II's debased world of aggression and desire.

In the drafts of the opening of part II, in which Self, we recall, is the sole voice, Yeats at first remains within the first person (employing both "I" and the "you"-of-self-address) when describing the Self's evolutionary formation. He dwells on the "impurity" of his intellect when it is governed by rage and desire (as before, I have conflated and regularized):

> What old [?miseries] must I endure—
> Rage that is thought's creator, desire that is
> Creator of all temporal images
> Have made your intellect impure—
>> (WS, 39)

In the finished part II, however, Yeats alternates interestingly (until the final first-person "we") between the first person singular ("I") and the third person ("he," "man"), probably because the use of the first person alone might seem to permit self-pity. After the first three lines of part II, he abandons the first person and depicts the Self's suffering in a generalized third person, enjambing his universalized autobiography over a stanza break:

> What matter if I live it all once more?
> Endure that toil of growing up;
> The ignominy of boyhood; the distress
> Of boyhood changing into man;
> The unfinished man and his pain
> Brought face to face with his own clumsiness;
>
> The finished man among his enemies?—

This great passage enters the poem early in the process of composition and remains essentially unchanged through all subsequent vicissitudes of revision. The list exhibits Yeats's brilliant verbal virtuosity, here in the deploying of nouns. What will be the umbrella-noun for "growing up"?—*toil.* What is suffered in "boyhood"?—*ignominy.* What noun accompanies adolescence?—*distress*. What characterizes young manhood?—*clumsiness*. What is the summarizing noun?—*pain*.[14] The stark attributes of Yeats's list of phases "endured" (*indurare*, to last long enough to harden into place) fix themselves in the memory. Growing up is "toil"—an intellectual toil as well as a physical one, exhausting, incessant, and unrewarded. Boyhood suffers "ignominy"—chiefly, one supposes in Yeats's case, at school—an ignominy springing from learning difficulties, an unconventional family, and relative poverty. As the etymology of "ignominy" tells us, he was *sine nomen*—unknown as the person he interiorly knew himself to be. While "growing up" is incremental external work and "boyhood" a state, adolescence brings, as a daily norm, an embarrassing changingness: "the distress / Of boyhood *changing* into man." "Distress"—from *di* ("twice") and *stringere* ("hold tightly")—denotes the intolerable antipodal stresses, the irreconcilable wishes, of the boy and the man he is turning into. And when the adolescent has become a man, he experiences further pain in finding himself physically and sexually mature while still emotionally immature; the disarticulation of mature body and immature soul issues in the agonizing social "clumsiness" of the would-be wooer or man of action. Finally, as this Everyman becomes a "finished man," the process might seem to be over. But he awakes from "all that toil" to discover that he is surrounded by malicious enemies, defaming him in the public arena until he almost thinks himself to be the caricature they have created.

No lines of Yeats's are more accurate and more telling in their simplicity than these impersonal verses in which Self tracks the formation of selfhood. The Soul knows nothing of such gradual and incremental processes; it knows only absolutes and polarities, sins and perfections. Because the harsh Soul is physically one with the imperfect Self, when the Self enters the public arena he is plunged into conflict: shall he stay in that arena, where honor demands he be, or shall he flee the debased public image of himself and the malicious enemies who have constructed it? As "honor" contends with the impulse to escape, the Self has a bitter foretaste of itself owning nothing but its honor, cast out, like Lear, into "the wintry blast":

> How in the name of Heaven can he escape
> That defiling and disfigured shape
> The mirror of malicious eyes
> Casts upon his eyes until at last
> He thinks that shape must be his shape?
> And what's the good of an escape
> If honour find him in the wintry blast?

It is not merely the conflict of private self-image against public mirror-image—that confusion caused by the presence of enemies—that arouses contrary impulses within the Self. (Yeats emphasizes the public process by the mirroring chiasmus enacted by "shape: eyes :: eyes: shape," as well as by the forced juxtaposition of "that shape must be his shape.") Also present is the harsher conflict between the Self's past actions and its present Soul-influenced judgment of them as "folly" and "degradation." The draft is even more explicit than the printed poem, exhibiting the same oscillation between "I" and "he" (I have regularized lightly, as with most of my transcriptions):

> I am content to live through it all again . . .
> Through that false, foul, most fecund ditch of all
> Of the folly that he does
> Or must suffer, if he woes
> A proud woman not kindred to the soul;
> For I must trace my folly
> Trace all that degradation to its source.
> (WS, 52, 53)

Impurity of intellect, folly in love, and moral degradation in action are (in these passages) the Self's verdict on its own past. The Self seems, in short, to have interiorized the inimical values of the Soul—for this is how the Soul would judge the lengths to which a "barren passion" has led the Self. There are yet earlier indications in the drafts of the Self's adoption of the Soul's standards: "The sword & silk have made mankind impure" (WS, 40, 41). If the Self truly believes that sword and embroidery are consecrated and sacred, he should not call his dedication to them "impurity" or "degradation." (Although the word "impure" remains in the finished poem, it is attached to the "ditches" of the social world and not to "mankind" or "the intellect.") And although the naming of love as "folly" survives in the finished poem (as the word "degradation" does not), it is no longer merely the Self's private failing: it is the very condition of the act of love, which not only causes active folly in oneself but also makes one the victim of the folly of the beloved. Under the spell of Eros, man does *and* must suffer folly. In conceding the double nature of folly, Self admits his self-critique but also excuses himself from personal sin by universalizing the folly that both drives sexual desire and results from it.

The anterior literary works presiding over "A Dialogue of Self and Soul" (as the drafts make evident) are *King Lear* and "The Rime of the An-

cient Mariner." A phrase of Lear's ("O I am bound upon a wheel of fire"),
although censored out of the finished poem, underlies Yeats's "What can
man's soul but mourn, for it is bound / Upon the wheel of life" (*WS*, 40, 41).
And the Mariner's blessing of the water-snakes ("O happy living things!") is
visible in Yeats's treatment of self-forgiveness:

> Upon the [?instant] so great my [?sweetness]
> I shall understand all living things
> & bless all living things.
>             (*WS*, 42, 43)

The final version of these lines drops the Coleridgean "living things" in fa-
vor of the abstract "everything":

> When such as I cast out remorse
> So great a sweetness flows into the breast
> We must laugh and we must sing,
> We are blest by everything,
> Everything we look upon is blest.

The Soul's felt presence is still generating some of the terms here. Against
the Soul's proposed "dumb" silence, the Self will "sing." But Yeats goes be-
yond a mere contradiction of Soul by unexpectedly prefacing "sing" with
the Blakean word "laugh"; laughing is not an act we associate with Lear or
the Ancient Mariner. The representation of joy in the internal trochaic te-
trameter couplet of this final stanza of "A Dialogue of Self and Soul"—"We
must laugh and we must sing, / We are blest by everything"—has a Blakean
childishness, and would not be out of place in the trochaic opening of *Songs
of Innocence:* "On a cloud I saw a child, / And he laughing said to me, /
'Pipe a song about a lamb!'"

The apparently worsted Soul having disappeared from view after part I,
Yeats would seem to have transformed the intimidating dialogue of Self
and Soul into a triumphant soliloquy of Self alone. However, the soliloquy
of part II retains, for a while, a shadow of the anterior dialogue, as the Self,
suddenly thrown on its own resources, at first shouts back at the Soul,
"What matter if the ditches are impure? / What matter if I live it all once
more? . . . / How in the name of Heaven [that Soul-word] can [a man] es-
cape?" "And what's the good of an escape?" These alternately defiant and
helpless questions, which disturb the integrity of the stanza-quatrains, are

"answered" by the steady rhythmic reiteration of assertion in the last two stanzas:

> I am content to live it all again
> And yet again, . . .
>
> I am content to follow to its source
> Every event.

These assertions climax at the close, when self-makers such as the poet "cast out remorse":

> We must laugh and we must sing,
> We are blest by everything;
> Everything we look upon is blest.

The Self's final chiasmus—blest: everything :: everything: blest—representing, as chiasmus does, both forethought and a completed circle—declares by its form that no further progress need be made. This is not an announcement of perfect mutuality: we do not read "We are blest by everything / [and] We bless everything," or "We are blest by everything . . . / [and] Everything is blest [by us]." The asymmetry of relation, in which everything can confer blessing, and everything looked upon by the blest is blest, leaves the speaker a receiver, rather than a source, of the great sweetness which has flowed into his breast. His activity is restricted by all the carefully distinguished verbs which he has enumerated: he will historically "follow to its source" his every action or thought; he will "measure the lot" with analytic eyes; he will "forgive myself the lot" (constituting himself a judge with the power to bind or loose); and he will then "cast out remorse" as though it were seven devils that had occupied his Soul. This self-exorcism in life is the final victory of the Self (contradicting the statement of the Soul that "only the dead can be forgiven"). These activities prove to be sufficient to make an unexpected external sweetness "flow" into the breast; they generate the compulsion to joy, phrased in necessitarian fashion as "We *must* laugh and we *must* sing" (italics mine) rather than in a future narration: ["We shall laugh and we shall sing"].

In writing a dialogue between Self and Soul, Yeats was setting up, one could say, an abstract version of the antinomy of sacred and secular explored in "Sailing to Byzantium." He was never seriously about to place himself permanently in the Soul's artifice of eternity, though he could not excuse himself from investigating its appeal to him. It was only when he advanced into the second part of the "Dialogue," to the more vexing dialogue of Self with Self, that he could describe the deep antinomy between the idealized "pure" Self and the realized Self of desire and rage, and thereby find words to overwrite the initial terms of debate established by the repressive Soul.[15]

I return now to the question of Yeats's choice of two embraced quatrains *(abbacddc)* as the stanza form for "A Dialogue of Self and Soul." How is the effect created by this form different from the effect of the Gregory stanza, with its two rhyming couplets followed by a single embraced quatrain *(aabbcddc)*? The two embraced-rhyme quatrains in the "Dialogue" stanza differ from each other in shape. The first embraced quatrain is not symmetrical: the two lines constructing the *"a"* rhyme (lines 1 and 4) differ in line-length—line 1 has five beats, while line 4 has only four—so that the first quatrain of each stanza reads metrically 5-5-5-4. The second embraced quatrain, by contrast, is symmetrical. Lines that rhyme together in the *cddc* quatrain are of equal length: 5-4-4-5. In poetry, we find it reassuring when two quatrains resemble each other, when the pattern, once established, repeats itself. The quatrains of the "Dialogue" stanza fall upon the ear entirely differently, and are therefore unsettling, suggesting something unresolvable within each stanza. It might seem that the Self, when it claims the floor in part II and tries to repudiate the Soul's commands, would choose a new stanza form, but he is constrained to live with the Soul, who has set the tune. The unease, therefore, can never entirely subside; the most Yeats can do is provide the grateful trochees of blessing. Earlier, in the Soul's departing lines of theological exposition, after the tetrameter "lightness" of the envisaged ascent to heaven, the blunt heaviness of the ten-word monosyllabic conclusion had made itself strongly felt:

> That is to say, ascends to Heaven;
> Only the dead can be forgiven;
> But when I think of that my tongue's a stone.

When we play this against the six-word closing lightness of the disburdened Self's envoi in part II—"Everything we look upon is blest"—we recognize that the Self has done all it can to "correct," by accepting the folly of life, the heavy tread of the Soul up the broken stair.

Throughout "A Dialogue of Self and Soul," Yeats's "willful" disregard of quatrain-borders and even of a stanza-barrier (in part I, we recall, the first stanza ran over into the second) contributes to our sense of precariousness as we experience the poem. A stanza form that "ought" by the symmetries of its embraced quatrain-rhymes to create agreeable enclosures *(abba cddc)* instead creates a repeated rhythmic and syntactic waywardness, suggesting the primeval unforeseeability of existence, which both Soul and Self, in their different ways, are attempting to organize. At the end, the Self is shown—by his final chiasmus of song—to be able to organize spiritual difficulties into sweetness, refusing the offered sublimities of the Soul's principles of organization, which depend on a determined linear "ascent" to "Heaven" and a subsidence into silence.

The "spacious lyrics" that I have been considering, decisively compressed into hard-to-manage stanzas of irregular line-lengths, acquire because of their "wayward" stanza forms their effect of exertion, of obstacles met and overcome, of intermittent outbreaks of frustration, of unexpected moments of stricken silence, or (by contrast) of sweetness revealed. Although *ottava rima* can also embody a sense of difficulty, instability is not natural to that stanza (as Yeats recognized by needing to bring "Among School Children" back to its more equable stanzaic form in the close). But exertions and detours *are* natural to Yeats's variously irregular eight-line stanzas (and to their cousins, the irregular nine-line stanza of "Chosen"[16] and the ten-line stanza invented for "All Soul's Night"). These irregular stanzas, as they unwind in their formally predestined but rhythmically and aurally unstable evolution, have the combined certainty and uncertainty of the unpredictable spiral gyre—always repeating itself, but ensuring that each new higher or lower parallel turn is slightly unlike the last.

## XII

# ∂— PRIMITIVISM AND THE GROTESQUE:
## "SUPERNATURAL SONGS"

"Supernatural Songs" (1934), a sequence of twelve poems (554–563), is a late and often grotesque work. Yeats's purpose in it is to parody, and blaspheme against, Christian doctrine, in order to clear the way for a new primitivism. In the descriptions that follow I give first a general overview of the whole sequence, and then proceed (with some inevitable repetition, for which I ask the reader's patience) to a consideration of each of these twelve difficult poems in turn.

In the first five poems of the sequence, we meet an imagined early Irish Christian monk named Ribh, whose "Druidic" Christianity is still interwoven with paganism. The evangelizer Patrick has recently arrived in Ireland, and, to Ribh's disgust, he is preaching a doctrine that Ribh has never before encountered—that God is a masculine trinity, composed of Father, Son, and Holy Spirit. Ribh jeers at this fiction, which he ascribes to Platonic Hellenism, as an "abstract Greek absurdity." Yeats's long "Commentary on Supernatural Songs" explains his premise for the sequence at some length:

> A famous philosopher believed that every civilization began, no matter what its geographical origin, with Asia, certain men of science that all of us when still in the nursery were, if not African, exceedingly Asiatic. Saint Patrick must have found in Ireland, for he was not its first missionary, men whose Christianity had come from Egypt, and retained characteristics of those older faiths that have become so important to our invention. . . .
>
> While this book [*The King of the Great Clock Tower*] was passing through the press I wrote the poems for that old hermit Ribh. I did not explain the poems in [the play] *The King of the Great Clock Tower,* nor will I explain these. I would consider Ribh, were it not for his ideas about the Trinity, an orthodox man. (837)

At the opening of the sequence, Ribh is discovered by some passersby; they see that although it is night, he appears to be reading a book. He informs them (drawing on Yeats's knowledge of Swedenborg) that the intercourse of "angels"—by which he means lovers who have passed on to the afterlife—generates light, and by that light he reads his "holy book."[1] As the sequence progresses, Ribh announces his own transvaluation of Christianity; he says he will "study hatred," rather than Christian love, since "hatred of God may bring the soul to God." Although his hearers do not understand the "broken sentences" that Ribh has let fall during his visionary ecstasy, their incomprehension does not disturb him; his function is to communicate, after the fact, as much as he can of his vision, so that his listeners may in turn relate his tale to others. At this point, at the close of part V— with seven more poems to come in the sequence—Ribh's voice falls silent.

Poem VI, as we shall see, is a "hinge" (quoting a female voice) between Ribh's portion and the last six poems of "Supernatural Songs." Although Ribh has disappeared, some of his doctrines, including a counter-trinity to Patrick's (a sexual trinity consisting of man, woman, and child), begin to enact themselves bizarrely on the page, while other doctrines are voiced from an impersonal and oracular point of view which surveys all of being from a great cosmic distance. And yet the second portion (poems VII–XII) of this "supernatural" sequence ends with one of Yeats's great worldly poems, a Shakespearean sonnet called "Meru"; this poem contrasts a Western tragic world-view of the successive self-destructions of past civilizations with the detached Eastern world-views of Hindu hermit-ascetics, who are both like and unlike the Irish hermit Ribh with whom the sequence began.

The very length of this sequence creates a problem. In its 1934 magazine publication, and in the 1934 volume *The King of the Great Clock Tower,* "Supernatural Songs" had only eight poems. But Yeats, before printing the sequence in the 1935 volume *A Full Moon in March,* added to it four more poems, of a sort that rendered the grotesque even more salient as an aesthetic effect within the whole. The chief questions we find rising in us as we read the "Supernatural Songs" are these: Why does Yeats want to write about the "supernatural" at all? Why does he drop the persona of the Irish monk Ribh halfway through? Why is the grotesque so insistent in these songs? Why did Yeats compose in the meters and stanza forms that we see here? Why are the poems arranged in their present order? Why were the late-inserted poems placed in the positions they ultimately took?

Before turning to the individual poems, which are often bizarre parodies of Christian belief and ritual, I propose, as an explanation for Yeats's intent in the songs, Victor Hugo's brilliant remarks (in the Preface to his drama *Cromwell*) on the necessity of the grotesque in art:

The modern muse . . . will realize that everything in creation is not humanly *beautiful,* that the ugly exists beside the beautiful, the unshapely beside the graceful, the grotesque on the reverse of the sublime. . . . In the idea of men of modern times . . . the grotesque plays an enormous part. It is found everywhere; on the one hand it creates the abnormal and the horrible, on the other the comic and the burlesque. It fastens upon religion a thousand original superstitions, upon poetry a thousand picturesque fancies. . . . How boldly it brings into relief all the strange forms which the preceding age had timidly wrapped in swaddling clothes! . . . We need a little rest from everything, even the beautiful. . . . The grotesque seems to be a . . . starting-point whence one rises toward the beautiful with a fresher and keener perception.[2]

"How boldly [the grotesque] brings into relief all the strange forms which the preceding age had timidly wrapped in swaddling clothes!" What we see in Yeats's "Supernatural Songs" is the antagonism of one modern poet when he contemplates Christian forms, which he feels have now become so conventionalized as to seem "natural." Such forms of ritual, prayer, and habit perhaps once represented the beautiful: the ascetic life seemed a noble liberation from the distortions of sensuality; the masculine Trinity offered a seemly Greek homogeneity; the love of God represented the path toward perfection. But now the forms are outworn, and no longer serve as viable forms of the beautiful. The way to the new beautiful (implies Yeats through Ribh's utterances) must pass through the grotesque and the parodic; Ribh's hatred of "God" (as God has been understood in Christian theology) may bring the soul to "God"—that is, to God as He would be if He represented a modern, not an archaic, sublime.[3] But the new perfection cannot yet be envisaged; before it can be glimpsed, the old must be purged. It is this sometimes violent purging that we see in "Supernatural Songs," many of which are written in primitive forms proper to a new point of origin. Where can a new spiritual energy be found? Can we identify the primitive energies driving the dynamism of the whole universe, on which any new sacredness must be founded? The "Supernatural Songs" aim to discover, at any cost, a new vigor of beginnings, one that will extirpate any nostalgia we may feel for the old forms and rituals. (It is important, in reading these wilder poems of Yeats's old age, to remember that they are arrantly symbolic. They do not present a practical program for the invention of a new religion.)

I turn now to the two elements of the formal scheme that Yeats invented for this sequence, a scheme that is indubitably significant. One element—rhyme—is used to stand for the primitive (except in parts I, V, and XII, as we shall see). The other, less visible, element of the scheme is the ordering of the parts in a "concentric" shape, to stand for the primacy—embodied in the central part VI—of what Yeats referred to as his "centric form," the ambivalent sexual conjunction of woman and man, moon and sun.

Yeats first composed, as I have mentioned, a sequence of eight poems, published in 1934 in *Poetry* and *The London Mercury*. The original eight are now numbered, in the augmented twelve-part version, I–II, V–VI, and IX–X–XI–XII. Between journal publication and the 1935 volume publication, Yeats inserted the four additional poems, not simply adding them but locating them in a careful way: he placed III and IV to the left of the central pair V–VI, and VII and VIII to the right of that pivotal pair. What, we can ask, made him arrange the four new poems in these locations, and what relation do the new poems bear to the eight poems earlier composed? Why are the late-inserted poems grouped in twos—III, IV; VII, VIII? And why are they allowed to "interrupt," at two distinct moments, the earlier continuity of the sequence? I will come back to these questions, but I begin by offering a chart that clarifies the formal aspects of the poems in this sequence. The four late additions are printed in boldface and starred:

| Poem | Meter | Rhyme Scheme | Stanzas | Lines |
|---|---|---|---|---|
| I Ribh at the Tomb | 5 | blank verse | 3 (unequal) | 27 |
| II Ribh Denounces Patrick | 6 (+) | *aaa* (× 4) | 4 | 12 |
| **III\* Ribh in Ecstasy** | **5** | ***aa* (× 4)** | **1** | **8** |
| **IV\* There** | **4** | ***aa* (× 2)** | **1** | **4** |
| V Ribh Considers | 5 | *aabccb* (× 4) | 4 | 24 |
| VI He and She | 3 | *abcbdb* (× 2) | 2 | 12 |
| **VII\* What Magic Drum?** | **6 (+)** | ***aaa* (× 2)** | **2** | **6** |
| **VIII\* Whence Had They** | **5** | ***aa* (× 6)** | **1** | **12** |
| IX The Four Ages of Man | 4 | *aa* (× 4) | 4 | 8 |
| X Conjunctions | 4 | *aa* (× 2) | 2 | 4 |
| XI A Needle's Eye | 4 | *aa* (× 2) | 1 | 4 |
| XII Meru | 5 | Shakespearean sonnet | 1 | 14 |
| | | | Total = | 135 |

Various facts are made evident by this summary. The sequence, we see, is framed by complex Renaissance forms—a blank-verse prelude and a coda in the form of a Shakespearean sonnet. Given these lofty frames for the sequence, we are perplexed by the primitive nature of the rhymes of its inner members. Of all the formal aspects of the sequence, these rhymes are the strangest and most conspicuous. Of the ten inner members, eight (II, III, IV, VII, VIII, IX, X, and XI) rhyme in *aa* couplets or *aaa* tercets. Yeats, normally a master of variety in rhyme, especially (as we have seen in Chapter III) in sequences, has confined himself in these eight (of ten) inner poems to "knowing" only these two simplest of all rhyme-schemes: *all* the stanzas of these eight poems are built from these "primitive" *aa* or *aaa* components. The only two of the ten inner lyrics that do not conform to this pattern adjoin each other at the middle of the poem so as to form the central pair, V and VI. Poem VI, the center-poem quoting a female voice, rhymes in an adaptation of another "primitive" form, the six-line ballad stanza, *abcbdb*. Poem V (Ribh's last word) is the only one of all the inner poems to have a "developed" rhyme scheme *(aabccb)*, which breaks the pattern of "primitiveness" dominating its neighbors.

When we inspect the poems *added* for book publication, we see that the new **III** matches the new **VIII** (both are *pentameter* poems rhyming in couplets), and that the new **IV** matches the old IX, X, and XI (all are *tetrameter* poems rhyming in couplets). We also note that the new "trinitarian" **VII** matches the old "trinitarian" II: both are written in long-lined, irregular, single-rhymed *aaa* tercets. In short, when Yeats inserted his four "extra" poems—**III, IV, VII,** and **VIII,** all in "primitive" *aa* couplets or *aaa* tercets—he made unmistakably salient his intent to emphasize the most basic forms of rhyme: couplets and single-rhyme tercets (any quatrains present are composed of couplet-rhymes). The positions into which Yeats inserted his four additional poems make the sequence, formally speaking, a roughly concentric one around parts V and VI:

I matches XII (as frame-poems),
II matches VII (tercet poems),
III matches VIII (pentameter couplet-poems),
IV matches IX (tetrameter couplet-poems),
and V (with its six-line stanza) matches VI (with *its* six-line stanza).
X and XI (as two four-line tetrameter couplet-poems) together create an
    eight-line "match" to IX (an eight-line tetrameter couplet-poem).

Graphically represented, Yeats's arrangement looks like this:

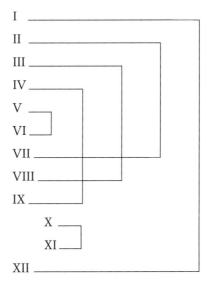

I mention these deliberately "concentric" arrangements made by Yeats because they too require explanation.

Yeats was at the end of his sixties when he wrote this sequence, one that has not been much attended to (except for "Meru") by critics. "Meru," the remarkable Shakespearean sonnet that closes the group, was written first, and in one draft was given the title "The summing up."[4] In it, Yeats projects his own sense of approaching death (and perhaps the recent death of Lady Gregory in 1932) onto the historical plane of the deaths of empires, and onto the cosmic plane of an Indian meditative knowledge that has existed for so long that it seems "supernatural." Yeats's personal and cultural *données* for "Supernatural Songs," then, were his own approaching death, the foreseeable (or already actual) death of Anglo-Irish culture, and (for "Meru") an encompassing Hindu view that aims to rise above the cultural nostalgia of one's own moment. In looking away from Christianity for a religious model that did not depend on the comfort of a personal afterlife, Yeats here found, not for the first time, Indian asceticism. Yet (once he had completed "Meru") he knew he could not convincingly impersonate an Indian hermit throughout his sequence, and so he persuaded himself that early Irish Christianity must have had something in common with Eastern religion.[5] The hermit who speaks for him within the sequence would not, therefore, be one of the Indian ascetics of "Meru" but an Irish analogue to those monks, Ribh, conceived as the authentic voice of an early Irish Christianity which preserves relics of paganism and also has (unknown to Ribh) affinities with Hinduism. Yeats allowed himself to surmise, in his "Commentary on Supernatural Songs," that by reaching back through Christianity to an earlier blend of the pagan and the Christian, to "older faiths," one might find the bearers of early virtue: "Perhaps some man young enough for so great a task might discover there men and women he could honour— to adapt the words of Goethe—by conferring their names upon his own thoughts; perhaps I myself had made a beginning" (837).

"Supernatural Songs" aims to hold in tension two irreconcilable sources of ecstatic energy: the first source is the ascetic life (like the monks of "Meru," Ribh is celibate, unmated, lost in meditation); the second source, incompatible with the first, is the sexual life described by Ribh as necessary for propagation on all planes, from the divine to the bestial. Ribh asserts that the supernatural sexual act of the self-generating Godhead is the primordial original of which every terrestrial sexual act is a copy. Human sexual coupling "descends" to ordinary procreation; if the human self had the purity of intention of the Godhead, it would derive its procreation from itself (says Ribh) in the fashion of his pagan trinity. If the Godhead is the master of sexual energy, the ascetic hermit-watcher is the master of the alternate source of energy, that of ascetic knowledge. (Yeats's syncretism is willing, by now, to incorporate aspects of any number of explanatory systems: the lore of the "Egyptian" Hermes Trismegistus, figures from astrology—Mars and Venus, Jupiter and Saturn—Hindu wisdom-literature, prehistoric nature worship, and Viconian gyres.)

Ribh's instructional prelude, as we saw in Chapter IX, is cast into blank verse, the form Yeats commonly used for doctrinal poems; and it is voiced in what we are accustomed to call Yeats's metaphysical style—gnomic, sustained, theological, learned. Theological language has long interested poets because of its self-referential nature: the invisible subjects of theological discourse are constituted by the very sentences purporting to describe and explain them. And doctrines of "the supernatural," offering to reveal the primitive origin of all things in the divine, tend to lead language into strange realms, several of which Yeats exploits in this sequence—especially in the four poems added after magazine publication, where his investment in "the primitive" is most noticeable.

Yeats's notion of the primitive is enacted not only in the elementary rhymes of this sequence but also in the "primitive" genres into which he casts individual poems. These are some of the oldest genres in Western lyric, associated as they are with the practice of religion, and they include the riddle, the myth of origin, the doctrinal exposition, the prayer, theological polemic, the genre asserting correspondence between the human and the divine, the report of mystic experience, the cosmological poem, and the portrayal of an afterlife. But these individual genres matter less than the effect they produce when thus assembled: eviscerated of their traditional Christian content, they provide old bottles into which Yeats can pour the new wine of his fantastic and blasphemous imagination.

The first such genre we encounter in the "Songs" is hagiography, which generates the opening poem, "Ribh at the Tomb of Baile and Aillinn." The language of hagiography is an accommodated one that seeks to make plausible to the laity the miracles, visions, and translated states of the saints, and hagiographic narrative is spoken or written by a mediator presumed to have insight into those "supernatural" actions or states. It is as hagiographer that we first meet Ribh, as he tells onlookers (who are surprised to find him reading his book in the dark) that he reads by the light generated from the energy of the afterlife intercourse of the mythical Irish lovers Baile and Aillinn, whose story they know.

That story had been told earlier (in tetrameter couplets) by Yeats in his beautifully lyrical 1901 poem "Baile and Aillinn." A prefacing "Argument" tells the plot:

> *Baile and Aillinn were lovers, but Aengus, the Master of Love, wishing them to be happy in his own land among the dead, told to each a story of the other's death, so that their hearts were broken and they died.*

In Yeats's tetrameter-couplet poem, the lovers' story, after their death, is inscribed on a "fan-book" (a term given to me by Warwick Gould) made of alternating leaves of apple wood (for Aillinn) and yew (for Baile):

> And poets found, old writers say,
> A yew-tree where his body lay;
> But a wild apple hid the grass
> With its sweet blossom where hers was;
> And being in good heart, because
> A better time had come again
> After the deaths of many men,
> And that long fighting at the ford,

> They wrote on tablets of thin board,
> Made of the apple and the yew,
> All the love stories that they knew.
>
> (197)

Yeats can say of the lovers, in "Ribh at the Tomb of Baile and Aillinn," that "All know their tale," and can be confident in saying so, because he has already written his long lyrical version of their story. In fact, Ribh may be using as his "holy book" (Warwick Gould speculates) a fan-book containing the lovers' story. It is not their life-tale that Ribh will recite; rather, he represents the lovers' miraculous intercourse on the anniversary of their death, which is also the anniversary of their first embrace. Here is the opening of "Ribh at the Tomb," with Ribh addressing the onlookers:

> Because you have found me in the pitch-dark night
> With open book you ask me what I do.
> Mark and digest my tale, carry it afar
> To those that never saw this tonsured head
> Nor heard this voice that ninety years have cracked.
> Of Baile and Aillinn you need not speak,
> All know their tale, all know what leaf and twig,
> What juncture of the apple and the yew,
> Surmount their bones; but speak what none have heard.

By their miraculous death at the command of Aengus, the lovers have been translated into "glorified" bodies (the theological term for bodies which have regained their souls on the Last Day). Yet these bodies are still able to have intercourse, thanks to Yeats's reading of Swedenborg:

> The miracle that gave them such a death
> Transfigured to pure substance what had once
> Been bone and sinew; when such bodies join
> There is no touching here, nor touching there,
> Nor straining joy, but whole is joined to whole;
> For the intercourse of angels is a light
> Where for a moment both seem lost, consumed.

As Ribh explains to his unseen auditors the nature of the miraculous light generated (but only to his eyes) by the intercourse of the lovers, he resorts to three different forms of discourse: the theological language of "miracle," "transfigured," "purified," "holy," and "angels"; the philosophical discourse of "pure substance" and "whole is joined to whole"; and the literary discourse of "tale," "tragedy," and the "pages [of a] holy book." These are all second-order discourses. The poem never enters the internal drama of an actual first-order supernatural experience: Ribh and his auditors remain fixed on earth; nobody but Ribh sees or can understand his "vision"; and Ribh cannot articulate it intelligibly while he is experiencing it.

From the habitual "when"—"when such bodies join"—Ribh moves to the actual moment of his lyric, the "now" and the "here" of his vision:

> Here in the pitch-dark atmosphere above
> The trembling of the apple and the yew,
> Here on the anniversary of their death,
> The anniversary of their first embrace,
> Those lovers, purified by tragedy,
> Hurry into each other's arms[.]

And Ribh closes by explaining why only he can see the transcendent embrace of the lovers:

> . . . these eyes,
> By water, herb and solitary prayer
> Made aquiline, are open to that light.
> Though somewhat broken by the leaves, that light
> Lies in a circle on the grass; therein
> I turn the pages of my holy book.
> (554–555)

The problematic relations among the supernatural, the natural, the philosophical, and the literary, upon which this opening poem is founded, pervade the rest of the sequence. Holy events, such as "the intercourse of angels," must be retold in human words ("my tale"). The clarifying and perpetuating role of literature—written and oral—supports Ribh's insistence that he not only watches the angelic lovers but reads his holy book, not only contemplates the divine but narrates its features to others ("Mark and digest my tale"). These actions distinguish Ribh from his silent Hindu counterparts in "Meru," who have passed beyond vision and hagiography into pure knowing, a state of immanent awareness in which reading, writing, and narrating are forgotten—a state Yeats may envy, but one to which, as a writer, he cannot truly aspire. The energy radiating from the intercourse of Baile and Aillinn, unseen by others, must diffuse itself into Ribh's tale of holy light, and pass thence to his audience.

If blank-verse instruction in hagiography and theology organizes the first poem of "Supernatural Songs," the polemic so natural to theological disputes organizes the second. "Ribh Denounces Patrick" (originally called "Ribh Prefers an Older Theology") asks whether God is one or three, and whether the triune Godhead is sexual or not. Ribh insists that "All natural or supernatural stories" run the same way—"Man, woman, child"—that the energy of heterosexual begetting, as everyone knows, drives all life. But now Patrick has arrived, preaching (says Ribh) a ridiculous new Greek concept (one might even say a homosexual concept) of a God who is purely masculine, and who begets himself on himself in a masculine Trinity—Father, Son, and Holy Spirit—with not a woman or child in the story. Anyone who would preach such an unlikely story, Ribh jeers, has taken leave of his senses. Ribh's denunciation of Patrick (in poem II) is uttered in parodic trinitarian tercets, raggèd in meter but carefully tricked out in trinitarian rhyme (*aaa*):

> An abstract Greek philosophy has crazed the man—
> Recall that masculine Trinity. Man, woman, child (a daughter or a
>    son),
> That's how all natural or supernatural stories run.

Yeats's long impatience with Irish sexual prudery explodes in Ribh's testy refutation of Patrician theology. The lines continue, polemically, Ribh's sexualized theology in the prelude, which so urbanely accounted for the energy radiating from the intercourse of Baile and Aillinn.

Theological discourse is founded on the belief that the cosmos is intelligible, while philosophical discourse allows for the possibility of a blank where cognitive intelligibility ends (Wittgenstein's "Whereof one cannot speak, thereof one must be silent"). Yeats's appetite for totalizing statement generates Ribh's Blakean universe, where everything below is a copy of things above, and "natural and supernatural with the self-same ring are wed." Just as the child-speaker of Blake's "The Lamb" asserts (even if naïvely) the unity in Christ of all orders of existence ("I a child and thou a lamb, / We are callèd by his name"), so Yeats's Ribh makes (but in a grotesque manner) a comparable assertion. The correspondence extends to all orders: "As man, as beast, as ephemeral fly begets, Godhead begets God-head." This unwieldy and preposterous statement crams into itself four lev-els of being—insect, beast, human, and divine—as Ribh's cosmic theology of begetting forces the line-unit to a length able to contain the Great Chain of Being. When Ribh quotes the "Great Smaragdine Tablet" of Hermes Trismegistus, Yeats is parodying theology's favorite resource, the argument from authority. A parody of theological discourse, Yeats suggests, may be the only possible modern vehicle for acceptable theological discourse. We can see here both Yeats's long-sustained desire for a theological system and his self-subversion whenever he writes one down. The stanza form itself en-acts the conflict between Ribh and Patrick: Ribh's unwieldy tercets (based on, but often exceeding, the hexameter) suggest the sexually differentiated form of his trinity of unlike members, while his identical "trinitarian" tercet rhymes *(aaa)* confirm that he is dueling with Patrick's triply masculine neo-platonic Trinity (which, if expressed in verse, would surely manifest itself in three lines perfectly equal in length).

The third poem in the sequence, "Ribh in Ecstasy," does not produce ec-static discourse proper, offering instead a *post hoc* view of ecstasy. When the onlookers complain to Ribh that they could not understand the "broken sentences" he uttered during his ecstatic trance, he scorns their criticism. Like Ribh's opening explanation, this mystic experience is voiced in pentam-eter, but Yeats will not cast this new poem into the doctrinal blank verse of Ribh's prelude, since ecstasy, even recounted in retrospect, demands rhyme to signify that its nature is lyric rather than instructional. The rhyme re-mains restricted to the "primitive" couplet, *aa*, because the content of Ribh's ecstatic experience is simple, even tautological: "Godhead on God-head in sexual spasm begot / Godhead." The pressure to continue within the fugitive rapt moment is signified by the driven enjambments of Ribh's report on ecstasy:

> My soul had found
> All happiness in its own cause or ground.
> Godhead on Godhead in sexual spasm begot
> Godhead. Some shadow fell. My soul forgot
> Those amorous cries that out of quiet come
> And must the common round of day resume.

It is perhaps to be expected that the ecstatic would speak only in "broken sentences," but no poet, not even the mystic poet, can remain in the ineffable. Ecstasy is summarized by Ribh only after he issues from it, and we are given no examples of those mid-ecstasy "broken sentences" overheard by his audience. Such sentences are beyond literature, and mark the point at which the supernatural becomes useless to the poet.

After Ribh's ecstasy a strange new internal form, which will reappear, enters the sequence: that of an inflexible syntactic template. Yeats resorts to this figure, I believe, to represent the pure stasis of eternity, in which pure energy resides. Stasis is energy's condition in eternity, preceding and following its dynamism in time. To the given rigid template, several or all lines of a given poem must be made to conform. The first example of such a template appears in Yeats's eschatological epigram "There," the fourth poem in the sequence. Its two end-stopped couplets maintain, with their monosyllabic end-words, the sequence's attachment to "primitive" forms of rhyme, but they add Yeats's new feature of the primitive: the invariant template "There all the [Plural Noun Subject] [Plural Verb Predicate]." The first line contains things material, the second mythical, the third historical, the fourth—as the list expands to its limit—cosmological, but all conform to the template:

> There all the barrel-hoops are knit,
> There all the serpent tails are bit,
> There all the gyres converge in one,
> There all the planets drop in the Sun.

In spite of the apparent syntactic symmetry of all four lines, there is one crucial asymmetry: the first two verbs are in the passive voice, as the separate barrel-staves of time are hooped into permanent form by the invisible Cooper and the temporal Ouroboros has been self-compelled to join head to tail; but the second two verbs are active, as gyres converge and planets drive themselves into the ultimate energy-source. The visually powerful knit barrel-hoops and bit serpent-tails are torsions that contain the boundless energy-in-eternity which would be released into time if the hoops burst or the serpent uncoiled. These metaphors replace the feebler geometrical nouns in the drafts: "Every circle there is knit / All the tails by teeth are bit."[6]

"There," like other poems in the sequence, becomes a parody of religious discourse, here the eschatological language of Revelation: "There shall be no night there . . . and there shall be no more curse . . . and there shall be no night there; and they need no candle, neither light of the sun;

for the Lord God giveth them light" (Rev. 21:25; 22:3–5). Yeats's diction, however, is drawn from vastly dissimilar linguistic sources (coopering, the Ouroboros, the Viconian gyres, cosmology, Revelation), and it alternates between the tension of force bounded by a superior will, and the free will of the turning gyres and planets seeking an energetic eternal stasis. The Yeatsian eschatology in "There" deliberately renders itself imagistically incoherent, unlike religious eschatologies, which are inscribed within a homogeneous and culturally understood code.

The next religious discourse to be parodied by Ribh is that of the Christian theology of love, transvaluated as "Hatred of God may bring the soul to God."[7] By hating man, woman, or event, in fact by hating even God as he is usually conceived, the soul may define herself and her idea of God in a new midnight asceticism, animated by emotional energy (rather than the sexual energy of Ribh's tale of Baile and Aillinn). "Ribh Considers Christian Love Insufficient" is Ribh's third pentameter poem, joining itself to his initial blank-verse doctrinal exposition and his couplet-account following his ecstatic experience. But now, as Yeats enters the first positive theological hope of the sequence, he confers upon the pentameter a beautiful and "developed" six-line lyric stanza form, in which a "primitive" couplet *(aa)* like those of "Ribh in Ecstasy" surprisingly adds to itself a quatrain using embraced rhymes *(bccb)*. The epigrammatic bite of the initial couplet is fully brought into play by Yeats in stanzas 1, 2, and 4:

> Why should I seek for love or study it?
> It is of God and passes human wit.
>
> Why do I hate man, woman, or event?
> That is a light my jealous soul has sent.
>
> At stroke of midnight soul cannot endure
> A bodily or mental furniture.

These are the opening assertions of someone defiantly sure of his ground. The quatrains that follow these couplets, though they continue the strong strain of assertion, enjoy the suspense of their longer expository arc, in which one has to wait out three pentameter lines to find the recurrence of the *b*-rhyme. In stanza 2, for instance, Yeats suspends the word "can"—the line-ending modal auxiliary—while he retells retrospectively (with modal links in *can, may,* and *could*) the whole history of the soul from postlapsarian

redemption ("freed") to prelapsarian innocence "before such things began."
There is a 30-syllable wait until "can" is allowed to find its rhyme in the sec-
ond syllable of the word "began":

From terror and deception freed it **can**
Discover impurities, *can* show at last / How soul *may* walk when all such things are past, / How soul *could* walk before such things **began**.

The effect of such suspension of rhyme is to make us feel that the speaker
"is thinking" as he works toward the completion of his thought in the last
word, the last rhyme.

In the latter half of "Ribh Considers Christian Love Insufficient," how-
ever, Yeats breaks the earlier-established pattern of an epigrammatic cou-
plet followed by an effortful arc-like quatrain. In stanza 3, the six lines are
divided not into two-plus-four but into three-plus-three, and the poem, in
this climactic symmetry, moves away from doctrinal exposition into the as-
sertive "shall learn" of religious prophecy, followed by Ribh's glorious dis-
missal of the unworthy garment of thought. But Ribh's vision of the soul
as bride declines into the merely hopeful "may bring" that closes the stanza:

> Then my delivered soul herself shall learn
> A darker knowledge and in hatred turn
> From every thought of God mankind has had.
> Thought is a garment and the soul's a bride
> That cannot in that trash and tinsel hide:
> Hatred of God may bring the soul to God.

Ribh cannot yet see past the dark of the final midnight, when the bride-soul
will cast off "bodily and mental furniture." As prophecy lapses, the poem
daringly takes on the burstingly energetic stasis of eternity, which, as in
"There," imposes an inflexible template. Here, the template is "[Interroga-
tory Word] can she [Active Verb] until (till) [God] [Subjunctive Verb]!" The
quatrain portion, anticipating the soul's future, reads:

> What can she take until her Master give!
> Where can she look until He make the show!
> What can she know until He bid her know!
> How can she live till in her blood He live!

The exclamation point replacing the expected question mark (which had
appeared briefly in the manuscript drafts)[8] is part of Ribh's defiant assertive-

ness in repudiating Christian "love." As in "There," the rigidity of the template does allow some internal variation: the first imagined eternal conjunction between the soul and God is that of gratitude (He will give, she will take); the second is that of contemplation (He will make the show, she will look); the third approaches epistemological coalescence (He will bid her know, she will know); and the fourth almost achieves identity (He will live in her, she will live). I have been rephrasing these lines in the prophetic future, but Yeats, though he began with indicatives in the draft, would not retain them: crossing out the indicatives and replacing them with the subjunctive (from "bids" to "bid," from "makes" to "make," from "lives" to "live"),[9] he intimates only the helplessness of the posthumous soul in eternity until a greater energy should intervene. The tolling interrogative phrases (*"What* can she . . . *Where* can she . . . *What* can she . . . *How* can she") transmit the intensity of waiting with no answers in sight. Syntactic templates of the stasis-energy of eternity, as in these closing questions of "Ribh Considers Christian Love Insufficient" and in the rigid framework of "There," remain important to the sequence. They will reappear in poems VIII ("Whence Had They Come?"), IX ("The Four Ages of Man"), and X ("Conjunctions").

Poem VI ("He and She"), placed (in both magazine and volume appearance) at the center of the sequence, embodies, as Yeats wrote, his "centric myth,"[10] but it "solves" nothing with respect to the original problem set by the sequence: How are we to reclaim the primitive and its energies, especially when it seems to be lodged in an inaccessible eternal realm, a "There"? What is the "best" template with which to represent the formal nature of primal energy? We have already seen several notions of the primitive. It appears first in the person of the archaic Ribh who, representing an earlier "antithetical" or subjective sexual era, repudiates the "primary" or "objective" Trinitarian era introduced by the Christian Patrick; we have also seen Ribh's reactive attempt to "start over" in religious discourse by inventing a new parodic theology of vigorous "hatred"; and we have noticed the rudimentary rhyme-schemes of couplets and tercets by which Yeats symbolizes primitive religion (including Ribh's pagan heterosexual trinitarian myth).

After poem V, Ribh, representing the old order, disappears from the sequence. (It is true that poem IV, "There," is impersonally voiced, but because it is followed immediately by another "Ribh poem," we ascribe it to Ribh rather than to a different, unspecified voice.) The poems from VII on are voiced impersonally, and they never refer specifically to Ribh and his vision. Why, we wonder, did Yeats make his sequence change orientation in this way? In "Supernatural Songs" Ribh's utterances are first-person ones, and they are situated within a crucial moment of Irish "history," the loss of the primitive fusion of the pagan and the Christian brought about by the swerve to "Roman" Catholicism, represented by Patrick. But in the second half of the sequence, when Yeats, adopting a cosmic distance, begins to reveal a "divine" perspective on how things are in the universe, he adopts an impersonal and unascribed voice that speaks from poem VII onward.

Poem VI, however, "He and She"—the central poem of "Supernatural Songs"—appears to be spoken neither by Ribh nor by the impersonal later voice. It is unique in the sequence because its undefined speaker quotes directly from the woman-moon, offering her estimate of the joys and perils of sexual conjunction:

He and She

As the moon sidles up
Must she sidle up,
As trips the scared moon
Away must she trip:
'His light had struck me blind
Dared I stop'.

She sings as the moon sings:
'I am I, am I;
The greater grows my light
The further that I fly'.
All creation shivers
With that sweet cry.

Yeats's "centric myth" of sexual conjunction is here represented by its fluctuations of proximity, symbolized by the waxing and waning of the moon. Yeats had earlier alluded to a comparable myth in his introduction to *The Holy Mountain* of Bhagwan Shri Hamsa:

> The visionary must have seen . . . a conflict between Moon and Sun, . . . between a Moon that has taken the Sun's light into itself, . . . and the Moon lost in the Sun's light. . . . The Eastern poet saw the Moon as the Sun's bride; now in solitude; now offered to her Bridegroom in a self-abandonment unknown to our poetry. (*E & I*, 470)

Adopting the metaphor of the Moon as the Sun's bride, and showing her alternating between almost joining with the Sun and fleeing from him, Yeats once again exemplifies, in "He and She," a Blakean "natural" correspondence among all orders—cosmological, biological, and theological—in their "primitive" state. As the moon is to the sun, so woman is to man, and so (implicitly) is the soul to God. The moon's temptation is to "drop in the sun," thereby ending sexual tension, time, and change, but she knows she would be blinded and eventually annihilated if she approached so close to him. In her wariness, the moon resists, emblematically, the soul's mystical absorption in the eternal divine, the female absorption in the male. She chooses to remain independent, singing in her slender trimeters "I am I, am I"—a claim biblically ascribed to Yahweh, but here endorsed, humanized, and universalized by Yeats's anonymous speaker, who declares that "All creation shivers / With that sweet cry."

In the persona of the female Soul, Yeats encounters, but will not submit to, the eternal "There," that Sun into which "all the planets drop." The tautological trimeter of the soul's cry, "I am I, am I," departs as far as possible from those philosophical pentameters and tetrameter complexities that had filled the scholastic discourse of Ribh's earlier doctrinal poems. Phrases such as "sidling up" and "tripping away" are far distant, in linguistic reference, from the weightier Latinate language—"the intercourse of angels," "the conflagration of their passion"—that Ribh used of sexuality. At this moment in the sequence, a pure first-person song[11] of the female, describing her relation to the male in the dyadic sexual myth (with no mention of procreation, but rather with an emphasis on female individuality), replaces not only Ribh's masculine expository discourse and endorsement of a familial trinity, but also his theological subtlety and gnomic riddles. In this transparent lyric of free will, the sequence has reached, one might say, confidence in its own mythological center, as the moon becomes a self-delighting voice. After this full-moon, fifteenth-phase climax, with its affirmation (in the new Yeatsian dispensation) of the theological centrality of sexual attraction on the one hand, and the resistant individuality of the soul on the other, the sequence begins to unravel what it has knit together, declining toward the dark of the moon and the extinction of free will in a deterministic universe. (A complementary representation of both the dark of the moon and the full of the moon will be seen, in Chapter XIII, in "The Double Vision of Michael Robartes.")

The second half of "Supernatural Songs" begins with a grotesque enactment of the heterosexual myth of divine self-procreation proclaimed earlier by Ribh. Since Ribh's trinitarian poem denouncing Patrick's concept of a masculine Trinity had declared that "all things below are copies," the second half of the sequence must oppose to Patrick's Christian myth the "true" myth of pagan trinitarian begetting—"man, woman, child." By this late insertion of a second *aaa*-rhymed long-lined trinitarian poem, "What Magic Drum?", which exemplifies in content, and matches in form, Ribh's earlier denunciatory one, Yeats begins to reshape his sequence into a "concentric" form. Yeats imagines himself here as the Godhead-begetting-Godhead seen by Ribh—a God part beast, part human, part divine—who from himself generates and embraces "Primordial Motherhood," thereby engendering a divine cub, whose glimmering belly will be licked into life by the same tongue that moves sexually down the breast and body of Primordial Motherhood:[12]

> He holds him[13] from desire, all but stops his breathing lest
> Primordial Motherhood forsake his limbs, the child no longer rest,
> Drinking joy as it were milk upon his breast.
>
> Through light-obliterating garden foliage what magic drum?
> Down limb and breast or down that glimmering belly move his
>     mouth and sinewy tongue.
> What from the forest came? What beast has licked its young?[14]

As we have seen, Yeats created Ribh to embody a supposed primitive Ireland, complete with Hermetic pre-Christian Celtic imaginings of God, an Ireland that might enable us to go "behind" Christianity to an anthropologically richer sense of the universe. The Ribhian Godhead himself, once Yeats's poem brings him on stage, can scarcely believe his own sense of natural joy in the prelude to and completion of divine begetting: "He holds him[self] from desire, all but stops his breathing," lest he split again into the three separate persons who have now momentarily joined in self-begetting. This primitive divine Trinity is almost indistinguishable from the human triad—father, mother, child—and the animal triad—sire, dam, and cub. The momentary unstable equilibrium of divine, human, and animal being is reflected in Yeats's wavering and unpredictable rhythmic effects, while his trinitarian rhymes *(aaa)* are a reprise of those of Ribh's earlier denunciation of Patrick. The divine trinitarian selving is accompanied (as we see from the title-phrase—"What Magic Drum?"—and its repetition within the poem) by the most primitive form of music: the rhythm of an unaccompanied "magic drum."[15]

But the visible free will of this "pagan" Trinity in poem VII and of the moon-woman-soul in VI—"I am I, am I"—is immediately challenged within "Supernatural Songs" by the appearance of a wholly deterministic historical panorama in the late-inserted poem VIII, "Whence Had They Come?" Here Yeats declares that human beings, whatever their illusions of personal freedom, are in fact puppets, emitting words not their own but uttered by the invisible Dramatis Personae of a drama conceived by an unknown Puppet-Master (a demiurgic image-relative of the Ringmaster of "The Circus Animals' Desertion," a coercive persona implicitly repudiated by Yeats at the end of that poem). This determinism, in a bleaker dark-of-the-moon fashion, is repeated, as we shall see in the following chapter, in part I of "The Double Vision of Michael Robartes."

The Zeitgeist, according to poem VIII, speaks through human actors unaware of the roles they are fated to enact in history. Our passions—sexual, religious, political—are themselves but the instruments of the "hand or lash" of the unseen dramatist, the First Mover. Yeats here resumes the pentameter of discursive effect, and shapes it—as he did in poem III (Ribh's report of his ecstasy)—into epigrammatic *aa* couplets. "Whence Had They Come?" ends in yet another set of static questions ("Whence," "What") comprising a reiterative template that enables a glimpse of the energy-instasis of the Puppet-Master in his eternity. The religious genre invoked here is that of Providential historiography:

> Whence had they come,
> The hand and lash that beat down frigid Rome?
> What sacred drama through her body heaved
> When world-transforming Charlemagne was conceived?

These questions resemble the homiletic astonishments of religious commentators, but the parodic substitution of the historical Charlemagne for Jesus in the nativity scene makes this "supernatural song" as remote as its companions from the Christian supernatural narrative. As we live our lives, we are not permitted to see clearly either the Dramatist or his Dramatis Personae whose words are "channelled" through us. "Whence Had They Come?" makes us realize that Yeats uses the word "supernatural" for human experience contemplated in its more baffling or mysterious aspects. Here, the mystery motivating the poem is the inexplicable emotional drivenness of sexual passion, and its shocking and unpredictable results.

The three short gnomic poems that follow Yeats's "sacred drama" of predestinarian history belong to the "primitive" religious genre of oracular sayings, and are spoken in a stern voice that has abjured the personal. As Yeats remarked in the 1937 essay "A General Introduction to My Work":

> All that is personal soon rots; it must be packed in ice or salt. . . . I must choose a traditional stanza, even what I alter must seem traditional. . . . Talk to me of originality and I will turn on you with rage. I am a crowd, I am a lonely man, I am nothing. . . . Imagination must dance, must be carried beyond feeling into the aboriginal ice. (*E & I*, 522–523)

In his "impersonal" style, Yeats graphs the processes of growth and age in the most universalized way possible: he becomes "man" struggling in turn with body, heart, mind, and God. Another rigid template, but now a thematic one—"He fought and in each case lost"—once more confines the verse into epigrammatic *aa* couplet-stanzas, here in a martial tetrameter line driven by strong downbeats of inevitability. Three of life's four battles are past, says the remote voice of poem IX, but the final war is yet to be fought:

### The Four Ages of Man

He with body waged a fight,
But body won; it walks upright.

Then he struggled with the heart;
Innocence and peace depart.

Then he struggled with the mind;
His proud heart he left behind.

Now his wars on God begin;
At stroke of midnight God shall win.

Although the preordained course of life is registered in the inflexible plot-template of the ever-defeated man, each successive loss has nonetheless been a victory for the man's expanding consciousness. Because learning to walk upright, finding passion, and gaining intellectual capacity have one by one superseded helpless infancy, we suspect that man's last defeat will also, paradoxically, be a victory, as man, dying, at last knows his life as a completed whole.

The other two oracular poems in the sequence, X and XI, each of four lines, try to describe, "supernaturally," individual fate and then the universal dynamic of history. The first, "Conjunctions," takes up the mystery of individual character, "explaining" the natures of Yeats's son and daughter by their planetary horoscopes. Here, the "centric myth" of the conjunction of male and female is embodied once again—this time not in the myth of Baile and Aillinn nor in the relation of sun and moon, nor even in the engendering embrace of the Primordial Parents, but rather in a primitive religious practice, the casting of horoscopes. Because the vocabulary of horoscopes alludes (via the planetary names) to classical myth, Yeats can "humanize" the horoscopes, drawing them into classical and Christian narratives (the dynastic struggle between the titan Saturn and Olympian Jupiter; the adulterous love of Mars and Venus; and the crucifixion of Jesus). Michael Yeats is an "antithetical" (subjective) spirit born under the conjunction of Jupiter and Saturn, Anne a "primary" (objective) one born under Mars and Venus. According to Yeats's letter on the poem to Olivia Shakespear (*L*, 827–829), "The Christian is the Mars-Venus—it is democratic," whereas "the Jupiter-Saturn civilization is born free among the most cultivated, out of tradition, out of rule." Between the two classical myths of his children's horoscopes, Yeats squeezes the brief era of Christian dominance:[16]

Conjunctions

If Jupiter and Saturn meet,
What a crop of mummy wheat!

The sword's a cross; thereon He died:
On breast of Mars the goddess sighed.

These conjunctions introduce a chink of possibility into the determinism of the latter half of "Supernatural Songs": epochal change has returned to the sequence. True, Patrick's widening gyre will replace Ribh's declining one, as Christianity replaces the classical past; but one has only to wait and a new version of the subjective will return to replace Christian "objectivity." The "mummy wheat" found in Egyptian tombs, when moistened, began (according to legend) to sprout; so (in Michael's horoscope) the mummy wheat of the subjective will renew itself. And though the crucifixion of Jesus indeed took place, the names of Mars and Venus, symbols of classical sexual conjunction, follow triumphantly after Christianity in the second half of Yeats's diptych. In these Frazerian verses on his children, Yeats, with the indifference of the impartial historian, brackets the central Christian symbol, the "primary" crucifixion, with the "pagan" dynastic personages of Jupiter and Saturn on the left, and on the right, the equally "pagan" lascivious personages of Mars and Venus. Yeats's couplets "defeat" Christianity by representing it as a brief one-line "interruption" of paganism; the inflexible *aa* couplet-form of both horoscopes tells us that such alternations are cosmologically determined.

The epigrammatic tetrameter couplet-stanzas of the horoscopes in "Conjunctions," like those of perpetual defeat in "The Four Ages of Man" or the preceding pentameter couplets of unknown Dramatis Personae in "Whence Had They Come?", offer no room for speculation, fleshed-out narrative, or emotional expression. Like its two predecessor-poems, "Conjunctions" fits human life into an ordained scheme. Such a scheme may be one invented by an unseen Puppet-Master, or it may be one of a universally imposed Four Ages of Man, or it may be the procession of successive myths (classical; Christian; classical); but in no case can the scheme be resisted or modified. "Supernatural Songs" seems at this point to have forgotten its own center, the sidling up and back of the moon, her celebration of her self-proclaimed identity, which she determinedly keeps apart from the ultimate power of the sun. And we are not reassured by the next poem (XI), the epigrammatic quatrain-in-couplets "A Needle's Eye," which reads history at a chilling astronomical distance, seeing it as the unceasing cosmic motion of a "stream" of events too far away to allow observers to see individual lives within the "roaring" current. This totalizing metaphor, adapted from Jesus' saying about the eye of a needle and (David Clark suggests) from the Upanishads' notion of a thread linking all worlds,[17] is the ultimate myth of origin, applying to all things without exception:

> All the stream that's roaring by
> Came out of a needle's eye;
> Things unborn, things that are gone,
> From needle's eye still goad it on.

Just as Yeats's children become (in their horoscopes) impersonal examples of antithetical and primary dispensations, so all of history now becomes a vocal gyre expanding out of an unknowable and minute point of origin, goaded on by the contents of a reversed cornucopial gyre behind the needle's eye. The pressure of what is past and what is to come drives the stream of what is passing. "The created world is a stream of images in the human mind . . . ; this stream is Time. Eternity is the abyss which receives and creates," Yeats wrote in his essay on Shelley's *Prometheus Unbound* (*E & I*, 419). In the stream, when seen at such a distance, there is no distinction of objects. They are all "things," the unborn and the vanished and the present alike (we are far from the specificity of the Byzantine golden bird's chronicle). Those human dimensions brought up earlier in "Supernatural Songs"—including sexuality, a "family" Godhead, and personal individuality—seem to have vanished altogether; this absence, for Yeats, represents the dark of the moon, when a "philosophical" view of human unimportance, given the unimaginable age of the physical universe, wipes out our scale of value. The primitive oracular tetrameter couplets (mostly trochaic) of "A Needle's Eye" are like axioms from a harsh cosmological geometry of the gyres.

And so we reach again the coda that was the genetic origin of the sequence, and that now formally ends it—the Shakespearean sonnet "Meru." (As a sonnet, it has appeared earlier, in Chapter VI.) At this point we can, I think, see the whole effort of the "Supernatural Songs." They are, first of all, one of the many nineteenth- and twentieth-century works stimulated by the inquiries into comparative religion that so excited nineteenth-century archaeologists, anthropologists, and classicists. Hoping to discover the primitive religion of mankind, scholars dreamed also of finding the roots of language, the matrix of social institutions, and the origins of art. Anthropology seemed about to disclose the common origins of religious systems, pagan or Christian. "I am convinced," Yeats wrote in the General Introduction to his work, "that the natural and supernatural are knit together, that to escape a dangerous fanaticism we must study a new science; at that moment Europeans may find something attractive in a Christ posed against a background not of Judaism but of Druidism, not shut off in dead history, but flowing, concrete, phenomenal" (*E & I*, 518). The "Supernatural Songs" are the flowing, concrete, phenomenal expression of Yeats's wish to track the civilized back to the primitive, even as far back as the original "needle's eye" and beyond. But the Yeatsian prose just quoted does not suggest the aspects of parody and grotesquerie that are introduced by a poetry in which the old genres of religious expression—hagiography, homily, the oracular utterance, theological polemic, the myth of origin, the doctrinal poem, the gnomic riddle, and so on—reappear in a pagan "Druidic" context filled with new blasphemous doctrines.

Readers have on the whole preferred the Yeats who looks through an eye more natural than supernatural. In the latter half of "Supernatural Songs" especially, Yeats's personal eye, in subjecting itself to primitive and oracular lyric forms, consents to be frozen in what he called "the aboriginal ice" of impersonality. Perhaps his respect for that metaphorical "ice" made him particularly notice, when he read *The Holy Mountain* (a monk's account of his pilgrimage to Mount Kailās, in myth called Mount Meru),[18] the ice and snow of the ordeal. There was, first, a "climb of five thousand feet," then a vigil on the icy floor of a frozen lake, then "terrible hardships." The monk recounts his struggle:

> Bitter cold, piercing winds, incessant snow, inordinate hunger, and deadly solitude combined to harass the mind; the body became numb and unable to bear the pangs. Snow covered me up to my breast and, till after midnight, I was fighting desperately with my mind.[19]

This narrative generated the sestet of "Meru," in which Indian hermits eventually gain superiority over their suffering, attaining indifference to man's monuments:

> Hermits upon Mount Meru or Everest,
> Caverned in night under the drifted snow,
> Or where that snow and winter's dreadful blast
> Beat down upon their naked bodies, know
> That day brings round the night, that before dawn
> His glory and his monuments are gone.[20]

But what precedes, in the sonnet, this quietist knowing? Yeats opens the octave of "Meru" with a universal picture in which "civilisation" is perpetually driven to destroy the rules and ideologies and illusions that artificially create and constrain it:

> Civilisation is hooped together, brought
> Under a rule, under the semblance of peace
> By manifold illusion . . .

The internal tension of such a rule, such an ideological peace, eventually causes its breakdown, as it is subjected to human inquiry:

> . . . but man's life is thought,
> And he, despite his terror, cannot cease
> Ravening, raging, and uprooting that he may come
> Into the desolation of reality.

It is the Keatsian word "desolation" that is salient here, simply because it abandons the harsh "r's" dominating the last three lines. If the ravening intellect is symbolized by the Miltonic hard "r's," then external fate is symbolized by the brutal "d's" and "b's" of the "dreadful blast" beating down on the bodies of the monks in the snow. The phonemes of man's "glory" and "monuments" do not participate in the previous play of "d's" and "b's": they stand out as non-combative, purely elegiac. The octave of "Meru" isolates the desolation generated by the ravaging hunger of thought, while the close of the sestet commemorates—even as they vanish—the glory and monuments created by successive flourishings of that same unstoppable thought. Between desolation and lament, however, at the very beginning of the sestet, Yeats fixes the monks' impervious and stoic knowledge.

If it were not for the gallant bravado of the salute closing the octave— "Egypt and Greece, good-bye, and good-bye, Rome!"—the supernatural "objective" eye might not seem worth having, since what it pitilessly registers is the extent of human suffering and the ephemerality of human accomplishment. In 1909, Yeats had taken the measure of that suffering in the passage in *Autobiographies* that was the kernel for "Meru":

> All civilisation is held together by the suggestions of an invisible hypnotist—by artificially created illusions. The knowledge of reality is always in some measure a secret knowledge. It is a kind of death.[21]

But the large mental freedom of the cry, "Egypt and Greece, good-bye, and good-bye, Rome!"—the cry of a citizen of space and time rather than of a single country or a single century—reminds us of the substantial advantages, for a poet, of an anthropological and panoramic perspective. In reformulating the "primitive" literary genres of Judeo-Christian tradition, Yeats undoes received religious discourse. There is no literary strategy more powerful than eviscerating a known cultural form and filling it with analogous but transgressive new content, new discourses, and new cultural codes. By replacing, within songs he labeled "supernatural," Christian saints with strange new sexually active "angels" such as Baile and Aillinn; by replacing St. Patrick with the anti-Trinitarian monk Ribh and the monks on Everest; by suggesting a polysexual Trinity instead of an asexual or homosexual one; by an anthropological equating of Christ with Charlemagne as initiators of new historical cycles; by a recommendation of hatred as a theological virtue; and by an appeal to the esoteric knowledge not of Christian mystics but of Indian monks, Yeats created a set of recognizable yet arrogantly distorted religious gestures.

And yet, in spite of all their alien material filling up old genres, these songs are not, finally, "supernatural" in the sense of envisaging a new religion to replace the one that modernity has lost. "A stream of images in the human mind" is all that is created—flowing, concrete, phenomenal. The title "Supernatural Songs" is wistful; the self-portrait as Ribh is a piece of "Druidic" nostalgia; the imagining of self as polymorphously sexual is a fantasy that Freud would have recognized. Yeats's attraction for the wilder shores of myth meets, here, his modernist cold eye. That eye singles out four kinds of primitive energy as driving the whole universe: the material cosmic energies goading it on; the emotional energies creating the drama of human historical action; the sexual energies directing animal continuity; and the ascetic energies seeking and finding knowledge. Energy—not any single cultural system or system of belief—is what is permanent.

"Supernatural Songs" would not be an original sequence were it not for its formal modulations: its initial theological scene of blank-verse instruction, its subsequent formal departures into primitive couplets and trinitarian tercets, and its striking distortions of line-length as its grotesque Trinity displays itself. The sequence generates interest (and amusement) by its parodic use of religious genres and religious discourse. But why should a sequence defining the primitive form of religion represented by an archaic Irish hermit and by gnomic oracular utterance end with a Shakespearean sonnet—the least primitive, the most courtly, the most intellectual of forms? The return to the primitive has certainly been enacted formally in earlier parts of the sequence; but what does the complex Shakespearean sonnet enact? It puts forth, I think, the kind of knowledge that Yeats believes he himself can have. He does not belong to the new Rough-Bestial (or the old Ribhian) primitivism; he does not subscribe to the European Christian belief-system; nor is he an adherent of Hindu quietism. He is, as he composes "Meru," his worldly and sophisticated self. He is still a spectator of the vicissitudes of history, but not from the astrological cosmic distance

of the watcher who sees history as a "roaring" stream. He is a watcher on
the macrocosmic human scale, one who has absorbed the legacy of Egypt
and Greece and Rome, but sees their present exhaustion: "Egypt and Greece,
good-bye, and goodbye Rome!"

The sonnet genre that Yeats now adopts as his own is the one in which
the ruins of Time have been most eloquently lamented in English; but to
the Shakespearean elegiac pathos of monuments (with which he closes the
sonnet) Yeats adds three un-Shakespearean, but very Irish and Yeatsian, in-
gredients: the first is the "gay good-night" to Empire; the second is the cor-
rection offered by Indian mystical practice to Western elegy; and the third is
the presence of those grim enjambments representing thought's ravening
drive to extinguish the very empires it has created. When Yeats speaks, at
the end of "Supernatural Songs," through the form identified with Shake-
speare, he puts forward Shakespeare as the best singer of a human song in
which "natural and supernatural with the self-same ring are wed." After all,
Shakespeare exhibits in the *Sonnets* a sympathetic understanding of those
essential sexual energies defended by Ribh and the moon, and also—espe-
cially in the history plays—a stoic knowledge of time's vicissitudes compa-
rable to that possessed by the ascetic monks. And Shakespeare, by his un-
equaled ingenuities in sonnet form, is the ultimate ratifier of the poet's
passion to make form embody meaning. (Even in "Meru," however, Yeats
avoids perfect rhyme in the final couplet, offering "dawn" and "gone" in-
stead.)[22] Yeats's deliberately varied forms in this sequence represent, in their
range, both the ultimately primitive and the ultimately civilized, all cen-
tered around the "centric myth" of sexual freedom and individual will; part
VI becomes the crucial point of reference for the other poems that wheel in
"concentric" orbits around it, no matter how deterministic they at times be-
come.

The striking contrast between the Frazerian "Supernatural Songs" and
Yeats's historical sequences such as "Nineteen Hundred and Nineteen" and
"Meditations in Time of Civil War" arises from the wish of the poet to
imagine, in "Supernatural Songs," an archetype—that of the inevitable
succession of human cultural systems—rather than to give the poem a
wholly human center. The feats of imagining that drive these "Supernatural
Songs" do not all succeed; but they present, in their strange verse-forms and
rhyme-schemes, a fascinatingly deliberate self-limitation on the part of a
writer. That Yeats, the accomplished stylist, should confine his thoughts
into couplets and tercets; that Yeats, the lover of shapeliness, should write
the ungainly tercets of the primitive Trinity; that Yeats, the anxious com-

poser of "A Prayer for My Daughter" and "A Prayer for My Son," should abstract his children into their mythical horoscopes; that the poet who for so long avoided the Shakespearean sonnet should write his envoi in Shakespearean form—all these contradictions make these songs a remarkable and unforeseeable excursus, toward the end of Yeats's life, into a strange modernist reconsideration of the "primitive" and its energies, dark with determinism at times, but at times radiant with free will.

## XIII

## ◇— RARE FORMS

There are, as we have seen, many forms that Yeats turns to again and again—the ballad, the *abab* trimeter quatrain, tetrameter, *ottava rima*. These offer him a known set of resources, within which he experiments in almost innumerable ways. But there are forms, too, that occur only once or twice in the *Collected Poems:* unrhymed (for the most part) hexameters ("Beautiful Lofty Things"); rhyme royal ("A Bronze Head" and "Hound Voice"); a twin-set of invented stanzas in an odd combination of pentameters and trimeters, 5-5-3-3, rhyming respectively *abab* and *aabb* (appearing only in "The Double Vision of Michael Robartes"); an irregularly but fully and perfectly rhymed form of (rhythmically) free verse ("Broken Dreams"); a strange sixain composed of a tetrameter *abab* quatrain followed by a pentameter couplet rhyming *cc* ("At Algeciras"); and the *terza rima* of Yeats's penultimate poem ("Cuchulain Comforted"). There are other rare forms as well: the dialogue-poem "An Image from a Past Life," with its seven-line *(abcccab)* stanza that wanes and waxes and wanes in line-breadth (5-4-2-3-4-5-3); "Demon and Beast," which (like "My Table" in "Meditations in Time of Civil War") uses a "top-heavy" (4-4-3-3) stanza of two couplets, *aabb*.

These inventions (and the motivations generating them) are all worthy of study, as are Yeats's repeated decisions, in several poems, to employ irregularly rhymed lines containing so many inexact rhymes that the poem in which they appear seems casually unrhymed (see, for instance, the eight-line poem "A Thought from Propertius," in which the rhyme-words are *head, knees, line, altar, images, side, centaur,* and *wine*—a group that one would not immediately perceive as an *abcdbadc* list, since the only "perfect" rhyme links "line" and "wine," the two rhyme-words furthest away from each other in the poem). I cannot describe all of Yeats's rare forms here, but I will consider two classes of them: those in which the form has a conventional ideological import (rhyme royal, for instance, and "epic" hexameter), and those in which the form, though rare, seems more arbitrarily matched with its content.

But first I want to comment in general on a poet's experience of rare forms. For the poet, the first time he tries *any* form it is a "rare form," because it has not yet found a place in his stylistic repertoire. Although a form such as *ottava rima* can (and did for Yeats) become "domesticated" as a familiar resource (although still demanding originality in each instance), certainly Yeats's first creation in *ottava rima* meant that he took up what was for his own practice at the time a "rare form." Yeats's search for technique in the early poems, recounted in Chapter IV, demonstrated his relish in the pursuit of all aspects of form: rhythmic, stanzaic, structural, generic, and "magical." Each successful venture in a new form must have given him (along with the misery of actual composition) the intense happiness that attends aesthetic discovery. We can imagine him writing, for instance, the dizain "A Coat" (320), choosing for it a two-part form he had not previously used. "A Coat" opens with a trimeter/tetrameter embraced quatrain *(abba)*; this is followed (with no intervening space) by an "embracing" tetrameter sestet, its two tercets bound together by their middle lines, which rhyme; the whole sestet rhymes *cdc ede* (for clarity, I have separated the parts). Dizains are not common in Yeats, and the only one preceding "A Coat" in the *Collected Poems* ("He Hears the Cry of the Sedge") uses a less symmetrical (and less successful) rhyme-scheme *(ababcdeced)* and a more wandering syntactic distribution. (In "A Coat" the sense-units coincide with the rhyme-units, in Yeats's preferred fashion at the time.) So, for the Yeats of *Responsibilities*—who usually had written rhymes in multiples of four, quatrains and octaves—the ten-line "A Coat" was, at the moment of writing, a "rare form":

> I made my song a coat
> Covered with embroideries
> Out of old mythologies
> From heel to throat;
> But the fools caught it,
> Wore it in the world's eyes
> As though they'd wrought it.
> Song, let them take it,
> For there's more enterprise
> In walking naked.

"A Coat," which serves as the end-poem of *Responsibilities,* is a manifesto declaring the end of Yeats the Romantic, enveloped in his long ("heel to throat") coat embroidered with mythological symbols (rather like Glaucus's cloak in *Endymion*). The first four lines linger nostalgically (in their quadrisyllabic "embroideries" and "mythologies") on the poet's labor and the resultant luxury of the coat he will never wear again. He is resigning it—at first reluctantly—to the "fools" who have plagiarized his style. The suitably "traditional" *abba* embraced rhyme allows (with intent) the fanciful modifiers of "coat" to intervene before "coat" finds its rhyme:

> I made my song a **coat**
> Covered with embroideries / Out of old mythologies / From heel to **throat.**

(The poet's heel touches the earth; his throat produces his song.)

We now might expect further embraced-rhyme quatrains. Instead, in a syntactically self-contained tercet rhyming *cdc,* "A Coat" stiffens into accusation of the thieving "fools." And the poem concludes with a second tercet, which, to our surprise, turns away from the speech-act of the first seven lines (narration) in favor of a bracing address by the poet to his poor denuded "song," shivering in its new nakedness. The poet, giving away his embroidered and mythological coat, uses the forward-looking word "enterprise" (later to reappear so plangently in "Among School Children") to hearten his uncertain song. With a single telling offhand rhyme, he joins the giving away of the old style ("let them take it") and his new self-presentation ("walking naked").

The units of "A Coat"—quatrain and sestet—are redolent, when they take a pentameter form, of Renaissance poetic tradition; but when they are reduced to a trimeter/tetrameter form, as here, they enact the poet's discarding of Renaissance discursive amplitude. Although Yeats may be willing to divest himself of mythologies, he does noticeably retain the "embroidery" of rhyme—rhyme that calls attention to itself as it links the polysyllabic "embroideries" and "mythologies" in its cloaked "Romantic" quatrain, and groups the monosyllabic phrases "caught it," "wrought it," and "take it" in its stripped Modernist sestet. Finally, it should be noticed that the poem is not called "Walking Naked," but rather "A Coat," asserting the poet's continued allegiance to what his coat meant to him before it was stolen by others. Once he had written this dizain, Yeats never again repeated its total form (although he did use its form of sestet-rhyme in the six-line "Memory"). The form of "A Coat" became for Yeats a nonce whole, reserved to this manifesto-poem and no other. He may have even vowed that singularity as he wrote the poem.

Yeats's decision to find a rare form that suits the matter at hand is evident as he casts his proto-elegy for Maud Gonne, the 1937 "A Bronze Head" (618–619), into "rhyme royal" (supposedly so called because James I of Scotland composed in it). Only a royal rhyme would suit the woman who was "it may be, a queen" ("Presences").[1] The rhyme royal seven-line pentameter stanza *(ababbcc)* begins with a "heroic quatrain," as it is sometimes called—a pentameter rhyming *abab,* awakening the reader's expectation either of more heroic quatrains, or of another *ab* (if the stanza were going to become *ottava rima*), or of a couplet, *cc* (if the stanza were going to become the *Venus and Adonis* stanza, *ababcc*). Instead, in rhyme royal, the quatrain unexpectedly delays, repeating its *b*-rhyme; and only after that self-extension can the quatrain advance to its final couplet. The effect is to prolong in line 5 the reflection carried out in the quatrain, and Yeats (especially in the first stanza of "A Bronze Head," but also in the second and fourth) takes advantage of this potential. There is no doubt in my mind that it was the "royal" nature of the rhyme that made the form attractive to Yeats for a "final" poem about Maud Gonne, but there is also no doubt that he "contested" with his language his chosen form, wishing that Maud had not lowered herself to hurl "the little streets upon the great" or teach "to ignorant men most violent ways." The poem is an attempt to reconcile Maud's "queenly" aspect with her "revolutionary" one, and the form suits sometimes the one aspect, sometimes the other, as we shall discover.

As Yeats enters the Dublin Municipal Gallery, he is shocked to see a bust (bronze in appearance, but in actuality painted plaster) of Maud Gonne in old age. So many of the figures represented in the Gallery are already dead (see "The Municipal Gallery Revisited") that this effigy seems to portray Maud, too, as one almost dead, her eye the only feature still alive, her dark spirit aloft in "the distant sky" rather than at its usual haunt, the tombs of the dead (the graves, perhaps, of executed patriots). In Yeats's arresting verbless beginning, the "royal" person of the bust has already arrived at a form of life perhaps more superhuman than human, provoking his question about the nature of her soul, still "empty" because not fulfilled or at rest:

### A Bronze Head

> Here at right of the entrance this bronze head,
> Human, superhuman, a bird's round eye,
> Everything else withered and mummy-dead.
> What great tomb-haunter sweeps the distant sky

(Something may linger there though all else die;)
And finds there nothing to make its terror less
*Hysterica passio* of its own emptiness?

The *hysterica passio* of Lear, an overmastering rise of emotion, a "climbing sorrow," denotes a character guided by volcanic feeling—in Maud's case, political feeling—rather than reason. The rhyme royal is not allowed to fall into its usual gracious form, but stops dead, on the word "dead," at the end of the opening tercet, "unable" to complete its first quatrain.

As in "Among School Children," the poet immediately recoils from Maud's image in old age and regresses to an idealized memory of her younger self, where she exhibits the royal virtue of "magnanimity," and is implicitly likened, in her "gentle" beauty, to the full moon of Yeats's Phase 14 (radiating a light indubitably royal, if paler than that of the "kingly" sun):

> No dark tomb-haunter once; her form all full
> As though with magnanimity of light,
> Yet a most gentle woman; who can tell
> Which of her forms has shown her substance right?
> Or maybe substance can be composite. . . .

In the opening quatrain in his second stanza (this time allowed to complete itself), the poet raises the metaphysical enigma of Maud's many contradictory self-manifestations. According to Aristotelian philosophy, her multiple forms necessarily all spring from a single "simple" (uncompounded) underlying "substance." But was Aristotle right in declaring substance simple? Perhaps not. Perhaps substance may be composite, says the fifth line, prolonging the problem of the quatrain. Yeats turns to a modern neo-Hegelian authority, J. McT. E. McTaggart (1866–1925), who has dared to assert that substance can be composite, or (as Yeats phrases it) that substance can contain in a phenomenon as ordinary as a breath, a single mouthful of air, the Blakean contraries of life and death:[2]

> Or maybe substance can be composite,
> Profound McTaggart thought so, and in a breath
> A mouthful hold the extreme of life and death.[3]

In reassuring himself that *all* of Maud's forms have "shown her substance right" (and by rhyming "light" and "right" with "composite"—against the "dark" tomb-haunter already presented), Yeats regains the courage to complete accurately (and thereby complicate) the former partial image of a Maud who was in youth "a most gentle woman." Now he can admit that even then, when she was a young creature "at the starting post" of her life's race, there was a "wildness" in her soul: her soul had been "shattered" by an intuition about its own future, "a vision of terror that it must live through." This admission of weakness in Maud strips from her both the "superhuman" quality of stanza 1 and the royal "magnanimity" of stanza 2, but at the cost of reducing her (in the eyes of her anxious lover) to the status of a child. The poet recalls that as he himself approached, by imaginative empathy, her "vision of terror," he caught, as if by contagion, the "wildness" of his beloved and became "wild" himself, pitying her as a doomed "child." Rhyme royal here loses its composure, hurtling down the page, after its first line, with no end-line pauses:

> But even at the starting-post, all sleek and new,
> I saw the wildness in her and I thought
> A vision of terror that it must live through
> Had shattered her soul. Propinquity had brought
> Imagination to that pitch where it casts out
> All that is not itself: I had grown wild
> And wandered murmuring everywhere, "My child, my child!"

This moment of repeated enjambment, in which the poet both patronizes the shattered beloved and is made wild himself, endangers the "queenliness" of the stanza-patterning. A second recoil on the poet's part re-confers her momentarily lost regality on Maud, who is now not merely "superhuman" but entirely "supernatural." Her round eye, the only living part of her, is perhaps not hers alone but is serving as a lens for a "sterner eye," one able to survey the whole world in its Gibbonian "decline and fall." Maud gains a starker royalty, that of prophetic vision:

> Or else I thought her supernatural;
> As though a sterner eye looked through her eye
> On this foul world in its decline and fall;
> On gangling stocks grown great, great stocks run dry,
> Ancestral pearls all pitched into a sty,
> Heroic reverie mocked by clown and knave,
> And wondered what was left for massacre to save.

If I am not mistaken, Yeats here permits his final stanza to end on an alexandrine, borrowing that beautiful Spenserian effect for salient closure. (Although it is barely possible to squeeze the last line into five beats, it falls more naturally, as a terminal cadence, into six: "And wondered what was left | for massacre to save.")

Yeats never wrote more violently than in this concluding stanza, in which the "decline and fall" of Maud's "realm" enrages him. The poem's terrible speculation—that a commitment to "massacre" might save "heroic reverie" along with what remains of "great stocks" and "ancestral pearls"—suggests a means too evil to be justified by the end at which it aims. Yeats grieved more deeply over the tragedy of Maud's acquiescence in violence in the service of a "United Ireland" (she remained an unregenerate Republican, opposed to the compromise that established the Free State) than he did over the "decline and fall" of his own cultural group, foreseen in "Upon a House Shaken by the Land Agitation." Only if the eye that "looked through her eye . . . / And wondered what was left for massacre to save" is the eye of Destiny, the ultimate Ruler, is the ruthlessness of the line understandable.

No other rhyme royal poem (except Yeats's own "Hound Voice") so disrupts its courtly form and offers so lurid a drama. And though Yeats "observes" the potential of the fifth line, the sheer strangeness of the chaotic content of the poem—as it ranges from tomb-haunter to McTaggart to gangling stocks to massacre, with *hysterica passio,* pearls, and a sty thrown in for good measure—ensures that it will not resemble any conventional rhyme royal predecessor. The incoherence of content corresponds to the vision that has shattered Maud's soul, and her shattered soul, in its turn, keeps the world (as she sees it) from reflecting back any sustaining harmony. "A Bronze Head"—by conforming itself to Maud's long-lived vision of terror, while recalling her beauty in youth and summoning up her gauntness in age—becomes a stanza-by-stanza recreation of her composite substance. The poem also tallies, in its atmosphere of wreckage, the poet's afflicted love for Maud as it has been damaged over the years. The elegy would not be so tragic were it not haunted by the ornamental and celebratory rhyme royal of the past, that form suited to pearls and heroic reverie.

Maud had appeared earlier in another nonce form—in the rough, mostly unrhymed hexameters, commemorating a Yeatsian pantheon, of "Beautiful Lofty Things."[4] Surely, in deciding to honor "all the Olympians" in hexameter, Yeats wanted to echo the epic hexameter. Epic is also our earliest source for the enumerative catalogue (of ships, for example), and that is the structure into which Yeats has placed his terse vignettes of persons important to his emotional life: three "fathers" (the revolutionary patriot John O'Leary; his own father, J. B. Yeats; and the historian Standish O'Grady); a "mother" (his patron Augusta Gregory); and a beloved (Maud Gonne). Although the poem has its own competent aural patterns (including some rhyme), its principal means are pictorial, as it creates a memorial gallery populated by these five indispensable figures in Yeats's life:

Beautiful Lofty Things

Beautiful lofty things: O'Leary's noble head;
My father upon the Abbey Stage, before him a raging crowd:
'This Land of Saints,' and then as the applause died out,
'Of plaster Saints'; his beautiful mischievous head thrown back.
Standish O'Grady supporting himself between the tables
Speaking to a drunken audience high nonsensical words;
Augusta Gregory seated at her great ormolu table,
Her eightieth winter approaching: 'Yesterday he threatened my life.
I told him that nightly from six to seven I sat at this table,
The blinds drawn up'; Maud Gonne at Howth station waiting a train,
Pallas Athene in that straight back and arrogant head;
All the Olympians; a thing never known again.

The individual sketches resemble portrait busts: O'Leary's head; J. B. Yeats's head; O'Grady's speaking head (though also his arms); Augusta Gregory's head visible through the window; Maud Gonne's arrogant head. The poem's economy of means makes us move swiftly from the title phrase "beautiful lofty things" (repeated in the first line) to its matching plural phrase at the close: "All the Olympians." But then, when the "beautiful lofty *things*" are suddenly condensed, in the closing half-line, into a singular— "*a thing*" never known again—an era sweeps up its varied inhabitants into a single group and consigns them to history. By his metamorphosis of "things" into "thing," Yeats ensures in his poem a Platonic overtone, as the Many, in their historical immortality, are absorbed into the One.

We can easily understand Yeats's choice of the non-arbitrary rare forms I have looked at so far in this chapter: his casting of his manifesto "A Coat" in a never-to-be-repeated dizain shape; his desire to do a wrenching sort of justice to Maud Gonne in rhyme royal; his wish to salute his "beautiful lofty things" in an epic catalogue of sculptural and painterly sketches, and—in the equally non-arbitrary form with which I will close this chapter—his portrayal of Cuchulain's afterlife in *terza rima*. It is less easy to say why he takes up other rare forms, arbitrary ones. Here I will look at only two such forms: the one found in the 1928 poem "At Algeciras—A Meditation upon Death" (493–494), and the double-form present in the 1919 "Double Vision of Michael Robartes" (382–384).

In "At Algeciras" Yeats invents a new stanza form—a narrative tetrameter quatrain supported on the plinth of a pentameter couplet (4-4-4-4-5-5), rhyming *ababcc*. The rhyme-scheme—a quatrain followed by a couplet—is a familiar one, used by Shakespeare in *Venus and Adonis*. But Shakespeare's poem attaches the rhyme-scheme to unchanging pentameters, while here, the disproportion between the shorter lines of the opening quatrain and the longer lines of the couplet draws attention to itself precisely because of its difference from the *Venus and Adonis* stanza. The five-beat couplets at the close enable the stanza to broaden out and end conclusively, and give the poem its distinctive and arresting shape.

But the strangest aspects of this three-stanza poem are its diction and its discontinuity. What other poem on "last things"—death and judgment—would begin with repellent lines concerning "The heron-billed pale cattle-birds / That feed on some foul parasite"? What such poem would proceed from the exoticism of a rich Moroccan midnight to a reminiscence of childhood voiced in artless first-person speech ("Often at evening when a boy"), as the poet recalls bringing shells gathered at Rosses Point to an older friend for his approval? And how does the poem leap from such disparate beginnings to an imagined posthumous appearance before the "Great Questioner"? In no other Yeats poem do the successive stanzas seem more emotionally and intellectually discontinuous than here. The terse power of this late poem remains to be accounted for. To clarify its strange opening lines, Yeats announces in the title that he is writing from Algeciras, in southern Spain, near the Straits of Gibraltar. Across the water is Morocco, where the birds live by day:

> At Algeciras—A Meditation upon Death
>
> The heron-billed pale cattle-birds
> That feed on some foul parasite
> Of the Moroccan flocks and herds
> Cross the narrow Straits to light
> In the rich midnight of the garden trees
> Till the dawn break upon those mingled seas.

Often at evening when a boy
Would I carry to a friend—
Hoping more substantial joy
Did an older mind commend—
Not such as are in Newton's metaphor,
But actual shells of Rosses' level shore.

Greater glory in the sun,
An evening chill upon the air,
Bid imagination run
Much on the Great Questioner;
What He can question, what if questioned I
Can with a fitting confidence reply.

Such a poem develops not logically but associatively. The unnatural-looking, unnaturally-living, unnaturally-hyphenated "cattle-birds" (with their "heron-bills") endure an unnatural life during the day, spending their time with species not their own and feeding on the foul parasites found on Moroccan sheep and cows. For a striking example of how Yeats transformed life into art, one has only to compare the repellent opening above with Yeats's two letter-versions of the same sight: "Many white herons perched among the dark leaves of the trees close to my window every night" (#5049), and "At sunset some hundred or so white herons will come flying from beyond Gibralter & go to sleep in some dark trees" (#5046). His correspondents might have been unpleasantly surprised to receive a letter saying "The heron-billed pale cattle-birds . . . feast on some foul parasite," etc. We do not at first know why the innocent epistolary birds have been so changed, but we sense the enormous contrast between their origin and their destination. Their days are "foul," but in the nights they can, by crossing the narrow Straits of Gibraltar, live—if only temporarily—in another world, the exotic paradise of southern Spain where, in the rich European midnight, fragrant garden trees cluster by the mingled seas of the Mediterranean and the Atlantic. At dawn, alas, the birds must return to Africa and their disagreeable feeding. This fierce alternation suggests that the "rich midnight" is much to be preferred to repellent day—or (as Yeats's subtitle implies) that the coming night of death may bestow a wealth no longer obtainable from the miserable conditions of daily life.

But Yeats has not yet reached that "rich midnight" of the unknown future; he is aware, however, that his evening is descending. In fact, an "evening chill" is upon the air, as we will learn in the closing stanza. The poet evades, for a moment, admitting the presence of the evening chill by recalling more rewarding evenings early in his life, when, as a boy, although he had taken idle joy in gathering shells at Rosses Point near Sligo, he carried them to an older friend in the hope of "more substantial joy" when an older mind would "commend" his naturalist endeavors. This digression into childhood memory does not, however, succeed in blotting out approaching death; adulthood makes its way into the stanza with the intrusion of the mature poet's recollection of Newton's wistful comments about his life's work: "To myself I seem to have been only like a boy, playing on the seashore, and diverting myself, in now and then finding another pebble or prettier shell than ordinary, while the great ocean of truth lay all undiscovered before me" (*NC*, 292). Although humorously setting aside "Newton's metaphor" by insisting on the "actual shells" he gathered, the poet has allowed his adult reading of Newton into what would otherwise have been a limpid recollection of childhood; he cannot, on the sophisticated shore of Spain, regress unimpeded to the "naïve" shore of Sligo.

It is only after that touching, but temporizing, invoking of a childhood "evening" that the present "evening" can be allowed into consciousness, and the solacing pathetic fallacy of the birds' rich evening garden-sojourns dismissed. But the present moment is not one solely of elegiac "chill"; the final stanza begins, unexpectedly, with praise: "Greater glory in the sun." This is a repudiation of Wordsworth's valedictory and mournful image of the sunset in the Intimations Ode:

> The clouds that gather round the setting sun
> Do take a sober coloring from an eye
> That hath kept watch o'er man's mortality.

For Yeats, the setting sun, immune to the surrounding chill, keeps its own coloring, its own (Wordsworthian, unvanished) "glory." The sheer appreciation of the expanding glory of the evening is one of the paradoxical blessings conferred on Yeats by age and illness (a variant title for the poem was "A Meditation Written During Sickness at Algeciras"). The superb left-right balance of "Greater glory in the sun, / An evening chill upon the air," suggests an equable mind confronting its own end, aware of both the magnificence and the indifference of nature. The particular judgment in which God weighs the merits of an individual soul immediately upon death then rises in Yeats's mind and is secularized into his appearance before a Newtonian "Great Questioner." It is this philosophical Deistic Abstraction that generates the diction not only of the penultimate line, with its stately chias-

mus ("What He can question, what if questioned I"), but also of the final
line, with its eighteenth-century restraint in hoping for "a fitting confi-
dence" with which to reply. Yeats's persistent skepticism resides in the frail
"if"—"what **if** questioned I / Can . . . reply"—and also in the concession
that it is the imagination, rather than faith, that is bidden to "run much" on
the Great Questioner.

What does the stanza form contribute to this strict and magnificently
reticent poem? To feel the formal importance of Yeats's stanza, one need
only rewrite the poem entirely in tetrameter, without the broadening re-
flectiveness of the closing pentameters:

> [the . . . birds
> Cross the narrow Straits to light
> At midnight on the garden trees
> Till dawn makes bright the mingled seas.]
>
> [. . . Did an older mind commend—
> Not shells from Newton's metaphor
> But shells from Rosses' level shore.]
>
> [. . . the Great Questioner;
> What to his questions then can I
> With fitting confidence reply.]

The sing-song of these tetrameter-effects—immediately audible—deletes all
emotional weight from the stanza-conclusions, which need their pentame-
ter gravity to remain steady and serious.

The distinctions in effect among the tetrameters of "At Algeciras" also
need to be felt. If we compare the laden—indeed over-laden—tetrameters
of the first stanza with those of the last, we sense acutely the drop in "life-
thickness." The adjectival burden of the first four lines—*heron-billed, pale,
cattle-, foul, Moroccan, narrow*—lessens in the next set of tetrameters (*sub-
stantial, older*) and disappears into abstraction in the last (*greater, evening,
Great*). The turn in each stanza from the narrative tetrameters to the re-
flective pentameters reveals the deathward tendency of the aging speaker's
mind. He cannot think of anything—from the cattle-birds to childish shell-
gathering to the present chill in the temperature—without its bringing his
mind, in the closing pentameters of each stanza, to his last end (mirrored in
the rich midnight, in Newton's late reflections, and in the imagined reply to
the Great Questioner). At this final point of life, philosophy constantly su-
pervenes on each event, no matter how disparate the events may be or how

far removed they are from each other in time. The approach of death introduces itself at every discrete moment, whether the moment is richly languid in late-life appreciativeness, gently reminiscent of childhood, or somberly apprehensive of objective judgment. We now perceive the reason for the (originally disturbing) lack of connection among the stanzas. They *must* appear widely separate if they are to present three distinct moments in the mind; the fact that they all lead inexorably to the same meditation on possible aspects of death is what startles and then gratifies us as we gradually perceive the underlying coherence of the three disparate parts. The two-part stanza form so well fits the motion of the poet's thoughts—event, reflection; event, reflection; event, reflection—that aesthetic satisfaction attends upon it. Its constant stanzaic return to breadth of reflection, as much as anything else in the poem, creates the firm representation of "an old man's eagle mind." So, although the form of "At Algeciras" at first appears to be an arbitrary one, having no thematic tradition that would link it to death or old age, it becomes in the end, thanks to Yeats's content, mimetic of an equable disposition of mind in illness and a firm stoic resolve.[5]

Yeats's strangest poem using rare forms is the difficult *three*-part sequence called (at first sight perplexingly) "The *Double* Vision of Michael Robartes" (382–384; italics mine). When we examine this poem, several puzzling questions arise: Given its three Roman-numeraled parts, why does it have "double" in its title? Why do the quatrains of part I rhyme alternately *(abab)* when those of *both* part II and part III rhyme in couplets *(aabb)*? And why, if this is a *double* vision, is the prosodic measure (5-5-3-3) of *all three* parts identical? We know that Yeats must have had something in mind underlying these choices; what does he convey by these discrepancies and identities?

Some possibilities present themselves almost immediately. The noun of the title is, after all, expressed in the singular: it may indeed be a *double* vision that Michael Robartes is vouchsafed, but the vision itself is one: "*The . . . Vision.*" And both parts of the double vision (parts I and II) begin with identical words: "On the grey rock of Cashel . . . ," while the post-hoc part III, though remaining in the same place, changes the wording to "In Cormac's ruined house." Because throughout all *three* parts the setting is unchanged—the rock of Cashel, in Tipperary, with the ruin of a twelfth-century Gothic church ("Cormac's chapel") upon it—all *three* parts of the sequence must be unchanging in measure, 5-5-3-3. But if Michael Robartes remains (as he does) in a single place throughout the whole poem, why does Yeats tell us, through his Roman numerals, that there are in fact three "stations"—three *different* perspectives of Robartes' mind—embodied in the poem? We can understand that since the two halves of the vision are distinguishable—it is a *double* vision—the rhyme-scheme of part II of the vision *(aabb)* should differ from that of part I *(abab)*. But why does Yeats cast part III in the same rhyme-scheme as that of part II *(aabb)* rather than in that of part I (or in some other rhyme-scheme entirely)?

In order to explore these formal conditions, and answer the last question, we must look at the subject-matter and conduct of the sequence, which is spoken throughout by a single Yeatsian persona, Michael Robartes. Part I contains his evocation of the spirits who preside at the dark of the moon (for Yeats, the nadir of being). At this moment Robartes feels that everything in his life is determined, that he does not now have, and never has had, free will: "When had I my own will? / O not since life began." As we shall see, part II of his vision, by contrast, is vouchsafed to him at the full of the moon (the zenith of being): "I saw by the moon's light / Now at its fifteenth night." The second, full-moon part of the vision, exemplifying free will, is exactly twice as long (eight quatrains) as the first, dark-of-the-moon deterministic part (four quatrains). This discrepancy of length, like the discrepancy of rhyme, presents a problem: a "double vision" ought, we feel, to exhibit two equal parts. Can it be that the dreadful dark quatrains of part I weigh twice as much as the full-moon quatrains of part II? And what will be the point of adding, to the already-articulated double vision, the five-quatrain part III?

Here is the first part of "The Double Vision," in which Michael Robartes has, by calling up "the cold spirits that are born" at the dark of the moon, a grim vision of human beings as bodies who are "constrained, arraigned, baffled, bent and unbent" by bizarre choiceless marionettes who are obeying the will of some hidden magical power:

I

On the grey rock of Cashel the mind's eye
Has called up the cold spirits that are born
When the old moon is vanished from the sky
And the new still hides her horn.

Under blank eyes and fingers never still
The particular is pounded till it is man.
When had I my own will?
O not since life began.

> Constrained, arraigned, baffled, bent and unbent
> By these wire-jointed jaws and limbs of wood,
> Themselves obedient,
> Knowing not evil and good;
>
> Obedient to some hidden magical breath.
> They do not even feel, so abstract are they,
> So dead beyond our death,
> Triumph that we obey.

As this very peculiar initial poem opens, the "mind's eye" *(Hamlet)* calls up spirits who are indifferent servants to some blank-eyed restless-fingered demiurge, who with some unspecified tool "pounds" the "particular" (a cluster of elementary particles, perhaps) "till it is man." Yeats is drawing here on his description of Phase One in *A Vision:*

> Mind has become indifferent to good and evil, to truth and falsehood;
> body has become undifferentiated, dough-like . . . ; and mind and body
> take whatever shape, accept whatever image is imprinted upon them. . . .
> There may be great joy; but it is the joy of a conscious plasticity; and it is
> this plasticity, this liquefaction, or pounding up, whereby all that has
> been knowledge becomes instinct and faculty. . . . All plasticities . . . are
> alike in being automatic.[6]

(The demiurge who "pounds" the body's dough into obedience seems to be a demonic version of Blake's God who, with his forge and his "immortal hand or eye," hammers fire into the form of the tiger.)

Realizing his domination by this hidden power, Robartes despairingly questions, in two trimeters, whether he has ever, since his life began, possessed free will: "When **had** I my **own will?** / O not since life began." The "cold spirits" of the dark are the demiurge's delegates, his wooden wire-jointed puppets; they know neither evil nor good, and are merely obedient to his "hidden magical breath." We in turn obey, helplessly, the demiurge's inhuman robots, who are so abstract, so "dead," that they cannot even take pleasure in our obedience to them. The universe presented by part I is a chain of automata: demiurge, spirits, ourselves.

By the end of its unfolding, part I of "The Double Vision" has made its metric clear—5-5-3-3.[7] But even when we have understood the metrical arrangement, the fact remains that the rhythm is jerky, resistant, at times almost unsayable—as we try, for instance, to construct a trimeter out of

"When the old moon is vanished from the sky." It can be done: "When the **old** moon is **van**ished from the **sky.**" We read the line as a trimeter more confidently when we perceive its syntactic alignment—by noun, verb, noun—with the unmistakable trimeter that follows it:

> When the **old** moon is **van**ished from the **sky,**
> And the **new** still **hides** her **horn.**

The ungainliness of the meter asserts itself in another way in the pentameters of lines 9 and 10. Their overburdened rhythms reproduce the conditions of our life on earth, when we are

> Con**strained**, ar**raigned**, **baffled**, **bent** and un**bent**
> By these **wire-joint**ed **jaws** and **limbs** of **wood** . . .

The gait mimicked by such lines—irregular, halting, stiff-kneed—is of course the point. When we feel we have no free will, we resist our fate, even while being forced to advance within it. As contorted as the rhythm is, the syntax of the final stanza of part I is even more so, as we see when we map it (I have added parentheses to clarify Yeats's *sotto voce* asides):

| WE | THE PUPPETS | | THE DEMIURGE |
|---|---|---|---|
| Constrained, arraigned, baffled, bent and unbent | | | |
| | By these wire-jointed jaws and limbs of wood, | | |
| | (Themselves | obedient, | |
| | Knowing not evil | and good); | |
| | | Obedient to | |
| | | | some hidden magical breath, |
| | They do not even feel, | | |
| | (so abstract are they, | | |
| | So dead beyond our death), | | |
| | Triumph that | | |
| we obey. | | | |

As we read these gaunt and constantly interrupted phrases, we absorb, almost unconsciously, the fact that they are meant to express, in their deformity, what it feels like to be bound and manacled, to be certain you have never had any free will, not at any time in your life. The dark of the moon represents, for Yeats, the triumph of "objectivity," the rule of the communal, in which no room exists for individual subjectivity.[8]

The "cold spirits" had been sketched earlier by Yeats in the previous year's dialogue-poem, "The Phases of the Moon": there, Owen Aherne questions Michael Robartes concerning the spirits of the dark of the moon—"And what of those / That the last servile crescent has set free?" Robartes replies that such spirits of darkness are other than human, cast out beyond the boundaries of human existence:

> They are cast beyond the verge, and in a cloud,
> Crying to one another like the bats;
> And having no desire they cannot tell
> What's good or bad, or what it is to triumph
> At the perfection of one's own obedience;
> And yet they speak what's blown into the mind;
> Deformed beyond deformity, unformed.
>
> (376)

Indeed, it is these cold spirits of the dark of the moon, perfectly obedient to the demiurge, unable to distinguish good from bad, that "speak what's blown into the mind" of Michael Robartes as he evokes them in the first half of his double vision. They are "dead beyond our death"; even the word "dead" is insufficient to describe their mechanical and soulless being.

It appears that the second half of the double vision, the vision of free will countering that of determinism, is more complicated for the poet to unveil, since it requires twice as many stanzas. As part II opens, Michael Robartes tells us that while still on "the grey rock of Cashel" he "suddenly saw," by the light of the full moon, the tableau of the second half of his double vision. We deduce that it was only by evoking and facing the cold spirits, and admitting the truth of the determinism they symbolize, that Michael Robartes was "suddenly" rewarded by the compensatory vision of free will. No longer formed in the alternately rhymed quatrains of part I, the stanzas of part II unroll their asymmetrical couplets rhyming *aa* (5-5) and *bb* (3-3) to set out, first of all, the three elements of this vouchsafed revelation of free will—Sphinx, Buddha, and dancer:[9]

II

> On the grey rock of Cashel I suddenly saw
> A Sphinx with woman breast and lion paw,

A Buddha, hand at rest,
Hand lifted up that blest.

And right between these two a girl at play
That, it may be, had danced her life away,
For now being dead it seemed
That she of dancing dreamed.

Although I saw it all in the mind's eye
There can be nothing solider till I die;
I saw by the moon's light
Now at its fifteenth night.

For Robartes/Yeats, it is not enough merely to present these three figures: in the next three stanzas he must also (in the same order) interpret them. The Sphinx, he says, represents intellect; the Buddha, love; and the dancer, perfection:

One lashed her tail; her eyes lit by the moon
Gazed upon all things known, all things unknown,
In triumph of intellect
With motionless head erect.

That other's moonlit eyeballs never moved,
Being fixed on all things loved, all things unloved,
Yet little peace he had,
For those that love are sad.

O little did they care who danced between,
And little she by whom her dance was seen
So she had outdanced thought.
Body perfection brought[.]

Yeats, we perceive, is redescribing the human self. Conventionally, the two faculties of the soul were thought to be the Intellect and the Will. Yeats is content to retain the word "intellect," but in representing it not by Reason but by a Sphinx, he defines the intellect as a presenter of enigmas, rather than a solver of them. The Will (seeking the good established by the intellect) was generally conceived of as conative, working toward an envisaged end. Because the desired end for Yeats is human creative art (the dance) rather than instrumental work, he places, as the complementary pole to intellect, not a conative will but compassionate love and pity (expressed by the Buddha's hand-gestures). The dancer oscillates between the two poles of intellect and love, embodying the moment (as described in "The Phases of the Moon") at which the non-human "spirits of the full of the moon" come into being:

> All thought becomes an image and the soul
> Becomes a body: that body and that soul [are]
> Too perfect at the full to lie in a cradle,
> Too lonely for the traffic of the world:
> Body and soul cast out and cast away
> Beyond the visible world.
>
> (375)

Surely, we think, the second half of Robartes' "double" vision must now be complete, after three stanzas of formal emblem-presentation and three subsequent stanzas of emblem-interpretation. We have seen thought become image, as the dancer "outdanced" thought; we have seen perfection realized in the body. What remains? To our surprise, Yeats appends to his six emblem-stanzas a two-stanza further interpretation, which, paraphrased, is a definition of the moment of contemplation, that timeless hiatus in which the "mind moves upon silence" (visually presented in "Long-Legged Fly" in the successive moments of contemplation of Caesar, "Michael Angelo," and Helen of Troy). In "The Double Vision," the only powers that can silence the restless intellect are those of "eye and ear" as they note the sensuous particulars of human life. The "minute particulars" of Blake counter the blank particles pounded by the demiurge. The last two stanzas of part II of Michael Robartes' double vision are self-reflective, contemplating an allegorized image of contemplation. Sphinx, Buddha, dancer—mind, love, image—are caught in the complete mutation of soul into dynamic corporeal form, as reflection and passion are transformed into embodied art, which is paradoxically "alive" (in perpetuity) even if "dead" to actual life:

> For what but eye and ear silence the mind
> With the minute particulars of mankind?
> Mind moved yet seemed to stop
> As 'twere a spinning top.
>
> In contemplation had those three so wrought
> Upon a moment, and so stretched it out
> That they, time overthrown,
> Were dead yet flesh and bone.

As all the human faculties move together—as intellect scans things known and unknown, passion scans things loved and unloved, and body transmits those activities into kinesthetic patterned energy—contemplation reaches its apogee (as in "Among School Children") in dance-form. Free will is seen to be so complex that it outdoes determinism in its recruiting of human forces, requiring, as it does, eight stanzas to determinism's four.

In "The Phases of the Moon" Yeats had already described the moment of contemplation, when the soul is "Caught up in contemplation, the mind's eye / Fixed upon images that once were thought" (375). Since the cold spirits of the dark of the moon and the perfect spirits of the full had been delineated in "The Phases of the Moon," why, we wonder, did Yeats need to compose "The Double Vision of Michael Robartes"? The later poem implicitly repudiates blank verse as the expository vehicle for doctrine, so we can infer that to Yeats his earlier blank-verse passages did not seem the only form in which doctrine could be cast. The blank-verse doctrinal poems were written "to some extent . . . as texts for exposition," as Yeats said in his note to "The Phases of the Moon" (821). But in his letter of July 15, 1918, to Ezra Pound about "The Double Vision" (#3461), Yeats describes it not as a text for exposition but rather as a "strange and beautiful symbol." It is the beauty conveyed by a song-measure (rather than the more pedestrian blank-verse exposition) that he feels as he chooses the prosodic form for "The Double Vision."

In the 1921 Preface to *Michael Robartes and the Dancer,* Yeats characterizes the poet's work as searching for illumination in a dark room until the objects of inquiry become visible. Gradually (looking for candlestick and matches), the poet passes from speculative thought to conviction, to emotion, to images, until finally he can actually look at "the objects in the room":

> It is hard for a writer, who has spent much labour upon his style, to remember that thought, which seems to him natural and logical like that style, may be unintelligible to others. The first excitement over, and the thought changed into settled conviction, his interest in simple, that is to say in normal emotion, is always I think increased: he is no longer looking for candlestick and matches but at the objects in the room. (853)

It is perhaps almost comic to think of demiurge, cold spirits, Sphinx, Buddha, and dancer as "the objects in the room," but in comparison to the more abstract speculations in "The Phases of the Moon," the double vision's spirits and persons symbolizing determinism, on the one hand, and intellect, love, and art, on the other, inhabit an atmosphere more lyric than expository. We can understand why Yeats felt it necessary to reify by images and new rhythms, through Michael Robartes, his "first excitement" of thought which he had rendered in the doctrinal blank verse of "The Phases of the Moon."

We have now seen Michael Robartes' "double vision," both parts of it: both are in quatrains, but the *abab* suspenseful dark quatrains of deterministic manipulation of humans by puppets exist in contrast with the succinct *aabb* couplets of the moonlit tableau of the dancer's free will. Robartes seems in complete emotional possession of his vision; he has unfolded and distinguished the halves of it with exemplary deliberateness and order. We are perplexed, then, when the double vision receives an unexpected supplement in part III. To our astonishment, Michael Robartes breaks down emotionally, explaining that he has been undone by his double vision, brought to "a pitch of folly . . . / Being caught between the pull / Of the dark moon and the full." Robartes, we now perceive, is himself the suffering site of the contest between determinism and freedom. His language becomes obscene as he describes (replicating the *aabb* "free will" form of the quatrains of part II) his prolonged erotic nightly dreams of a girl embodied (he now realizes) in the dancer of the second half of his vision. Those dreams always flee as he wakes, leaving him in a state of frustrating sexual arousal:

> III
> I knew that I had seen, had seen at last
> That girl my unremembering nights hold fast
> Or else my dreams that fly
> If I should rub an eye,
>
> And yet in flying fling into my meat
> A crazy juice that makes the pulses beat[.]

This coarse language comes from substituting the body's erotic vision for the mind's contemplative one, reminding us that the privileged moment of contemplation is just that—a moment—from which one awakes just as crazed in mind and as passionate in body as before, abasing oneself before an indifferent beloved:

> A crazy juice that makes the pulses beat
> As though I had been undone
> By Homer's Paragon

> Who never gave the burning town a thought;
> To such a pitch of folly I am brought,
> Being caught between the pull
> Of the dark moon and the full,
>
> The commonness of thought and images
> That have the frenzy of our western seas.

"The commonness of thought" arises from the tyranny of the collective during the reign of "objectivity" in the dark of the moon; the "images / That have the frenzy of our western seas" are those of the Homeric Helen and all her radiant lunar successors, who are the causes of the erotic madness described elsewhere by Yeats as "the folly that man does / Or must suffer if he woos / A proud woman not kindred of his soul" ("A Dialogue of Self and Soul").

"Undone," "caught," his genitals suffused with a "crazy juice," Michael Robartes, once he has fallen out of his visionary trance, is merely human—torn between thinking himself determined or believing that he is free, simultaneously subject to collective thought and impassioned by images of desire. It is only after Michael Robartes completes his last two stanzas that we understand why it is that part III has retained the rhyme-scheme, *aabb*, of the full-moon segment of the double vision:

> Thereon I made my moan,
> And after kissed a stone,
>
> And after that arranged it in a song
> Seeing that I, ignorant for so long,
> Had been rewarded thus
> In Cormac's ruined house.[10]

This ritual thanksgiving—in which Michael Robartes must first moan at his own distressed and conflicted human state, then must make obeisance, by kissing a stone, to the sacred place where he was rewarded with his double vision—must precede Robartes' final task, "arranging" the vision "in a song"—which, we realize as we reach the end of this Möbius strip, is the song of the double vision, parts I and II, which we have just experienced.

We are now able, with hindsight, to deduce the poet's state of mind *before* the double vision solaced him. He had been tormented by a sexual passion available only in dream, ending always in frustrated arousal; he had felt himself both helplessly driven toward, and freely choosing, his Helen-like "paragon"; he had been roused by passion and perplexity to such a pitch of folly in his daily life that he was ashamed. "When will my dreams cease to torture me; am I compelled or am I free in this passion; why do I long for a woman indifferent to me; is it despair or joy I feel as I oscillate back and forth between my apparent erotic compulsion and my interior conviction of free choice?" These questions have driven equanimity from Robartes' mind until—as though miraculously formulating themselves—his two half-visions (the obverse and reverse of his introspection) show him that he is at once driven *and* free, helpless *and* self-choreographing, obedient to the demiurge's puppets *and* a creature of intellect, love, and contemplation.

But as quickly as it came, the double vision vanishes, and Robartes is left alone in the ruined chapel on the bare rock with its archaic stones. He has seen, however, in his double vision, a remarkable personal revelation of a double truth: determinism is real, and it is only by evoking its cold spirits that one can "suddenly see" that free will is also real. Robartes need no longer berate himself for folly, denigrate his sexual arousal, condemn his erotic abjection. His former "ignorance" is replaced by the "reward" not only of a wider philosophical understanding of the two forces always embedded in human nature and driving human action, but also by his perception that the vision is in truth a single one, its two halves dialectically related. He is grateful for his ability to "arrange in a song" his enlarged perceptions.

Into what form, then, have we seen Yeats cast this long "song" as he arranges it? A: into a single form—the quatrain—for all three parts of his sequence. But also B: in two quatrain-versions, one for each half of the double vision (*abab* and *aabb*). But what form will Yeats choose for Robartes' remarks as a "real person," now awakened from his vision, in part III? We see that Robartes' commentary in part III carries the *nachschein*, the afterglow, of the solacing full moon: he clings at the close to the *aabb* form of his vision of free will. Somehow his mind has taken, during the second half of his vision, the impress of the full moon; henceforth her measure will be the one that reverberates in his song. By the end, Robartes is less a creature of the demiurge, more than before a member of the contemplative trio ravished out of time. Though he is still, like all human beings, "caught between the pull / Of the dark moon and the full," he is grateful for the clarification of his state generated by his double vision—and he thereby becomes freer and more composed in mind than the frustrated and abject person he had been before he both evoked and was granted the vision.

Unless we perceive that Yeats's two rhyme-forms preserve the same prosodic measure, we do not understand them as obverse and reverse of the same 5-5-3-3 "overform" that remains stable through all three parts of the poem. Until we remark the persistence of the "free-will" form of part II into the "real world" of part III, we do not understand the extent of Robartes' "reward." And until we recall that Robartes has had to bring his tormented self to the "ruined" house of Irish kingly history in order to receive his vision, we do not understand this poem as a nationalist utterance. Erotic and philosophical torment can be soothed, but that solace can come only through a felt local connection to one's fellows of which the rock of Cashel is the symbol. The historical Cormac—and not only the sinister magical demiurge and the trio symbolizing free being—bears a part in constituting Robartes' freed selfhood.

In my own case, an exasperation attended the first reading of this poem, and continued for some time in subsequent encounters with it. It may be years before the driving power of "The Double Vision" becomes enlightening, before its images begin to seem familiar. It may be even longer until the reason for the disturbing language of the "crazy juice" becomes apparent. It may be only later that the metrical forms obtrude themselves and pose their insistent questions. By the time Yeats was composing *The Wild Swans at Coole,* he had decided to let at least some of his poems issue from his capacious and eclectic mind without too much explanation; he had a superb confidence that one day they would be understood. There is something winning about the indifference of such poems to a ready interpretation. They lie quietly in the *Collected Poems,* waiting for someone to relish them. It was a long time before I could relish "The Double Vision of Michael Robartes." Now it seems to me a great poem, sited on historic Irish soil, of determinism, free will, inner torment, and partial solace; I would not want to be without it, or without its strange and meaningful verse-forms, its originally opaque choice of three parts for two half-visions.

There are of course other nonce forms in Yeats, some (mostly early ones) less successful than others. And there are sure to be felicities of invention I have missed in the poems I have just glanced at (not to speak of the poems left unmentioned). But there were very few such felicities left unexplored by Yeats. We respect in him his insouciant way of thinking, "I haven't yet done *this*"—and then, even on his deathbed, doing it. What better companion at the end than Dante's ghost, inhabiting Yeats's perfectly cadenced *terza rima?* "Cuchulain Comforted" (634–635), dated January 13, 1939, and therefore Yeats's penultimate poem, was conceived the preceding December as a "sequel—strange too, something new"[11] to the play the poet had recently completed, *The Death of Cuchulain.* The poem was cast into *terza rima* because it unfolds a Dantesque encounter, in which the famous warrior Cuchulain finds himself after death in the company of elusive birdlike creatures referred to as "Shrouds." In Yeats's purgatorial afterlife myth, enunciated in *A Vision,* one phase ("the Shiftings") requires that the dead person experience the opposite of the emotional and moral code he had adopted during his life on earth, in order (as is said in "The Man and the Echo") to "complete his partial mind."[12] Cuchulain, who has always lived by the code of the warrior, is instructed to discard his arms, take up a length of linen, and sew a shroud as his new companions do. It is only after he obeys and begins to sew that the Shrouds tell him the nature of their character and the experience he can expect to undergo with them in this phase: they are "'Convicted cowards all, by kindred slain // 'Or driven from home and left to die in fear.'" After this revelation the Shrouds begin to sing, their voices transmuted to birdsong. Here is the poem—peculiar, quiet, eerie, moving:

### Cuchulain Comforted

A man that had six mortal wounds, a man
Violent and famous, strode among the dead;
Eyes stared out of the branches and were gone.

Then certain Shrouds that muttered head to head
Came and were gone. He leant upon a tree
As though to meditate on wounds and blood.

A Shroud that seemed to have authority
Among those bird-like things came, and let fall
A bundle of linen. Shrouds by two and three

Came creeping up because the man was still.
And thereupon that linen-carrier said:
'Your life can grow much sweeter if you will

'Obey our ancient rule and make a shroud;
Mainly because of what we only know
The rattle of those arms makes us afraid.

'We thread the needles' eyes, and all we do
All must together do.' That done, the man
Took up the nearest and began to sew.

'Now must we sing and sing the best we can,
But first you must be told our character:
Convicted cowards all, by kindred slain

'Or driven from home and left to die in fear.'
They sang, but had nor human tunes nor words,
Though all was done in common as before;

They had changed their throats and had the throats of birds.

On January 1, 1939, Yeats speaks in a letter of his newly completed play, *The Death of Cuchulain,* and adds a word about the poem that was being conceived as a "sequel" to the play: "I think my play is strange and the most moving I have written for some years. I am making a prose sketch for a poem—a kind of sequel—strange too, something new."[13] The "prose sketch" of "Cuchulain Comforted" was dictated, according to Mrs. Yeats, on January 7, a week before the dying poet composed the finished verses (dated January 13). By comparing the prose with the poem, we are able to see how Yeats went about constructing the *terza rima* that his imagination had proposed, in homage to Dante, for this afterlife-material. In the quotation that follows, I have put in **bold** the words of the dictated prose that appear in the poem, and I have set in *italics* the subject-matter that, in some synonymous form, is retained in the poem:

**A** shade recently arrived went through **a** valley in the Country of **the Dead; he** had **six mortal wound**s, but he had been a tall, strong, handsome **man.** *Other shades looked* at him from the **trees.** Sometimes **they** *went near to him and then went away quickly.* At last he sat down, he seemed very tired. *Gradually the shades gathered round him,* and *one of them who seemed to have some* **authority among** the others *laid a parcel of* **linen** *at his feet.* One of the others **said:** "I am not so **afraid** of him now that he is sitting **still.** It was the way his **arms rattled.**" Then another shade **said:** "**You** *would be* **much** *more comfortable* if **you** would **make a shroud** and wear it instead of the **arms.** We have brought **you** some **linen.** If **you make** it yourself **you** will be **much** happier, but of course we will **thread the needles,** so that when we have laid them at your feet **you** will **take** whichever you like best." The man with the **six wounds** saw that nobody had ever **threaded needles** so swiftly and so smoothly. He **took** the **threaded needles and began to sew,** and one of the shades said: *"***We** will **sing** to **you** *while you sew, but* **you** *will like to* **know** *who we are. We are the people who run away from the battles. Some of us have been put to death as* **cowards,** but others have hidden, and some even died without people knowing they were cowards." *Then* **they began to sing,** *and* **they did not sing** *like men and women, but like linnets* that had been stood on a perch and taught by a good singing master.[14]

The surprising thing about Yeats's prose sketch is how *few* words and phrases it provided for the poem: **A, the, dead, he, six, mortal, wounds, tree[s], they, authority, among, linen, said, afraid, still, arms, rattle[d], you, much, make, shroud, thread, needles, took, and, began, to** (infinitive), **sew, we, sing, know, cowards**—only thirty-two words in all. The first necessity for the poet, then, after completing his prose sketch, is simply to muster *more words,* keeping in mind that many of them will have to provide the rhymes necessary for the *terza rima.* When we consider the twenty-five rhyme-words of the finished poem, we see that only nine of them—**man, dead, tree, authority, still, said, know, afraid,** and **sew**—have been borrowed from the prose, and that only seven of these rhyme with each other: **dead, said,** and **afraid; tree** and **authority; know** and **sew.** Yeats takes up the prose's nine potential rhyme-words and begins to find additional rhymes for them as he constructs Cuchulain's story: **"man"** calls up "gone," "can," and "slain"; the three words **"dead," "said,"** and **"afraid"** summon up—in the masterstroke of the composition—"Shroud" (as well as "head" and "blood"); **"tree"** and **"authority"** generate "three"; **"still"** creates "fall" and "will"; **"sew"** and **"know"** attract "do." We perceive that the very last rhyme-words of the poem—"character," "fear," and "before," as well as "words" and "birds"—do not correspond to any words in the prose story; the words of the sketch have now been "used up" as sources of rhymes. (Some of the words *not* used, such as the feminine-ending words **"rattle"** and **"needles,"** are self-evidently not qualified for the masculine rhymes of Yeats's *terza rima;* others which might have made plausible entries, such as **"began"** or **"sing,"** apparently proved unproductive.) It remains for Yeats, as he begins to conclude the poem, to construct new rhymes not indebted to the prose as he produces and sustains, in twenty-five lines, a haunting death-drama.

Yeats creates the dramatic impetus of the poem through unexplained initial verbs and through stringent cuts in the prose story. The brief camera shots of the opening of the poem, alternating between Cuchulain and the Shrouds, occur in curt sentences animated by the first unsettling verbs, deliberately repeated: "The man **strode;** eyes **stared** and **were gone;** Shrouds that **muttered . . . came and were gone;** he **leant;** a Shroud **came, and let fall;** Shrouds **came creeping up.**" These active sentences of the first half of the poem draw us into the plot, preparing us for the second half, which consists solely of speeches, individual and collective, by the Shrouds. To these speeches the recently slain Cuchulain makes no answer. He silently accepts the invitation to sew a shroud for himself; and (as we know from the title) he is comforted by joining this unlikely company of ghostly cowards. He will eventually participate (once he has assumed his shroud) in the final choral singing, as the Shrouds, by an etherealizing metamorphosis, sing like birds, non-verbally, abandoning laborious words in favor of tunes that are beyond human capacity.

As Yeats replaces the prose's rather faint "shades" by reified (and alliterating) "Shrouds," he also deletes from the poem the prose's palpable aura of dilatory Irish folk-tale, so clearly present in its homely specification ("At last he sat down, he seemed very tired"), its colloquial hyperbole ("The man with the six wounds saw that nobody had ever threaded needles so swiftly and so smoothly"), its frequent repetitions, and its social prescriptions ("[They sang] like linnets that had been stood on a perch and taught by a good singing master"). Yeats chooses Dante's *terza rima* not only because the poem recounts an encounter with shades, but also because the form itself confers a religious dignity on "Cuchulain Comforted." (We are reminded, too, that Yeats put himself and Dante in the same phase—Phase 17, The Daimonic Man—of the psychology elaborated in *A Vision*.) The excisions that Yeats made in his prose sentences are crucial; a folk-tale diction ("We are the people who run away from the battles") could not have described the Shrouds so cuttingly as the harsh alliterative phrasing of the poem, as the Shrouds reveal their "**character; / Convicted cowards** all, by **kindred** slain." We know from their self-characterization that although their collectivity is replacing, in the afterlife, the former uniqueness of the "famous" individual, their group is not an inclusive tribal one. Rather, it is a collective of social outcasts (slain by their own kindred or driven by their kin from home and left to die). It is a group determined by shame and fear, emotions not native to Cuchulain. Though he too will sing, it will be with a completed mind, in which the warrior he used to be has fused with the coward he will now, for a time, become.

Although "Cuchulain Comforted" is Yeats's sole venture into *terza rima,* it is as accomplished as anything else he wrote. When we try to imagine the material of the prose sketch cast into a different container—a tetrameter narrative? a ballad? a sonnet?—we realize that few forms could bear so well the gravity of Cuchulain's entrance into the underworld as Dante's own *terza rima,* in one of its milder tonalities. A reader ignorant of *terza rima* could read "Cuchulain Comforted" appreciatively, but would miss the bridge across space and time to the *Divine Comedy,* and would not perceive the quasi-religious dignity with which Yeats wanted to invest the events of his poem. In this self-elegy, Yeats-as-Cuchulain, feeling his body failing, implicitly agrees to disavow his own fantasy of a famous and aggressive life, and join the anonymity of the meek collective dead. However, as we have seen in Chapter V, Yeats recoils from that resigned stance in his final, and defiant, poem, "The Black Tower." The two deathbed poems ratify the *Collected Poems* (as well as Yeats's other writings) in revealing the double Yeats: the poet assenting to the deterministic completion of his partial mind; and the "oath-bound" nationalist asserting the freedom of the will.

In his Preface to *Endymion,* Keats wrote, "I hope I have not in too late a day touched the beautiful mythology of Greece and dulled its brightness." I hope I have not, in touching the forms of the beautiful poems of Yeats, dulled their brightness for the reader. Description in words of what a trained ear would perceive without mediation is in part an ungrateful task; yet perhaps others will enjoy finding out what it has taken me a long time to understand and articulate. Yeats himself was no doubt thinking of Keats when he adopted Keatsian enjambed couplets for "Adam's Curse," a poem about the pang of unrequited love, but also about the effort of verse. It has not always been understood, I think, that everything the young Yeats says in that poem is not a mere conversational exchange (though it is made to seem so); every word is directed not toward the interlocutor, Maud Gonne's sister, but toward the silent Maud. The young poet speaks; the sister ("that beautiful mild woman")[15] speaks; but Maud says nothing. The young Yeats first tells his two companions (but speaking really only to Maud) how hard it is to turn oneself into a poet; but Maud says nothing. Then (after her sister's remark—not exactly what he had hoped for—that it is also hard to make oneself into a beautiful woman), he tries again, saying that he has tried to write with the "high courtesy" of lovers of olden days, quoting "with learned looks / Precedents out of beautiful old books," but adds, self-deprecatingly, "Yet now it seems an idle trade enough." He is hoping that

Maud will reply that it is not an idle trade, and that he has won her love by his ardent courtship and his beautiful words. But Maud says nothing. His implicit pleading has failed; Maud remains silent, and, as the "worn" moon rises, he knows that his beloved will never be his. He has something more he wants to say to Maud, but not in the presence of her sister; he wants to tell her of his heartbreak, and speak of the incomprehensible ways of fate, but in this public moment he must painfully stifle his words:

> I had a thought for no one's but your ears:
> That you were beautiful, and that I strove
> To love you in the old high way of love;
> That it had all seemed happy, and yet we'd grown
> As weary-hearted as that hollow moon.

Yeats's lifelong effort to invent ways of persuading Maud Gonne to love and understand him may have impelled him to some of those feats of poetic discovery that we have seen in his pages. He, at least, sometimes thought so; as he said in "Words,"

> [E]very year I have cried, 'At length
> My darling understands it all,
> Because I have come into my strength,
> And words obey my call';
>
> That had she done so who can say
> What would have shaken from the sieve?
> I might have thrown poor words away
> And been content to live.
>                 (255–256)

But of course it was not only to explain himself that Yeats composed poetry; it was to satisfy his ardor for the permutations and combinations of shaped and musical language, the desire "to articulate sweet sounds together." The resulting strong and decisive poems of formal mastery appeared, and kept appearing, throughout his fifty years of writing.

As a poet, Yeats knew what it is to be a reader of poetry:

> A poetical passage cannot be understood without a rich memory, and like the older school of painting appeals to a tradition, and that not merely when it speaks of 'Lethe's Wharf' or 'Dido on the wild sea-

banks' but in rhythm, in vocabulary; for the ear must notice slight varia-
tions upon old cadences and customary words, all that high breeding of
poetical style.[16]

To know Yeats as a poet, we must see how he mastered and transformed
the "old cadences and customary words" of inherited genres and forms so
that they would convey the full urgency of his experience, both personal
and national; we must come to understand that "high breeding of poetical
style" which he so intently absorbed from the past, and which he regener-
ated, with tireless and tenacious originality, in his own fifty years of verse.

## ⌒ Abbreviations

The following abbreviations are used in the text and notes:

CL        *The Collected Letters of W. B. Yeats,* General Editor John Kelly, 4 vols. (Oxford: Oxford University Press, 1986–2005)

DWL       *Letters on Poetry from W. B. Yeats to Dorothy Wellesley* (London: Oxford University Press, 1964)

E & I     W. B. Yeats, *Essays and Introductions* (New York: Macmillan, 1961)

Foster    R. F. Foster, *W. B. Yeats: A Life,* 2 vols. (Oxford: Oxford University Press, 1997, 2003)

L         *The Letters of W. B. Yeats,* ed. Allan Wade (New York: Macmillan, 1955)

Myth      W. B. Yeats, *Mythologies,* ed. Warwick Gould and Deirdre Toomey (London: Macmillan, 2005)

NC        A. Norman Jeffares, *A New Commentary on the Poems of W. B. Yeats* (London: Macmillan, 1984)

PF        *"Parnell's Funeral" and Other Poems from "A Full Moon in March":* Manuscript Materials, ed. David R. Clark (Ithaca, N.Y.: Cornell University Press, 2003)

WS        *The Winding Stair* (1929): Manuscript Materials, ed. David R. Clark (Ithaca, N.Y.: Cornell University Press, 1995)

## Preface

1. W. B. Yeats, *Memoirs,* transcribed and edited by Denis Donoghue (New York: Macmillan, 1972), 211.
2. Numbers within parentheses, preceded by the number sign, refer to accession numbers of letters in the InteLex database of Yeats's *Collected Letters,* John Kelly, General Editor (Oxford: Oxford University Press, InteLex Electronic Edition, 2002).

## I. Lyric Form in Yeats's Poetry

1. W. B. Yeats, *Essays and Introductions* (New York: Macmillan, 1961; rpt. 1968), 243. Hereafter cited in the text and notes as *E & I.*
2. This revision, and others that I'll mention, can be found in *The Wild Swans at Coole:* Manuscript Materials, by W. B. Yeats, ed. Stephen Parrish (Ithaca, N.Y.: Cornell University Press, 1994), 63.
3. It needs to be said that the intonational emphasis on Kiltartan is contrastive: "*My* country is Kiltartan Cross, / *My* countrymen Kiltartan's poor" (i.e., "My country is *not* Britain, in whose armed forces I have enlisted"). Similarly, "or" needs to be said pointedly: "No likely end could bring them loss / *Or* leave them happier than before." It doesn't matter to Kiltartan how Great Britain fares.
4. W. B. Yeats, *The Variorum Edition of the Poems,* ed. Peter Allt and Russell K. Alspach (New York: Macmillan, 1940; 4th printing, 1968). Subsequent quotations of poems from this volume will be identified by page number alone following the poem.
5. Yeats thought of substituting "The lone impulse of my delight," but thought better of it, probably on both musical and tonal grounds.
6. For confirmation that the poem concerns Olivia Shakespear, see the letters of Yeats to Shakespear of December 16 [1929], #5327, and October 24 [1933], #5956.
7. *Words for Music Perhaps:* Manuscript Materials, by W. B. Yeats, ed. David R. Clark (Ithaca, N.Y.: Cornell University Press, 1999), 491–497. Here, as elsewhere, I have lightly regularized the manuscript for intelligibility.
8. By the time he writes "Blood and the Moon," Yeats has understood that not even decrepitude can confer wisdom: "For wisdom is the property of the dead, / A something incompatible with life."

9. *E & I*, 521–522.

10. #3204 (March 28, 1917): "Please be very careful with the Rebellion poem" (enclosing an early version of "Easter 1916").

11. Roy Foster, *W. B. Yeats: A Life*, 2 vols. (Oxford: Oxford University Press, 1997, 2003), II, 63. Hereafter the biography is cited parenthetically as Foster. Foster draws Maud's remark from Anna MacBride White and A. Norman Jeffares, eds., *The Gonne-Yeats Letters, 1893–1938: Always Your Friend* (London: Hutchinson, 1992), 384.

12. In the extant manuscripts the distinction between stanza 3 and the other stanzas is present from the beginning. See *Michael Robartes and the Dancer*: Manuscript Materials, by W. B. Yeats, ed Thomas Parkinson with Anne Brannen (Ithaca, N. Y.: Cornell University Press, 1994), 69–87. In the drafts for the poem, the individual stanzas are prefaced by Roman numerals. Perhaps Yeats decided that the poem was not a sequence in the sense that his Roman-numeraled poems normally are—that it is governed not by different meditations on various aspects of the case, but rather by the single conflict between ideological fixity and the fluency of natural life.

13. That Yeats realized that only *active* versions of the verb "to change" could appear in this stanza is evident in his work on this line. He had at first written, of the shadow of cloud, that it "Changes minute by minute"; then, wanting variation perhaps, he crossed out "Changes" and wrote above it "Is changed minute by minute." Then, realizing he had thereby ruined his central contrast between changing and being changed, he crossed out "Is changed," and put *stet* next to his original, active "Changes." See draft, *Michael Robartes and the Dancer*, Manuscript Materials, 73.

14. Yeats had first written "Can petrify the heart." His wish always to make his abstractions concrete and his language "natural" leads him to substitute an actual "stone" for the Latinate abstract verb.

15. Warwick Gould has suggested to me that there are closer, Irish, sources for the phrase "a terrible beauty." In the letter (#2950) in which Yeats says "I am trying to write a poem on the men executed; terrible beauty has been born again," he adds that Maud Gonne's "main thought" about the event "seems to be tragic dignity has returned to Ireland." The "terrible beauty" of the plot of Wilde's "The Doer of Good" is remarked on by Yeats in *Autobiographies*, ed. William H. O'Donnell and Douglas N. Archibald (New York: Scribner, 1999), 224. Gould cites as "the closest example" of Irish use of "terrible beauty" Sheridan Le Fanu's poem "The Legend of the Glaive" (*Dublin University Magazine*, February 1816, 210–216); the lines in question (216) read:

> Fionula the Cruel, the brightest, the worst,
> With a terrible beauty the vision accurst
> Gold filleted, sandalled, of times dead and gone—
> Far looking, and harking, pursuing, goes on.

"The Legend of the Glaive," Gould adds, was included in Stopford A. Brooke and T. W. Rolleston, eds., *A Treasury of Irish Poetry* (New York and London:

Macmillan, 1900), a volume to which Yeats was a contributor. My preference for Blake as Yeats's source for the phrase, whenever he used it (without entirely discounting Le Fanu), is that in Le Fanu the context is erotic, not political. Gonne's phrase, "tragic dignity," although it has a superficial resemblance to "terrible beauty," puts the aesthetic word first, the moral one second; but Blake's and Yeats's phrases put the moral word first ("fearful" and "terrible") and the aesthetic word second ("symmetry" and "beauty"). The parallel seems to me to make a strong case for a reminiscence of Blake's Tyger, that revolutionary creature.

16. Yeats included "The Wearing of the Green" in the "anonymous" section of his 1895 *A Book of Irish Verse,* while noting that "This is not the most ancient form of the ballad, but it is the form into which it was recast by Boucicault, and which has long taken the place of all others." See the modern reprint of Yeats's anthology with a new introduction by John Banville (London: Routledge, 2002), 162, 176.

17. The number symbolism was pointed out to me by my Ph.D. student at Harvard, Nathan Rose.

18. Warwick Gould queries the theory of number symbolism, seeing the 16-line and 24-line lengths of the stanzas as merely a mathematical consequence of the poem's being written in quatrains. He notes that the number symbolism proffered here does not explain why both the 16-line and the 24-line stanzas are repeated, alternately. I can give no answer except to say that the reiteration impresses on the reader the inequality in stanza-length, and might provoke a question about why the stanzas employ this number of lines here, that number there. I cannot find that Yeats uses in any other lyric the technique of alternating matching stanzas of unequal length.

## II. Antechamber and Afterlife

1. As we saw in Chapter I, Yeats originally affixed Roman numerals to the stanzas of "Easter 1916," but then removed them, I believe because an emphasis on four-partness would obscure the fundamentally binary conflict of the poem—that between ideological fixity and natural fluency.

2. Yeats's well-known rearrangement of the order of the stanzas in "The Wild Swans at Coole" changes entirely the implicit argument of the poem. (The same is true, for example, of Harriet Monroe's changes in the order of Wallace Stevens's "Sunday Morning.")

3. As has been frequently remarked, the whole of "Sailing to Byzantium" is in dialogue with Keats's "Ode to a Nightingale"; the dialogue is established by the echoes in Yeats of Keats's "bird," "generations," "passing," and "Emperor":

> Thou wast not born for death, immortal Bird!
> No hungry generations tread thee down;
> The voice I hear this passing night was heard
> In ancient days by Emperor and clown[.]

Yeats changes the pathos of Keats's adjective in "passing night" to something objective, when he refers to himself as the detached commentator on what is "passing" instead of writing "what is past, or present, or to come," the more natural series.

4. Warwick Gould points out to me that "hammered gold and gold enamelling" is "an extraordinary sonic form of chiasmus, whereby the inner symmetry is that of the repeated word 'gold' and the outer [brackets] are purely sonic: 'hammer[ed]' and 'ename[lling].'"

5. Warwick Gould argues that one can see stanza III as an intermediate zone in which the speaker's heart is "consumed away" in order to be alchemized into gold, and that the sages have become (as they were asked to be) the speaker's "singing masters," enabling him to sing as the golden bird. "So, 'once out of nature' seems to express the state after 'alchemical' purgation by the holy fire and the sages and before refashioning as a singing artefact," says Gould. I can see the logic of fire and singing masters producing gold and singing, but it does not seem to me that Yeats would have suggested alchemical transformation by the intensive verb "consume away" (rather than, for example, "transmute") nor can I think that one can "progress" from the artifice of eternity to the artifice of time. Once in eternity, one stays there.

6. The late Professor Oliver Edwards of Queen's University, Belfast, once recited, at the Yeats International Summer School at Sligo, "Byzantium" as it was enunciated by Yeats (who, at Edwards's impassioned request, had read it aloud to him several times). What was most striking in Edwards's rendition was its resonance: the depth, fullness, and slowness of the Yeatsian vowels, the rolling of the "r's," and the prolongation of final consonants. The final line sounded out all of these: "That dollphinnn toorrrnnn, that gonggg-tooorrrmennted sea."

7. In answer to a letter from T. Sturge Moore, Yeats wrote on October 4 [1930], (#5390):

> My dear Sturge-Moore
> Yes I have decided to call the book "Byzantium". I enclose the poem from which the name is taken, hoping that it may suggest symbolism for the cover. The poem originates from a criticism of yours. You objected to the last verse of "Sailing to Byzantium" because a bird made by a goldsmith was just as natural as anything else. That showed me that the idea needed exposition.

8. Plotinus, *The Enneads,* trans. Stephen MacKenna, 3rd ed. revised by B. S. Page (London: Faber and Faber, 1962), 16–17.

9. The Poussin painting formerly thought to represent the marriage of Peleus and Thetis has been retitled as *Acis and Galatea.*

10. On February 6, 1938, replying to Dorothy Wellesley about her poem "The Shell," Yeats wrote, "It is charming and profound and full of good words—eyebright, Pangloss, formality, copulate" (#7175).

11. See *CL* I, 411, and George Bornstein, "Remaking Himself: Yeats's Revisions of

His Early Canon," TEXT: *Transactions of the Society for Textual Scholarship* (1991), 339–358; the cited passage is on p. 348.

12. Letter of June 30, 1932, to Olivia Shakespear (#5692).

13. Tzvetan Todorov, *The Poetics of Prose,* trans. Richard Howard (Ithaca, N.Y.: Cornell University Press, 1977), 245.

14. "Yeats's Byzantium Poems: A Study of Their Development," in *Yeats: A Collection of Critical Essays,* ed. John Unterecker (Englewood Cliffs, N.J.: Prentice-Hall, 1963), 93–130. This is a revised version of Bradford's original essay by the same name in *PMLA* 75 (March 1960), 110–125. He is, I believe, mistaken in his interpretation of "Sailing to Byzantium" when he says that Yeats has his protagonist "beseech the sages to . . . enter the gyre again in order that they . . . may help him . . . enter the 'artifice of eternity,' help him, that is, to become a golden bird singing on a golden bough" (112). This is a frequent mistake. Why would holy sages want a human being to turn into a golden bird? The protagonist, as I say above, asks the sages to make him of their company, to gather him up to where they are, in God's holy fire—not to make him a denizen of the Emperor's palace. It is interesting that the "sages" were once "saints and apostles," or "saints and martyrs" (or even an "angel") in the mosaic: "Saints and apostles in the gold of a wall / Symbolic of God's love await my prayer" (101). It is revealing that Yeats suspected that his prayer to become holy would remain unanswered: "As if God's love will refuse my prayer" (101). Various cancellations in Yeats's drafts show his revulsion from the fixed ideology of religious sages: "Make me what you were . . . Rigid, abstracted, and fanatical" . . . (cancelled in favor of "Unwavering, indifferent, and fanatical," which is in its turn cancelled in favor of "Unfaltering, indifferent, fanatical" (102–104). The drafts that Bradford cites may be seen fully in W. B. Yeats, *The Tower:* Manuscript Materials, ed. Richard J. Finneran with Jared Curtis and Ann Saddlemyer (Ithaca, N.Y.: Cornell University Press, 2006).

## III. The Puzzle of Sequence

1. See Yeats's note (827) on "Meditations in Time of Civil War": "These *poems* were written at Thoor Ballylee . . . The sixth *poem* is called *The Stare's Nest by My Window* . . . In the second stanza of the seventh *poem* occur the words 'Vengeance upon the murderers'" (italics mine).

2. *L*, 668. Hillis Miller, in *The Linguistic Moment: From Wordsworth to Stevens* (Princeton: Princeton University Press, 1985), sees the whole sequence as a manifestation of the whirling of the gyres, as image succeeds image in rapid succession. Whether all of the sections whirl deconstructively around "an absent center" seems more debatable; Yeats's center—atrocity through the ages—is all too present.

3. Foster, II, 193 n. 83.

4. *W. B. Yeats: The Poems,* ed. Daniel Albright (London: J. M. Dent, 1990), 651.

5. *Lady Gregory's Journals*, 2 vols., ed. Daniel J. Murphy (Gerrards Cross: Colin Smythe, 1978), I, 197.

6. Compare the slightly more extended account of the Troubles around Kiltartan Cross in Yeats's address to the dead Robert Gregory in "Reprisals":

> Half-drunk or whole-mad soldiery
> Are murdering your tenants there.
> Men that revere your father yet
> Are shot at on the open plain.
> Where may new-married women sit
> And suckle children now? Armed men
> May murder them in passing by
> Nor law nor parliament take heed. (791)

7. Dame Alice Kyteler was accused, in 1324–25, "of being at the head of a band of sorcerers in the city of Kilkenny, and of offering sacrifice to demons. Her incubus, to whom she had made the sacrifice of nine red cocks and nine peacocks' eyes, sometimes made his appearance as a cat or black dog, sometimes as a black man." See W. B. Yeats, *Mythologies*, ed. Warwick Gould and Deirdre Toomey (London: Macmillan, 2005), 289 n. 7; hereafter cited as *Myth*. Yeats's note in the *Variorum* (433) adds, "My last symbol, Robert Artisson, was an evil spirit much run after in Kilkenny at the start of the fourteenth century."

8. Jeffares, following Henn (*NC*, 234), speculates that Yeats, in collectivizing Salome's dance into the dance of "the daughters of Herodias," may have been prompted not only by the medieval naming of the Sidhe, who, as Yeats noted in *The Wind Among the Reeds*, "journey in whirling winds that were called the dance of the daughters of Herodias in the Middle Ages" (800), but also by Arthur Symons's poem "The Dance of the Daughters of Herodias." Warwick Gould suggests to me that Symons's poem "may take its title from Yeats's preoccupation with this subject as in the note to *The Wind Among the Reeds* rather than the other way around."

9. Warwick Gould finds here an allusion to Richard II (2.1.72): "What comfort, man? How is't with aged Gaunt?"

10. He turns to it again for part II ("My House") of "Meditations in Time of Civil War." There, it is composed in a vortex-structure, in which external features of Ballylee (bridge, farmhouse, acre of ground) lead (in stanza 2) to entering the tower, going up the winding stair, finding a chamber and its fireplace, and finally, at the narrowed point of the vortex, stopping at "A candle and a written page." This "gyre-structure" is repeated, in reverse, to show Yeats's literary ancestry, beginning with the single figure of Milton's "Platonist" toiling "in some like chamber," and widening out to the "benighted travellers" passing outside who see his "lighted candle glimmering." The third vortex in the poem is one of time, not space: it begins with the ancient founder of the tower among his score of men; descends to Yeats, the present occupant; and at its narrowest point looks forward to his "bodily heirs." The vortex may be seen as a version of the labyrinth and of the gyre.

11. It might seem that line 9 of the Loie Fuller stanza has four beats, not three; but a glance at the other stanzas of this pattern reveals that Yeats always intends lines 6, 7, 8, and 9 to be trimeters. The correct scansion is probably "**All** men are **dan**cers and their **tread**."

12. "All Souls' Night" was written in November 1920; Yeats began the composition of "Nineteen Hundred and Nineteen" on April 9, 1921. See #3899 and #3900.

13. Recall two other Yeatsian uses of the word "labyrinth": "The labyrinth of her days" ("Against Unworthy Praise") and "the labyrinth of another's being" ("The Tower," II, line 112).

14. These include *bronze/bronzed; old wrong/new right and wrong/the old; habits/ habit; thought, thought, thought/thoughts/thought; triumph/triumph; solitude/soli- tary/solitude/solitude; break/break; vanishes/vanish/vanish; dragon-ridden/dragon; traffic/traffic; work/master-work/works; show/show; shriek/shrieked; winds/ winds/wind/wind/wind/wind/wind/wind; labyrinth/labyrinth; image/image/ imagined/images; eyes/eyes; sun's/sun.* This list does not mention all the internal repetitions within single poems, which are numerous; it gives only repetitions *across* from one poem in the sequence to another.

15. See Ben Jonson's verse-preface to his *Epigrams*, "To My Book":

    > It will be looked for, booke, when some but see
    >> Thy title, *Epigrammes*, and nam'd of me,
    > Thou should'st be bold, licentious, full of gall,
    >> Wormewood and sulphure, sharp and tooth'd withal,
    > Become a petulant thing, hurle ink, and wit
    >> As mad-men stones: not caring whom they hit.

    *Poems*, ed. George Burke Johnston (Cambridge, Mass.: Harvard University Press, 1960), 7.

16. The categories appear as well in lines 81–83 of Shelley's "Mont Blanc," in which the mountain's voice is "Not understood / By all, but which the wise, and great, and good / Interpret."

17. Derek Attridge, perhaps unaware of this venture of Yeats into a backwards- ballad stanza (with an added line), invents (for his catalogue of rhythms) a 3-4- 3-4 stanza, and comments, "It's an invented example, since such stanzas don't occur normally in the tradition. . . . The movement of the stanza is ungainly. . . . If we rearrange the lines [so as to give a 4-3-4-3 stanza], they take on the fa- miliar lilt which tells us immediately that we're reading a deeply-ingrained rhythmic structure." See his *Poetic Rhythm: An Introduction* (Cambridge: Cam- bridge University Press, 1995), 61.

18. Warwick Gould argues that Yeats would ascribe the human practice of vio- lence not to sexual desire but to "belief in the supernatural," citing the passage in *Autobiographies* (ed. O'Donnell and Archibald, 298–299) in which Yeats recalls accompanying Lady Gregory "from cottage to cottage collecting folklore":

    > My object was to find actual experience of the supernatural, for I did not
    > believe, nor do I now, that it is possible to discover in the text-books of the

schools, in the manuals sold by religious booksellers, even in the subtle reverie of saints, the most violent force in history.

Yeats's scenes in part VI of "Nineteen Hundred and Nineteen" are indeed expressed with the "supernatural" symbols of the Sidhe, the Daughters of Herodias, and Robert Artisson; but the hand attempting to touch one of the daughters, and Alice Kyteler in her subjection to her incubus, are human beings motivated by sexual desire.

19. It is also the mode with which Yeats decides to end "Meditations in Time of Civil War." There, too, he has a tripartite vision, as his subtitle tells us: "I See Phantoms of Hatred and of the Heart's Fullness and of the Coming Emptiness." The Phantoms of Hatred are medieval Templars crying for vengeance on the murderers of their Grand Master, Jacques Molay; the Phantoms of the Heart's Fullness are female figures riding upon unicorns, who represent the moment (Phase 14) when "all thought becomes an image" ("The Phases of the Moon"); the Phantoms of the Coming Emptiness are brazen hawks whose wings have put out the moon; these hawks are symbols, according to Yeats, of "the straight road of logic, and so of mechanism" (827). But after this tripartite vision, Yeats adds—as he does not in "Nineteen Hundred and Nineteen"—a personal postscript. He turns away from the local soldiers representing the life of action, and recommits himself to his poetic vocation: "The abstract joy, / The half-read wisdom of demonic images, / Suffice the ageing man as once the growing boy." Since this closing statement does not adopt a new form, but is included within the hexameter octaves of Yeats's tripartite vision, it does not undo the visionary Romance-mode that ends the sequence. The resemblance of the close of "Meditations" to the ending of the later "Nineteen Hundred and Nineteen" is striking, although by closing "Nineteen Hundred and Nineteen" with "Romance" pentameter sixains, Yeats distinguishes it from "Meditations," with its "Renaissance" hexameter octaves *(ababcdcd).*

20. "My Table," part III of "Meditations," written in the same strange measure as "Demon and Beast" (4-4-3-3, *aabb*), breaks the pattern of resemblance to "Nineteen Hundred and Nineteen." The 32 lines of part III appear as one unbroken block (while the 50-line "Demon and Beast" is divided into stanzas of unequal length). Because "Demon and Beast" adds a two-line 4-4 coda, it exhibits a more stable close than "My Table."

21. The drafts of "Blood and the Moon" show that part I was originally in tetrameter, and part III in hexameter. Yeats quickly decided on the non-linear *abba* rhyme scheme for part I, but the pentameter for part III was longer in arriving. Part II always had its "spiring" staircase-shape in ungainly tercets. See *The Winding Stair* (1929): Manuscript Materials by W. B. Yeats, ed. David R. Clark (Ithaca, N.Y.: Cornell University Press, 1995), 61–99.

22. Warwick Gould recalls that in Yeats's tale *Rosa Alchemica*, Swift and his ilk were to be found "joking and railing" on the staircase of the narrator's house in Dublin. See *Myth*, 179.

23. The pictorial quality of this statement may recall Blake's engraving of a long

ladder reaching from earth toward the moon, with the caption referring to the cry of the child at the foot of the ladder yearning for the moon: "I want! I want!"

24. It may not be too fanciful to think that Yeats is here reversing George Herbert's famous window-looks in "The Elixir," which Yeats had imitated in his look at and through the mosaic in "Sailing to Byzantium":

> A man may look on glass,
> And on it stay his eye,
> Or if he pleaseth, through it pass,
> And then the heaven espy.

In "Blood and the Moon," Yeats, dissatisfied with espying the heaven and its moon, chooses to "stay his eye" on the surface; he replaces Herbert's stained glass with the multicolored butterflies. (In one of his more creative spellings in the drafts, Yeats refers to "tortashel" butterflies, proving how much the sound, rather than the derivation, of words mattered to him.)

25. Yeats was originally unwilling to give unequivocal glory to the lunar light. In the drafts, we read two antitheses: "Wisdom has no stain, / Whether a crescent or a waning moon, / Whether unclouded, or in clouds beset" (*WS*, 95). If the moon is "waning," or "beset" by clouds, it might seem diminished in power, even in its own celestial realm. In "Blood and the Moon," Yeats finally decides that there can be no commerce between ideal power and political power: the moon remains full and unstained, the tower is irremediably tainted by blood.

## IV. "Magical" Techniques in the Early Poems

1. This chapter, the first written of this book, was called into being when Warwick Gould devoted an issue of the *Yeats Annual* to the commemoration of Richard Ellmann, and asked me to be a contributor. In the event, illness intervened and my essay was printed one issue after the commemorative one, but it was still dedicated to that genial and learned and generous man, a dedication I want to repeat here. As I say in my Acknowledgments, Richard Ellmann was the anonymous reader of my first book on Yeats, and he kindly allowed the publisher to use (and attribute to him) some of his remarks as jacket copy. Dick and I were acquaintances for years, and I always felt better after having encountered him. The last time I saw him was at Oxford, when he invited me to dinner at New College. He never seemed more in his element, or happier. Whenever I teach or write on Yeats, I recall with admiration his pioneering and gifted scholarship, and I remember my continuing gratitude for his sponsorship of my first work.

2. Marjorie Perloff, *Rhyme and Meaning in the Poetry of W. B. Yeats* (The Hague: Mouton, 1970), *passim*.

3. Samuel Taylor Coleridge, "Epitaph," *Poems*, ed. Ernest Hartley Coleridge (London: Oxford University Press, 1961), 491–492.

4. William Shakespeare, *Timon of Athens*, ed. H. J. Oliver (London: Methuen, 1959); see the editor's note on p. 140. The fact that Plutarch says that the last portion of the epitaph was written by Callimachus would also have recommended it to Yeats's attention. In a May 18, 1938, letter (#7239) Yeats compares himself, writing *On the Boiler*, to Timon: "It looks to me as if I may spend my remaining life . . . in a fierce Timon like propaganda."

5. *Last Poems: Manuscript Materials*, ed. James Pethica (Ithaca, N.Y.: Cornell University Press, 1997), xxxvi–xli.

6. In its appearance as a proem to *The Celtic Twilight*, printed in italics, the last three lines read: "But, kindly old rout / Of the fire-born moods, / You pass not away." Though he rightly dropped the "kindly" which damages the sublimity of the moods, Yeats preserved in revision the double nature of the seven-line form. See *Myth*, 433.

7. From the 1895 essay "The Moods," *E & I*, 195.

8. The much-worked drafts of "The Song of Wandering Aengus" show Yeats, in his revisions, always moving toward a closer "magical" connection between words, deleting non-alliterating words in favor of alliterating ones, or deleting nonce words in favor of the repetition of earlier words. See *The Wind Among the Reeds: Manuscript Materials of W. B. Yeats*, ed. Carolyn Holdsworth (Ithaca, N.Y.: Cornell University Press, 1993), 56–57.

## V. Tales, Feelings, Farewells

1. I refer the reader to *The New Princeton Encyclopedia of Poetry and Poetics*, ed. Alex Preminger and T. V. F. Brogan (Princeton: Princeton University Press, 1993). Under "Ballad Meter," the *Encyclopedia* (118–120) reads as follows, much condensed:

> The nature of the ballad meter had been the subject of much dispute. . . . One may say that all its varieties are based on a quatrain of lines each having 4 stresses (or 3) rhyming abcb or abab. . . . Much influenced by the common alternation of stress and slack in the *later* ballads, Stewart (G. R. Stewart, Jr., *Modern Metrical Technique as Illustrated by Ballad Meter* [1700–1920]) considers all ballad meter essentially foot verse and treats variations under such rubrics as trisyllabic substitution and monosyllabic feet. . . . Treating ballad meter as accentual verse is intuitively appealing, for the isochronism of the line is apparent in a great many cases. . . .
>
> Another set of terms for ballad meter was developed out of the metrical psalter tradition. . . . Though terms vary somewhat, the following are traditional (numbers denote stresses per line): Long Meter: 4-4-4-4; Common Meter: 4-3-4-3; Short Meter: 3-3-4-3; and (rarely) Half Meter: 3-3-3-3. . . . Those scholars who accept either the musical or accentual origin of ballad meter have ensured the symmetry of the whole typology by inserting a *metrical pause* . . . for the missing fourth stresses in the 3-stress lines. . . . Common Meter is thus:

X / X / X / X /
X / X / X / (p)
X / X / X / X /
X / X / X / (p).

2. In these early ballads, a trimeter is sometimes substituted in place of a tetrameter, as the *Princeton Encylopedia* mentions.

3. As late as 1936, Yeats defended regular rhyme in ballads: "In narrative verse we want to concentrate the attention on the fact or the story, not on the form. The form must be present as something we all accept—'the fundamental sing-song.' I do not know a single example of good narrative where the rhyme scheme is varied" (#6619, letter of July 21, 1936, to Dorothy Wellesley).

4. I read the meter in "The Blessed" as dactylic rather than anapestic because the stressed syllables usher in a downbeat: "O | **bless**edness | **comes** in the | **night** and the | **day**." The anapestic version would read: "O **bless**- | edness **comes** | in the **night** | and the **day**." In either reading, the lilt is patent.

5. Lane, an art dealer and collector, and Augusta Gregory's nephew, drowned when the *Lusitania* was torpedoed on May 7, 1915. The ballads alluding to the Lane controversy include "To a Wealthy Man" and "To a Friend Whose Work Has Come to Nothing" (discussed in Chapter VII). Another poem, "To a Shade," which alludes to the Lane affair although addressed to Parnell, is written in "heroic" (pentameter) quatrains, rhyming *abab;* but the quatrains are printed in a solid block, without stanza breaks. The Lane affair is elegiacally commemorated in the *ottava rima* of "The Municipal Gallery Revisited."

6. Warwick Gould points out to me the ancestor of "September 1913," Thomas Davis's street-ballad "The Green Above the Red," in Davis's *National and Historical Ballads, Songs, and Poems: A New and Revised Edition* (Dublin: James Duffy and Sons, 1876), 190–192:

> Sure 'twas for this Lord Edward died, and Wolfe Tone sunk serene—
> Because they could not bear to leave the Red above the Green;
> And 'twas for this that Owen fought, and Sarsfield nobly bled—
> Because their eyes were hot to see the Green above the Red.

Gould adds: "The reuse [by Yeats] of tropes familiar from Davis's poem shows a shrewd rhetorical strategy of cultural inclusiveness. But it also extends the noble concept of the wild geese well beyond its original metaphorical sense of Irish soldiers fighting in Irish regiments to a more inclusive embrace of more recent exiles and expatriates. And it dares ask for closure: 'But let them be, they're dead and gone.'"

7. "The Dolls" is one of a set of paired poems (like the Byzantium and Oracle poems we have already seen) in which Yeats treats the "same" subject in formally different styles; its companion poem is "The Magi." The two poems were written on the same day (*NC,* 126), and from *Responsibilities* until the 1933 *Collected Poems* they were published together as a single sequence, with Roman numerals I and II before their respective titles.

8. Why does Yeats insist on the extra syllable constructing (by means of the final

trochee) a nine-syllable line in positions 1 and 3 of the stanza in lieu of the ex-
pected octosyllabic lines that would match the other lines of the stanza? He
does it, I believe, in part to link line 1 directly with line 2 and line 3 with line 4,
using the "extra" syllable to bridge the pause between the lines. This practice
serves to distinguish the syllabic pattern of the quatrain that opens each stanza
(9-8-9-8) from the "pure" octosyllabic couplet (8-8) that concludes each stanza
("hour" and "tower" in lines 11–12 are of course monosyllabic in British pro-
nunciation). The stanzas of "Under the Round Tower" could be said, then, to
take on, as we hear them, the following form, with the two purely octosyllabic
lines conferring a final mimetic spin on the dance:

> Of golden king and silver lady, Bellowing up and bellowing round,
> Till toes mastered a sweet measure, Mouth mastered a sweet sound,
> Prancing round and prancing up
> Until they pranced upon the top.

9. David Clark points out, in his introduction to *Words for Music Perhaps and Other Poems*: Manuscript Materials by W. B. Yeats (Ithaca, N.Y.: Cornell University Press, 1999), xliv, that in the initial printing of "A Man Young and Old" in *The Tower* (1928), the closing chorus from *Oedipus at Colonus* does not appear within the sequence. However, it follows the sequence in *The Tower* (separated from it only by "The Three Monuments").

10. Line 5 of each of the two sixains of this poem contains a singsong "folk-song" internal rhyme ("away/stay" and "alone/stone"). This feature does not occur anywhere else in "A Man Young and Old."

11. David R. Clark, ed., *The Winding Stair* (1929): Manuscript Materials (Ithaca, N.Y.: Cornell University Press, 1995), xxvi.

12. Ibid., xxvi.

13. These are, in their great variety: "Her Triumph," an alternating-rhyme pentam-eter douzain; "Parting," an aubade dialogue-"sonnet" of interwoven trimeter rhymes; "Her Vision in the Wood" in *ottava rima*; "From the 'Antigone'" in ir-regularly rhymed tetrameter stanzas of varying lengths (6 lines; 7 lines; 3 lines); and "Chosen," which is written in an irregular nine-line stanza adapted from Donne. Yeats's three-part *rhyme-scheme* in the stanzas of "Chosen" is identical to that of Donne in "A Nocturnall on St. Lucie's Day": in both, an opening em-braced quatrain *(abba)* is followed by a tercet *(ccc)*, followed by a couplet *(dd)*. But Yeats introduces a noticeable change in *line-length*. Donne's line-lengths for these three parts are as follows: 5-5-4-4, 3-5-5, 5-5; Yeats, when he arrives at the middle tercet, makes each line grow by a foot, 3-4-5. Yeats wishes to imitate, in this departure, the swelling and subsidence of sexual climax, as it builds in the 3-4-5 of the tercet and subsides in the 5-5 stability of the closing pentameter couplet. In the first of the two stanzas, the crescendo of desire in the woman, rising to "breast," is interrupted by the departure of her sun-lover:

> Scarce sank he from the west                    (3)
> Or found a subterranean rest                     (4)

> On the maternal midnight of my breast            (5)
> Before I had marked him on his northern way,     (5)
> And seemed to stand although in bed I lay.       (5)

But in the second stanza, the climax is implicitly allowed its entire unfolding, from arousal to union to the depicted completion in stillness:

>           . . . I take
> That stillness for a theme              (3)
> Where his heart my heart did seem      (4)
> And both adrift on the miraculous stream    (5)
> Where—wrote a learned astrologer—           (5)
> The Zodiac is changed into a sphere.          (5)

The "growth in length" of successive lines is also visible in the nonce form of "An Image from a Past Life," written in seven-line stanzas *(abcccab)* scanned 5-4-2-3-4-5.

14. See Clark, ed., *The Winding Stair,* Introduction, xix–xxvi, for remarks on the "contemporaneity and interpenetration" (xx) of the two sequences.

15. For "Crazy Jane on the King" (in eight-line tetrameter stanzas rhyming *aabcddcb* and with the refrain, *"May the devil take King George"*) see Clark, ed., *Words for Music Perhaps: Manuscript Materials,* 579–603.

16. See *Letters on Poetry from W. B. Yeats to Dorothy Wellesley* (London: Oxford University Press, 1964), 69–82. Hereafter cited as *DWL.*

17. The Chambermaid's adjectives (in an earlier draft) are memorably defended by Yeats in answer to Dorothy Wellesley's flinching: "The worm is right," he replies, "its repulsiveness is right—so are the adjectives—'dull', 'limp', 'thin', 'bare', all suggested by the naked body of the man, & taken with the worm by that body abject & helpless. All suggest [the chambermaid's] detachment, her 'cold breast', her motherlike prayer" (#6731). Yeats dropped "thin" and "bare" in his final version of "The Chambermaid's Second Song." For versions of the earlier drafts sent to Wellesley and Ethel Mannin in November 1936, see *L,* 867–870, and #6717, 6716, 6722, and 6733.

18. The convergence in Yeats's sequence of the refrain *"Lord have mercy on us"* and a persistent set of dimeters may remind some readers of Nashe's dimeter lament in time of plague: "Adieu, farewell, earth's bliss"; Yeats's lover's opening lines, rhyming "air" and "where," may be unconsciously recalling Nashe's most famous lines:

> Brightness falls from the air,
> Queens have died young and fair;
> Dust hath closed Helen's eye.
> I am sick, I must die.
>      Lord, have mercy on us.

19. Warwick Gould tells me that this expression (and therefore the Lady's song, in part) derives from the bawdy *ballade* "The Hay Hotel" by Oliver S. John Gogarty. Its closing stanza, preceding the envoi, runs:

> Where is Piano Mary, say,
> Who dwelt where Hell's Gates leave the street,
> And all the tunes she used to play
> Along your spine beneath the sheet?
> She was a morsel passing sweet
> And warmer than the gates of hell.
> Who tunes her now between the feet?
> Go ask them at the Hay Hotel.

(A. Norman Jeffares, *The Poems and Plays of Oliver S. John Gogarty* [Gerrards Cross: Colin Smythe, 2001], 302.)

It will be seen that Yeats (rhyming in couplets without white space) did not borrow Gogarty's rhymes *(ababbcbc)* nor his stanzas. The resemblance is confined to Yeats's line, "And he plays tunes between your feet." Yeats knew such poems by Gogarty, writing to Olivia Shakespear (of "The Old Pianist") that it was "one of those many poems on which [Gogarty's] fame depends, poems that pass by word of mouth, & are only written down by some chance. Obscene & yet full of tragic poetry" (#5942).

20. For the drafts and the alternate titles of "Three Marching Songs" (which began life as "Three Songs to the Same Tune"), see *Last Poems:* Manuscript Materials by W. B. Yeats, ed. James Pethica (Ithaca, N.Y.: Cornell University Press, 1997), 149–187. Remarks on intermingled drafts of "The Black Tower" can be found on pp. 175 and 181. The title "Three Revolutionary Songs" appears on p. 150.

21. See A. Norman Jeffares, *W. B. Yeats: Man and Poet* (London: Kyle Cathie, 1996), 337 n. 4.

22. Foster, II, 648.

23. Foster, II, 648–649, quoting an "abandoned fragment" of a draft of "The Black Tower," says it "makes the approach of [Yeats's] own death manifest," but does not apply that interpretation to the finished poem.

24. "Easter 1916" is and is not a ballad. Its Half-Meter trimeters, its *abab* rhyme scheme, and its refrain pull it within the ballad sphere of influence, but its refusal to separate its quatrains, its departures from ballad diction, and its omission of the refrain after its third stanza (among other features) keep us from thinking of it purely as a ballad.

25. It should be noted, however, that the old cook—who swears the king is still living—adds another dimension to the poem. Seamus Heaney says of the poem and its men, "The ironist and questioner is their old cook, who represents a kind of unheroic life force, a scuttling principle of survival and self-preservation. . . . Yet the cook's thoroughly creditable skepticism is resisted by the *comitatus;* they persist at their post even as they are pestered by his rumours and heckling." See *The Place of Writing* (Atlanta: Scholars Press, 1989), 34.

26. *The Book of Irish Ballads* and *The Songs of Ireland,* ed. D. F. McCarthy and Michael J. Barry (Dublin: James Duffy, 1848), 36–37.

## VI. Troubling the Tradition

1. It can be found in *The Early Poetry*, II, ed. George Bornstein (Ithaca, N.Y.: Cornell University Press, 1994), 361.
2. Warwick Gould called my attention to the allusion to Shelley.
3. *CL*, I, 3.
4. I have reprinted Yeats's first wording, from *The Countess Kathleen* (1892).
5. Here is the original Ronsard poem:

> Quand vous serez bien vieille, au soir, à la chandelle,
> Assise auprès du feu, dévidant et filant,
> Direz, chantant mes vers, en vous émerveillant:
> Ronsard me célébrait du temps que j'étais belle.
>
> Lors vous n'aurez servante oyant telle nouvelle,
> Déja sous le labeur à demi someillant,
> Qui au bruit de mon nom ne s'aille réveillant,
> Bénissant votre nom de louange immortelle.
>
> Je serai sous la terre et fantôme sans os,
> Par les ombres myrteux je prendrai mon repos:
> Vous serez au foyer une vieille accroupie,
> Regrettant mon amour et votre fier dédain.
> Vivez, si m'en croyez, n'attendez à demain:
> Cueillez dès aujourd'hui les roses de la vie.
>
> *(Sonnets pour Hélène,* 1587)

In English translation, the Ronsard sonnet would read:

> When you are very old, at evening, seated by the fire,
> Spinning and winding wool by the light of a candle,
> You will say, reciting my verses, in wonderment,
> "Ronsard celebrated me when I was beautiful."
> Then not one among your servants, hearing this word,
> Though already half-sleeping at her work,
> But will stir to waking at the sound of my name,
> Blessing your name with immortal praises.
>
> I shall lie underground, a ghost lacking bones;
> By myrtle shades I shall take my rest:
> You will be an old woman hunched at the hearth
> Regretting my love and your disdainful pride.
> Live for now, believe me, don't wait till tomorrow,
> Pluck from this day onward the roses of life.

6. Although Ronsard does introduce the first person, in the possessive adjective "mes," early in the poem ("Direz, chantant mes vers," etc.), that form of minor mention has nothing of the spectral force of "Je serai sous la terre." Yeats takes

care to suppress the first person, preserving impersonality in his third-person formulations, "this book" and "one man."

7. In rewriting the poem in 1925, Yeats made the girl more Homeric and created enjambment between the second and third quatrains, attempting to give the poem classical loftiness and greater momentum; he also made the final symbols more explicit—"an empty sky," "that lamentation of the leaves."

8. The article was omitted in the first printing in *The Countess Kathleen* (1892); it was inserted in the 1895 *Poems*.

9. It was printed for the first time as a separate poem in the Dramatical Poems, volume II of the 1906 *Poetical Works*, where it serves as a second proem to *The Shadowy Waters*.

10. He had been preceded in his abandoning of sonnet-rhyme by Keats, in "Oh thou whose face hath felt the Winter's wind."

11. In the original dramatic version of *The Shadowy Waters*, from which Yeats extracted this sonnet, Forgael's truncated blank-verse line is continued by a speech of Dectora's:

> *Forgael.* And from that hour he has watched over none
> But faithful lovers.
> *Dectora. (Half rising)*        Something glitters there—
> There—there—by the oar. (762)

12. Quiet and her wild heart appear elsewhere in the same 1903 volume in the narrative poem "Baile and Aillinn," in which the narrator, praising the translated lovers of the title, says: "What were our praise to them? They eat / Quiet's wild heart, like daily meat[.]"

13. Yeats considered several different titles for the poem. In *McClure's Magazine* (December 1910) it was entitled "To a Certain Country House in Time of Change," suggesting that the poem should be read as addressed to the house itself. In *The Green Helmet,* it was called "Upon a Threatened House" (which, because it did not specify the threat, could suggest terrorism rather than the threat of new legislation). The final title keeps the meditative "Upon" rather than the *viva voce* "To."

14. The drafts of the poem show that the word "luckier" (repeated in line 9 as "luck") was arrived at after some deliberation. The earlier word was "better." W. B. Yeats, *"In the Seven Woods" and "The Green Helmet and Other Poems"*: Manuscript Materials, ed. David Holdeman (Ithaca, N.Y.: Cornell University Press, 2002), 201.

15. *NC*, 94, gives the original French, but errs in saying that "the [Yeats] poem is very close to the original sonnet." On the contrary, Yeats freely invents many of his lines. The original reads, in approximate translation:

> Tyard, they blamed me, when I began to write,
> Saying I was obscure to the common people;
> But today they say that I have become the opposite,
> And that I contradict myself, speaking too vulgarly.
> You, whose labor learnedly gives birth

> To immortal books, tell me, what should I do?
> Tell me, since you know everything, how I should please
> This headstrong monster, so contrary in its judgments?
>    When I thunder in my verses, it is afraid to read me;
> When my voice deflates itself, it slanders me for that.
> Tell me by what rope, power, pincers, or nails
>    I can hold still this Proteus who changes constantly?
> Tyard, you're right, we must let it have its say,
> And laugh at it just as it laughs at us.

16. The ode opens as follows:

> Come leave the loathed Stage,
> And the more loathsome Age,
> Where pride and impudence in faction knit,
>    Usurpe the Chair of wit:
> Inditing and arraigning every day,
>    Something they call a Play.
> Let their fastidious, vaine
> Commission of the braine,
> Runne on, and rage, sweat, censure, and condemn:
> They were not made for thee, lesse thou for them.

See *Poems of Ben Jonson,* ed. George Burke Johnston (Cambridge, Mass.: Harvard University Press, 1960), 298.

17. Yeats's first "hybrid" sonnet, "The Veiled Voices and the Questions of the Dark" (1883–1884), reprinted as a reading text in William Butler Yeats, *Under the Moon: The Unpublished Early Poetry,* ed. George Bornstein (New York: Scribner, 1995), 61, is a somewhat incoherent poem, beginning "As me upon my ways the tram car whirled." The octave presents two "veiled voices"—the first that of a lonely "Pharisee" within a Shakespearean quatrain *(abab)* followed by the second voice which releases laughter over tears in a Petrarchan quatrain *(cddc);* the sestet, presenting a third "veiled voice," that of a fallen female, consists of a couplet *(ee)* followed by a Petrarchan quatrain whose inner rhymes echo the couplet *(feef).* This rhyme-scheme bestows on each of the "veiled voices" a different rhyme "enclosure." Yeats would later have seen hybrid sonnets among the "Holy Sonnets" of John Donne; he could also have encountered hybrid sonnets earlier, among Keats's poems (notably "On Sitting Down to Read *King Lear* Once Again").

18. So named in the Table of Contents for *Responsibilities and Other Poems* (1916).

19. In its first publication in *The New Statesman* (February 7, 1914), it was entitled "Notoriety / *(Suggested by a recent magazine article.)*"

20. The phrase "the dull ass's hoof" comes from the close of Jonson's *The Poetaster:*

> There's something come into my thought,
> That must, and shall be sung, high and aloofe,
> Safe from the wolves black jaw, and the dull asses hoofe.

See Ben Jonson, *Poetaster* (Workes 1616), in *English Prose Drama Full-Text Database* (Cambridge: Chadwyck-Healey, 1997).

21. Cf. "On the New Forcers of Conscience under the Long Parliament":

> Dare ye for this adjure the civil sword
> To force our consciences that Christ set free,
> And ride us with a classic hierarchy
> Taught ye by mere A. S. and Rutherford?

Milton frequently enjambs one quatrain into another, and runs the octave over the *volta*. His sestets are on the whole regularly rhymed in alternating rhymes or quatrains plus couplets, but occasionally (see "Lawrence of virtuous father virtuous son" with its sestet rhyme *cdceed*) he does not adhere to the more regular patterns. His use of proper names (including the location-name "Mile-End Green") can also be seen in "A book was writ of late called *Tetrachordon*." Yeats mentions in *Memoirs* (53), in connection with his early acquaintances with nationalists, J. F. Taylor, the barrister and orator, who "seemed to know by heart whole plays of Shakespeare and all the more famous passages in Milton," which the young Yeats must have heard him recite.

22. "'The Second Coming': Coming Second; Coming in a Second," *Irish University Review* (Spring 1992), 92–100. The citation is from pp. 94–95.

23. See W. B. Yeats, *Michael Robartes and the Dancer:* Manuscript Materials, ed. Thomas Parkinson with Anne Brannen (Ithaca, N.Y.: Cornell University Press, 1994), 151. As Curtis Bradford remarked long ago, "Though beginning a poem in the first person is a frequent practice with Yeats, it would have been more frequent still had he not in instance after instance removed his I-persona from the onset of a poem late in the process of composing it. . . . Many of Yeats's greatest poems begin with the setting of their symbolic scenes . . .; then the persona arrives, so to speak, and when he does Yeats's meditative exploration of the scene begins. . . . The type of opening chosen involves the question whether Yeats wants the point of view to be controlling, or the view itself, or both equally." See Bradford, *Yeats at Work* (Carbondale: Southern Illinois University Press, 1965), 52–53.

24. The most lengthy reading of "Leda and the Swan" is that of Elizabeth Butler Cullingford in *Gender and History in Yeats's Love Poetry* (Cambridge: Cambridge University Press, 1993), which has undergone some historicizing revision in her recent essay "Yeats and Gender" in *The Cambridge Companion to Yeats* (Cambridge: Cambridge University Press, 2006), 167–184. She finds ambiguities (e.g., in the mutuality of the sexual climax) where I do not. Yeats has taken such pains to distinguish the agents of actions by pronouns and pronominal adjectives ("he," "her") that when he drops such proprietorial forms (in "body," "that white rush," and "the strange heart") he is preparing for the unascribed phrasing, "A shudder in the loins." Cullingford is inclined to take the sonnet more literally, as a rape, than I find credible. Naturalistic commentary (treating the event as a "rape" in the human legal sense, and arguing that even if a rape victim experiences orgasm she is not "consenting" to the rape) seems to me off

the mark with respect to the situation of the poem. Zeus's right to inaugurate destiny by his chosen means is not disputed by the poem, or by Yeats's sources. And congress with the divine, as one is "caught up" into its "feathered glory" and "white rush," does not, presumably, resemble the "caught" experience of naturalistic rape. The bas-relief which was Yeats's inspiration, like most of the visual depictions of the scene, from Leonardo to Correggio, implies seduction rather than rape, as does Spenser's retelling of the story in *The Faerie Queene*, III, Canto XI, stanza 32 (called to my attention by Warwick Gould):

> Then was he turnd into a snowy Swan,
> To win faire *Leda* to his louely trade:
> O wondrous skill, and sweet wit of the man,
> That her in daffadillies sleeping made,
> From scorching heat her dainty limbs to shade:
> Whiles the proud Bird ruffling his fethers wyde,
> And brushing his faire brest, did her invade;
> She slept, yet twixt her eyelids closely spyde
> How towards her he rusht, and smiled at his pryde.

25. See W. B. Yeats, *The Tower* (1928): Manuscript Materials, ed. Richard J. Finneran with Jared Curtis and Ann Saddlemyer (Ithaca, N.Y.: Cornell University Press, 2006), 328–332. An interpretive account of some of the manuscript evidence for "Leda and the Swan" can be consulted in Thomas Parkinson, *W. B. Yeats: The Later Poetry* (Berkeley: University of California Press, 1964), 136–142.

26. In its original magazine appearances, "Meru" was printed with white space separating octave from sestet, making the poem more obviously a sonnet. However, from its first appearance in a volume (the 1934 Cuala edition of *The King of the Great Clock Tower*), the poem was printed as a solid block, giving it a suitably "Shakespearean" appearance, in spite of its internally "Italian" structural division into octave and sestet.

27. See William O'Donnell's note: "Mount Kailās (elev. 22,030 feet), in the Himalayan range, Tibet; it is called Mount Meru in the epic *Mahābhārata* and in the Vedas." W. B. Yeats, *Later Essays*, ed. William H. O'Donnell (New York: Scribner's, 1994), 375 n. 22.

## VII. The Nationalist Measure

1. Yeats's "iambic" trimeters use so many trochaic substitutions that it would sometimes seem suitable, as in "The Dolls," to represent them as "iambic/trochaic" trimeters. The reader will notice a succession of emphatic downbeats, especially in the initial foot, in such poems.

2. There are almost no irregularities in this group of poems. However, "On Woman," "Upon a Dying Lady," and "The Tower" all have a single "defective" quatrain, in which a line is "missing."

3. When trimeter quatrains occur in song, they are usually cast into an anapestic measure, often entailing feminine rhymes:

> He said that the sword had enslaved us—
> > That still at its point we must kneel—
> The liar!—though often it braved us,
> > We cross'd it with hardier steel!

("He said that he was not our brother" by John Banim, in *The Book of Irish Ballads* and *The Songs of Ireland*, ed. D. F. McCarthy and Michael J. Barry [Dublin: James Duffy, 1848], from *The Songs of Ireland*, 139.)

Stephen Burt reminds me that *A Shropshire Lad* contains both trimeter quatrains (in III, XIV, XXVIII, XXXIII, LIV, and LXIII) and also five-line trimeter stanzas rhymed *ababb* (XXI, XXIX). The *a* rhymes, however, he adds, often have feminine endings, whereas Yeats's have masculine endings; and Housman does not enjamb his trimeter quatrains as Yeats does.

4. Cecil Day-Lewis, "The Poet," in *Complete Poems* (London: Sinclair Stevenson, 1992), 329.

5. The relevant lines from "The Madness of King Goll" are:

> > I *laughed* aloud and hurried on
> > By *rocky* shore and rushy fen. . . .
>
> > [I] saw where this old *tympan* lay
> > Deserted on a doorway seat,
> > And bore it to the woods with me;
>
> > When my *hand* passed from *wire to wire*
> > It quenched, with sound like falling dew,
> > The whirling and the wandering fire.
> > > (83–86; italics mine)

Yeats's father drew and painted his son as the mad King Goll. The lines above, especially the words I have italicized, would seem to be Yeats's source for the "laughing string / Whereon mad fingers play / Amid a place of stone."

6. > Only a sweet and virtuous soul,
> > Like season'd timber, never gives;
> But though the whole world turn to coal,
> > Then chiefly lives.

7. Wallace Stevens, "The immense poetry of war," in *Wallace Stevens: Collected Poetry and Prose* (New York: Library of America, 1997), 251.

8. I am grateful to Professor Eamon Duffy of the University of Cambridge for pointing out to me the probable relation between the Yeatsian trimeter and the lyric hexameters of the Young Ireland poets.

9. Parts II and IV depart a bit in rhyme form from the "pure" *abab* quatrain form: the eleven-line section II (concerning Mabel's artist-friends and the works they bring her) has a defective quatrain (lines 5–7, in which line 6, which "ought" to rhyme with the "phantom" line 8, is rhymed with lines 2 and 4 in the preceding quatrain to make it "belong," a technique that Yeats uses elsewhere, e.g., at the close of "The Tower"); and the eight-line section IV ("The End of Day," about Mabel's decline) connects its two quatrains by adding a linking "*b*" rhyme-

sound *(ababcbcb)* and a rhyme-word that links the two (the last *"b"* rhyme-word, "play," turns out to be the same as the first *"b"* rhyme-word, to make the poem a closed circle). If we admit these two sections (as I think we might in spite of their irregularities) to the trimeter-quatrain group, Mabel Beardsley's sequence becomes visibly dominated (with four sections out of seven) by trimeter *abab* quatrains. The other three parts are written—unsurprisingly, given Mabel's physical heroism as Yeats's subject—in "free" hexameters, Yeats's "epic" measure. Two of these three parts rhyme in the same manner as the trimeter parts, *abab.* The third, a dizain, although in hexameters rather than pentameters, combines a "Shakespearean" quatrain with a "Petrarchan" sestet, rhyming *ababcdcede.* The "hybridity" of the form symbolizes the "hybridity" of the afterlife in which Yeats imagines Mabel ("I have no speech but symbol"); in that afterlife she will meet, Yeats says, a heterogeneous group of inhabitants, all of whom "have lived in joy and laughed into the face of Death." We can see here—as Mabel is to meet first the Celtic figure Grania, then "some old cardinal" once painted by Giorgione, and finally "Achilles, Timor, Babar, Barhaim"—Yeats's fore-sketch for the comparably heterogeneous historical and mythological afterlife of "News for the Delphic Oracle."

10. It was not always a sentence-fragment. In the original magazine publication in *The New Republic* and *The Criterion,* the first line of the second stanza read, "And at the loophole there," making a full sentence. But that sentence did not make an explicit analogy between the creation of art and the creation of a jackdaw's nest; in replacing "And" with "As," Yeats achieved his simile at the expense of his syntax.

## VIII. Marches and the Examination of Conscience

1. Yeats borrowed the notion for "The Wheel," and some of its phrasing, from a passage in the notebooks of Leonardo da Vinci which he had freely paraphrased almost a quarter-century earlier in "The Tables of the Law" (1896):

    Leonardo da Vinci . . . has this noble sentence: "The hope and desire of returning home to one's former state is like the moth's desire for the light; and the man who with constant longing awaits each new month and new year, deeming that the things he longs for are ever too late in coming, does not perceive that he is longing for his own destruction" *(Myth,* 197).

    *Mythologies* (416 n. 40) gives the original quotation from Yeats's source: *The Literary Works of Leonardo da Vinci,* compiled and edited from the original manuscripts by Jean Paul Richter (London: Sampson Low, Marston, Searle and Rivington, 1883), II, 291:

    Now you see that the hope and the desire of returning home and to one's former state is like the moth to the light, and that the man who with constant longing awaits with joy each new spring time, each new summer, each new month and new year—deeming that the things he longs for are ever too late in coming—does not perceive that he is longing for his own

destruction. But this desire is the very quintessence, the spirit of the ele-
ments, which finding itself imprisoned with the soul is ever longing to re-
turn from the human body to its giver. And you must know that this same
longing is that quintessence, inseparable from nature, and that man is the
image of the world.

2. This list would mutate, in the later Yeats, into the contents of the "rag-and-
bone shop of the heart" in "The Circus Animals' Desertion," discussed in
Chapter X with Yeats's other *ottava rima* poems.

3. This title (first appearing in *Responsibilities*), with its opening dactyl and subse-
quent trochees and its alliteration in *p*—**If** It Were **Proved** the **Peop**le **Want**ed
**Pict**ures—replaced (and spectacularly improved, acoustically and rhetorically)
the actuarial-sounding 1913 title in *The Irish Times* of January 11: "The Gift /
To a friend who promises a bigger subscription than his first to the Dublin Mu-
nicipal Gallery if the amount collected proves that there is a considerable 'pop-
ular demand' for the pictures."

4. The single most solid kind of four-beat quatrain unit in Yeats may be the late-
employed double-couplet quatrain *aabb*, which appears only in the thirties, in
"A Needle's Eye" (1934), "There" (1935), and "A Stick of Incense" (1939):

> There all the barrel-hoops are knit,
> There all the serpent-tails are bit,
> There all the gyres converge in one,
> There all the planets drop in the Sun.
>
> (557)

Although "perfect" and therefore comparable to the *abab* quatrain (by contrast
to the "imperfect" *abcb* quatrain), the double-couplet form is "airless"—there is
no space between the initial appearance of a rhyme-sound and its immediate
echo. The *abab* quatrain used in "To a Wealthy Man" allows for some air be-
tween the first appearance of a rhyme-sound and its recurrence, but not so
much as an *abcb* quatrain does. The "airless" aspect of the double-couplet qua-
train makes it particularly suited to the dry tightness of the epigram, visibly ex-
ploited above in "There." The danger in using the double-couplet quatrain
form is that it will separate into two separate couplet-units; Yeats avoids this
hazard in "There" by the initial anaphora and rigid template that bind together
the first and second couplets.

5. Two other Pollexfen brothers, not mentioned in the elegy, had predeceased Al-
fred: William died at the age of two, and William Middleton, who had died in
1913, had gone insane. Of the five Pollexfen sisters, only Yeats's mother, the el-
dest, was dead; she had died in the same year, 1900, as her brother John, the
missing sailor, who, like Susan, "should" have been laid in this Sligo tomb.

6. See WBY to AG, January 4, 1900 (*CL*, II, 485).

7. *Autobiographies*, ed. William H. O'Donnell and Douglas N. Archibald (New
York: Scribner, 1999), 52.

8. Although the first stanza of "Parnell's Funeral," part I, has only seven lines
(*ababacc*), the other stanzas are in *ottava rima*. Compare the absence of a line in

"The Municipal Gallery Revisited," part V *(ababacc);* originally the stanza had eight lines (see p. 603, line 37a). Yeats refused to pad the stanza and deleted the weak line. As I say below, in Chapter X, there is evidence, in the extant manuscript drafts, of the missing sixth line for the first stanza of "Parnell's Funeral," part I. The needed line has to rhyme with "blown" and "down": Yeats thought of writing, "Through all that animal blood what shudders run." See *"Parnell's Funeral" and Other Poems,* Manuscript Materials by W. B. Yeats, ed. David R. Clark (Ithaca, N.Y.: Cornell University Press, 2003), 25. Given the "missing" lines in the poems above, and in "In Memory of Alfred Pollexfen," we can perhaps ratify the absence, in the final printing of "Under Ben Bulben," of the cancelled line "The soul's perfection is from peace," an absence that renders the "quatrain" incomplete.

9. Curtis Bradford, in *Yeats at Work,* says, "Almost the first thing Yeats did when starting to work on a poem was to establish his form, a practice illustrated by most of the manuscripts I reproduce" *(Yeats at Work* [Carbondale: Southern Illinois University Press, 1965]), 9. The drafts of "In Memory of Eva Gore-Booth" (see the following note) show the embraced quatrain appearing on the first of the nine draft-pages for the poem, as Yeats calls up "pictures of the mind":

> Pictures of the mind recall
> That table & the talk of youth
> Two girls in silk kimonos, both
> Beautiful, one a gazell[e].
>
> (WS, 3)

10. Citations of Yeats's drafts of "In Memory of Eva Gore-Booth and Con Markiewicz" are taken from *The Winding Stair* (1929), Manuscript Materials by W. B. Yeats, ed. David R. Clark (Ithaca, N.Y.: Cornell University Press, 1995), 3–17. Page references to *WS* are given in parentheses following each quotation from a draft. In the citations, I have regularized Yeats's hazarded spelling. See also Jon Stallworthy's *Between the Lines: Yeats's Poetry in the Making* (Oxford: Clarendon Press, 1963), 164–176, for a discussion of the drafts.

11. Stephen Burt suggests that Yeats's "wreath" here may be a source for the "ring-wreath-style composition" in Paul Muldoon's 1987 poem "7, Middagh Street," which, just as it jokes (in Auden's voice) on the later poem "The Man and the Echo," jokes (in the voices of Carson McCullers and Louis MacNeice) about this poem, too:

> CARSON
> Two girls, I thought, two girls in silk kimonos.
> LOUIS
> Both beautiful, one a gazebo.

See Muldoon's *Poems: 1968–1998* (New York: Farrar, Straus and Giroux, 2001), 178, 189.

12. In the drafts, an alternate stanza is planned (I have regularized the draft):

> Some great bellows to a pyre
> Has not widow Nature still

> All those cradles left to fill
> And works of intellectual fire

Warwick Gould reminds me of this passage, and that the cancelled "intellectual fire" turns up in the middle-unit "stair" of "Blood and the Moon": "Everything that is not God consumed with intellectual fire" (481).

13. Yeats remembered "marching down O'Connell Street [in his youth] with many thousands of Irishmen and . . . we smashed £10,000–worth of plate glass." See *W. B. Yeats: Interviews and Recollections,* ed. E. H. Mikhail, 2 vols. (London: Macmillan, 1977), II, 348.

14. In one of the drafts for this passage, Yeats places himself in the position of maximum guilt: "I the great gazebo built / They [the sages] brought home to me the guilt." The alteration by which Yeats replaces his "I" with a collective "We" reveals how completely the poet places himself within the circle of guilt in which he had originally, by his scorn, placed the sisters alone. The transition from "you" to "I" to "we," marking the moral advance in the speaker's mind, is the unobtrusive inventive triumph of the poem.

15. Seamus Heaney has brilliantly made this argument—about an imaginative response to savagery needing to be made on an altogether different plane—using as his example the incident in which Jesus, asked whether the woman taken in adultery should be stoned, bends down and silently writes some words on the ground, without at first orally responding to the question at all. See "From 'The Government of the Tongue'" in *Finders Keepers: Selected Prose 1971–2001* (New York: Farrar, Straus and Giroux, 2002), 207–208.

16. In contrast to stanza 1 and the refrain, the other stanzas are in their four expository lines almost entirely iambic (with perhaps a single initial pyrrhic substitution, "We are"). Stanza 3 has no trisyllabic feet at all; in both stanza 2 and stanza 4 there is a single anapest—"and the key" and "We had fed."

17. This line, which, after many tetrameter and other drafts, became "That if nothing drastic is done," should be a tetrameter like all its fellows. But it is impossible, I think, to feel it as anything but a trimeter. The discourse of the "hysterical women" has been established as a rapid one by the line "For everybody knows or else should know"—which tumbles over into "That if nothing drastic is done." Yeats in fact had considered keeping the line a tetrameter; in one draft he corrected the trimeter line to read: "That if nothing drastic can be done." See W. B. Yeats, *New Poems:* Manuscript Materials by W. B. Yeats, ed. J. C. C. Mays and Stephen Parrish (Ithaca, N.Y.: Cornell University Press, 2000), 31. Yeats so rarely disobeys his own metrical laws that I cannot account for this discrepancy except by comparison to his other disobediences (e.g., in "Parnell's Funeral," part I, "The Municipal Gallery Revisited," "In Memory of Alfred Pollexfen," and "Under Ben Bulben"), always in avoidance of padding a line or a stanza. As Jon Stallworthy remarks of this revision, "The colloquial rhythm of 'That if nothing drastic is done' is wholly lost once the line is changed." See *Vision and Revision in Yeats's Last Poems* (Oxford: Clarendon Press, 1969), 55.

18. Some editors have decided to adopt (against the *Variorum Edition*'s "The Man

and the Echo") the title "Man and the Echo," present in the first appearances of the poem in January of 1939, in *The Atlantic Monthly* and *The London Mercury*. Yeats's draft listing the contents of *Last Poems* simply says "Man & Echo"—perhaps an abbreviation rather than a decided-upon title, but in its resemblance to "Self and Soul" it clearly implies two antagonists. See *Last Poems:* Manuscript Materials, ed. James Pethica (Ithaca, N.Y.: Cornell University Press, 1997), 466. However, in the 1939 *Last Poems and Two Plays* of the Cuala Press, the piece was printed as "The Man and the Echo," a title closer to the first-person stance of the poem. The poem does not concern universal "Man"; it concerns *a* man, *the* man of the title, who is confronting his antagonist, the echo, as he considers the last questions of existence. The draft-title "Man and Echo" suggests two singular entities confronting each other, an idea borne out by the poem's two named speakers, *"Man"* and *"Echo."* This equality of antagonists is paralleled by the title "The Man and the Echo" but not by "Man and the Echo," in which "Man" has to mean "Humankind" (which it does not in "Man and Echo"). Although the poem aspires, toward its close, to a collective "we"—"What do we know but that we face / One another in this place?"—it is deflected from such philosophizing generalizations by the cry of a stricken rabbit, a cry reported in the first person by the speaker, "the" man: "And its cry distracts my thought." This is an individualized speaker, a man, the man.

19. Paul Muldoon, "7, Middagh St.," in *Poems: 1968–1998* (New York: Farrar, Straus and Giroux, 2001), 178.

20. He seems to have borrowed the name (while altering it) from the 1938 poem "The Gyres," in which he addresses an unidentified being as "Old Rocky Face."

## IX. The Medium of Instruction

1. There is one notable mostly unrhymed poem in hexameters, "Beautiful Lofty Things," discussed in Chapter XIII on Yeats's "rare forms." I think Yeats left it unrhymed because it too, like some of the other mature unrhymed poems I discuss here, offers not merely anecdote but a form of doctrine, in this case the philosophical doctrine of the One and the Many. The poem demonstrates the perfect "fit" of *many* "beautiful lofty *things*" into *one* paradigmatic *Thing:* "All the Olympians: *a thing* never known again" (italics mine). It has to be added that there are some rhymes in "Beautiful Lofty Things," including *rime riche;* see my discussion in Chapter XIII.

2. The division of Yeats's poems, in the 1933 edition, into lyric (placed first) and narrative and dramatic (placed second) was done for marketing reasons, but agreed to by Yeats. Warwick Gould, commenting on the amount of blank verse present in "The Old Age of Queen Maeve," "The Two Kings," and "The Gift of Harun Al-Rashid," says, in a personal communication: "When these 570 lines or so are added to WBY's blank verse pile, interspersed where he had wanted them among lyric and meditative and conversation poem contexts, I think the impact of the blank verse is curiously impressive." Yet these poems are primar-

ily narratives, and so I exclude them here, since they are not, to my way of thinking, "lyric" blank verse. "The Gift of Harun Al-Rashid" has affinities with the blank verse poems conveying instruction, but it is not a poem of pure instruction, like "The Phases of the Moon" or "Ego Dominus Tuus." It is primarily a verse-epistle containing a narration which itself contains some doctrine.

3. Yeats once wrote, concerning *The Land of Heart's Desire,* in a 1912 letter to James Stephens, "No young man writes good blank verse" (#1908).

4. Why is "A Dialogue of Self and Soul" not in blank verse? Or the dialogue in "Vacillation" between the Soul and the Heart? By the time of his late verse, Yeats's phase of exposition in blank verse had, I think, exhausted itself, since the excitement of formulating *A Vision,* which had elicited his middle blank verse, was over.

5. Between "In the Seven Woods" (1902) and "The People" (1915), Yeats wrote two sub-Tennysonian blank-verse narratives, "The Old Age of Queen Maeve" (1903) and "The Two Kings" (1912). These are still employing a blank verse of considerable monotony, and neither reveals anything new in Yeats's management of the medium.

6. It was of course preceded by the beautiful rhymed-in-couplets "reported conversation" in the 1904 "Adam's Curse."

7. *NC,* 166, quoting J. M. Hone, *W. B. Yeats, 1865–1939* (London: Macmillan, 1962), 305.

8. See "Introduction to 'A Vision'" in *A Vision* [B] (London: Macmillan, 1962), 19.

9. Yeats did, however, have subsequent lapses. The blank verse of the 1918 narrative poem "The Gift of Harun Al-Rashid" seems to me, as blank verse, relatively uninteresting in its movement, though of course the poem has attracted attention because its content deals with Yeats's marriage and the automatic writing. (The poem is a verse-epistle written by "Kusta Ben Luka"—addressing "Abd Al-Rabban," Treasurer of the Caliph—which encloses a dialogue between Kusta and the Caliph, leading to Kusta's discovery of the woman whom he marries.)

## X. The Renaissance Aura

1. An earlier version of this chapter appeared as "Yeats and *Ottava Rima*" in the *Yeats Annual,* No. 11, ed. Warwick Gould (Basingstoke: Macmillan Press Ltd., 1995), 26–44.

2. The first stanza of "Parnell's Funeral" has only seven lines, rhyming *ababacc.* The missing last *b* line appears partially and briefly (choosing among "ran," "runs," and "run" for its rhyme-word) in the single extant draft (*Parnell's Funeral,* 25). As I interpret the confused phrases of its several incarnations, it reads:

> A shudder runs through all their wolfish blood
> Through all their wolfish blood a shudder runs
> Through all that animal blood what shudders run

Apparently dissatisfied with all his attempts to find a third *"b"* rhyme, Yeats suppressed line 6 of his first stanza altogether. Stanzas 2, 3, and 4 of "Parnell's Funeral" exhibit regular *ottava rima*.

3. Seamus Heaney, *The Place of Writing* (Atlanta: Scholars Press, 1989), 29.

4. The phrase "empty purse" originates in "The Compleint of Chaucer to his Empty Purse," which (as Warwick Gould tells me) was how the poem now known as "The Complaint of Chaucer to his Purse" was entitled in Yeats's World's Classics and Kelmscott Press editions of Chaucer.

5. A more complete account of both "The Circus Animals' Desertion" and "Among School Children" can be found in the chapter on Yeats in my *Poets Thinking: Pope, Whitman, Dickinson, Yeats* (Cambridge, Mass.: Harvard University Press, 2004), 92–119.

6. The six-week span is confirmed by Yeats's complaint of barrenness in the letters of the period. See, e.g., #7093 (October 13, 1937, to George Yeats): "Since I came to England I have been upset because, though I tried every day, I could not find a theme for poetry. I thought I was finished."

7. Compare the similar "entanglement" of the words *mire, blood, fury, mire, veins,* and *complexities* in "Byzantium," where Yeats is also creating the texture of introspection.

8. Yeats establishes "Oisin" and "The Countess Kathleen" as [pagan] "truth" and [Christian] "counter-truth" in his description of them in the preface to "The Countess Kathleen and Various Legends and Lyrics" (London, 1892):

> The greater number of the poems in this book, as also in 'The Wanderings of Oisin,' are founded on Irish tradition. The chief poem ["The Countess Kathleen"] is an attempt to mingle personal thought and feeling with the beliefs and customs of Christian Ireland; whereas the longest poem in my earlier book endeavoured to set forth the impress left on my imagination by the Pre-Christian cycle of legends. The Christian cycle being mainly concerned with contending moods and moral motives needed, I thought, a dramatic vehicle. The tumultuous and heroic Pagan cycle, on the other hand, having to do with vast and shadowy activities and with the great impersonal emotions, expressed itself naturally—or so I imagined—in epic and epic-lyric measures (845).

9. As late as the first typescript of *Last Poems*, Yeats was using, and not cancelling, in his last stanza of "The Circus Animals' Desertion," a blustering insistence on tragic gaiety and armed violence:

> O hour of triumph come and make me gay,
> If burnished chariots are put to flight
> Why brood upon old triumph, prepare to die;
> Even at the approach of the un-imaged night
> Man has the refuge of his gaiety,
> A dab of black enhances every white,
> Tension is but the vigor of the mind,
> Cannon the god and father of mankind.

See W. B. Yeats, *Last Poems:* Manuscript Materials, ed. James Pethica (Ithaca, N.Y.: Cornell University Press, 1997), 383.

10. See *The Tower* (1929): Manuscript Materials by W. B. Yeats (Ithaca, N.Y.: Cornell University Press, 2006), 386, 387.

11. In one version of the drafts (380, 381) the verb attached to the glance was (for reasons of alliteration) "glittering": "O body swayed to music, O glittering glance." But "glitter" is a steady-state, frequentative verb (like Keats's "twitter") and, unlike "brighten," does not increase over time. Yeats rarely sacrificed an alliteration so seductive as "glittering glance"; but he clearly wanted the creative *increase* of invention to be included in his participial adjective, so he decided on a progressive rather than a frequentative verb.

## XI. The Spacious Lyric

1. Quoted here from Abraham Cowley, *Poems*, ed. A. R. Waller (Cambridge: Cambridge University Press, 1905), 32–37.

2. Cowley's trimeters in the Hervey poem occur more often in lines 6 and 7 than in line 4, but they can appear there as well. Cowley does not distinguish trimeters from tetrameters by a further indentation; one could say that his poem consists of "long lines" (the pentameters) and "shorter lines" (the equally indented tetrameters and trimeters). (George Herbert, by contrast, usually keeps his indentations accurate to the different measures of his poem.) Here is a Cowley stanza with trimeter substitutions in lines 6 and 7:

> Large was his *Soul;* as large a *Soul* as ere
> Submitted to *inform a Body* here.
> High as the Place 'twas shortly in *Heav'n* to have,
> > But low, and humble as his *Grave.*
> So *high* that all the *Virtues* there did come
> > As to their chiefest seat
> > Conspicuous and great;
> So *low* that for *Me* too it made a room.

3. There is one exception to this rule: in "A Dialogue of Self and Soul," Yeats did allow himself a trimeter in line 62 ("The folly that man does") when he could not, it seems, find a way to make an acceptably terse tetrameter. He attempted a tetrameter (*WS,* 59) in trying out "The folly that a man does," but revised it to its present trimeter state before publication.

4. In placing all his lines flush left, Yeats may have been influenced (as Warwick Gould reminds me) by Jonson's similar practice in the Cary-Morison ode. Although Gould suggests that the closing quatrain-pattern in the Gregory stanza matches that of Jonson's second quatrain in "The Stand" sections of the ode, the quatrains match only in using embraced rhyme. They do not match in meter: Yeats's quatrain is 5-4-4-5, while Jonson's is 5-3-3-4.

5. See my "Four Elegies," in *Yeats, Sligo, and Ireland,* ed. A. Norman Jeffares (Gerrards Cross: Colin Smythe, 1980), 216–231.

6. "Soldier, scholar, horseman, he, / As 'twere all life's epitome" derives, as Warwick Gould remarks, from Dryden's *Absalom and Achitophel:* "A man so various, that he seemed to be / Not one, but all mankind's epitome." Gould continues (personal communication): "Is it not odd that WBY should create his rhetoric of praise and encomium in imitation of the list of roles and the 'epitome' from a wonderful piece of Dryden's satirical butchery?"

7. See the account of the oblique reflections, in Yeats's work, of his mother and her predicament, in Deirdre Toomey's "Away" in *Yeats and Women,* ed. Deirdre Toomey (Basingstoke: Macmillan, 1997), 135–167. The article appeared originally in *Yeats Annual* 10 (1993), 3–32. The most startling revelation in the essay is the connection in Yeats's mind between his mother's inert presence after her stroke and paralysis and the inert material bodies of those whose spirits had been taken away by the fairies. Toomey sketches all the childhood absences of Yeats from his mother, seeing them as possible causes for his difficulty in intimate relations with women.

8. *Michael Robartes and the Dancer:* Manuscript Materials by W. B. Yeats, ed. Thomas Parkinson with Anne Brannen (Ithaca, N.Y.: Cornell University Press, 1994), 175. The editors say of these latter stanzas which address the daughter, "here . . . are drafts for the poem as a letter to, rather than a prayer for, the daughter" (185). But there is precedent in Yeats for a change from a third-person reference to a second-person address without presuming that Yeats is composing a "letter": see, e.g., "In Memory of Eva Gore-Booth and Con Markiewicz." After referring to the sisters as "the older . . . the younger," Yeats turns to them directly: "Dear shadows, now you know it all." Similarly, as the poet's thoughts speed ahead while he prays for his daughter, he addresses her as she will be at twenty-five. There is no need to postulate a "letter" here; there is merely a decision to cast his voice forward in time to address the adult Anne.

9. Ibid., 171.

10. Only two among the poem's twelve stanzas lack an initial couplet offering a self-sufficient statement. Instead, they enjamb the opening couplet with line 3. The first of these is the late-inserted stanza on Gregory's prowess in horse-riding, requested by his wife Margaret:

> When with the Galway foxhounds he would ride
> From Castle Taylor to the Roxborough side
> Or Esserkelly plain . . .

and the second is the concluding stanza:

> I had thought, seeing how bitter is that wind
> That shakes the shutter, to have brought to mind
> All those that manhood tried . . .

11. Yeats had the good sense to delete lines in the draft that show him brandishing Sato's sword:

> I stand
> Scabbard & silk & sword above my head [33].

In the printed poem, the blade ended up more stably, on his knees. But Richard

Ellmann, in *The Identity of Yeats* (London: Faber and Faber, 1964), 8, recounts that during a visit by the Indian Professor Bose, Yeats "strode swiftly across the room, took up Sato's sword and unsheathed it dramatically and shouted, 'Conflict, more conflict!'"

12. W. B. Yeats, *The Winding Stair* (1929), Manuscript Materials, ed. David R. Clark (Ithaca, N.Y.: Cornell University Press, 1995), 23–60.

13. One of the drafts (*WS*, 53), which exhibits the striking misspelling of "woos" as "woes," attempts to regularize the meter of the penultimate stanza with two awkward internal tetrameters, thus:

> Through that false, most fecund ditch of all
> Of the fall that he does
> Or must suffer, if he woes
> A proud woman not kindred to the soul[.]

In the end, Yeats let his anomalous trimeter ("The folly that man does") stand in the published work. It foretells, perhaps, his substitution of trimeters for tetrameters in the embraced quatrains of "Byzantium" (1930).

14. Yeats had considered, in the drafts (*WS*, 39), attaching the noun "agony" to "childhood," but that would have started his drama too far up the scale of pain, so he changed it to the similar-in-sound "ignominy," predicating it of "boyhood"; he thought at first of emphasizing the length of adolescence by attaching the Tennysonian "drear" ("Mariana") to "distress," but then cancelled it as melodramatic and archaic.

15. I have resisted identifying the harsh Soul as the Freudian superego. They have something in common, of course; but Soul represents the holy (not simply repressive conscience), and Self is not merely libidinal.

16. In a letter to Professor H. C. Grierson, editor of the poems of John Donne, on February 21, 1926, Yeats wrote, "I have been reading your Donne again . . . especially that intoxicating 'St. Lucies Day.' . . . I have used the arrangement of the rhymes in the stanzas for a poem of my own, just finished" (*L*, 710). In "Chosen" (534–535), Yeats indeed retains the *rhyme-scheme* of the nine-line stanza of Donne's "A Nocturnall upon St. Lucie's Day" *(abbacccdd)*, but he changes the *metrical length* of one line. Donne's line-lengths are 5-5-4-4-3-5-5-5-5, whereas Yeats replaces the pentameter in line 6 with a tetrameter. In Donne's poem, the three lines which rhyme *ccc* are 3-5-5 in length, while in Yeats (a poet always thinking of gyres) they successively grow by a foot each: 3-4-5. In the second stanza of "Chosen," these are the lines rhyming *theme, seem, stream,* and they are obviously meant to mimic that "utmost pleasure," the growing intensity of the lovers' union:

> If questioned on
> My utmost pleasure with a man
> By some new-married bride, I take
> That stillness for a theme (3)
> Where his heart my heart did seem (4)
> And both adrift on the miraculous stream . . . (5)

## XII. Primitivism and the Grotesque

1. Yeats speaks in a letter (#5836) of Swedenborg: "He somewhere describes two spirits meeting, & as they touch they become a single conflagration."

2. Victor Hugo, Preface to *Cromwell,* cited (in the English translation quoted in the text) from *Dante in English,* ed. Eric Griffiths and Matthew Reynolds (London: Penguin Classics, 2005), lxxvi. The original reads as follows:

    La muse moderne . . . sentira que tout dans la création n'est pas humainement *beau,* que le laid y existe à côté du beau, le difforme près du gracieux, le grotesque au revers du sublime. . . . Dans la pensée des modernes . . . le grotesque a un rôle immense. Il y est partout; d'une part, il crée le difforme et l'horrible; de l'autre, le comique et le bouffon. Il attache autour de la religion mille superstitions originales, autour de la poésie mille imaginations pittoresques. . . . Comme il fait hardiment saillir toutes ces formes bizarres que l'âge précédent avait si timidement envelopées de langes! . . . On a besoin de se reposer de tout, même du beau. . . . Il semble . . . que le grotesque soit un temps d'arrêt, . . . un point de départ d'où l'on s'élève vers le beau avec une perception plus fraîche et plus excitée.

    See *Oeuvres Complètes de Victor Hugo présentées par Jeanlouis Cornuz,* vol. 11 (Paris: Éditions Rencontre, 1967), 19, 21, 22.

3. In *The Tables of the Law* (as Warwick Gould reminds me), "Owen Aherne had moved beyond hatred of others to hatred of the God of conventional belief, and that hatred of God eventually brought him back to believing it would be a good thing to be able to believe." See *Myth,* 197–199. But *The Tables of the Law* does not use the words "Hatred of God," etc. It is not easy, formally speaking, to connect the vague distresses of Owen Aherne with the crisp determination of Ribh.

4. See *"Parnell's Funeral" and Other Poems from "A Full Moon in March"*: Manuscript Materials, ed. David R. Clark (Ithaca, N.Y.: Cornell University Press, 2003), 253; cited hereafter in this chapter as *PF.*

5. See P. S. Sri, "The Influence of Vedanta on Yeats's 'Supernatural Songs,'" *Yeats Annual,* No. 16 (London: Palgrave Macmillan, 2005), 113–129, describing Yeats's simultaneous projection, in Ribh, of "early Christian Ireland and . . . Indian mysticism." Yeats says in a letter, about a comparable problem, "I could not make Robartes a Buddhist because I required a man whose thought was not too far from European tradition" (#6017, To F. P. Sturm, March 7, 1934).

6. *PF,* 169.

7. "The [?voice] once said, 'to think about hatred' / . . . The growing hatred among men has long been a problem with me." The "voice" came from George Yeats's trance. See *PF,* 171.

8. Ibid., 185.

9. Ibid.

10. *L,* 829.

11. Interestingly, the poem began (as the drafts show) as a ballad alternating tetrameters and trimeters. The ballad is indeed a "primitive" form, but its basic premise is narrative. Yeats finally succeeded in making all but one of the lines of "He and She" into trimeters: he shortened the tetrameter "I am I, I am I," for instance, to "I am I, am I." One line resisting coercion remained in its tetrameter form, "**She** sings **as** the **moon sings**," after the others had become trimeters (*PF*, 203). Yeats reluctantly (we infer) forced it in the draft into trimeter form: "As **sings** the **moon** she **sings**" (*PF*, 205). But very quickly Yeats restored the original tetrameter, presumably because of its better formulation of the comparison he is engaged in making, with its beat on "she" and "moon" rather than on "sings" and "moon." In its unusual tetrameter presence among the trimeters, this line allows a ghost of the ballad stanza to drift through this "singing" lyric.

12. As David Clark points out in *"Parnell's Funeral" and Other Poems* (xl), the drafts leave no doubt that the intent of the passage is to depict the male, after holding off on penetration, performing oral sex on the female: "Down & around those dark declivities travel his mouth & tongue" (*PF*, 207). See Yeats's use of the same phrase in the 1926 "Parting," in which the young woman says, "I offer to love's play / My dark declivities" (536).

13. The "him" refers to the Godhead, and the verb is a reflexive one: "He holds him[self] from desire," lest he break the spell as he generates from his own substance Primordial Motherhood and cub. The "him" does not refer to the yet-to-be-mentioned child. And the "child" is a different aspect of the Godhead from the female aspect ("Primordial Motherhood"). Critics have been misled on these two points, but Daniel Albright gets it right: "God is at once the father, the mother, and the child." But although Ribh in poem III regarded this act as a "sexual spasm," Yeats in "What Magic Drum?" emphasizes the moment of stillness, of abnegation from desire, and of identity-fulfillment within a sexual pause. Albright is mistaken, I believe, in calling the act in this poem "a frenzy of self-begetting." W. B. Yeats, *The Poems*, ed. Daniel Albright (London: J. M. Dent, 1990), 764.

14. Yeats drew here on the mystical experience described by the Hindu monk Bhagwan Shri Hamsa, who heard a mysterious voice singing the Mandukya Upanishad. Then, after enduring long cold and solitude on Mount Kailās (the Himalayan counterpart to the mythological Mount Meru), the monk beheld the Lord Dattatreya: "My Master lifted me up like the Divine Mother and hugged me to His breast and caressed me all over the body" ("The Mandukya Upanishad," *E & I*, 479). This Indian story, rejecting the separation of body and soul, belongs therefore to the anti-Christian polemic of Yeats's whole sequence.

15. For a long time, a Byzantine décor of cathedral and gong persisted as part of the atmosphere of the poem (*PF*, 221, 223). Only in the final draft is "the magic gong" replaced by "what magic drum."

16. In its first draft (*PF*, 237), the poem began with the crucifixion of Christ, giving it pride of place. Subsequent drafts interchanged the position of the two stan-

zas, "reducing" the Christian moment to a subordinate position between two classical eras.

17. See *PF,* xlvi–xlvii.

18. According to the *Encyclopaedia Britannica* (1991), vol. 8, 44, quoted by David Clark in *PF,* xlvii, "Mount Meru reaches down below the ground, into the nether regions, as far as it extends into the heavens." If Yeats had known about this belief, he would have seen Mount Meru as a double gyre, making it doubly attractive as a symbol.

19. Bhagwan Shri Hamsa, *The Holy Mountain,* quoted in Yeats's essay "The Mandukya Upanishad" (*E & I,* 478).

20. Yeats significantly altered the last two lines in order to remove agency from man. Originally, the lines read (I have normalized the chaotic draft): "Why everything must end, why man must break / Whatever thing his days of glory make" (*PF,* 251).

21. W. B. Yeats, *Autobiographies,* ed. William H. O'Donnell and Douglas Archibald (New York: Scribner, 1999), 356.

22. Warwick Gould reminded me of the imperfect rhyme in the couplet, Yeats's non-Shakespearean touch.

## XIII. Rare Forms

1. There is only one other poem composed in rhyme royal, written close in time to "A Bronze Head": this is "Hound Voice" (621–622), of which Jeffares oddly remarks, without explanation, "The poem was written in a spirit of mockery" (*NC,* 420). This strangely violent poem groups the women Yeats loved—still loyal, like himself, to wild rather than "settled" ground—under a single rubric: "'Hound Voices' were they all." The terror that "shattered" Maud Gonne in "A Bronze Head" has assailed these other women and the poet as well:

> We picked each other from afar and knew
> What hour of terror comes to test the soul,
> And in that terror's name obeyed the call.

As the poem draws to its close, poet and women know "the hunt is on," and with their "ancient hounds" they pursue the quarry until "the kill beside the shore";

> Then cleaning out and bandaging of wounds,
> And chants of victory amid the encircling hounds.

To my mind, no critical discussion of "Hound Voice" has yet offered a convincing explanation of this "plot" of a gory hunt, nor can I venture one myself. Warwick Gould speculates that Yeats may have drawn his rhyme royal in this instance from William Morris's enormous poem-of-many-meters, *The Earthly Paradise* (rather than from medieval or Renaissance sources).

2. Cf. Yeats's song from the 1934 *The King of the Great Clock Tower:* "O, what is life but a mouthful of air; / *Said the rambling, shambling travelling man*" (788).

3. I have corrected the *Variorum Edition*'s printing of "held" to "hold." In the origi-

nal journal publications of March 1939 *(The New Republic, The London Mercury)*, the line read "hold," but it was corrected for volume preparation (probably by Mrs. Yeats) to read "held." A recently discovered typescript confirms that Yeats intended "hold": "Or maybe substance can be composite . . . and in a breath, a mouthful, [substance] can hold the extreme of life and death." See the discussion (confirming "hold" as the proper reading) by James Pethica in W. B. Yeats, *Last Poems:* Manuscript Materials (Ithaca, N.Y.: Cornell University Press, 1997), xlix–li.

4. Stephen Burt has called to my attention the fact that "Beautiful Lofty Things" does contain a full rhyme at the close ("train/again"), as well as a consonant rhyme ("head/crowd") and some *rime riche* ("head/heads"; "tables/table/table"). Nonetheless, I think a reader's impression would find this an unrhymed poem, but would note that there are many repeated words.

5. Warwick Gould has generously reminded me that "At Algeciras" was originally part I of a two-part diptych called "Meditations upon Death," in which part II contained the verses now known as "Mohini Chatterjee." In the end, Yeats split "Meditations" into two distinct poems, separating them by "The Choice." "These three poems," says Gould (personal communication), "clear the intellect before the great vision of 'Byzantium.'" He continues, citing the drafts and Yeats's commentary, to summarize: "The 'dark breast' of the trees, then, is the nurse's breast, the great examiner (a boyhood recollection) becomes the great questioner, and [together with] the evening chill suggest not only three 'distinct moments in the mind,' [but] their 'wide separation' in fact registers something of three of the four ages of man."

6. *A Vision* (London and Basingstoke: The Macmillan Press, 1937; reissued with corrections, 1962), 183–184.

7. This does not obviate the difficulty of reading line 3 as a trimeter, nor line 6 as a pentameter. There exist in the poem lines that could be, taken alone, scanned in two ways: either as trimeter ("When **had** I my **own** will?") or as tetrameter ("**When** had I my **own** will?"). But the 5-5-3-3 ground-plan of the stanza, as well as its syntactic parallels to the following line, constrains us to read this line as a trimeter.

8. Yeats had quoted these lines ("Constrained . . . we obey") in "The People's Theatre" *(Explorations* [1962], 258–259), prefacing them with an account of the "tyranny" of which the demiurge and its cold spirits are emblems. Were it not, he asserted, for the countervailing gyre of subjectivity, "we would fall in a generation or so under some tyranny that would cease at last to be a tyranny, so perfect our acquiescence" *(NC,* 182).

9. Warwick Gould suggests to me that aspects of the figures of the Buddha and the Sphinx are owed, respectively, to the Buddha episode of Flaubert's *La Tentation de Saint Antoine,* and to Huysmans' *À Rebours* (the dialogue of the Chimera and the Sphinx as ventriloquized to Des Esseintes by the prostitute).

10. Compare this solacing ritual ending with that of the much later "Crazy Jane on the Mountain," which is tragic: "Thereupon, / Propped upon my two knees, /

I kissed a stone; / I lay stretched out in the dirt / And I cried tears down." See Chapter V for further treatment of Crazy Jane's last poem.

11. *L*, 922.

12. *A Vision* (1962), 231. In Book III of *A Vision*—called "The Soul in Judgment"—Yeats writes (in part VII): "At the end of the second state [of the afterlife], the events of the past life are a whole and can be dismissed; the emotional and moral life, however, is but a whole according to the code accepted during life. The *Spirit* is still unsatisfied, until after the third state . . . , called the *Shiftings,* where the *Spirit* is purified of good and evil. In so far as the man did good without knowing evil, or evil without knowing good, his nature is reversed until that knowledge is obtained."

13. *L*, 922.

14. *NC*, 410, citing Dorothy Wellesley's account of Yeats reading the sketch aloud, in *DWL*, 193.

15. The sister was transformed for the purposes of the poem into a "close friend" of the beloved; a sibling might have been distracting to the intention of creating an unspoken dialogue between poet and beloved.

16. "Certain Noble Plays of Japan," *E & I*, 227–228.

# ‿ Selected Bibliography

## General Works

Attridge, Derek. *Poetic Rhythm: An Introduction*. Cambridge: Cambridge University Press, 1995.

Bornstein, George. "Remaking Himself: Yeats's Revisions of His Early Canon." *Transactions of the Society for Textual Scholarship* (1991), 339–358.

Bradford, Curtis. *Yeats at Work*. Carbondale: Southern Illinois University Press, 1965.

——— "Yeats's Byzantium Poems: A Study of Their Development." In *Yeats: A Collection of Critical Essays*, ed. John Unterecker. Englewood Cliffs, N.J.: Prentice-Hall, 1963.

Brooke, Stopford A., and T. W. Rolleston, eds. *A Treasury of Irish Poetry*. New York and London: Macmillan, 1900.

Coleridge, Samuel Taylor. *Poems*, ed. Ernest Hartley Coleridge. Oxford: Oxford University Press, 1961.

Davis, Thomas. *National and Historic Ballads, Songs, and Poems: A New and Revised Edition*. Dublin: James Duffy and Sons, 1876.

Foster, R. F. *W. B. Yeats: A Life*, 2 vols. Oxford: Oxford University Press, 1997, 2003.

Gogarty, Oliver S. John, *The Poems and Plays*, ed. A. Norman Jeffares. Gerrards Cross: Colin Smythe, 2001.

Gould, Warwick, ed. *The Yeats Annual*. London, 1982– .

Gregory, Augusta. *Lady Gregory's Journals*, 2 vols., ed. Daniel J. Murphy. Gerrards Cross: Colin Smythe, 1978.

Henn, T. R. *The Lonely Tower*. London: Methuen, 1950.

Jeffares, A. Norman. *A New Commentary on the Poems of W. B. Yeats*. London: Macmillan, 1984.

——— *W. B. Yeats: Man and Poet*. London: Kyle Cathie, 1996.

Jonson, Ben. *Poems*, ed. George Burke Johnston. Cambridge, Mass.: Harvard University Press, 1960.

Le Fanu, Sheridan. "The Legend of the Glaive." *Dublin University Magazine* (February 1816), 210–216.

McCarthy, D. F., and Michael J. Barry, eds. *The Book of Irish Ballads* and *The Songs of Ireland*. Dublin: James Duffy, 1848.

Miller, Hillis. *The Linguistic Moment: From Wordsworth to Stevens*. Princeton: Princeton University Press, 1985.

Parkinson, Thomas. *W. B. Yeats: The Later Poetry*. Berkeley: University of California Press, 1964.

Perloff, Marjorie. *Rhyme and Meaning in the Poetry of W. B. Yeats.* The Hague: Mouton, 1970.

Plotinus. *The Enneads,* trans. Stephen MacKenna, 3rd ed., revised by B. S. Page. London: Faber and Faber, 1962.

Preminger, Alex, and T. V. F. Brogan, eds. *The New Princeton Encyclopedia of Poetry and Poetics.* Princeton: Princeton University Press, 1993.

Shakespeare, William. *Timon of Athens,* ed. H. J. Oliver. London: Methuen, 1959.

Stallworthy, Jon. *Between the Lines: Yeats's Poetry in the Making.* Oxford: Oxford University Press, 1963.

———— *Vision and Revision in Yeats's Last Poems.* Oxford: Oxford University Press, 1969.

Todorov, Tzvetan. *The Poetics of Prose,* trans. Richard Howard. Ithaca, N.Y.: Cornell University Press, 1977.

Vendler, Helen. "New Wine in Old Bottles: Yeats's 'Supernatural Songs.'" *The Southern Review* 27, no. 2 (Spring 1991), 399–406.

———— *Poets Thinking: Pope, Whitman, Dickinson, Yeats.* Cambridge, Mass.: Harvard University Press, 2004.

———— "Technique in the Earlier Poems of Yeats." *Yeats Annual,* no. 8 (1991), 3–20.

White, Anna MacBride, and A. Norman Jeffares, eds. *The Gonne-Yeats Letters, 1893–1938: Always Your Friend.* London: Hutchinson, 1992.

## Works by Yeats

Yeats, W. B. *Autobiographies,* ed. William H. O'Donnell and Douglas N. Archibald. New York: Scribner, 1999.

————, ed. *A Book of Irish Verse* (1895), rpt. with an Introduction by John Banville. London: Rutledge, 2002.

———— *Collected Letters,* General Editor John Kelly, 4 vols. Oxford: Oxford University Press, 1986, 1997, 1994, 2005. I: John Kelly and Eric Domville, eds.; II: John Kelly, Warwick Gould, and Deirdre Toomey, eds.; III and IV: John Kelly and Ronald Schuchard, eds.

———— *Collected Letters,* General Editor John Kelly, InteLex Edition. Oxford: Oxford University Press, 2002.

———— *The Countess Kathleen, and Various Legends and Lyrics.* London: T. F. Unwin, 1892.

———— *Essays and Introductions.* New York: Macmillan, 1961; rpt. 1968.

———— *Explorations,* sel. Mrs. W. B. Yeats. London: Macmillan, 1962; New York: Macmillan, 1963.

———— *Letters,* ed. Allan Wade. New York, Macmillan, 1955.

———— *Letters on Poetry from W. B. Yeats to Dorothy Wellesley.* London: Oxford University Press, 1964.

———— *Mythologies,* ed. Warwick Gould and Deirdre Toomey. London: Macmillan, 2005.

———— *New Poems,* ed. J. C. C. Mays and Stephen Parrish. Ithaca, N.Y.: Cornell University Press, 2000.

———— *The Poems,* ed. Daniel Albright. London: J. M. Dent, 1990.

—— *Under the Moon: The Unpublished Early Poetry,* ed. George Bornstein. New York: Scribner, 1995.

—— *The Variorum Edition of the Poems,* ed. Peter Allt and Russell K. Alspach. New York: Macmillan, 1940; 4th printing, 1968.

—— *A Vision.* London: Macmillan, 1937.

—— *A Vision:* A Reissue with the Author's Final Revisions. New York: Macmillan, 1956.

## Manuscript Materials

*"In the Seven Woods" and "The Green Helmet and Other Poems":* Manuscript Materials, ed. David Holdeman. Ithaca, N.Y.: Cornell University Press, 2002.

*Last Poems:* Manuscript Materials, ed. James Pethica. Ithaca, N.Y.: Cornell University Press, 1997.

*Michael Robartes and the Dancer:* Manuscript Materials, ed. Thomas Parkinson with Anne Brannen. Ithaca, N.Y.: Cornell University Press, 1994.

*"Parnell's Funeral" and Other Poems from "A Full Moon in March":* Manuscript Materials, ed. David R. Clark. Ithaca, N.Y: Cornell University Press, 2003.

*Responsibilities:* Manuscript Materials, ed. William H. O'Donnell. Ithaca, N.Y.: Cornell University Press, 2003.

*The Tower:* Manuscript Materials, ed. Richard Finneran with Jared Curtis and Ann Saddlemyer. Ithaca, N.Y.: Cornell University Press, 2006.

*The Wild Swans at Coole:* Manuscript Materials, ed. Stephen Parrish. Ithaca, N.Y.: Cornell University Press, 1994.

*The Wind Among the Reeds:* Manuscript Materials, ed. Carolyn Holdsworth. Ithaca, N.Y.: Cornell University Press, 1993.

*The Winding Stair* (1929): Manuscript Materials, ed. David R. Clark. Ithaca, N.Y.: Cornell University Press, 1995.

*Words for Music Perhaps:* Manuscript Materials, ed. David R. Clark. Ithaca, N.Y.: Cornell University Press, 1999.